Images of
CHRIST
Ancient and Modern

edited by Stanley E. Porter,
Michael A. Hayes & David Tombs

ROEHAMPTON INSTITUTE LONDON PAPERS, 2

Sheffield
Academic Press

Copyright © 1997 Sheffield Academic Press

Published by Sheffield Academic Press Ltd
Mansion House
19 Kingfield Road
Sheffield S11 9AS
England

Printed on acid-free paper in Great Britain
by Bookcraft Ltd
Midsomer Norton, Bath

British Library Cataloguing in Publication Data

A catalogue record for this book is available
from the British Library

ISBN 1-85075-658-9
ISBN 1-85075-812-3 pbk

CONTENTS

'Images of Christ: Ancient and Modern' was the title of a conference held at Roehampton Institute London on 24th and 25th February 1996 and this collection of essays derives directly from it.

It was the belief of the organizing committee—Professor Stanley Porter, Father Michael Hayes and myself—that the phrase 'images of Christ' would attract a rich diversity of papers, and so it proved to be. There was consideration of representations of Christ in sacred texts, in theology, in literature, in the visual, dramatic and musical arts, and in religious cultures other than Christianity. As it turned out, there are many fields we could have explored, and some of these are reflected in this book.

Conferences are often followed by the book of the conference. This is entirely as it should be. A good conference offers many delights. There are the speakers, sometimes famous, sometimes unknown, and there are their papers and the substance of what they have to say. There is the silent or vocal participation of the delegates in the papers and workshops they have attended. There is the fellowship, the eating and drinking and talking, the networking, the backbiting and the new friendships that are forged. Everyone has a unique experience, their own narrative or argument deriving from those parts of the complex whole with which they engaged. Meanwhile, and mysteriously, everyone has a sense of the whole and of wholeness as the living organism that is the conference grows to fulfilment.

But where there is a book of the conference, that fulfilment is greater, even though deferred, first till publication and then, perhaps indefinitely, till the book has done its work in shops, in studies and in university libraries. For the speakers turned authors the book allows for revision of what they said in the light of the experience of the conference and the necessary recasting for a new kind of audience—the reader rather than the listener. For those who attended, it allows for nostalgia but, more importantly, renewed acquaintance with the papers that the reader attended and the opportunity to find out about what was missed. For all these people it complements, in its different format, configuration, rhythm and pace, and in its permanence, the very different and transitory thing that was the conference itself.

For those who were not there it is a book of essays on a common theme. And, in this case, that theme could hardly be more interesting: how is God made flesh?

This was the second annual conference on a religious theme sponsored and organized by the Faculty of Arts and Humanities, the Centre for Advanced Theological Research and Digby Stuart Chaplaincy, and it attracted speakers and delegates from the USA, Canada and Italy as well as universities throughout the United Kingdom. I would like to thank not only all those who attended, for their participation, but those unsung heroes and heroines working (relatively silently) behind the scenes—among them Reeva Charles, Liz Jones, Káren North and Brook Pearson during and in the period leading up to the event, and Stanley Porter, Michael Hayes and David Tombs in the months that followed while they have edited the manuscripts resulting from it.

Neil Taylor
Dean of Arts and Humanities
Roehampton Institute London
October 1996

ABBREVIATIONS

AB	Anchor Bible
ABD	D.N. Freedman (ed.), *Anchor Bible Dictionary*
ABRL	Anchor Bible Reference Library
AGJU	Arbeiten zur Geschichte des antiken Judentums und des Urchristentums
AnBib	Analecta biblica
ANRW	*Aufstieg und Niedergang der römischen Welt*
APAMS	American Philological Association Monograph Series
ATLA	American Theological Library Association
ATR	*Anglican Theological Review*
BA	*Biblical Archaeologist*
BARev	*Biblical Archaeology Review*
BASOR	*Bulletin of the American Schools of Oriental Research*
BBR	*Bulletin for Biblical Research*
BETL	Bibliotheca ephemeridum theologicarum lovaniensium
Bib	*Biblica*
BLE	*Bulletin de littérature ecclésiastique*
BNTC	Black's New Testament Commentaries
BZNW	Beihefte zur *ZNW*
CBQ	*Catholic Biblical Quarterly*
CBQMS	*Catholic Bibical Quarterly*, Monograph Series
CELAM	Episcopal Conference of Latin America
ConBNT	Coniectanea biblica, New Testament
ConBOT	Coniectanea biblica, Old Testament
CTQ	*Concordia Theological Quarterly*
EBib	Etudes bibliques
EHST	Europäische Hochschulschriften, Series 23: Theologie
EKKNT	Evangelisch-Katholischer Kommentar zum Neuen Testament
ELR	*English Literary Renaissance*
ETL	*Ephemerides theologicae lovanienses*
EvT	*Evangelische Theologie*
FB	Forschung zur Bibel
GNS	Good News Studies
HTKNT	Herders theologischer Kommentar zum Neuen Testament
HTR	*Harvard Theological Review*
HTS	Harvard Theological Studies
ICC	International Critical Commentary

JBL	Journal of Biblical Literature
JLT	Journal of Literature and Theology
JR	Journal of Religion
JSNT	Journal for the Study of the New Testament
JSNTSup	Journal for the Study of the New Testament, Supplement Series
JSOT	Journal for the Study of the Old Testament
JSP	Journal for the Study of Pseudepigrapha
JTS	Journal of Theological Studies
JWR	Journal of Women and Religion
KAI	H. Donner and W. Röllig, Kanaanäische und aramäische Inschriften
KJV	King James Version
NAC	New American Commentary
NCB	New Century Bible
NEB	New English Bible
NHS	Nag Hammadi Studies
NIBC	New International Bible Commentary
NICNT	New International Commentary on the New Testament
NIGTC	The New International Greek Testament Commentary
NovT	Novum Testamentum
NovTSup	Novum Testamentum Supplements
NRSV	New Revised Standard Version
NTAbh	Neutestamentliche Abhandlungen
NTS	New Testament Studies
NTTS	New Testament Tools and Studies
NumSup	Numen Supplements
OBO	Orbis biblicus et orientalis
OGIS	W. Dittenberger, Orientis graeci inscriptiones selectae I–II
PG	J. Migne (ed.), Patrologia graeca
PL	J. Migne (ed.), Patrologia latina
RHPR	Revue d'histoire et de philosophie religieuses
RILP	Roehampton Institute London Papers
RSV	Revised Standard Version
SANT	Studien zum Alten und Neuen Testament
SBL	Society of Biblical Literature
SBLDS	SBL Dissertation Series
SBLMS	SBL Monograph Series
SBLRBS	SBL Resources for Biblical Study
SC	Sources chrétiennes
SecCent	Second Century
SKKNT	Stuttgarter Katholisches Kommentar Neuen Testament
SNTA	Studiorum Novi Testamentum Auxilia, Leuven
SNTSMS	Society for New Testament Studies Monograph Series
SNTW	Studies of the New Testament and its World

SSEJC	Studies in the Scriptures of Early Judaism and Christianity
TF	Theologische Forschung
Theol	*Theology*
THKNT	Theologischer Handkommentar zum Neuen Testament
TLZ	*Theologische Literaturzeitung*
TS	*Theological Studies*
TTod	*Theology Today*
TU	Texte und Untersuchungen
ThWAT	G.J. Botterweck and H. Ringgren (eds.), *Theologisches Wörterbuch zum Alten Testament*
TynBul	*Tyndale Bulletin*
VC	*Vigiliae christianae*
WBC	Word Bibical Commentary
WF	Wege der Forschung
WMANT	Wissenschaftliche Monographien zum Alten und Neuen Testament
WUNT	Wissenschaftliche Untersuchungen zum Neuen Testament
ZNW	*Zeitschrift für die neutestamentliche Wissenschaft*
ZTK	*Zeitschrift für Theologie und Kirche*

List of Contributors

John Anonby, Trinity Western University, Langley, BC, Canada

John Barber, London, England

Isobel H. Combes, London, England

Deane E.D. Downey, Trinity Western University, Langley, BC, Canada

Craig A. Evans, Trinity Western University, Langley, BC, Canada

David J. Graham, Glasgow Bible College, Scotland

Susan Lochrie Graham, Wycliffe College, University of Toronto, Canada

Mary Grey, Le Sainte Union, University of Southampton, England

Suman Gupta, Roehampton Institute London, England

Richard S. Hess, Roehampton Institute London, England

Kevin McCarron, Roehampton Institute London, England

Clive Marsh, University College of Ripon and York St John, England

Gerald O'Collins, Gregorian University, Rome, Italy

Barbara Pell, Trinity Western University, Langley, BC, Canada

Pat Pinsent, Roehampton Institute London, England

Stanley E. Porter, Roehampton Institute London, England

Wendy J. Porter, Roehampton Institute London, England

Mona Siddiqui, University of Glasgow, Scotland

R.S. Sugirtharajah, Selly Oak Colleges, Birmingham, England

John O. Thompson, University of Wales, Cardiff

David Tombs, Roehampton Institute London, England

Pamela Tudor-Craig, Huntingdon, Cambridgeshire, England

INTRODUCTION

Stanley E. Porter, Michael A. Hayes and David Tombs

Images of Christ come in various forms, shapes, sizes and descriptions. The conference that first heard these papers was a vital part of the continuing conceptualization and re-conceptualization of Christ that has continued without interruption from the first century to the present day. These papers, duly revised and edited for publication in the light of the conference and further reflection, present a more permanent form of the discussion. Each is now here presented for a larger audience to scrutinize and contemplate.

The papers in this volume are organized around presentations of Christ in four major areas: the Bible, Theology, Literature and the Arts. Although several of them would be expected categories for exploration in a set of papers on this topic, each category recapitulates traditional and expected images of Christ but also offers something new and different.

It is appropriate that treatment of the image of Christ begins with the Bible. What may surprise some, however, is that this discussion begins in the Old Testament, with Richard Hess's paper, 'The Image of the Messiah in the Old Testament', setting appropriate groundwork for subsequent biblical discussion. The two following papers are concerned with the Gospels. Craig Evans, in 'Images of Christ in the Canonical and Apocryphal Gospels', surveys the varying images to be found in the Gospel sources, and argues that the complementary pictures of the canonical Gospels are of more value in the quest for the historical Jesus than the apocryphal sources. Using categories from literary theory, Susan Lochrie Graham turns the tables on two recent attempts to describe the historical Jesus found in the Gospels and exegetes the exegetes, in her 'The Life of Jesus as Comedy: Plot Structure in Two Contemporary Historical Jesus Portraits'. Turning to Paul, perhaps the first and arguably the most important conceptualizer of Christ, in

'Images of Christ in Paul's Letters', Stanley Porter explores the complexity of Paul's view, drawing out the fact that Paul does not appear to make the distinction between the historical Jesus and the Christ of faith that later interpreters have claimed that he made. This section concludes with a fascinating study of several other now rather less well-known images of Christ in the Church Fathers. Isobel Combes's 'Nursing Mother, Ancient Shepherd, Athletic Coach? Some Images of Christ in the Early Church' raises intriguing questions about the changing fortunes of the figurative language used to speak of Christ.

Although it may seem like a small and simple step from the biblical images of Christ to the theological ones, the papers in the second section on Theology reflect a much greater diversity than one might expect. Gerald O'Collins, in 'Images of Jesus and Modern Theology', provides a masterful overview and critique of recent treatments of christological titles by modern theologians. His paper is an apt reminder that re-imaging Jesus as Christ is still an important task for theologians, but one with many potential pitfalls. R.S. Sugirtharajah opens up neglected avenues of enquiry in his 'The Magi from Bengal and their Jesus: Indian Construals of Christ during Colonial Times'. His discussion of three important Hindu critiques of Christianity in terms of the problematic colonial ethos provides important insights for those who are only aware of Western contributions to the history of scholarly debates. Mona Siddiqui, in 'Images of Christ in Islam: Scripture and Sentiment', provides an examination of the role and place of Christ in Islamic thought, comparing his role to that of Muhammad and others, especially as depicted in the Qur'an. David Tombs presents the challenging ideas of the Sri Lankan Jesuit Aloysius Pieris in 'Liberating Christology: Images of Christ in the Work of Aloysius Pieris'. Mary Grey concludes this section with a thought-provoking exploration of various feminist conceptions of Christ, in particular the Christa image, in 'Who do you Say that I am? Images of Christ in Feminist Liberation Theology'. Rather than confining itself to Christian conceptions of Christ, this section offers alternative approaches to and alternative means of imaging Christ.

Literature has long been preoccupied with Christ figures and various images of Christ. Sometimes these images have found favour with critics and other times not. The papers in this third section explore the multi-faceted culturally and theologically complex nature of these portraits. In 'Images of Christ in *Corpus Christi* Medieval Mystery

Play Cycles', Deane Downey claims that the didactic and theological intent of the mystery plays does not detract from their appreciable literary qualities. In 'The Image of Christ in the Writings of Two Seventeenth-Century English Country Parsons: George Herbert and Thomas Traherne', Pat Pinsent explores the differing christological images in two well-known Christian writers with formal ties to the Church, even though both remain within the bounds of orthodoxy. John Anonby takes up the novels of arguably the best known and most important recent Kenyan novelist, Ngugi wa Thiong'o, and 'Images of Christ in East African Literature: The Novels of Ngugi wa Thiong'o' treats the various Christ images in his work. Barbara Pell, in 'Images of Christ in Canadian Literature: Faith and Fiction in the Novels of Callaghan, Hood and MacLennan', takes a critical look at three contemporary Canadian novelists, evaluating them according to their stated and implied intentions with regard to Christianity. She finds that expectations are not always fulfilled in literary practice, and that the 'Christian' novel is hard to write. In a study of the work of T.S. Eliot, recently much maligned in critical circles, Kevin McCarron traces important correlations between Eliot's and Dante's work, calling into question some of the criteria used to judge the Anglo-American poet. McCarron's '"The Sudden Look of Some Dead Master": T.S. Eliot and Dante' is an energetic defence of Eliot.

In the fourth and final section of the book, the Arts, some of the most challenging—as well as interesting—work of this book is found. Whereas it is difficult enough to verbally conceptualize Christ, when other media are employed the difficulties are often increased. In 'Jesus as Moving Image: The Question of Movement', John Thompson offers provocative analyses of the ways in which characters are depicted in film, illustrating the challenge that conception of Jesus offers to the medium. Similarly, in 'Christ Imagery in Recent Film: A Saviour from Celluloid?', David Graham examines in more detail various forms of Christ imagery in several recent films. Turning to the plastic arts, Pamela Tudor-Craig, in 'The Iconography of Corpus Christi', explores the image of Christ in several better and less well-known pieces of medieval religious art, challenging viewers to examine these icons again. In 'Images of Christ in the Works of Rembrandt', John Barber focuses upon Rembrandt's corpus. Although Rembrandt is well recognized as an image-maker of Christ, Barber as a practising artist brings his artistic sensibilities to play in this appreciative analysis. Two very stimulating essays address contemporary artists as well. Suman Gupta, in 'Images of Christ in the Paintings of Jamini Roy', and Clive Marsh, in 'Christ on the Road to Belleville: Christology through Conversation with Georges Rouault (1871–1958)', both offer sympathetic yet probing critical analyses of two modern artists concerned with depicting various kinds of images of Christ. In the final essay, 'Bach, Beethoven and Stravinsky Masses: Images of Christ in the Credo', Wendy Porter singles out the Credo section of the masses by these well-known composers to trace their strikingly different conceptions of Christ as illustrated through both text and music.

Although the images presented in these papers are various and diverse in their conception and articulation, and many of the authors would wish to disagree—sometimes quite strongly—with their co-authors in this volume, we believe that such responses are natural and in fact desirable. It is a mistake to think of any image of Christ as static. Of course, the image may remain the same on the page or on a tapestry or on a piece of celluloid, but the reactions that an image of such a figure is bound to elicit bring forth continuing articulation and re-articulation of traditional and modern, orthodox and revisionist, rationalistic and emotional responses.

Part I

BIBLE

THE IMAGE OF THE MESSIAH IN THE OLD TESTAMENT

Richard S. Hess

1. *Introduction*

Consideration of 'the image of Christ' in the Old Testament must avoid the danger of anachronism, especially the temptation to read the character of the Jesus of the New Testament into the Old Testament texts. It is likely that the idea of Christ as it emerges in the New Testament draws upon several components that are found in the Hebrew Bible. One of the most important of these is the term, Messiah, 'the anointed one'.

As is well known, the Greek word for 'Christ', χριστός (*christos*), is a translation of the Hebrew root, משׁח (*mšḥ*), meaning 'to anoint'. There have been many word studies of this root.[1] However, it is worthwhile to re-examine the texts and to consider the implications of this 'title' as understood by the Hebrew Bible. It has been observed that this meaning in the Hebrew Bible is wide and varied and that it does not designate a future individual (except perhaps in Dan. 9).[2] However, this observation requires some qualification. The New Testament writers consistently referred to the Old Testament as their source for understanding the figure designated as the Christ. They most often referred to the Greek Bible, the Septuagint. It is therefore significant that the Greek word, χριστός, wherever it is used in the Septuagint to translate a Hebrew Bible text, always translates some form of the Hebrew root, משׁח.[3] This is remarkable, given the variety of translation techniques

---

1. See, e.g., the bibliographies in K. Seybold, 'מָשַׁח I *māšaḥ*', *ThWAT*, V, cols. 46-47; M. de Jonge, 'Messiah', *ABD*, IV, pp. 787-88.

2. M. Selman, 'Messianic Mysteries', in P.E. Satterthwaite, R.S. Hess and G.J. Wenham (eds.), *The Lord's Anointed: Interpretation of Old Testament Messianic Texts* (Carlisle: Paternoster; Grand Rapids: Baker, 1995), pp. 282-85. Selman himself goes on to qualify this observation with a discussion of other components that con‐stitute the picture of the Messiah.

3. This conclusion is based on an examination of the Septuagint text edition of

used by the writers of the Septuagint. The converse is not true. The Hebrew root, מָשַׁח, is usually but not always translated by the Greek, χριστός, or some form of its cognate verb, χρίω 'I anoint'.[4] Nevertheless, the correspondence between the title and the Hebrew root that it translates invites an examination of its use in the Hebrew Bible. The result may not coincide in every detail with the New Testament writers' image of the Christ, but it will provide a picture that must form the starting point for understanding the development of this concept in later Judaism and Christianity.

In the Hebrew Bible, this root occurs in verbal and noun forms. The closest form related to 'Christ' is the noun form, מָשִׁיחַ (*māšîaḥ*), 'anointed one' or 'messiah'. Apart from this special use as a nominal form, the root, מָשַׁח, occurs at least ninety-three times in the Hebrew Bible. This study will first examine the other uses of the root מָשַׁח and then focus on the occurrences of מָשִׁיחַ, 'anointed one', in the Hebrew Bible.

2. *The Extrabiblical Context of* מָשַׁח *and the Practice of Anointing*

Forms of this root occur in Akkadian, Amorite, Ugaritic, Aramaic and Arabic.[5] An Akkadian verb related in form and meaning is *pašāšu(m)* 'to anoint, rub in', with its corresponding nominal forms, *paššum* 'anointed', *piššatu* 'anointing oil', *pašīšu(m)* 'anointer' (= a priest).[6] In Mari and elsewhere in the early second millennium BCE, Amorite personal names occur with the *mšḥ* root (using a *qātīl*-form of the root, *mšḥ*), *Ma-si-ha-an* and *Ma-si-ḥu-um*.[7] Thus hundreds of years before

---

A. Rahlfs (ed.), *Septuaginta* (Stuttgart: Württembergische Bibelanstalt, 1935), using the *acCordance Septuagint (LXX)* (Vancouver, WA: The GRAMCORD Institute, 1995).

4. See Gen. 31.13; Num. 3.3; 2 Sam. 3.39; Isa. 21.5; and Dan. 9.24.

5. This review follows Seybold, 'מָשַׁח I *māšaḥ*', cols. 47-48.

6. W. von Soden, *Akkadisches Handwörterbuch* (Wiesbaden: Otto Harrassowitz, 1959–1981), pp. 843, 845, 869.

7. H.B. Huffmon, *Amorite Personal Names in the Mari Texts: A Structural and Lexical Study* (Baltimore: The Johns Hopkins University Press, 1965), pp. 145, 232; M. Birot, J.-R. Kupper and O. Roualt, *Répertoire Analytique. II. Tomes I–XIV, XVIII et textes divers hors-collection: première partie: noms propres* (Archives Royales de Mari, 16.1; Paris: Paul Geuthner, 1979), pp. 150-51; I.J. Gelb *et al.*, *Computer-*

the title, מָשִׁיחַ 'anointed one', occurs in the Hebrew Bible, a similar form appears as personal names of men and women. In Ugaritic, *mšḥ* 'to anoint' occurs.[8] In one mythic text it refers to the god Baal anointing the horns of the goddess Anat for battle.[9] Aramaic *mšḥ* occurs from Old Aramaic onwards.[10] In eighth-century BCE Old Aramaic inscriptions it may occur both as a noun ('oil') and a verb ('to anoint [the breasts?]').[11]

Anointing with oil had a variety of uses in the ancient Near East.[12] Oil could be applied for cosmetic and hygienic reasons. It could be used to seal various legal agreements and to create kings. Among the Hittites, holy objects and statues of deities were anointed with oil after they were washed. As part of his accession to the throne and the priesthood of the sun god, the Hittite king was anointed with oil.[13] Of special interest is a

Aided Analysis of Amorite (Assyriological Studies, 21; Chicago: The Oriental Institute of the University of Chicago, 1980), pp. 24-25, 325.

8. For the occurrence of the verb, see C.H. Gordon, *Ugaritic Textbook: Grammar* (Rome: Pontifical Biblical Institute, 1965), p. 439; M. Dietrich, O. Loretz and J. Sanmartín, *The Cuneiform Texts from Ugarit, Ras Ibn Hani and Other Places* (Münster: Ugarit-Verlag, 2nd edn, 1995), KTU 1.10, II, lines 22-23. Fabry reconstructs KTU 1.107 line 48 as *[šm]n.mšḥt.ktpm* 'the anointing oil of the magicians'. In this Fabry follows J. Nougayrol, *Ugaitica V: Textes Suméro-Accadiens des archives et bibliothèques privées d'Ugarit* (Mission de Ras Shamra, 16; Paris: Imprimerie Nationale, 1968), pp. 578, 601. However, the first word is uncertain and therefore *mšḥt* may be either a noun or a verb. See D. Pardee, *Les textes para-mythologiques de la 24e campagne 1961* (Ras Shamra-Ougarit, 4; Paris: Éditions Recherche sur les Civilisations, 1988), p. 254.

9. N.H. Walls, *The Goddess Anat in Ugaritic Myth* (SBLDS, 135; Atlanta: Scholars Press, 1992), p. 91, with discussion of the earlier literature.

10. J. Hoftijzer and K. Jongeling, *Dictionary of the North-West Semitic Inscriptions. Part Two. M-T* (Leiden: Brill, 1995), p. 699.

11. For the verb, *ymsḥ*, see Sefire A 21 (= KAI 222 line 21), J.A. Fitzmyer, *The Aramaic Inscriptions of Sefire* (Biblica et Orientalia, 19; Rome: Pontifical Biblical Institute, 1967), pp. 14-15, 42; H. Donner and W. Rollig, *Kanaanäische und Aramäische Inschriften* (Wiesbaden: Otto Harrassowitz, 1962–1963), I, p. 41, II, p. 247. For a possible noun formation, *mšḥ*, see the analysis of the Zincirli inscription of Barrākib to king Panamuwa II in J. Tropper, *Die Inschriften von Zincirli* (Abhandlungen zur Literatur Alt-Syrien-Palästinas, 6; Münster: Ugarit-Verlag, 1993), pp. 111-12.

12. See Å. Viberg, *Symbols of Law: A Contextual Analysis of Legal Symbolic Acts in the Old Testament* (ConBOT, 34; Stockholm: Almqvist & Wiksell, 1992), pp. 92-93.

13. H.A. Hofner, 'Oil in Hittite Texts', *BA* 58 (1995), pp. 111-12.

fourteenth-century BCE text that describes how the Egyptian pharaoh installed a vassal ruler in a Syrian province.[14] This was done by means of putting oil on the head of the vassal. Thus the pharaoh made kings by anointing them with oil. In addition to personal and legal uses, oil was applied to stone monuments as part of festival rituals in the Late Bronze Age at the Syrian city of Emar.[15] If the stones represent deities, the anointing may represent their preparation for a divine gathering. At the same city a chief female religious functionary, the NIN.DINGIR, had oil poured on her head on the first day of her installation festival.

3. *General Biblical Uses of* מָשַׁח

The Pentateuch uses מָשַׁח exclusively with reference to anointing objects and persons for religious purposes. In Genesis its use is restricted to anointing the pillar at Bethel (Gen. 31.13) in preparation for the vow that Jacob made to God. In Exodus it is part of the ceremony by which Aaron and his sons are made priests (Exod. 28.41; 29.7, 29; 30.30; 40.13, 15; Lev. 6.20; 7.36; 8.12; Num. 3.3). Indeed, it is a special qualification for the priest who presides at the Day of Atonement ritual (Lev. 16.32) and for the high priest whose death signals the end of the unintentional killer's exile in a town of refuge (Num. 35.25). The altar and its implements are anointed to prepare it for consecration (Exod. 29.36; 40.10, 11; Lev. 8.10, 11; Num. 7.1, 10, 84, 88). The same action is done to the tent of meeting and its contents (Exod. 30.26; 40.9; Num. 7.1). The verb, מָשַׁח, describes the adding of oil to cakes that are used in the Tabernacle worship (Exod. 29.2; Lev. 2.4; 7.12; Num. 6.15). All the Tabernacle and priestly applications use a special type of 'anointing oil' (שֶׁמֶן הַמִּשְׁחָה *šemen hammišḥâ*; Exod. 29.7; 40.9; Lev. 8.10, 12).

Cultic or religious uses for מָשַׁח are also found outside the Pentateuch. Dan. 9.24 describes a future time when a 'most holy place' in Jerusalem will be anointed. Ezra records that both Cyrus and Darius decreed that

14. El Amarna text 51, lines 6-7, discussed by Viberg, *Symbols of Law*, pp. 93-94. The text reads, 'when Manaḫpiya, the king of Egypt, your ancestor, made [T]a[k]u, my ancestor, a king in Nuḫašše, he put oil on his head...' W.L. Moran (ed. and trans.), *The Amarna Letters* (Baltimore: The Johns Hopkins University Press, 1992), p. 122.

15. D.E. Fleming, 'More Help from Syria: Introducing Emar to Biblical Study', *BA* 58 (1995), pp. 143-45.

the priests in Jerusalem should receive sufficient oil for their work (Ezra 6.9; 7.22; cf. 6.3?). The Aramaic for this is מְשַׁח (*mᵉšaḥ*). The association of olive oil with the priestly ritual is not only attested in the Bible but also by archaeological excavations in Israel. The presence of an olive oil processing installation at the 'high place' sacred area of tenth/ninth-century BCE Dan (Tel Dan), and the presence of more than a dozen horned altars among more than one hundred olive oil installations at seventh-century BCE Ekron (Tel Miqne) attest to a cultic association of olive oil.[16] If Amos 6.6 is part of a description of a marzeah festival and if this festival has religious associations, then the anointing with oil that is described there also occurs in a religious context, although one that is not approved by the prophet.[17]

In Joshua and Judges the only reference to anointing occurs in Jotham's fable about the trees of the forest who seek to anoint the olive tree and the thorn bush as king (Judg. 9.8, 15). This act of anointing has nothing to do with any specifically Yahwistic activity. Instead, it suggests that the custom of anointing is synonymous with that of appointing or officially recognizing kingship. When Samuel anoints Saul (1 Sam. 9.16; 10.1; 15.1, 17) and David (1 Sam. 16.3, 12, 13; 2 Sam. 2.4 [1 Chron. 11.13], 7; 3.39; 5.3, 17 [1 Chron. 14.8]; 12.7) as leaders, the act of anointing, though divinely ordained, is in itself not primarily a consecration to God but rather a divine recognition that first Saul and then David have achieved a certain status over the people. In David's case this appointment does not immediately establish him as king in Israel. Instead, it signals a feature present in all the specific descriptions of royal anointing in Judah and Israel: they occur especially at times when the succession is irregular; that is,

16. L.E. Stager and S.R. Wolff, 'Production and Commerce in Temple Courtyards: An Olive Press in the Sacred Precinct at Tel Dan', *BASOR* 243 (1981), pp. 95-102; S. Gitin, 'Ekron of the Philistines. Part II: Olive-Oil Suppliers to the World', *BARev* 16.2 (1990), pp. 32-42, 59; *idem*, 'Seventh Century BCE Cultic Elements at Ekron', in A. Biran *et al.* (eds.), *Biblical Archaeology Today, 1990: Proceedings of the Second International Congress on Biblical Archaeology. Jerusalem, June–July 1990* (Jerusalem: Israel Exploration Society and Israel Academy of Sciences and Humanities, 1993), pp. 248-58.

17. The text usually identified with this festival is Amos 6.4-7. See P.J. King, *Amos, Hosea, Micah—An Archaeological Commentary* (Philadelphia: Westminster Press, 1988), pp. 137-61. For the Canaanite texts, see R.J. Clifford, 'Phoenician Religion', *BASOR* 279 (1990), pp. 55-64, esp. p. 58.

when the anointed king is not the eldest son of his predecessor.[18] David was not Saul's son, but this act of anointing gave him the recognition necessary to justify both his own aspirations of military leadership and Saul's attempts to quash them.

The same is true of the anointing of Solomon as king (1 Kgs 1.34, 39, 45; 5.1; 1 Chron. 29.22). That it is done by Zadok the priest seems less a statement about the act's religious associations than it does a public recognition of Solomon's office by a prominent official. In addition, reference is made to the anointing of Absalom (2 Sam. 19.10 [Heb. 11]), Hazael (1 Kgs 19.15), Jehu (1 Kgs 19.16; 2 Kgs 9.3, 6, 12; 2 Chron. 22.7), Joash (2 Kgs 11.12 [2 Chron. 23.11]), and Jehoahaz (2 Kgs 23.30) as kings, and to the anointing of Elisha (1 Kgs 19.16) as a prophet. The one(s) who anoint(s) could be an assembly, as in the Jotham fable, or a single individual, as in most of the occurrences. When a prophet is involved in anointing, God may be credited with the decision to anoint.[19]

In the book of Jeremiah, the verb, מָשׁח 'to anoint', occurs once. Jer. 22.14 describes the activities of an unrighteous ruler who oppresses the people in order to build a fine palace. Part of the palace decoration involves decorating the building. Our root is used to describe this action by means of an infinitive absolute. It has nothing to do with the anointing of a king but it is an act performed by a king.

The occurrences of the verbal form in the Psalms and Isaiah also are used of kingship. Here we return to a use that describes the anointing of the king. However, these occurrences move the act of anointing beyond that of an official designation of a ruler to a clearly religious matter. That is because both designate God as the one who

18. Viberg, *Symbols of Law*, pp. 98, 106. Viberg denies any legal significance to this act and the anointing of Saul in 1 Sam. 10.1. He bases this on the use of the term, *nāgîd*, rather than the customary term for 'king', *melek*. It is likely that in both cases Samuel is avoiding the appointment of each figure as king immediately. For Saul, see J.J.M. Roberts, 'In Defense of the Monarchy: The Contribution of Israelite Kingship to Biblical Theology', in P.D. Miller, Jr, P.D. Hanson and S.D. McBride (eds.), *Ancient Israelite Religion: Essays in Honor of Frank Moore Cross* (Philadelphia: Fortress Press, 1987), pp. 377-96. However, this is not to suggest that anointing to the office of *nāgîd* is not also a legal act with ramifications for both Saul and David.

19. De Jonge ('Messiah', pp. 777-88 [778]) emphasizes Yahweh as the agent responsible for anointing the priests and the kings of Israel. It is true that in many texts Yahweh commands prophets to anoint and priests to be anointed.

anoints. Ps. 45.7 [Heb. 8] refers to God's anointing of a king of Jerusalem. Ps. 89.20 [Heb. 21] describes God's anointing of David בְּשֶׁמֶן קָדְשִׁי (*bᵉšemen qodšî*) 'with my holy oil'. The special oil described recalls that oil which was set apart for use in the priestly rituals at the Tabernacle and Temple. Thus the act of anointing the king has become religious as well as political in its significance. There is only one other occasion when God does the anointing. That is in the description of the spirit-endowed servant of Isa. 61.1 whom Yahweh has anointed to perform a mission (RSV):

> The Spirit of the LORD God is upon me,
> because the LORD has *anointed* me
> to bring good tidings to the afflicted;
> he has sent me to bind up the brokenhearted,
> to proclaim liberty to the captives,
> and the opening of the prison to those who are bound;
> (2)
> to proclaim the year of the LORD's favour,
> and the day of vengeance of our God;
> to comfort all who mourn;
> (3)
> to grant to those who mourn in Zion—
> to give them a garland instead of ashes,
> the oil of gladness instead of mourning,
> the mantle of praise instead of a faint spirit;
> that they may be called oaks of righteousness,
> the planting of the LORD, that he may be glorified.

This text refers to a future individual who will perform deeds of justice and righteousness often associated with rulers. Richard Schultz has revived an earlier interpretation that connects this passage with the Servant Songs of Isaiah 40–55.[20] If so, then this 'servant' is related to the one who brings comfort to Israel and yet who also suffers and dies for the guilt of others. Situated in a context rich in imagery of Israel's exodus, the figure portrayed in the Servant Songs is rightly identified with a 'second Moses' by Gordon Hugenberger.[21] The picture of a 'second exodus', with its comfort to the oppressed, its freedom from oppression and its divine vengeance, is also found in Isa. 61.1-3. This

20. R. Schultz, 'The King in the Book of Isaiah', in Satterthwaite, Hess and Wenham (eds.), *The Lord's Anointed*, pp. 141-65, esp. p. 160.

21. G. Hugenberger, 'The Servant of the Lord in the "Servant Songs" of Isaiah', in Satterthwaite, Hess and Wenham (eds.), *The Lord's Anointed*, pp. 105-40.

figure is not designated a king in Isaiah 61 but he is one who is anointed and who acts like a king in many ways.

Other than for religious and royal purposes, the root, מָשַׁח, occurs in military contexts as a description of the care of a shield. In 2 Sam. 1.21, David's eulogy for King Saul describes his shield as not 'anointed' with oil. This term carries a double meaning in its present context. On the one hand it refers to the proper care given to a shield by a warrior.[22] Thus Isa. 21.5 exhorts the leaders of the armies that attack Babylon to anoint their shields. In 2 Samuel, the shield will no longer receive its appropriate care since its owner has fallen. On the other hand, there is a wordplay with David's use of the Lord's 'anointed' מְשִׁיחַ יהוה (*mᵉšîaḥ yhwh*). In the Hebrew Bible this is the only spelling of the root, מָשַׁח, in the form, מָשִׁיחַ, 'anointed one' or 'messiah', in which the word does not refer to a person or people but to a shield. As will be seen, the most frequent use of מָשִׁיחַ, 'anointed one' or 'messiah,' is found in David's descriptions of Saul and his reason for not killing the old king. David regularly describes Saul as 'Yahweh's anointed'. His concern to avoid any responsibility for Saul's demise and the consequent blood guilt ends with Saul's death in battle. The anointed of God has been cut down so that for the present there is no 'anointed one' to challenge David's rise to kingship, whether it be the former king or the representation of the divine defence of his person in the form of a shield.

A survey of the uses of מָשַׁח 'to anoint', not including the uses of 'the anointed one', reveals that the verb tends to cluster around royalty and religious figures and objects. In the Pentateuch, the emphasis is on the cult and the anointing of priests and objects used in the worship of Israel's God. Throughout the rest of the Bible there is an emphasis on anointing as part of the ceremony used to make a king. These pre-dominant uses are supplemented by uses in other contexts that suggest that the verb could be used in nonroyal and noncultic contexts. Prophets are anointed, houses are decorated and shields are rubbed with oil. However, even these occurrences of the verb can be related to religious or royal concerns. Thus the reader of the Hebrew Bible, when coming upon this verbal root, will expect to find a description dealing with either kings or with religious figures or objects. The same is true of

22. L.E. Stager, 'The Archaeology of the Family in Ancient Israel', *BASOR* 260 (1985), p. 9; A.R. Millard, 'Saul's Shield Not Anointed with Oil', *BASOR* 230 (1978), p. 70.

the extrabiblical uses. With these conclusions about the general uses of
the root in mind, it is possible to turn our consideration to the specific
occurrences of the form מָשִׁיחַ.

4. *Specific Biblical Uses of* מָשִׁיחַ

The Septuagint translates nearly all the appearances of the nominal
form, מָשִׁיחַ 'anointed one', with a form of χριστός. The three exceptions (Lev. 4.3; 2 Sam. 1.21 already discussed; and Dan. 9.25-26) use
a cognate form of χριστός.[23] מָשִׁיחַ 'anointed one' occurs four times in
the Pentateuch, all in chs. 4 and 6 of Leviticus (4.3, 5, 16; 6.22). It
always describes the priest who is anointed to perform the sacrifices
of the sin offering and the burnt offerings. Thus the use of this noun
form corresponds to the general use of the root משׁח 'to anoint', in the
Pentateuch. Outside of these five books, its normal use is to designate
the king. It appears seventeen times in the books of Samuel, first of all
occurring in Hannah's song in parallel to מֶלֶךְ (*melek*) 'king', and thus
signalling this new use (1 Sam. 2.10; cf. also 2.35). The word identifies
a specific king, Saul, as Samuel refers to him (1 Sam. 12.3, 5). It is
used by Samuel to designate Saul's replacement as king (1 Sam. 16.6).
Its most frequent use is by David to identify Saul as מָשִׁיחַ יהוה 'the
anointed one of Yahweh'. David uses this expression nine times with
reference to Saul (1 Sam. 24.6 [twice], 10; 26.9, 11, 16, 23; 2 Sam.
1.14, 16). In every case, David describes the need to protect Saul and
consequently David's own absolute refusal to allow any harm to come
to him.

This use becomes the primary theme of the remaining biblical texts
that use מָשִׁיחַ 'anointed one'. David himself is so identified three times
at the end of 2 Samuel. It is used as part of his title in 23.1 and it
occurs in Abishai's words that suggest death for any who curse David,
the anointed of Yahweh (19.21). Although in the books of Samuel and
Kings it is only used specifically of Saul and David, among all the
kings of Israel and Judah, it does occur in the poem of 2 Sam. 22.51
where it widens to include all royal descendants of David (RSV):

> [God] shows steadfast love
> to his anointed

---

23. In Lev. 4.3, a participial form occurs to describe the anointed priest
(κεχρισμένος *kechrismenos*). 2 Sam. 1.21 uses a passive aorist form, ἐχρίσθη
(*echristhē*). In Dan. 9.25-26, the common noun, χρῖσμα (*chrisma*), occurs.

> to David
> and to his descendants
> for ever.

This statement is also found in the parallel text, Ps. 18.50 [Heb. 51]. There it provides a clue for the eight remaining occurrences of the singular מָשִׁיחַ 'anointed one' in the Hebrew Psalter. These appearances describe conditions in which the anointed one is threatened by earthly forces (2.2; 89.51 [Heb. 52]), but directs pleas for deliverance to God (84.9 [Heb. 10]; 132.10) and is confident of salvation (20.6 [Heb. 7]; 28.8) and of promised blessing (132.17). In Psalm 89 the psalmist blames God for rejecting the anointed one (v. 38 [Heb. 39]), but even here the Psalm ends with a cry to the same deity to rescue the anointed one from those who mock and taunt (v. 51 [Heb. 52]). Although the anointed one is normally understood as the king, in the psalm of Hab. 3.13 the term is used in parallel with the people of God (RSV):

> Thou wentest forth
> for the salvation of thy people (עַמֶּךָ *'ammekā*),
> for the salvation of thy anointed.

Here the Septuagint renders the singular Hebrew 'anointed one' with the plural, 'your anointed ones' τοὺς χριστούς σου (*tous christous sou*). The people of Israel are also designated this way in Ps. 105.15 which is placed in the mouth of David by the Chronicler (1 Chron. 16.22). Here it describes the people of Israel as divinely protected during their early period of wandering from nation to nation. They are called both anointed ones and prophets, and these titles bestow upon them a special privilege and protection given by God.[24]

Elsewhere, Solomon refers to himself in this way. At the conclusion of his prayer to dedicate the Temple, he requests that God remain with him and bless him (2 Chron. 6.42). God designates Cyrus, the king of Persia, as 'my anointed one' in Isa. 45.1. The purpose of this unusual attribution of divine anointing to a non-Israelite has to do with Cyrus's conquests that allow Israel to return to Jerusalem. A mysterious future figure is designated as מָשִׁיחַ 'anointed one' in Dan. 9.25-26. This ruler will be associated with the future restoration of Jerusalem but will be cut off before the time of the city's subsequent destruction.

The association with both royal and priestly figures may find support

---

24. See also Lam. 4.20 where the anointed of Yahweh are caught by the enemy, despite their belief that their status would protect them.

in the postexilic prophecies of Zechariah. In chs. 4–6 the prophet praises Zerubbabel the governor of the Jerusalem community, and Joshua the high priest. In Zech. 4.14, in the context of a vision of a lampstand and olive trees, the two are described as בְּנֵי־הַיִּצְהָר (*bᵉnê-hayyiṣhār*), literally 'sons of olive-oil', but actually a reference to their possession of an anointing so that they 'stand before the lord of all the earth'.[25] This text is unique in its explicit association of both Jerusalem's civil leader and priest with anointing.

5. *Conclusion*

This survey of the occurrences of מָשִׁיחַ 'anointed one' in the Hebrew Bible leads to a number of observations.

First, מָשִׁיחַ 'anointed one' has a wide ranging use that includes non-Israelites as well as Israelites, priests as well as kings, groups of people as well as individuals. Therefore, it was not used only of a single person or even a group or type of person.

Secondly, many occurrences of מָשִׁיחַ 'anointed one' share common features. It is not possible to be categorical about these traits but there are characteristics that most figures share. The מָשִׁיחַ 'anointed one' tends to be an individual or group whose life is threatened by enemies and who is often engaged in military matters. The מָשִׁיחַ 'anointed one' also is a figure who is chosen and protected by God, and therefore can expect God to act with mercy and salvation.

Thirdly, the most numerous occurrences of מָשִׁיחַ 'anointed one' are those by David used to describe Saul. These uses suggest a divinely appointed ruler whose authority extends over all the people of God and whose protection and support is their responsibility. It is not clear that it describes a personal or intimate relationship between God and the anointed one.[26] The Cyrus text (Isa. 45.1) is particularly difficult to explain in this way. It is better to understand in the act of anointing an assignment to an office or responsibility that carries with it authority for the leadership of the people, whether in religious, civil or military matters. In Israel's context this authority is divinely given and the person bearing the office, whether prophet, priest or king, must ulti-

---

25. M. de Jonge, 'Christ', in K. van der Toorn, B. Becking and P.W. van der Horst (eds.), *Dictionary of Deities and Demons in the Bible* (Leiden: Brill, 1995), col. 371.

26. De Jonge, 'Messiah', p. 779.

mately answer before God for his or her exercise of this authority.

Fourthly and finally, the act of anointing with oil was a practice that formed part of the West Semitic culture, both within the Bible and outside. In the texts we have looked at, its religious and royal function was understood to authorize and empower the anointed one to priestly, cultic, military and prophetic functions. Although the image of the anointed one in the Hebrew Bible and its larger cultural context could reflect a variety of practices, its most frequently attested roles in the texts that have been preserved are those of priest and king. The occurrences of these referents in the extrabiblical texts and in the uses of the root, משׁח, and of the form, מָשִׁיחַ, in the Hebrew Bible provide an image of 'Christ' for both modern and ancient readers which places an emphasis on priestly and royal elements.

IMAGES OF CHRIST IN THE CANONICAL
AND APOCRYPHAL GOSPELS

Craig A. Evans

A review of the images of Christ in the canonical and apocryphal Gospels is no easy task. This is so because of the number and complexities of these documents. These complexities involve problems such as poor preservation of sources, uncertain literary relationships among the documents themselves, and even less certain knowledge of their respective provenances. In short, we know little about the individuals and communities (the latter often no more than an assumption) which generated and transmitted them.

Closely related to the images of Christ in the Gospels is the question of the historical Jesus. A modest, but reasonably certain, portrait of the historical Jesus is necessary in order to highlight the respective images of Christ. But the task of Jesus research brings with it many complications and uncertainties. More problematic still, there is a great deal of debate about just what the goal of Jesus research is and what, therefore, we should hope to learn from the canonical and apocryphal Gospels. Are we inpursuit of the pre-Easter Jesus, or the risen Christ who casts the pre-Easter Jesus into a new light? Are we attempting to recover the *real* Jesus, or is such a quest misguided and ultimately impossible?[1] The present essay does not address this complicated dimension of the problem, but it does bear it in mind.

---

1. On this latter point, see J.P. Meier, *A Marginal Jew: Rethinking the Historical Jesus* (ABRL; New York: Doubleday, 1991), pp. 21-40; L.T. Johnson, *The Real Jesus: The Misguided Quest for the Historical Jesus and the Truth of the Traditional Gospels* (San Francisco: HarperCollins, 1995). Johnson's entire book is addressed to these difficult questions. In my view, his criticisms leveled against much of the recent Jesus research and its questionable assumptions and methods, especially those associated with the North American Jesus Seminar, are right on target and deserve careful consideration.

In this essay I shall attempt a modest survey and limited analysis of the various portraits of Jesus[2] presented in the canonical and apocryphal Gospels. The canonical Gospels will not be accorded privileged status (nor will such be accorded the apocryphal Gospels). My hope is to clarify the nature of the material out of which portraits of Jesus could be composed and to identify significant tendencies. Nevertheless, lying behind this survey is a concern to recover a picture of the historical Jesus and to determine its relationship to the images of Christ as they came to expression in the Gospels in and outside of the canon. This picture will serve as a point of reference as the various portraits of Christ are considered.

Assessing the Sources and the Methods: Preliminary Considerations

When we think of the 'Canonical' Gospels, we usually have in mind Matthew, Mark, Luke, and John. But, depending upon one's solution to the synoptic problem and the question of the development of the Johannine tradition, we may have six, not four canonical sources. The synoptic problem attempts to explain the literary relationship among the first three Gospels. The majority of Gospel scholars believe that Mark and the sayings source called Q were the literary sources upon which the Matthean and Lukan evangelists later drew in composing their respective Gospels. If this solution is correct, and I believe that it is,[3] then in reality we have four synoptic sources: Q, Mark, Matthew, and Luke (in the probable order of their composition).[4] With regard to the Fourth Gospel, many scholars believe that a document consisting

2. I shall refer to 'Jesus', instead of 'Christ', because the latter term is confessional and more theologically charged than the former. My concern is not so much with what Christians believed about Jesus (i.e. Christology; or how one is supposed to believe 'in' him), but how they remembered and depicted him (i.e. historiography). I am well aware that Christology influenced historiography.

3. I summarize what I regard to be the primary arguments in favor of the Two Source hypothesis in C.A. Evans, 'Source, Form and Redaction Criticism: The "Traditional" Methods of Synoptic Interpretation', in S.E. Porter and D. Tombs (eds.), *Approaches to New Testament Study* (JSNTSup, 120; Sheffield: Sheffield Academic Press, 1995), pp. 17-45, esp. pp. 20-26.

4. Some scholars add two more sources: 'M' (a source utilized by the Matthean evangelist) and 'L' (a source utilized by the Lukan evangelist). These hypothetical sources are much debated. Along with many others, I am not convinced that there ever were such sources, at least as distinct, coherent literary works.

largely of Jesus' miracles, referred to as 'signs', was incorporated. If this view is correct, and again I think it is,[5] then we have two Johannine sources: the signs source and the Johannine Gospel itself. Thus, all together we may very well have six sources preserved in the four New Testament Gospels; and, conceivably, we could have six distinct images of Jesus.

Once we step outside of the New Testament, we are confronted with several Gospels, preserved for the most part as fragments and excerpts in later sources. The portraits of Jesus preserved in these writings display a great deal of variety. As we shall see, our knowledge of their provenance is limited. Our conclusions must remain tentative, though, as we shall see, there are some who believe that they can infer a great many things from these writings.

Scholarly study of the Gospels entails several important tasks, which are achieved through the application of three methods: (1) source criticism, (2) form criticism, and (3) redaction criticism. In recent years several other aspects of these critical methods have been developed that in various ways grow out of the three older critical methods.

Source criticism of the Gospels has addressed itself primarily to the already mentioned synoptic problem. Scholarly investigation has resulted in the discovery of two primary sources (Q and Mark) and two later sources (Matthew and Luke, along with their special sources and traditions). Source critics have also explored the relationship of John to the synoptic Gospels. It appears that most scholars today think that John was literarily independent of the Synoptics, though synoptic-like tradition may have been known to the fourth evangelist. Source criticism lays the groundwork for ongoing critical study.

Form criticism of the Gospels is concerned with the history and development of the dominical tradition, from its oral to its written transmission. Ascertaining the 'form' (or *genre*) of individual units of tradition and their 'function' in the life of the community (or *Sitz im Leben*) constitutes the principal task of this method. *Historical criticism* and *tradition criticism* grew out of form criticism. The former is concerned with the question of what can be learned of the historical Jesus from the Gospels, while the latter traces the development of certain themes, ideas, and interpretations. Form critics, especially the German pioneers, often rendered historical judgments, claiming that this saying

---

5.   On this question, see the discussion and bibliography below.

or that derived either from the historical Jesus or from the early community.

Redaction criticism is concerned with the manner in which the respective evangelists edited the material they inherited and how they composed their respective Gospels. Redaction critics hope to infer from this editorial activity information about the circumstances of the evangelists and their communities. Recognizing the presence of redaction is important for Jesus research, though it is not necessary to assume that all redaction is unhistorical and, when it concerns the words of Jesus, inauthentic. Several related methods have grown out of redaction criticism. Most fall under the general heading of literary criticism, much of which expresses itself in terms of 'close readings' of the text.[6] We now hear of new methods such as 'structuralism',[7] 'reader response' criticism,[8] 'rhetorical' criticism,[9] and 'social-scientific' criticism.[10]

Canonical Images of Jesus

We shall examine the canonical images of Jesus in the probable order of their production and publication. The oldest extant material, in all probability, is what we call Q, that is, the source extracted from Matthew and Luke. Next come Mark, Matthew, and Luke. How to fit the Johannine tradition into this sequence is difficult to determine. It is

6. See E.V. McKnight, *Postmodern Use of the Bible: The Emergence of Reader-Oriented Criticism* (Nashville: Abingdon Press, 1988); S.D. Moore, *Literary Criticism and the Gospels* (New Haven: Yale University Press, 1989).

7. See D. Patte, *What is Structural Exegesis?* (Philadelphia: Fortress Press, 1976); R.M. Polzin, *Biblical Structuralism* (Missoula, MT: Scholars Press, 1977).

8. See S.E. Porter, 'Why Hasn't Reader-Response Criticism Caught on in New Testament Studies?', *JLT* 4 (1990), pp. 278-92; *idem*, 'Literary Approaches to the New Testament: From Formalism to Deconstruction and Back', in Porter and Tombs (eds.), *Approaches to New Testament Study*, pp. 77-128, esp. pp. 106-28.

9. See D.L. Stamps, 'Rhetorical Criticism of the New Testament: Ancient and Modern Evaluations of Argumentation', in Porter and Tombs (eds.), *Approaches to New Testament Study*, pp. 129-69.

10. See B.J. Malina and R.L. Rohrbaugh, *Social-Science Commentary on the Synoptic Gospels* (Minneapolis: Fortress Press, 1992); P. Richter, 'Social-Scientific Criticism of the New Testament: An Appraisal and Extended Example', in Porter and Tombs (eds.), *Approaches to New Testament Study*, pp. 266-309.

I have deliberately omitted 'deconstructionism'. It is more of an assumption than a method, resting on confusion and misunderstanding of what language and literature attempt to and in fact usually do accomplish.

possible, and I think probable, that the signs source is early. But is it as early as Q, or one of the Synoptic Gospels? It could be, but because we do not know and because it would not be helpful to interrupt the synoptic sequence in our analysis, we shall treat the Johannine tradition last in this section.

Q

More than a century ago scholars began to refer to the large body of sayings shared by Matthew and Luke but not found in Mark as 'Q', from the German word *Quelle*, which means spring (of water) or source. In the last two or three decades there has been a marked increase in scholarly interest in ascertaining as precisely as possible the contents of Q and the nature of the Christian community that gathered and edited this material.[11] Q is popular with those involved in Jesus research because it is widely assumed to yield the most primitive and historical portrait of Jesus.

Q may indeed be quite old and its tradition may well be primitive, but in my view scholars say far too much about this hypothetical source. There is no Q document extant, but that has not stopped James Robinson and company from attempting to reconstruct it on the basis of what is found in Matthew and Luke.[12] How do we know that a sufficient amount of Q has been preserved to make such reconstruction possible, and the inferences that inevitably derive from it? Any description of the theology of Q and of the community alleged to have assembled and edited it must be circumspect.[13] But not all scholars heed these caveats.

11. One of the difficulties that attend Q research is the question of what form it took: was it written, oral, or part-written and part-oral? For a defense of Q as a written source, see J.S. Kloppenborg, *The Formation of Q: Trajectories in Ancient Wisdom Collections* (Studies in Antiquity & Christianity; Philadelphia: Fortress Press, 1987), pp. 41-51.

12. J.M. Robinson, 'The Sayings of Jesus: Q', *Drew Gateway* 54 (1983–84), pp. 26-38; *idem*, 'A Critical Text of the Sayings Gospel Q', *RHPR* 72 (1992), pp. 15-22; *idem*, 'The Sayings Gospel Q', in F. Van Segbroeck *et al.* (eds.), *The Four Gospels 1992* (F. Neirynck Festschrift; 3 vols.; BETL, 100; Leuven: Peeters and Leuven University Press, 1992), I, pp. 361-88.

13. Bibliography on Q is enormous. For recent work that speaks to issues that are pertinent to the present study, see V. Taylor, 'The Original Order of Q', in A.J.B. Higgins (ed.), *New Testament Essays: Studies in Memory of T.W. Manson* (Manchester: University of Manchester Press, 1959), pp. 246-69; D. Lührmann, *Die Redaktion der Logienquelle* (WMANT, 33; Neukirchen-Vluyn: Neukirchener Verlag,

We hear confident descriptions of the 'Christology of Q' and the 'community of Q'. We are even told, on the basis of silence, what the Q community did not regard as important, for example, Jesus' miracles, death, and resurrection. From these observations we now know, we are assured, that the Jesus of the Q community was substantially different from the portraits of Jesus preserved in the Synoptic Gospels.

The following materials, which according to convention are placed in the Lukan order, are thought by most scholars to belong to Q:

Lk. 3.7-9, 16-17	Preaching of John	Mt. 3.7-12
Lk. 4.1-13	Temptations	Mt. 4.1-11
Lk. 6.20-26	Beatitudes	Mt. 5.1-12
Lk. 6.27-36	Love of enemies	Mt. 5.39-42, 44-48; 7.12
Lk. 6.37-42	Admonitions	Mt. 7.1-5; 10.24-25; 15.14
Lk. 6.43-45	A tree and its fruit	Mt. 7.16-20; 12.33-35

1969); S. Schulz, *Q: Die Spruchquelle der Evangelisten* (Zürich: Theologischer Verlag, 1972); G.N. Stanton, 'On the Christology of Q', in B. Lindars and S.S. Smalley (eds.), *Christ and Spirit in the New Testament* (C.F.D. Moule Festschrift; Cambridge: Cambridge University Press, 1973), pp. 27-42; R.A. Edwards, *A Theology of Q* (Philadelphia: Fortress Press, 1976); J. Delobel (ed.), *Logia: Les Paroles de Jésus—The Sayings of Jesus (Mémorial Joseph Coppens)* (BETL, 59; Leuven: Peeters and Leuven University Press, 1982); A. Polag, *Fragmenta Q: Texthefte zur Logienquelle* (Neukirchen-Vluyn: Neukirchener Verlag, 2nd edn, 1982); D. Zeller, *Kommentar zur Logienquelle* (SKKNT, 21; Stuttgart: Katholisches Bibelwerk, 1984); Kloppenborg, *The Formation of Q*; R.A. Piper, *Wisdom in the Q-Tradition: The Aphoristic Teaching of Jesus* (SNTSMS, 61; Cambridge: Cambridge University Press, 1989); H. Koester, 'Q and its Relatives', in J.E. Goehring *et al.* (eds.), *Gospel Origins and Christian Beginnings* (Forum Fascicles; Sonoma, CA: Polebridge Press, 1990), pp. 49-63; A.D. Jacobson, *The First Gospel: An Introduction to Q* (Sonoma, CA: Polebridge Press, 1992); Van Segbroeck *et al.* (eds.), *The Four Gospels 1992*, I, pp. 361-688; D.R. Catchpole, *The Quest for Q* (Edinburgh: T. & T. Clark, 1993); B.L. Mack, *The Lost Gospel: The Book of Q and Christian Origins* (San Francisco: HarperCollins, 1993); J.S. Kloppenborg (ed.), *The Shape of Q: Signal Essays on the Sayings Gospel* (Minneapolis: Fortress Press, 1994); L.E. Vaage, *Galilean Upstarts: Jesus' First Followers according to Q* (Valley Forge, PA: Trinity Press International, 1994); R.A. Piper (ed.), *The Gospel behind the Gospels: Current Studies on Q* (NovTSup, 75; Leiden: Brill, 1995); C.M. Tuckett, *Studies on Q* (Edinburgh: T. & T. Clark, 1995).

For synopses that provide the Greek text of Q, see J.S. Kloppenborg, *Q Parallels* (Foundations and Facets; Sonoma, CA: Polebridge Press, 1988); F. Neirynck, *Q-Synopsis: The Double Tradition Passages in Greek* (SNTA, 13; Leuven: Peeters and Leuven University Press, 1988; 2nd edn, 1995).

Lk. 6.46-49	Two foundations	Mt. 7.21, 24-27
Lk. 7.1-10	Healing of the centurion's slave	Mt. 7.28a; 8.5-10, 13
Lk. 7.18-23	John's question	Mt. 11.2-6
Lk. 7.24-28	Jesus praises John	Mt. 11.7-11
Lk. 7.31-35	Fickle children	Mt. 11.16-19
Lk. 9.57-62	Would-be followers	Mt. 8.19-22
Lk. 10.2-12	The mission speech	Mt. 9.37-38; 10.7-16
Lk. 10.13-15	Woe on unbelieving cities	Mt. 11.21-23
Lk. 10.16	Hearing and rejecting	Mt. 10.40
Lk. 10.21-24	Praise of the Father	Mt. 11.25-27; 13.16-17
Lk. 11.2-4	Lord's Prayer	Mt. 6.9-13
Lk. 11.9-13	Ask, seek, knock	Mt. 7.7-11
Lk. 11.14-20, 23	Beelzebul accusation	Mt. 12.22-30; 9.32-34
Lk. 11.24-26	Return of unclean spirit	Mt. 12.43-45
Lk. 11.16, 29-32	Request for a sign	Mt. 12.38-42
Lk. 11.33	Lamp and bushel basket	Mt. 5.15
Lk. 11.34-35	Eye and light	Mt. 6.22-23
Lk. 11.39-52	Religious hypocrisy	Mt. 23.4, 6-7, 13, 23, 25-27, 29-32, 34-36
Lk. 12.2-12	Revelation and faith	Mt. 10.26-33; 12.32; 10.19-20
Lk. 12.22-31	On anxieties	Mt. 6.25-33
Lk. 12.33-34	On possessions	Mt. 6.19-21
Lk. 12.39-46	On preparedness	Mt. 24.43-51
Lk. 12.49-53	Sword, not peace	Mt. 10.34-36
Lk. 12.54-56	Knowing the times	Mt. 16.2-3
Lk. 12.57-59	Before the judge	Mt. 5.25-26
Lk. 13.18-21	Mustard seed and leaven	Mt. 13.31-33
Lk. 13.23-30	Two ways	Mt. 7.13-14; 25.10-12; 7.22-23; 8.11-12; 20.16
Lk. 13.34-35	Jerusalem indicted	Mt. 23.37-39
Lk. 14.11; 18.14	Exaltation and debasement	Mt. 23.12
Lk. 14.16-24	Parable of the Great Banquet	Mt. 22.2-10
Lk. 14.26-27	Hating one's family	Mt. 10.37-38
Lk. 14.34-35	Tasteless salt	Mt. 5.13
Lk. 15.4-7	Parable of Lost Sheep	Mt. 18.12-14
Lk. 16.13	Two masters	Mt. 6.24
Lk. 16.16	Law and prophets	Mt. 11.12-13
Lk. 16.17	Importance of the Law	Mt. 5.18

Lk. 16.18	On divorce	Mt. 5.32
Lk. 17.1	Millstone	Mt. 18.7
Lk. 17.3-4	On forgiveness	Mt. 18.15, 21-22
Lk. 17.6	On faith	Mt. 17.20
Lk. 17.23-24, 26-30, 33-35, 37	The coming of the Son of Man	Mt. 24.26-28, 37-41; 10.39
Lk. 19.12-27	Parable of the Noble Man	Mt. 25.14-20
Lk. 22.28-30	On twelve thrones	Mt. 19.28

An image of Jesus can be tentatively extracted from this material. A first impression is that Jesus is a sage, a teacher of a way of life. Much of the material found in the Sermon on the Mount/Plain falls into this category. Many of the teachings found in Q reflect themes found in Jewish wisdom tradition, as found, for example, in Proverbs, Sirach, and Wisdom of Solomon. Only one miracle story is told (Lk. 7.1-10 = Mt. 8.5-10, 13) and the point mostly has to do with faith ('Not even in Israel have I found such faith!'). There is no story of the passion; nor is the resurrection mentioned. But we cannot infer from these omissions that the 'Q community', if there was one, had no interest in the death and resurrection of Jesus. To make such a claim would be an inappropriate use of the argument from silence. This is so for two reasons: (1) The purpose of the Q collection may have been primarily paraenetic. Therefore, miracle stories and the passion story were unnecessary. (2) Because we have no way of knowing how much of Q is missing, we cannot be certain that it originally did not contain references to the passion and resurrection.

Q does contain some important elements of Christology. John's question ('Are you the Coming One?') and Jesus' positive reply, in which he alludes to passages from Isa. 35.5-6 and 61.1-2 (Lk. 7.18-23 = Mt. 11.2-6), should probably be understood as a messianic affirmation. This is probable because of the discovery of 4Q521 in which a similar allusion to the Isaian passages is found in the context of a description of the deeds of the Messiah. That is, John has asked Jesus if he is the Messiah, and Jesus has replied indirectly (as modesty and messianic tradition apparently required) that he is, as seen by his messianic deeds.[14] Elsewhere Jesus warns his generation of the danger

14. See the discussion in J.D. Tabor and M.O. Wise, '4Q521 "On Resurrection" and the Synoptic Gospel Tradition: A Preliminary Study', *JSP* 10 (1994), pp. 149-62; J.J. Collins, *The Scepter and the Star: The Messiahs of the Dead Sea Scrolls and*

of judgment for their lack of faith. They have no excuse, for a preacher greater than Jonah is present, and a sage wiser than Solomon is present (Lk. 11. 29-32 = Mt. 12.40-42). Indeed, he who acknowledges Jesus before people will be acknowledged before the angels of God (Lk. 12.8-9 = Mt. 10.32-33). On account of Jesus, families will be divided (Lk. 12.51-53 = Mt. 10.34-36). The allusion to Mic. 7.6 is significant here, for it appears in the Mishnah's only significant mention of the Messiah (cf. *m. Sota* 9.15). It is probable that in predicting family divisions on account of himself, Jesus implies that he is Israel's Messiah. Finally, the saying about the disciples sitting on thrones judging the twelve tribes of Israel (Lk. 22.28-30 = Mt. 19.28), at the time when the son of man is seated on his throne of glory (so Matthew), or when his disciples will sit at table with Jesus 'in [his] kingdom' (so Luke), clearly implies a messianic self-understanding on the part of Jesus.

Thus, although we may not be certain what views the author(s) of the Q material held with respect to the death and resurrection of Jesus (and silence gives us little to go on!), we cannot say that there is no Christology in Q or that Q's Christology is a low Christology. What Christology is present coheres, as we shall see, with the Christology present in the other New Testament Gospel sources.

Gospel of Mark

Mark's Gospel directly and boldly clarifies its image of Jesus: in the opening verse the evangelist declares that Jesus is the 'Christ, the son of God' (Mk 1.1).[15] Toward the end of his narrative, at the moment that

---

Other Ancient Literature (ABRL; New York: Doubleday, 1995), pp. 117-22. Wise and Tabor ('The Messiah at Qumran', *BARev* 18.6 [1992], pp. 60-65) were the first to recognize the significance of the parallel between 4Q521 and Jesus' reply to John the Baptist.

15. For selected studies, see W. Marxsen, *Mark the Evangelist: Studies on the Redaction History of the Gospel* (Nashville: Abingdon Press, 1969 [1956]); R.P. Martin, *Mark: Evangelist and Theologian* (Exeter: Paternoster; Grand Rapids: Zondervan, 1972); W. Schenk, *Der Passionsbericht nach Markus: Untersuchung zur Überlieferungsgeschichte der Passionstraditionen* (Gütersloh: Mohn, 1974); D.-A. Koch, *Die Bedeutung der Wundererzählungen für die Christologie des Markusevangeliums* (BZNW, 42; Berlin: de Gruyter, 1975); W. Kelber (ed.), *The Passion in Mark: Studies on Mark 14–16* (Philadelphia: Fortress Press, 1976); D. Juel, *Messiah and Temple: The Trial of Jesus in the Gospel of Mark* (SBLDS, 31; Missoula, MT: Scholars Press, 1977); H.C. Kee, *Community of the New Age: Studies in Mark's Gospel* (Philadelphia: Westminster Press, 1977); C.R. Kazmierski,

the crucified and apparently defeated Jesus dies, the Roman centurion confesses: 'Truly this man was the son of God!' (Mk 15.39). It is apparent that the Markan evangelist wishes to portray Jesus as the true 'son of God', in contrast to the Roman emperor or to any other savior or deliverer of the Graeco-Roman world. Mark's portrait of Jesus appears consciously to parallel aspects of ceremony and deification associated with the Roman emperor cult, as it was developing in the middle of the first century CE. These parallels can be observed at several points:

Jesus, the Son of God: A Study of the Markan Tradition and its Redaction by the Evangelist (FB, 33; Würzburg: Echter Verlag, 1979); E. Best, *Following Jesus: Discipleship in the Gospel of Mark* (JSNTSup, 4; Sheffield: JSOT Press, 1981); *idem, Disciples and Discipleship: Studies in the Gospel according to Mark* (Edinburgh: T. & T. Clark, 1986); A. Stock, *Call to Discipleship: A Literary Study of Mark's Gospel* (GNS, 1; Wilmington, DE: Michael Glazier, 1982); J.D. Kingsbury, *The Christology of Mark's Gospel* (Philadelphia: Fortress Press, 1983); *idem, Conflict in Mark: Jesus, Authorities, Disciples* (Minneapolis: Fortress Press, 1989); M. Hengel, *Studies in the Gospel of Mark* (Philadelphia: Fortress Press, 1985); B. van Iersel, *Reading Mark* (Edinburgh: T. & T. Clark, 1988); T.J. Geddert, *Watchwords: Mark 13 in Markan Eschatology* (JSNTSup, 26; Sheffield: JSOT Press, 1989); J. Camery-Hoggatt, *Irony in Mark's Gospel: Text and Subtext* (SNTSMS, 72; Cambridge: Cambridge University Press, 1992); A.Y. Collins, *The Beginning of the Gospel: Probings of Mark in Context* (Minneapolis: Fortress Press, 1992); Van Segbroeck *et al.* (eds.), *The Four Gospels 1992*, II, pp. 693-1183; C.A. Evans and W.R. Stegner (eds.), *The Gospels and the Scriptures of Israel* (JSNTSup, 104; SSEJC, 3; Sheffield: Sheffield Academic Press, 1994), pp. 196-278; H.T. Fleddermann, *Mark and Q: A Study of the Overlap Texts* (BETL, 122; Leuven: Peeters and Leuven University Press, 1995).

The following commentaries (with emphasis on English works) are recommended: H. Anderson, *The Gospel of Mark* (NCB; London: Oliphants; Grand Rapids: Eerdmans, 1976); J. Gnilka, *Das Evangelium nach Markus* (2 vols.; EKKNT, 2.1-2; Zürich: Benzinger; Neukirchen–Vluyn: Neukirchener Verlag, 1978 [1979]); W. Grundmann, *Das Evangelium nach Markus* (THKNT, 2; Berlin: Evangelische Verlagsanstalt, 8th edn, 1980); R.A. Guelich, *Mark 1–8:26* (WBC, 34A; Dallas: Word, 1989); R.H. Gundry, *Mark: A Commentary on his Apology for the Cross* (Grand Rapids: Eerdmans, 1993); M.D. Hooker, *The Gospel according to Saint Mark* (BNTC; London: A. & C. Black, 1991); L. Hurtado, *Mark* (NIBC, 2; Peabody, MA: Hendrickson, 1989); W.L. Lane, *The Gospel according to Mark* (NICNT; Grand Rapids: Eerdmans, 1974); R. Pesch, *Das Markusevangelium* (2 vols.; HTKNT, 2.1-2; Freiburg: Herder, 1979, 1991); V. Taylor, *The Gospel according to St Mark* (London: Macmillan, 2nd edn, 1966).

1. Various events related to the Roman emperor were called 'good news'. A calendrical inscription from Priene (OGIS 458), which describes the birthday of Augustus, provides a helpful example: ἦρξεν δὲ τῶι κόσμωι τῶν...εὐαγγελίων ἡ γενέθλιος τοῦ θεοῦ ('But the birthday of the god was...the beginning of the good news for the world'). Elsewhere (e.g. *P. Ryl.* 601; *P. Tebt.* 382; *P. Oslo* 26) Augustus is called 'son of God' (υἱὸς θεοῦ). Vespasian's accession to the throne (69 CE) was hailed throughout the empire as 'good news' (Josephus, *War* 4.10.6 §618; 4.11.5 §§656–57).

The appearance of the words ἄρχεσθαι ('to begin'; cognate to ἀρχή, 'beginning'), εὐαγγέλιον ('good news'), and θεός ('God') or υἱὸς θεοῦ ('son of God') in inscriptions in honor of the Roman emperor immediately reminds us of the opening words of Mark's Gospel: 'The beginning of the good news of Jesus Christ, the son of God' (ἀρχὴ τοῦ εὐαγγελίου Ἰησοῦ Χριστοῦ υἱοῦ θεοῦ). The Markan evangelist has employed the very words used in the Roman Empire to acclaim the emperor.

2. Omens surrounding birth, death, and other major events in the lives of Roman emperors were commonly reported. Caesar's murder was foretold to him by 'unmistakable signs' (Suetonius, *Divus Julius* 81.1), among which was the death of a small bird carrying a sprig of laurel (81.3). Several omens supposedly prior to, during, and shortly after the birth of Augustus were remembered, at least many years after the fact. Suetonius relates that the senate, fearing the fulfillment of the prophecy of a coming king, 'decreed that no male child born that year should be reared' (*Divus Augustus* 94.3). The parents of Augustus had portentous dreams, such that following his birth the child was regarded as the 'son of Apollo' (94.4). Jupiter appeared in one dream and foretold that Augustus would become the 'savior of his country' (94.8). The death of Augustus was preceded by many omens and signs. According to Suetonius, 'His [Augustus's] death...and his deification after death, were known in advance by unmistakable signs' (*Divus Augustus* 97.1). Suetonius states that various omens attended the death of Claudius, including the appearance of a comet (*Divus Claudius* 46). Finally, according to Cassius Dio, 'Now portents and dreams had come to Vespasian pointing to the sovereignty long beforehand' (*Hist. Rom.* 66.1.2).

Although Mark does not say anything about the birth of Jesus (as do the Matthean and Lukan evangelists—complete with omens, dreams, and prophecies), omens do attend the baptism (Mk 1.10-11), the transfiguration (9.2-8), and the crucifixion and death of Jesus: daytime darkness (15.33) and the tearing of the Temple veil (15.38). The most astounding omen of all was the subsequent discovery of the empty tomb and meeting the mysterious young man who proclaimed Jesus' resurrection (16.1-8).

3. Following a great victory a 'triumph' (θρίαμβος; *triumphus*) was held, at which time the emperor's sovereignty and divine status were reaffirmed (e.g. Suetonius, *Divus Augustus* 22). In Jewish history the most memorable triumph was celebrated in Rome following Titus's capture of Jerusalem in 70 CE (cf. Josephus, *War* 7.5.4-6 §§123–57). Two stone reliefs on the inside of the Arch of Titus depict this event. One historian comments: 'With the longing of the people for a saviour went at the same time the growth of the power of individuals, chiefly the great generals, to whom was accorded the triumph that was the closest thing in Roman state ceremony to deification'.[16]

In Mark, Jesus receives a mock 'triumph' at the hands of the Roman soldiers. His entry into the city of Jerusalem (Mk 11.1-11) may have impressed inhabitants of the Roman world as the prelude to a triumph of sorts, but that was as far as it went. Jesus received no honors and no acclaim. His affirmations of a close relationship with the Deity led to cries of blasphemy and to his condemnation to death (14.61-64). The Roman soldiers dressed Jesus in a purple robe and gave him a crown of thorns (instead of a laurel wreath); then saluted him: 'Hail, king of the Jews!' (15.16-20). How much of this scene may be attributed to Mark's literary skills and how much to history itself is hard to tell, but that Mark's readers would sense the parallels with their triumphs in honor of the emperor is certain.[17] But in his death— and here we encounter Markan irony—Jesus is hailed 'son of God' by a Roman centurion (Mk 15.39), and so in a certain sense his 'triumph' ends with deification after all.

4. Because of their divinity, it was believed that the Roman emperor could in some instances effect healing. According to Suetonius, 'A man of the people, who was blind, and another who was lame, came to [Vespasian] together as he sat on the tribunal, begging for the help for

16. L.R. Taylor, *The Divinity of the Roman Emperor* (APAMS, 1; New York: Arno, 1931; repr. Chico, CA: Scholars Press, 1975), p. 57.

17. T.E. Schmidt, 'Mark 15.16-32: The Crucifixion Narrative and the Roman Triumphal Procession', *NTS* 41 (1995), pp. 1-18.

their disorders which Serapis had promised in a dream; for the god declared that Vespasian would restore the eyes, if he would spit upon them, and give strength to the leg, if he would deign to touch it with his heel. Though he had hardly any faith that this could possibly succeed, and therefore shrank even from making the attempt, he was at last prevailed upon by his friends and tried both things in public before a large crowd; and with success' (*Divus Vespasianus* 7.2-3).

Jesus' astounding ability to heal is a prominent feature in Mark's Gospel. The story about Vespasian making spittle to restore the blind man's sight immediately recalls Mk 7.31-37, where Jesus spits and restores a man's speech (cf. Jn 9.1-12, where Jesus' spittle is used to restore a man's sight).

5. The Roman emperor cult included legends and traditions about the emperor seated or standing at the right hand of a god. A coin minted in Rome in 55 CE depicts 'divine' Claudius seated at the right hand of Augustus (who in *SB* 8895 is described as 'God from God'!) atop a chariot drawn by four elephants.[18] A later sculpture depicts Hadrian, dressed as Zeus, 'standing side by side with the image of Iuppiter/Zeus himself'.[19]

Here one thinks of Jesus' bold asseveration, uttered before the High Priest and members of the Jewish Council, that as 'son of man' he would be seen seated at the right hand of God (Mk 14.62; cf. Acts 7.56, where the martyred Stephen sees Jesus standing at the right hand). Although Jesus has alluded to the Jewish Scriptures (cf. Dan. 7.13; Ps. 110.1), a Roman audience would also be reminded of the emperor cult and the privileged position and status of their semi-divine emperor.

From all of this I think we can infer that one very important aspect of the Markan evangelist's portrait of Jesus is a comparison to the Roman emperor and the emperor cult. Given the obvious dangers, why did the evangelist do this? I think he did so partly in response to the historical circumstances in which he found himself. At the time of his writing, which was probably in the mid to late 60s, the Roman empire was in a state of political turmoil. The golden era of Augustus (30 BCE–14 CE)

18. H. Mattingly, *Coins of the Roman Empire in the British Museum* (London: British Museum, 1965), I, p. 201 + pl. 38.

19. H.S. Versnel, *Triumphus: An Inquiry into the Origin, Development, and Meaning of the Roman Triumph* (Leiden: Brill, 1970), p. 69; cf. Taylor, *Divinity*, pp. 44-45.

was over. Imperial succession had proven to be disappointing, to say the least. Whereas the Senate had deified Julius Caesar and his nephew Augustus, this honor had been denied to the eccentric and lecherous Tiberius (14–37 CE) and the cruel and murderous Gaius Caligula (37–41 CE). The honor was bestowed, out of pity, upon the stuttering and cowardly Claudius (41–54 CE), but was denied to his murderous and insane successor Nero (54–68 CE). Following Nero's assassination three would-be emperors filled the office in brief, rapid succession (Galba, Otho, and Vitellius). Suicide and murder were the order of the day. Morale in the Empire was waning. To compound the difficulties was the Jewish war, which exploded in 66 CE, catching Rome completely unprepared. The governor Gesius Florus (64–66 CE) had been murdered, the Roman squadrons stationed in Judea and Galilee had been annihilated, and the war, at least in its early stages, was not going well. Had Mark been written in 68 or 69, which seems probable, the social backdrop would have been one of anxiety and foreboding. One emperor after another, each seemingly worse and more impotent than his predecessor, had failed—and each one had been hailed 'son of God'![20] The emerging cynicism would have been equalled only by the growing fear and alarm. It was against this setting that the Markan evangelist dared to put forward the Christian gospel and declare that the true son of God was Jesus, the Messiah of Israel and 'king of the Jews', not some would-be Roman emperor.

Gospel of Matthew
The Matthean evangelist portrays Jesus as Israel's Messiah, the true son of Abraham and of David, the fulfiller of prophetic Scripture, a

---

20. Waiting until Jesus dies on the cross and the Roman centurion confesses him to be the true 'son of God' may explain—when we keep in mind the Roman tradition of deifying the emperor—Mark's messianic secret. That is, Jesus' sonship cannot be made public until his deification is recognized. The first to recognize it is the Roman centurion—the very person expected to recognize the deity of the Roman emperor during a triumph. The deification of Jesus is confirmed by the resurrection. Unlike the Roman caesars who die and are buried (and remain buried), Jesus is resurrected. Therefore, Jesus—not the Roman caesars—qualifies to be recognized as son of God. Exclamations of Jesus' divine sonship prior to his passion are, accordingly, premature. Demons are silenced (1.24-25, 34; 3.11-12), healed persons are hushed (1.44; 5.43), even Peter is told 'to tell no one about him' (8.30). Jesus' true identity cannot be proclaimed until his work—his triumph—is finished (9.9, 30-31).

new Moses who gives a new Law and teaches the way of righteousness.[21] The Christology of Matthew is consistent with that observed in

21. For selected studies, see G. Bornkamm *et al.*, *Tradition and Interpretation in
Matthew* (Philadelphia: Westminster Press, 1963 [1960]); D.R.A. Hare, *The Theme of
Jewish Persecution of Christians in the Gospel according to St Matthew* (SNTSMS, 6;
Cambridge: Cambridge University Press, 1967); M.J. Suggs, *Wisdom, Christology
and Law in Matthew's Gospel* (Cambridge, MA: Harvard University Press, 1970);
J.D. Kingsbury, *Matthew: Structure, Christology, Kingdom* (Philadelphia: Fortress
Press, 1975); *idem, Matthew as Story* (Philadelphia: Fortress Press, 1986);
O.L. Cope, *Matthew: A Scribe Trained for the Kingdom of Heaven* (CBQMS, 5;
Washington: Catholic Biblical Association, 1976); J.P. Meier, *Law and History in
Matthew's Gospel* (AnBib, 71; Rome: Biblical Institute Press, 1976); G.N. Stanton
(ed.), *The Interpretation of Matthew* (London: SPCK; Philadelphia: Fortress Press,
1983); *idem, A Gospel for a New People: Studies in Matthew* (Edinburgh: T. & T.
Clark, 1992); T.L. Donaldson, *Jesus on the Mountain: A Study in Matthean Theology*
(JSNTSup, 8; Sheffield: JSOT Press, 1985); D. Senior, *The Passion of Jesus in the
Gospel of Matthew* (Wilmington, DE: Michael Glazier, 1985); S.H. Brooks,
Matthew's Community: The Evidence of His Special Sayings Material (JSNTSup,
16; Sheffield: JSOT Press, 1987); D.R. Bauer, *The Structure of Matthew's Gospel: A
Study in Literary Design* (JSNTSup, 31; Sheffield: JSOT Press, 1988); L. Schenke
(ed.), *Studien zum Matthäusevangelium* (Stuttgart: Katholisches Bibelwerk, 1988);
M.J. Wilkins, *The Concept of Disciple in Matthew's Gospel* (NovTSup, 59; Leiden:
Brill, 1988); R.T. France, *Matthew: Evangelist and Teacher* (Grand Rapids:
Zondervan, 1989); J.A. Overman, *The Gospel of Matthew and Formative Judaism:
A Study of the Social World of the Matthean Community* (Minneapolis: Fortress
Press, 1990); D.L. Balch (ed.), *Social History of the Matthean Community: Cross-
Disciplinary Approaches* (Minneapolis: Fortress Press, 1991); Van Segbroeck *et al.*
(eds.), *The Four Gospels 1992*, II, pp. 1187-1448; Evans and Stegner (eds.), *The
Gospels and the Scriptures of Israel*, pp. 94-194.

The following commentaries (with emphasis on English works) are recommended:
D.C. Allison, Jr, and W.D. Davies, *A Critical and Exegetical Commentary on the
Gospel according to Saint Matthew* (2 vols. to date; ICC; Edinburgh: T. & T. Clark,
1988, 1991); F.W. Beare, *The Gospel according to Matthew: A Commentary*
(Oxford: Blackwell, 1981); J. Gnilka, *Das Matthäusevangelium* (2 vols.; HTKNT,
1.1-2; Freiburg: Herder, 1986, 1988); W. Grundmann, *Das Evangelium nach
Matthäus* (THKNT, 1; Berlin: Evangelische Verlagsanstalt, 1968); R.H. Gundry,
Matthew: A Commentary on his Handbook for a Mixed Church under Persecution
(Grand Rapids: Eerdmans, 1994); D.A. Hagner, *Matthew* (2 vols.; WBC, 33A and
33B; Dallas: Word, 1993, 1995); U. Luz, *Matthew 1–7: A Commentary* (vol. 1;
Continental Commentaries; Minneapolis: Augsburg, 1989); *idem, Das Evangelium
nach Matthäus* (vol. 2; EKKNT, 1.1-2; Neukirchen–Vluyn: Benzinger and
Neukirchener Verlag, 1990); L. Morris, *The Gospel according to Matthew* (Pillar
Commentary; Grand Rapids: Eerdmans, 1992); R.H. Mounce, *Matthew* (NIBC, 1;

Q and Mark, but there are important features which are highlighted. These entail fulfillment of Scripture, the nature of Jesus' Messiahship, and the implications of his Messiahship for the Gentile nations.

Matthew's portrait of Jesus takes on a whole new look by the addition of the infancy narrative. The reader is treated to an exciting story of adventure and suspense. King Herod learns of the child's birth and the significance of the heavenly omen. He tries to destroy the child in a way that is reminiscent of Pharaoh's attempt to eliminate the Hebrew threat in his day. Jesus and his parents hide in Egypt (where the infant Moses had been hidden), only returning after the death of the hated tyrant. In this story no fewer than five Old Testament prophecies are cited as fulfilled (1.22-23; 2.5-6, 15, 17-18, 23). In the Markan narrative Jesus' appearance on the public scene had been abrupt, but in Matthew it has been well prepared. Jesus had been a child of destiny, born under an omen, sought with respect by wise men from afar, sought with murder by a king at home, and protected through the directions of an angel. Such origins, Matthew's readers would have had to agree, surely pointed to future significance and greatness.

The Moses typology implicit in the infancy narrative returns in the temptation narrative (4.1-11). Making use of his Q source, the Matthean evangelist tells of Jesus' experience in the wilderness. Unlike the children of Israel who centuries ago had failed when tempted, Jesus passes every test, relying on the word of God, as written by Moses.[22] Shortly after the temptation narrative, Jesus ascends the mountain— again reminiscent of Moses—and gives his law (i.e. the Sermon on the Mount; Mt. 5–7). Jesus is the new law-giver, but he is more than Moses; he assumes the role of God himself who gives the Law (the antitheses; Mt. 5.21-48).[23] Six times Jesus says, 'You have heard it said, but I say to you' (Mt. 5.21-22, 27-28, 31-32, 33-34, 38-39, 43-44). What Moses said and how it was being interpreted by his students (i.e. those who 'sit on the seat of Moses'; 23.2) were inadequate. With greater authority Jesus taught the way of true righteousness.[24] Jesus had not come to

Peabody, MA: Hendrickson, 1991); R. Schnackenburg, *Matthäusevangelium* (2 vols.; Die neue echter Bibel; Würzburg: Echter Verlag, 1985, 1987).

22. B. Gerhardsson, *The Testing of God's Son (Matt 4.1-11 & Par.): An Analysis of an Early Christian Midrash* (ConBNT, 2.1; Lund: Gleerup, 1966).

23. See D.C. Allison, *The New Moses: A Matthean Typology* (Minneapolis: Fortress Press, 1993).

24. See B. Przybylski, *Righteousness in Matthew and his World of Thought*

break the Law, but to fulfill it (Mt. 5.17-20; cf. 11.13). Accordingly, his disciples are to be perfect (Mt. 5.48).

Perhaps for the Matthean evangelist the most important aspect of Jesus' identity lies in his divine sonship. Here the evangelist has seized upon a feature that, as we have already seen, was important for the Markan evangelist. But Matthew wishes to enrich the Markan depiction of Jesus as 'son'. Jesus is the 'son of David' (Mt. 1.1, 17, 20; 9.27; 12.23; 21.9, 15). Jesus' Davidic ancestry plays a prominent role in the evangelist's presentation of the genealogy, with the numerical value of the name 'David' (דוד) probably explaining the division of the genealogy into groups of fourteen.

As important as his Davidic descent and identity are, Jesus' divine sonship is much more important (Mt. 11.27). This divine sonship is expressed explicitly with the epithet 'son of God' (16.16; 26.63; 27.40, 43). But it is also implied with the enigmatic self-reference 'son of man' (13.37, 41; 16.13, 27, 28; 25.31). In Matthew there can be no doubt that the 'son of man' referred to the mysterious figure of Dan. 7.13, to whom was given the kingdom and authority. Drawing upon Q tradition, the Matthean Jesus assures his disciples that 'in the new world' the 'son of man will sit on his glorious throne' (19.28).

Jesus' Davidic and divine sonship qualifies him to be Israel's true Messiah. As Israel's Messiah he will subdue the Gentile nations. It is in this light that the Great Commission (Mt. 28.18-20) should be understood. In language that again is reminiscent of Daniel, the 'son', to whom all authority in heaven and on earth has been given, Jesus has sent forth his apostles to make disciples of all nations (i.e. Gentiles). Israel's dream of conquering her pagan neighbors, under the leadership of God's Anointed One, will be fulfilled.

Gospel of Luke

The Jesus of the Lukan Gospel is very much concerned for the socially marginalized.[25] This is not because Luke was the first Christian

(SNTSMS, 41; Cambridge: Cambridge University Press, 1980).

25. For selected studies, see H. Conzelmann, *The Theology of St Luke* (New York: Harper & Row, 1960 [1954]); W.C. Robinson, Jr, *Der Weg des Herrn: Studien zur Geschichte und Eschatologie im Lukas-Evangelium* (TF, 36; Hamburg and Bergstedt: Herbert Reich, 1964); L.E. Keck and J.L. Martyn (eds.), *Studies in Luke–Acts* (P. Schubert Festschrift; Philadelphia: Fortress Press, 1966); S. Brown, *Apostasy and Perseverence in the Theology of Luke* (AnBib, 36; Rome: Biblical

social worker. His teaching frequently touches on issues relating to one's attitude toward and use of wealth. He also expresses concern for 'sinners' (e.g. 15.1-32).

Lukan editing of Mark and Q (to the extent that it can be discerned) is quite revealing. Material unique to Luke (usually dubbed 'L') is no less revealing. Whereas Matthew punctuated his infancy narrative with fulfillments of Scripture, Luke has none. Instead, Luke treats his readers with several canticles and announcements which praise God for the salvation that is now at hand in the coming of John the Baptist and Jesus. These canticles and announcements (1.14-17, 32-33, 46-55, 67-79; 2.14, 29-33, 34-35) are laced with scriptural phrases. Jesus will be

Institute Press, 1969); F.W. Danker, *Jesus and the New Age according to St Luke* (St. Louis: Clayton, 1972); J. Jervell, *Luke and the People of God* (Minneapolis: Augsburg, 1972); G. Braumann, *Das Lukas-Evangelium: Die redaktions- und kompositionsgeschichtliche Forschung* (WF, 280; Darmstadt: Wissenschaftliche Buchgesellschaft, 1974); P. Zingg, *Das Wachsen der Kirche: Beiträge zur Frage der lukanischen Redaktion und Theologie* (OBO, 3; Göttingen: Vandenhoeck & Ruprecht; Freiburg: Universitätsverlag, 1974); G. Lohfink, *Die Sammlung Israels: Eine Untersuchung zur lukanischen Ekklesiologie* (SANT, 34; Munich: Kösel, 1975); W.E. Pilgrim, *Good News to the Poor: Wealth and Poverty in Luke–Acts* (Minneapolis: Augsburg, 1981); R. Stronstad, *The Charismatic Theology of St Luke* (Peabody, MA: Hendrickson, 1984); R.F. O'Toole, *The Unity of Luke's Theology: An Analysis of Luke–Acts* (Wilmington, DE: Michael Glazier, 1984); J. Ernst, *Lukas: Ein theologisches Portrait* (Düsseldorf: Patmos, 1985); C.H. Giblin, *The Destruction of Jerusalem according to Luke's Gospel: A Historical-Typological Moral* (AnBib, 107; Rome: Biblical Institute Press, 1985); D.L. Bock, *Proclamation from Prophecy and Pattern: Lucan Old Testament Christology* (JSNTSup, 12; Sheffield: JSOT Press, 1987); R.L. Brawley, *Luke–Acts and the Jews: Conflict, Apology, and Conciliation* (SBLMS, 33; Atlanta: Scholars Press, 1987); C.A. Evans and J.A. Sanders, *Luke and Scripture: The Function of Sacred Tradition in Luke–Acts* (Minneapolis: Fortress Press, 1993); Van Segbroeck *et al.* (eds.), *The Four Gospels 1992*, II, pp. 1451-1716; Evans and Stegner (eds.), *The Gospels and the Scriptures of Israel*, pp. 280-355.

The following commentaries (with emphasis on English works) are recommended: E.E. Ellis, *Luke* (NCB; London: Oliphants; Grand Rapids: Eerdmans, 2nd edn, 1974); C.A. Evans, *Luke* (NIBC, 3; Peabody, MA: Hendrickson, 1990); J.A. Fitzmyer, *The Gospel according to Luke* (AB, 28 and 28A; 2 vols.; Garden City: Doubleday, 1981, 1985); W. Grundmann, *Das Evangelium nach Lukas* (THKNT, 3; Berlin: Evangelische Verlagsanstalt, 1961); A.R.C. Leaney, *A Commentary on the Gospel of St Luke* (BNTC; London: A. & C. Black, 1958); I.H. Marshall, *The Gospel of Luke: A Commentary on the Greek Text* (NIGTC; Exeter: Paternoster; Grand Rapids: Eerdmans, 1978); R.H. Stein, *Luke* (NAC, 24; Nashville: Broadman, 1992).

'a light for revelation to the Gentiles' and will bring 'glory to [God's] people Israel' (2.32; cf. Isa. 49.6).

The Lukan evangelist extends the quotation of Isa. 40.3 that he found in Mk 1.3 all the way to Isa. 40.5: 'and all flesh shall see the salvation of God' (Lk. 3.4-6). The evangelist wishes to underscore his portrait of Jesus as Lord and Savior of Gentiles and not only the people of Israel. Several passages found only in Luke contribute to this portrait. The Parable of the Good Samaritan (10.29-37), the Parable of Great Banquet (14.15-24), the Parable of the Prodigal Son (15.11-32), the Parable of the Rich Man and Lazarus (16.19-31), and the Parable of the Pharisee and the Publican (18.9-14) illustrate in various ways how the Kingdom of God has been opened up to the marginalized, to the disenfranchised, and—according to the canons of conventional wisdom—to the nonelect.[26]

The Jesus of Luke—concerned with the socially and religiously marginalized—prepares the groundwork for the Church's mission, as described in the Lukan evangelist's second volume, the Book of Acts. In the sequel we find the apostles carrying out their master's ministry. The good news of the kingdom is extended to Israelites of the land of Israel, to Israelites of the diaspora, to the half-Israelite Samaritans, to the God-fearers and to the Gentile heathen. Following their master's teaching, early Christians worship together and share their possessions according to need.

Signs Booklet—The Beginning of Johannine Literature
The 'Signs Booklet' (or Signs Source, as many call it) is comprised of seven, or so, miracles of Jesus, which are now found incorporated in the Gospel of John.[27] Analysis of the Signs Booklet entails the same

26. On this theme, see J.A. Sanders, 'The Ethic of Election in Luke's Great Banquet Parable', in J.L. Crenshaw and J.T. Willis (eds.), *Essays in Old Testament Ethics* (New York: Ktav, 1974), pp. 245-71; repr. in Evans and Sanders, *Luke and Scripture*, pp. 106-20; C.A. Evans, 'Luke's Use of the Elijah/Elisha Narratives and the Ethic of Election', *JBL* 106 (1987), pp. 75-83; repr. in Evans and Sanders, *Luke and Scripture*, pp. 70-83.

27. For selected studies, see J. Becker, 'Wunder und Christologie: Zum literarkritischen und christologischen Problem der Wunder im Johannesevangelium', *NTS* 16 (1969-70), pp. 130-48; R.T. Fortna, *Gospel of Signs: A Reconstruction of the Narrative Source Underlying the Fourth Gospel* (SNTSMS, 11; Cambridge: Cambridge University Press, 1970); *idem*, *The Fourth Gospel and its Predecessor* (Philadelphia: Fortress Press, 1988); W. Nicoll, *The Semeia in the Fourth Gospel:*

cautions as in the analysis of Q. But the difficulty in this instance is even greater. Whereas the presence of Q can be easily detected in comparing the three Synoptic Gospels, the existence of the 'Signs Booklet'[28] is far from certain, and the extent of it remains much debated.

Although there is no consensus (such as whether or not the passion and resurrection belong in this hypothetical source), it is possible to summarize the general contents of the Signs Booklet:[29]

The Opening
1.6-7, 19-34 (the witness of John the Baptist); 1.35-49 (the call of the disciples)
Jesus' Signs in Galilee
2.1-11 (sign 1: turning water into wine); 2.12a + 4:46b-54 (sign 2: healing of the official's son); 21.1-14 (sign 3: miraculous catch of fish); 6.15b-25 (feeding of the 5,000 and walking on the sea)
Jesus' Signs in Jerusalem
5.2-9 (healing of lame man); 9.1-8 (healing of blind man); 11.1-4, 14-17, 32-35, 38-45 (raising of Lazarus)
The Culmination of Jesus' Signs
11.47-53 (plot to kill Jesus); 12.37-40 (failure to believe despite the signs)
The Closing
20.30-31 (signs are to produce faith, resulting in eternal life)

The Signs Booklet is made up of an opening, a closing, and seven miracles, 'signs' (σημεῖα), from which this hypothetical document

---

Tradition and Redaction (NovTSup, 32; Leiden: Brill, 1972); L. Cope, 'The Earliest Gospel Was the "Signs Gospel"', in E.P. Sanders *et al.* (eds.), *Jesus, the Gospels, and the Church* (W.R. Farmer Festschrift; Macon, GA: Mercer University Press, 1987), pp. 17-24; U.C. von Wahlde, *The Earliest Version of John's Gospel: Recovering the Gospel of Signs* (Wilmington, DE: Michael Glazier, 1989); F. Neirynck, 'The Signs Source in the Fourth Gospel: A Critique of the Hypothesis', in Neirynck, *Evangelica II* (BETL, 99; Leuven: Peeters and Leuven University Press, 1991), pp. 651-77.

28. I call this hypothetical source a 'booklet', because apparently that is what it called itself: 'Jesus performed many other signs... which are not written in this book(let) [βιβλίῳ]' (Jn 20.30). βίβλιον is often translated 'book', but given the brevity of the document in question, 'booklet' seems more appropriate.

29. In part, I follow the arrangement found in R.J. Miller (ed.), *The Complete Gospels* (Sonoma, CA: Polebridge Press, 1992), pp. 180-93. I do not accept, however, the inclusion of the passion and resurrection accounts. I believe that this material constitutes an integral part of the scriptural apologetic that gives the expanded Gospel of John its character and purpose.

derives its name. The Signs Booklet has a decided propagandistic edge to it. Its 'signs' are designed to stimulate faith in Jesus as Israel's true Messiah. The booklet in all probability opened with the witness of John the Baptist, remembered by Jews as a popular preacher who was wrongfully executed by the ambitious, but cowardly Herod Antipas (cf. Josephus, *Ant.* 18.5.2 §§116–19). This famous prophet and martyr had acknowledged the messiahship of Jesus and proclaimed him to be 'the son of God' (Jn 1.34). This anticipation helps mitigate the theological problem of Jesus' rejection, a problem with which early Christians were confronted. John's predictive words also anticipate the conclusion of the Signs Booklet, in which it is acknowledged that despite the many signs he performed, most of the Jewish authorities would not—indeed, could not—believe in him.

I believe this document had an evangelistic function in the context of Christian missionary activity largely in the context of the synagogue. The Signs Booklet was produced and employed by Christians, both Jewish and Gentile, in their efforts to persuade a skeptical synagogue that Jesus really was the Messiah, as proven by his numerous and impressive signs, something which Jews required of those claiming to have been sent from God (Mk 8.11; 1 Cor. 1.22). The closing portion of the booklet argues that the authorities found it necessary to eliminate Jesus, lest his popularity lead to an uprising. Therefore, despite the many signs, signs that should have led to faith, the religious leaders plot Jesus' death. In doing this they unwittingly fulfill Scripture. Then, very transparently, the Signs Booklet concludes with its statement of purpose: 'Many other signs Jesus performed before his disciples, which are not written in this booklet; but these are written that you might come to believe that the Messiah, the son of God, is Jesus, and that believing you should have life in his name' (Jn 20.30-31).

But what is Jesus' image in this hypothetical missionary booklet, or tract? What is surprising is the observation that in the Signs Booklet Jesus is essentially like the Jesus we have encountered in the Synoptic Gospels. Bereft of the highly symbolic and theologically-charged discourses, the Signs Booklet portrays Jesus in largely the same colors in which he is portrayed by the Synoptic evangelists.

The concern of the author of the Signs Booklet seems not so much to lie with his portrait of Jesus, which becomes a much greater concern when the booklet is expanded into the Gospel of John, as it seems to lie with its evangelistic interpretation of the significance of Jesus' ministry.

Whereas Jesus in the synoptic tradition refuses to offer a sign (σημεῖον) to his contemporaries (Mk 8.11-12), in the Signs Booklet all of his miracles are called 'signs' (σημεῖα). This is a deliberate and calculated literary and theological achievement on the part of the author of the Signs Booklet, and, in my judgment, represents his most significant contribution to the early history of the interpretation of Jesus. The historical Jesus may very well have refused to offer signs to his doubting contemporaries and religious opponents, but his miracles were, nevertheless, signs, signs that by all rights should have led to faith. That they did not do so is explained by Scripture (Jn 12.37-40, paraphrasing Isa. 53.1 and 6.10) and so should not deflect from the signifying and confirmatory value of the miracles.

The Signs Booklet evidently represents an early literary effort to support the Johannine community's evangelistic efforts in the context of a skeptical synagogue. How could this community claim that Jesus really was Israel's Messiah and son of God? What confirming sign did he perform? If he did perform signs, why did not the religious authorities respond in faith? And, if Jesus really was the Messiah, where is he now? What does he offer the people of Israel? Given the limited focus of the Signs Booklet, these latter questions were not convincingly answered. At some point the Johannine community was expelled from the synagogue, its evangelistic efforts falling short of convincing most. A new approach was needed, and with it a new literary effort.

Gospel of John
The evangelistic orientation of the Signs Booklet gives way, in its new context in the expanded narrative we now call the Gospel of John,[30] to

30. For selected studies, see C.H. Dodd, *The Interpretation of the Fourth Gospel* (Cambridge: Cambridge University Press, 1953); E.D. Freed, *Old Testament Quotations in the Gospel of John* (NovTSup, 11; Leiden: Brill, 1965); W.A. Meeks, *The Prophet-King: Moses Traditions and the Johannine Christology* (NovTSup, 14; Leiden: Brill, 1967); J.L. Martyn, *History and Theology in the Fourth Gospel* (New York: Harper & Row, 1968; 2nd edn Nashville: Abingdon Press, 1979); R. Kysar, *The Fourth Evangelist and his Gospel: An Examination of Contemporary Scholarship* (Minneapolis: Augsburg, 1975); O. Cullmann, *The Johannine Circle* (London: SCM Press; Philadelphia: Westminster Press, 1976 [1975]); M. de Jonge (ed.), *L'Évangile de Jean: Sources, rédaction, théologie* (BETL, 44; Leuven: Leuven University Press, 1977); J. Ashton (ed.), *The Interpretation of John* (London: SPCK; Philadelphia: Fortress Press, 1986); G.M. Burge, *The Anointed Community: The Holy Spirit in the Johannine Tradition* (Grand Rapids: Eerdmans, 1987); J.H. Neyrey, *An Ideology*

Images of Christ

an apologetic portrait of Jesus. In essence, the Johannine evangelist wishes to assure Christians and to reply to non-Christians that Jesus' rejection at the hands of Jewish religious authorities and execution at the hands of the Roman authorities do not invalidate the Christian belief in Jesus as Israel's Messiah and God's Son, through whom people may gain life in the world to come.

The fourth evangelist accomplishes this task in two principal ways: (1) he adds a great deal of distinctive teaching material; and (2) he punctuates his narrative with a series of quotations of Scripture designed to offer a compelling apologetic for the activities, rejection, and death of Jesus. The evangelist's achievement is nothing less than remarkable.

First, the Fourth Gospel's distinctive teaching material is principally made up of the lengthy 'I am' discourses (which at one time Rudolf Bultmann assigned to a gnostic 'discourse source'). Here we encounter a Jesus who repeatedly defines himself with Old Testament imagery: 'I am the bread of life' (6.35, 48); 'I am the light of the world' (8.12;

of Revolt: John's Christology in Social-Science Perspective (Philadelphia: Fortress Press, 1988); M.M. Thompson, *The Humanity of Jesus in the Fourth Gospel* (Philadelphia: Fortress Press, 1988); M. Hengel, *The Johannine Question* (London: SCM Press; Philadelphia: Trinity Press International, 1989 [rev. German edn, 1993]); J.H. Charlesworth (ed.), *John and the Dead Sea Scrolls* (repr. New York: Crossroad, 1990 [1972]); D. Burkett, *The Son of the Man in the Gospel of John* (JSNTSup, 56; Sheffield: JSOT Press, 1991); A.T. Hanson, *The Prophetic Gospel: A Study of John and the Old Testament* (Edinburgh: T. & T. Clark, 1991); A. Denaux (ed.), *John and the Synoptics* (BETL, 101; Leuven: Peeters and Leuven University Press, 1992); M. Scott, *Sophia and the Johannine Jesus* (JSNTSup, 71; Sheffield: JSOT Press, 1992); Van Segbroeck *et al.* (eds.), *The Four Gospels 1992*, III, pp. 1723-2221; Evans and Stegner (eds.), *The Gospels and the Scriptures of Israel*, pp. 358-474.

The following commentaries (with emphasis on English works) are recommended: C.K. Barrett, *The Gospel according to St John* (London: SPCK; Philadelphia: Westminster Press, 2nd edn, 1978); G.R. Beasley-Murray, *John* (WBC, 36; Dallas: Word, 1987); R.E. Brown, *The Gospel according to John* (2 vols.; AB, 29 and 29A; Garden City: Doubleday, 1966, 1970); D.A. Carson, *The Gospel according to John* (Grand Rapids: Eerdmans, 1991); W. Grundmann, *Das Evanglium nach Johannes* (ed. E. Fascher; THKNT, 4; Berlin: Evangelische Verlagsanstalt, 1968); B. Lindars, *The Gospel of John* (NCB; London: Marshall, Morgan & Scott; Grand Rapids: Eerdmans, 1972); J.R. Michaels, *John* (NIBC, 4; Peabody, MA: Hendrickson, 1989); R. Schnackenburg, *The Gospel according to St John* (3 vols.; repr. New York: Crossroad, 1987 [1980]); B.F. Westcott, *The Gospel according to St John* (repr. Grand Rapids: Eerdmans, 1973 [1881]).

9.5); 'I am the door of the sheep' (10.7, 9); 'I am the good shepherd' (10.11); 'I am the resurrection and the life' (11.25); 'I am the way, the truth, and the life' (14.6); and 'I am the true vine' (15.1). Just as Jesus performed seven signs, so Jesus utters seven 'I am' statements, several of which are intertwined with the signs miracles taken over from the Signs Booklet. For example, after feeding the 5,000 (6.15-25), Jesus describes himself as the 'bread of life', whose flesh must be eaten and blood must be drunk in order to have life (6.51-58). When he heals the man born blind (9.1-8), Jesus declares that he is the 'light of the world' (9.5). When he raises Lazarus (11.1-45), he says he is the 'resurrection and the life' (11.25). Other 'I am' sayings relate to the new narrative material that has been incorporated into the expanded Johannine Gospel. Because he is establishing a new way to God, a way that can no longer be found in the synagogue, Jesus asserts that he is 'the way, the truth, and the life', the only access to God the Father. Because he is establishing a new community, as opposed to Israel which has rejected him, Jesus describes himself as the 'true vine' and as the 'good shepherd' who will protect and care for his sheep.

Secondly, perhaps of even greater interest is the fourth evangelist's ingenuous use of Scripture. Part of the reason that the Signs Booklet failed to persuade most in the synagogue (we may surmise) was the lack of a convincing explanation of Jesus' rejection. After all, if Jesus really was the Messiah, why then did he die and why has not the kingdom of God appeared as promised? Jesus' death and the continuation of an unsatisfactory status quo seem to constitute clear evidence that Jesus was not the Messiah. From a Jewish perspective, the objection against Christian claims, on these grounds, would seem unanswerable. Nevertheless, the fourth evangelist makes a new attempt at providing a convincing explanation by greatly expanding the role of the witness of Scripture. Signs are not enough, especially not enough in the context of a synagogue of the diaspora. Scripture is the ultimate authority for Jewish life, especially in the aftermath of the destruction of the Jerusalem Temple and the cessation of sacrifices and an active priesthood.

The fourth evangelist's resourceful use of Scripture is seen in how each scriptural passage is introduced leading up to the passage that at one time appeared near the conclusion of the older Signs Booklet (i.e. 12.37-40), in which Jewish unbelief is explained by appeal to the texts from Isaiah. To this point in the Fourth Gospel every quotation of

Scripture is introduced in terms other than fulfillment. Jesus does and says things 'just as it is written' or as 'the Scriptures say' (e.g. 1.23, 45; 2.17; 5.46; 6.31, 45; 7.42; 8.17; 10.34; 12.14, 16). But commencing with the introduction of the passages from Isaiah in Jn 12.38-40, every passage is introduced as in *fulfillment* of this or that Scripture (e.g. 12.38, 39; 13.18; 15.25; 17.12; 18.9, 32; 19.24, 28, 36, 37). What is the significance of this pattern? The most probable explanation is that the fourth evangelist wishes to show that in his rejection and death on the cross, one Scripture after another has been fulfilled. Whereas in the first half of the Gospel (i.e. 2.1–12.36) Jesus performs his many 'signs' and conducts his ministry, 'as it is written'; in the second half of the Gospel (i.e. 12.37–19.37) Jesus' rejection and execution take place 'in order that Scripture be fulfilled'. Far from proving that Jesus was not Israel's Messiah (as is implied by such a statement as, 'We have heard from the Law that the Messiah remains forever' [12.34]), his rejection and death fulfilled Scripture and so proved that he really was the Messiah. The fourth evangelist has offered his contemporaries an apologetic that was meant to demonstrate the scriptural truth of the Christian message and to summon people to faith.[31]

To underscore this new portrait and apologetic of Jesus, the evangelist enriches the scene in which John the Baptist introduces Jesus. Jesus is now introduced by the Baptist not only as 'God's son' (1.34), but as the 'lamb of God, who will take away the sin of the world' (1.29, 36). This announcement prepares for Jesus' death, at Passover, as the lamb whose bones are not broken (19.31-37). Far from failure and defeat, Jesus' death is now portrayed as foreordained and efficacious, and even as a component of Israel's most revered holidays.

There are other aspects of the fourth evangelist's portrait of Jesus that cannot be investigated here. The role of wisdom tradition is an obvious and inviting one. The fourth evangelist's enhancement of the portrait of Jesus, in an attempt to serve apologetic ends and lift Jesus up above the earthly politics of the Roman world, departs so far from what might be regarded as the more or less conventional image found in the synoptics that Ernst Käsemann felt compelled to conclude that John's was a naive docetism, in which Jesus was portrayed as God

31. For further discussion of this understanding of the fourth evangelist's employment of Scripture, see C.A. Evans, *Word and Glory: On the Exegetical and Theological Background of John's Prologue* (JSNTSup, 89; Sheffield: JSOT Press, 1993), pp. 174-77.

striding on the earth.[32] Although Käsemann's assessment may have understated the humanity of Jesus,[33] his exaggeration does underscore the noticeable difference between the Fourth Gospel and the first three.

Extra-Canonical Images of Jesus

Interest in the extra-canonical Gospels has become in recent years a growth industry. Gospel-like writings, to which mainstream scholars throughout most of this century paid little attention, are now studied and debated with great interest.[34] Some scholars, notably those who participate in North America's Jesus Seminar, believe that many of these writings are independent of the New Testament Gospels and in some instances contain more primitive, even authentic materials.[35] In

32. E. Käsemann, *The Testament of Jesus: A Study of the Gospel of John in the Light of Chapter 17* (London: SCM Press; Philadelphia: Fortress Press, 1968 [1966]).

33. See the corrective offered by Thompson, *The Humanity of Jesus in the Fourth Gospel*.

34. Picking through hundreds of sayings attributed to Jesus, known as *agrapha* (i.e. sayings 'not written' in the New Testament Gospels), J. Jeremias (*Unbekannte Jesusworte* [Zürich: Zwingli, 1947; 2nd edn Gütersloh: Bertelsmann, 1951; 3rd edn, 1961]; ET *The Unknown Sayings of Jesus* [London: SPCK, 1957; 2nd edn, 1964]) thought that he had identified a small number of potentially authentic utterances, but nothing that would in the least alter critical assessments of the historical Jesus. In his recent reassessment of the *agrapha*, O. Hofius ('Unknown Sayings of Jesus', in P. Stuhlmacher [ed.], *The Gospel and the Gospels* [Grand Rapids: Eerdmans, 1991], pp. 336-60) expresses even less optimism than had Jeremias. The editors and contributors to E. Hennecke's and W. Schneemelcher's collection of New Testament apocrypha (*Neutestamentliche Apokryphen in deutscher Übersetzung. I Band: Evangelien* [Tübingen: Mohr (Siebeck), 1959; 6th edn (by Schneemelcher only), 1990]; ET *New Testament Apocrypha. Volume One: Gospels and Related Writings* [Cambridge: James Clarke; Louisville: Westminster/John Knox, rev. edn, 1991]; references will be to this edition) are on the whole very skeptical of the historical worth of these writings. For bibliography and a survey of the history of the discovery and evaluation of these writings, see J.H. Charlesworth, 'Research on the New Testament Apocrypha and Pseudepigrapha', *ANRW* II.25.5 (1988), pp. 3919-68. For further bibliography, see *idem*, *The New Testament Apocrypha and Pseudepigrapha: A Guide to Publications, with Excursuses on Apocalypses* (with J.R. Mueller; ATLA Bibliography Series, 17; London and Metuchen: ATLA, 1987); C.A. Evans, *Life of Jesus Research: An Annotated Bibliography* (NTTS, 16; Leiden: Brill, rev. edn, 1996), pp. 256-80.

35. Illustrative studies include H. Koester, *Synoptische Überlieferung bei den Apostolische Vätern* (TU, 65; Berlin: Akademie Verlag, 1957); *idem*, 'Apocryphal

my judgment, this claim is excessive,[36] but it has served to stimulate further research into the origins of the Gospels and into the question of the historical Jesus.

It is not easy to categorize these writings. One could attempt to do so according to date, but the dates are uncertain and, in a certain sense, are not necessarily helpful. One could attempt to categorize them according to language, but this too is problematic. Some writings survive in Latin, Coptic, and Syriac, but we suspect that they were originally in another language—usually Greek. Probably the best way to categorize these writings is according to genre and source. Is the writing a narrative, or a collection of sayings, or an apocalypse, with a surreal setting? Has the writing drawn upon what appears to be early material, or has it drawn upon later, imaginative material?

With these questions in mind, I suggest assigning the extra-canonical Gospels to three categories. First are the 'para-canonical' Gospels. By this I mean writings whose contents parallel closely those of the New Testament Gospels. In this category I place the Q-like *Gospel of Thomas*, the *Gospel of Peter*, the *Secret Gospel of Mark*, and several others, like the last mentioned, which exist only as papyrus fragments and brief quotations in patristic sources. Second are the 'gnostic' Gospels. The *Dialogue of the Savior*, the *Apocryphon of John*, the *Apocryphon of James*, and the *Gospel of Mary* belong in this category. *Thomas* could have been placed here also, but the gnosticizing tendencies now observable were in all probability not part of the original Greek version. The third category is made up of the 'infancy

and Canonical Gospels', *HTR* 73 (1980), pp. 105-30; *idem*, 'Überlieferung und Geschichte der frühchristlichen Evangelienliteratur', *ANRW* II.25.2 (1984), pp. 1463-1542; *idem, Ancient Christian Gospels: Their History and Development* (London: SCM Press; Philadelphia: Trinity Press International, 1990); R.D. Cameron, *The Other Gospels: Non-Canonical Gospel Texts* (Philadelphia: Westminster Press, 1982); J.D. Crossan, *Four Other Gospels: Shadows on the Contours of Canon* (Minneapolis: Seabury, 1985; repr. Sonoma, CA: Polebridge Press, 1992 [references are to reprint]); *idem, The Cross that Spoke: The Origins of the Passion Narrative* (San Francisco: Harper & Row, 1988); W.D. Stroker, *Extracanonical Sayings of Jesus* (SBLRBS, 18; Atlanta: Scholars Press, 1989); and, more recently, Miller (ed.), *The Complete Gospels*.

36. See Meier, *A Marginal Jew*, pp. 112-66; J.H. Charlesworth and C.A. Evans, 'Jesus in the Agrapha and Apocryphal Gospels', in B.D. Chilton and C.A. Evans (eds.), *Studying the Historical Jesus: Evaluations of the State of Current Research* (NTTS, 19; Leiden: Brill, 1994), pp. 479-533.

Gospels' and other 'orthodox' apocryphal Gospels. Best known are the *Infancy Gospel of Thomas* and the *Infancy Gospel of James.*

'Para-Canonical' Gospels
Gospel of Thomas.[37] The Prologue plus twenty-one sayings whole or in part are extant in *P. Oxy.* 1, 654, and 655, Greek fragments dating from the end of the second century and from the third century.[38] The

---

37. For selected studies, see C.-H. Hunzinger, 'Unbekannte Gleichnisse Jesu aus dem Thomasevangelium', in W. Eltester (ed.), *Judentum–Urchristentum–Kirche* (J. Jeremias Festschrift; BZNW, 26; Berlin: Töpelmann, 1960), pp. 209-20; R.E. Brown, 'The Gospel of Thomas and St John's Gospel', *NTS* 9 (1962–63), pp. 155-77; W. Schrage, *Das Verhältnis des Thomas-Evangeliums zur synoptischen Tradition und zu den koptischen Evangelienübersetzungen: Zugleich ein Beitrag zur gnostischen Synoptikerdeutung* (BZNW, 29; Berlin: Töpelmann, 1964); H.-W. Bartsch, 'Das Thomas-Evangelium und die synoptische Evangelien', *NTS* 16 (1965), pp. 449-54; J.-E. Ménard, *L'Évangile selon Thomas* (NHS, 5; Leiden: Brill, 1975); B. de Solages, 'L'évangile de Thomas et les évangiles canoniques: L'ordre des pericopes', *BLE* 80 (1979), pp. 102-108; B. Dehandschutter, 'L'évangile de Thomas comme collection de paroles de Jésus', in Delobel (ed.), *Logia: Les Paroles de Jésus*, pp. 507-15; *idem*, 'Recent Research on the Gospel of Thomas', in Van Segbroeck *et al.* (eds.), *The Four Gospels 1992*, III, pp. 2257-62; C.L. Blomberg, 'Tradition and Redaction in the Parables of the Gospel of Thomas', in D. Wenham (ed.), *The Jesus Tradition Outside the Gospels* (Gospel Perspectives, 5; Sheffield: JSOT Press, 1984), pp. 177-205; B.D. Chilton, 'The Gospel according to Thomas as a Source of Jesus' Teaching', in Wenham (ed.), *The Jesus Tradition Outside the Gospels*, pp. 155-75; Crossan, *Four Other Gospels*, pp. 3-38; R.D. Cameron and F.T. Fallon, 'The Gospel of Thomas: A Forschungsbericht and Analysis', *ANRW* II.25.6 (1988), pp. 4195-4251; J.-M. Sevrin, 'Un groupement de trois paraboles contre les richesses dans l'Evangile selon Thomas. EvTh 63, 64, 65', in J. Delorme (ed.), *Les paraboles évangéliques: Perspectives nouvelles* (Paris: Cerf, 1989), pp. 425-39; K.R. Snodgrass, 'The Gospel of Thomas: A Secondary Gospel', *SecCent* 7 (1989–90), pp. 19-38; H. Koester, 'Q and its Relatives', in J.E. Goehring *et al.* (eds.), *Gospel Origins and Christian Beginnings* (Sonoma, CA: Polebridge Press, 1990), pp. 49-63; M. Fieger, *Das Thomasevangelium: Einleitung, Kommentar und Systematik* (NTAbh, 22; Münster: Aschendorff, 1991); S.J. Patterson, *The Gospel of Thomas and Jesus* (Sonoma, CA: Polebridge Press, 1993); Charlesworth and Evans, 'Jesus in the Agrapha and Apocryphal Gospels', pp. 496-503. For additional bibli–ography, see Schneemelcher, *New Testament Apocrypha*, p. 110; Charlesworth, *The New Testament Apocrypha and Pseudepigrapha*, pp. 374-402.

38. J.A. Fitzmyer, 'The Oxyrhynchus Logoi of Jesus and the Coptic Gospel according to Thomas', *TS* 20 (1959), pp. 505-60; ed. and repr. in Fitzmyer, *Essays on the Semitic Background of the New Testament* (London: Geoffrey Chapman, 1971; repr. SBLSBS, 5; Missoula, MT: Scholars Press, 1974), pp. 355-433; O. Hofius,

whole of the document (the Prologue plus 114 sayings) is preserved as the second tractate in Codex II of the Nag Hammadi Library.[39] This Coptic codex has been dated to the middle of the fourth century. In this much discussed and hotly debated writing,[40] Jesus is portrayed as a mysterious personage. His teaching is enigmatic, esoteric, and elitist. There is no narrative, only questions (sometimes) and answers. There are traces of an anti-Jewish bias (e.g. §43, §60) and a cynical disposition toward society in general (e.g. §64, §80, §85).

Thomas begins with a Prologue that sets the tone for the document as a whole: 'These are the words which the living Jesus spoke, and which Didymus Judas Thomas wrote'. The opening saying heightens the esoteric element: 'He who shall find the interpretation of these words shall not taste death' (§1). Throughout *Thomas* we encounter a mysterious, unearthly Jesus whose words are far from transparent: 'On the day when you were one, you became two. But when you have become two, what will you do?' (§11); 'Where the beginning is, there the end will be' (§18); 'Seek a place of rest, that you may not become a corpse and be eaten' (§60); 'I am the light that is above them all. I am the all; the all came forth from me, and the all attained to me. Split wood, I am there. Lift a stone, and you will find me there' (§77). Often times a familiar saying is expanded, to bring out new meaning: 'Give to Caesar what is Caesar's; give to God what is God's; and give to me what is mine' (§100); 'A prophet is not acceptable in his own country, no doctor heals those who know him' (§31); 'It is not possible for a man to ride two

'Das koptische Thomasevangelium und die Oxyrhynchus-Papyri Nr. 1, 654 und 655', *EvT* 20 (1960), pp. 21-42, 182-92.

39. A. Guillaumont *et al.*, *The Gospel according to Thomas* (Leiden: Brill, 1959); H. Koester and T. Lambdin, 'The Gospel of Thomas', in J.M. Robinson (ed.), *The Nag Hammadi Library in English* (Leiden: Brill, rev. edn, 1988), pp. 124-38; B. Layton (ed.), *Nag Hammadi Codex II 2–7, together with XIII 2*, Brit. Lib. Or. 4926 (1) and P. Oxy. 1, 654, 655* (NHS, 20; Leiden: Brill, 1989).

40. Most of the debate revolves around the question of how the traditions of *Thomas* relate to those extant in the canonical Gospels. Are some of the sayings in *Thomas* independent of the canonical Gospels? If they are, are they more primitive, more reliable? Are some of the sayings which have no parallel in the canonical Gospels potentially authentic, in that they derive from the historical Jesus? For discussion of these questions, see Charlesworth and Evans, 'Jesus in the Agrapha and Apocryphal Gospels', pp. 496-503. In my view, *Thomas* is secondary to the canonical Gospels and offers little, if anything, of value to Jesus research.

horses or to stretch two bows; and it is not possible for a servant to serve two masters' (§47).

Thomas ends on a most politically incorrect note: 'Simon Peter said to them: "Let Mariam go out from among us, for women are not worthy of life!" Jesus said: "Behold, I will lead her that I may make her male, in order that she too may become a living spirit resembling you males. For every woman who makes herself male will enter the kingdom of heaven"' (§114).

Gospel of Peter.[41] Until the winter of 1886–87, when a large fragment was discovered in a monk's coffin, the *Gospel of Peter* was known

41. For selected studies, see A. Harnack, *Bruchstücke des Evangeliums und der Apokalypse des Petrus* (TU, 9; Leipzig: Hinrichs, 1893); *idem* and H. von Schubert, 'Das Petrusevangelium', *TLZ* 19 (1894), pp. 9-18; T. Zahn, *Das Evangelium des Petrus* (Erlangen: Deichert, 1893); P. Gardner-Smith, 'The Gospel of Peter', *JTS* 27 (1925–26), pp. 255-71; *idem*, 'The Date of the Gospel of Peter', *JTS* 27 (1925–26), pp. 401-407; L. Vaganay, *L'évangile de Pierre* (EBib; Paris: Gabalda, 1930); C.H. Dodd, 'A New Gospel', in Dodd, *New Testament Studies* (Manchester: Manchester University Press, 1953), pp. 12-52; K. Beyschlag, 'Das Petrusevangelium', in Beyschlag, *Die verborgene Überlieferung von Christus* (Munich and Hamburg: Siebenstern Taschenbuch, 1969), pp. 27-64; J. Denker, *Die theologiegeschichtliche Stellung des Petrusevangeliums: Ein Beitrag zur Frühgeschichte des Doketismus* (EHST, 36; Bern and Frankfurt: Lang, 1975); Cameron, *The Other Gospels*, pp. 76-82; J.W. McCant, 'Gospel of Peter: Docetism Reconsidered', *NTS* 30 (1984), pp. 258-73; D.F. Wright, 'Apocryphal Gospels: The "Unknown Gospel" (Pap. Egerton 2) and the *Gospel of Peter*', in Wenham (ed.), *The Jesus Tradition Outside the Gospels*, pp. 207-32; R.E. Brown, 'The Gospel of Peter and Canonical Gospel Priority', *NTS* 33 (1987), pp. 321-43; J.B. Green, 'The Gospel of Peter: Source for a Pre-Canonical Passion Narrative?', *ZNW* 78 (1987), pp. 293-301; J.D. Crossan, *The Cross that Spoke: The Origins of the Passion Narrative* (San Francisco: Harper & Row, 1988); *idem*, *Four Other Gospels*, pp. 87-127; Koester, 'Überlieferung und Geschichte', pp. 1487-88, 1525-27; *idem*, *Ancient Christian Gospels*, pp. 216-40; E. Schaeffer, 'The Guard at the Tomb (*Gos. Pet.* 8:28–11:49 and Matt 27:62-66; 28:2-4, 11-16): A Case of Intertextuality?', in E.H. Lovering (ed.), *Society of Biblical Literature 1991 Seminar Papers* (SBLSP, 30; Atlanta: Scholars Press, 1991), pp. 499-507; W. Rebell, *Neutestamentliche Apokryphen und Apostolischen Vätern* (Munich: Chr. Kaiser Verlag, 1992), pp. 92-99; Charlesworth and Evans, 'Jesus in the Agrapha and Apocryphal Gospels', pp. 503-14. For additional bibliography, see Schneemelcher, *New Testament Apocrypha*, p. 216; Charlesworth, *The New Testament Apocrypha and Pseudepigrapha*, pp. 321-27.

only through one clear reference in the fourth-century Church Father Eusebius, *H.E.* 6.12.2-6: τοῦ λεγομένου 'κατὰ Πέτρον εὐαγγελίου' ('called "the Gospel according to Peter"'). The newly discovered ninth-century Akhmimic Greek text was published five years later.[42] Two more Greek fragments, dating from the late second or early third-century, have since been discovered. The first, *P. Oxy.* 2949,[43] overlaps with a small portion of the Akhmimic text, while the second, *P. Oxy.* 4009,[44] overlaps with no part of the Akhmimic text, but nevertheless might belong to the *Gospel of Peter*.

The *Gospel of Peter* narrates the story of Jesus' crucifixion and resurrection. The Akhmimic fragment begins by stating that 'none of the Jews washed their hands' (1.1), presumably in contrast to Pilate who according to Mt. 27.24 did wash his hands. Jesus is then delivered up and crucified. Aspects of Christology are heightened, or at least the author thought he had heightened them. He tells us that Jesus 'felt no

42. U. Bouriant, 'Fragments du texte grec du livre d'Enoch et de quelques écrits attribués à Saint Pierre', in *Mémoires publiés par les membres de la Mission archéologique française au Caire* 9.1 (Paris: Librarie de la Société asiatique, 1892), pp. 137-42. Edited and corrected editions of the text can also be found in J.A. Robinson and M.R. James, *The Gospel according to Peter, and The Revelation of Peter* (London: C.J. Clay, 1892); H. von Schubert, *Die Composition des Pseudopetrinischen Evangelien-Fragments* (Berlin: Reuther & Reichard, 1893); *idem, The Gospel of St Peter* (Edinburgh: T. & T. Clark, 1893); H.B. Swete, *ΕΥΑΓΓΕΛΙΟΝ ΚΑΤΑ ΠΕΤΡΟΝ: The Akhmîm Fragment of the Gospel of St Peter* (London and New York: Macmillan, 1893); and more recently in M.G. Mara, *Évangile de Pierre* (SC, 201; Paris: Cerf, 1973).

43. For text of this papyrus, see R.A. Coles, 'Fragments of an Apocryphal Gospel (?)', in G.M. Browne *et al.* (eds.), *The Oxyrhynchus Papyri* (vol. 41; London: Egypt Exploration Society, 1972), pp. 15-16 (+ pl. II). See also D. Lührmann, 'POx 2949: EvPt 3–5 in einer Handschrift des 2./3. Jahrhunderts', *ZNW* 72 (1981), pp. 216-22.

44. For text of this papyrus, see D. Lührmann and P.J. Parsons, '4009. Gospel of Peter?', in Parsons *et al.* (eds.), *The Oxyrhynchus Papyri* (vol. 60; London: Egypt Exploration Society, 1993), pp. 1-5 (+ pl. I). See also D. Lührmann, 'POx 4009: Ein neues Fragment des Petrusevangeliums?', *NovT* 35 (1993), pp. 390-410. Lührmann has restored the text to read: '"...the harvest. But become innocent as doves and wise as serpents. You will be like sheep in the midst of wolves." I said to him, "When should we be torn asunder?" And answering, he says to me, "When the wolves have torn the sheep asunder, they are no longer able to do anything to it. Therefore I say to you, do not fear those who kill you and after killing no longer are able to do anything..."'

pain' (4.10). When Jesus cries out of the cross, he says: 'My power, O power, you have abandoned me!' (5.19). After his death, 'the Jews' perceived that they had committed a terrible sin (7.25-27). The scribes and Pharisees admit that Jesus had been righteous (8.28) and so request a guard to prevent the theft of his body and the subsequent rumor of resurrection (8.29-31). Pilate acquiesces and the Jewish religious leaders themselves take part in the watch, in a cemetery no less! (8.32-33; 10.38). They, along with the Roman soldiers, witness the resurrection. The stone covering the opening of the tomb is rolled aside. Two young men are observed to enter. Moments later they emerge, supporting a third. The heads of the two reach heaven, but the head of the third overpasses heaven. But they are not all that exit the tomb, the cross itself comes bounding out after them (10.39). A voice from heaven is then heard: 'Have you preached to them that sleep?' (10.41), and the cross (!) answers: 'Yes' (10.42).

The image of Jesus preserved in this fanciful writing is tinged with features alien to the canonical Gospels. Feeling no pain during the crucifixion, the loss of 'power', and being 'taken up' (though still on the cross physically) point to docetic tendencies. Jesus' divine sonship is heightened (3.6, 9; 11.45, 46). Indeed, there is much in the *Gospel of Peter* that bears the stamp of enthusiastic Christian exaggeration unrestrained by realistic knowledge of Jewish piety and customs. And, of course, the description of the risen Christ, accompanied by a talking cross, is the stuff from which fables are made. It is hard to understand why some scholars, among them John Dominic Crossan, attach a great deal of importance to this document and think that it contains tradition more primitive than that found in the canonical Gospels.[45]

Secret Gospel of Mark.[46] Embedded in a partially preserved letter penned by Clement of Alexandria, the 'Secret' (as opposed to the public)

45. See Crossan, *The Cross that Spoke*, p. 404.

46. For selected studies, see M. Smith, *Clement of Alexandria and a Secret Gospel of Mark* (Cambridge, MA: Harvard University Press, 1973); *idem, The Secret Gospel: The Discovery and Interpretation of the Secret Gospel according to Mark* (New York: Harper & Row, 1973); H. Merkel, 'Auf den Spuren des Urmarkus? Ein neuer Fund und seine Beurteilung', *ZTK* 71 (1974), pp. 123-44; R.E. Brown, 'The Relation of "The Secret Gospel of Mark" to the Fourth Gospel', *CBQ* 36 (1974), pp. 466-85; R.M. Grant, 'Morton Smith's Two Books', *ATR* 56 (1974), pp. 58-64; Q. Quesnell, 'The Mar Saba Clementine: A Question of Evidence', *CBQ* 37 (1975), pp. 48-67; F. Neirynck, 'La fuite du jeune homme en Mc 14, 51-52',

Gospel of Mark suggests that teaching regarding the kingdom of God was mysterious and secretive. Clement tells us that Secret Mark contains a passage (at Mk 10.34) that tells of Jesus raising a young man, who then returns to Jesus, wearing only a linen sheet, to be taught 'the mystery of the kingdom of God'. Evidently, this young man is to be identified with the young man who fled naked the night of Jesus' arrest (Mk 14.52).

Secret Mark, if there ever was such an edition of Mark, adds little to our gallery of portraits of Jesus. The late Morton Smith thought that it added much, lending support to his controversial depiction of Jesus as a magician, perhaps even homosexual.[47] But there are three reasons to hesitate before attaching too much credibility to this document: (1) its late, uncorroborated status (no one, besides Smith, has seen it; it remains unverified);[48] (2) Clement was gullible, passing on as genuine several other apocryphal writings; and (3) the canonical Gospels were freely edited and embellished in some circles. If there was a Secret *Gospel of Mark*, it probably was little more than a second-century revision of canonical Mark.[49]

Jewish-Christian Gospels. Scattered about in the patristic literature we find references to and brief quotations of three Jewish-Christian Gospels: the *Gospel of the Nazaraeans* (or *Nazoreans*), the *Gospel of*

ETL 55 (1979), pp. 43-66; H. Koester, 'History and Development of Mark's Gospel: From Mark to Secret Mark and "Canonical" Mark', in B.C. Corley (ed.), *Colloquy on New Testament Studies: A Time for Reappraisal and Fresh Approaches* (Macon, GA: Mercer University Press, 1983), pp. 35-58; *idem*, *Ancient Christian Gospels*, pp. 293-303; *idem*, 'Überlieferung und Geschichte', pp. 1501-1503; Crossan, *Four Other Gospels*, pp. 61-83; H. Merkel, 'Appendix: The "Secret Gospel" of Mark', in Schneemelcher (ed.), *New Testament Apocrypha*, pp. 106-109; P. Sellew, '*Secret Mark* and the History of Canonical Mark', in B.A. Pearson (ed.), *The Future of Early Christianity* (H. Koester Festschrift; Minneapolis: Fortress Press, 1991), pp. 242-57; Rebell, *Neutestamentliche Apokryphen*, pp. 120-24; Charlesworth and Evans, 'Jesus in the Agrapha and Apocryphal Gospels', pp. 526-32. For additional bibliography, see Schneemelcher, *New Testament Apocrypha*, p. 106; M. Smith, 'Clement of Alexandria and Secret Mark: The Score at the End of the First Decade', *HTR* 75 (1982), pp. 449-61; S. Levin, 'The Early History of Christianity, in Light of the "Secret Gospel" of Mark', *ANRW* II.25.6 (1988), pp. 4270-92.

    47. M. Smith, *Jesus the Magician* (New York: Harper & Row, 1978).

    48. See the concerns raised by Quesnell, 'The Mar Saba Clementine', pp. 48-67.

    49. For more discussion, see my comments in Charlesworth and Evans, 'Jesus in the Agrapha and Apocryphal Gospels', pp. 526-32.

the *Ebionites*, and the *Gospel of the Hebrews*.[50] The difficulties and uncertainties that attend study of these Gospels are numerous. There is debate about just how many Jewish-Christian Gospels actually existed (e.g. is the *Gospel of the Ebionites* to be identified with the *Gospel of the Hebrews*?) and how they relate to the canonical Gospels (e.g. are these Gospels recensions of Matthew?). Interpreters are faced with these difficulties largely because of confusing and contradictory statements in the patristic sources and because we possess only small portions of these long-lost writings. The brief, selected quotations found in patristic sources are useful, however, for they tend to draw attention to the distinctive features of these Gospels.

According to the *Gospel of the Nazaraeans*, which was probably originally composed in Aramaic,[51] Jesus asks, in response to a suggestion that he be baptized by John: 'How have I sinned that I should go and be baptized by him?' (§2; cf. Jerome, *Against Pelagius* 3.2). In his interview with the wealthy young man who asks about inheriting eternal life (cf. Mk 10.17-22), Jesus challenges the claim that the Law has been observed faithfully: 'How can you say that you fulfilled the Law and the Prophets? For it stands written in the Law: "Love your neighbor as yourself"; and behold, many of your brothers, sons of Abraham, are begrimed with dirt and die of hunger—and your house is full of many good things and nothing at all comes forth from it to them!' (§16; cf. Origen, *Commentary on Matthew* 15.14 [on Mt. 19.16-22]). This Jesus of practical-orientation is reminiscent of the admonitions found in James. One immediately thinks of the criticism leveled against him who does not provide for his brother or sister the necessities of life (Jas 2.14-16).

We shall pass over the *Gospel of the Ebionites*, since there is almost nothing attributed directly to Jesus. According to the *Gospel of the Hebrews*, which was probably originally composed in Greek, Jesus says: 'And never be joyful, except when you look upon your brother with love' (§5; cf. Jerome, *Commentary on Ephesians* 5.4). Elsewhere Jesus says that the gravest sinner is 'he who grieves the spirit of his brother' (§6; cf. Jerome, *Commentary on Ezekiel* 18.7). Following his resurrection, Jesus appears to James the Just and gives him bread, saying: 'My brother, eat your bread, for the son of man is risen from

50. See Schneemelcher, *New Testament Apocrypha*, pp. 134-78.
51. See Jerome, *Epistles* 120; *idem*, *Commentary on Matthew* 27.51: 'the Gospel which is written in Hebrew characters'.

among them who sleep' (§7; cf. Jerome, *On Famous Men* 2). A distinctive feature of the *Gospel of the Hebrews*, if we were to make an assessment on the basis of the surviving fragments, seems to be its portrait of a compassionate, brotherly Jesus.

Egerton (and other miscellaneous papyrus fragments).[52] It is very difficult to infer from these papyrus fragments a portrait of Jesus; there simply is not enough preserved material. *P. Egerton* 2 is apparently a blend of synoptic and Johannine elements. It consists of three fragments. Most of the material in the first two fragments can be read, restored, or reasonably inferred. Fragment 1 (*verso*) provides us with a Johannine-like debate between Jesus and accusing legalists. Jesus' demand to 'search the Scriptures', in which his accusers think they have life, is an unmistakable allusion to Jn 5.39. The debate continues onto the *recto* side of the first fragment. We are told that rulers laid hands on Jesus, hoping to stone him. But his hour had not yet come, so he was able to escape from them. The *recto* continues with the story of the leper who begs Jesus to cleanse him. The story is clearly a version of the synoptic story of the cleansing of the leper (Mk 1.40-45). Fragment 2 (*recto*) provides a version of the question of paying tax to Caesar (Mk 12.13-17), with a touch of other synoptic elements. The *verso* of fragment 2 is not as easily restored as the *recto*, for it tells an otherwise unattested story. People are perplexed at a strange question. Jesus stands at the bank of the Jordan River, stretches out his hand, which apparently is filled with seed, then sows it upon the river (though

---

52. H.I. Bell and T.C. Skeat, *Fragments of an Unknown Gospel and Other Early Christian Papyri* (London: British Museum, 1935), pp. 8-15, 26; *idem, The New Gospel Fragments* (London: British Museum, 1951), pp. 29-33; G. Mayeda, *Das Leben-Jesu-Fragment Papyrus Egerton 2 und seine Stellung in der urchristlichen Literaturgeschichte* (Bern: Haupt, 1946), pp. 7-11; Crossan, *Four Other Gospels*, pp. 41-57; M. Gronewald, 'Unbekanntes Evangelium oder Evangelienharmonie (Fragment aus dem Evangelium Egerton)', in *Kölner Papyri (P. Köln)* (vol. 6; Sonderreihe Papyrologica Coloniensia, 7; Cologne: Bibliothèque Bodmer, 1987), pp. 136-45; J. Jeremias and W. Schneemelcher, 'Fragments of Unknown Gospels', in Schneemelcher (ed.), *New Testament Apocrypha*, pp. 92-109; D. Lührmann, 'Das neue Fragment des PEgerton 2 (PKöln 255)', in Van Segbroeck *et al.* (eds.), *The Four Gospels 1992*, III, pp. 2239-55; Rebell, *Neutestamentliche Apokryphen*, pp. 88-91; Charlesworth and Evans, 'Jesus in the Agrapha and Apocryphal Gospels', pp. 514-25.

this is uncertain). Fruit is brought forth and the people rejoice (though again, this is uncertain). This vignette is reminiscent of one of the amusing stories found in the *Infancy Gospel of Thomas*, in which the boy Jesus sows a handful of seed resulting in an enormous crop. Almost nothing can be recovered from Egerton's third fragment; from the *recto* we can make out a few words ('I abide', 'stones', 'should kill him'), which again suggest a Johannine parallel.

Crossan and Koester have argued that this papyrus contains tradition that antedates the canonical Gospels, before the bifurcation of Johannine and synoptic traditions.[53] But this is very doubtful. The final portion, which is badly preserved, seems to recount a story all too familiar to us in the fanciful Gospels of later Christians, who wished to embellish the element of the marvelous and miraculous.

There are several other papyrus fragments of what might have been Gospels. Their limited contents make it impossible to decide with certainty whether they actually are Gospels, or are other types of writings which recite sayings and/or deeds of Jesus. *P. Oxy.* 840 (fourth or fifth century) tells of an angry exchange over baptism between Jesus and a few religious leaders in Jerusalem. *P. Oxy.* 1224 (early fourth century) offers the remains of two pages of a papyrus book (pages 175 and 176). The first page parallels Mk 2.16-17 in which Pharisees and priests com-plain of Jesus' dining with sinners. The second page parallels Mt. 5.44 in which Jesus enjoins his followers to pray for their enemies. *P. Cairo* 10735 preserves a fragment of the infancy narrative, with the *recto* paralleling Mt. 2.13, where the angel speaks to Joseph, and the *verso* paralleling Lk. 1.36, where Mary is told of the pregnancy of Elizabeth. Finally, the Fayyum Fragment preserves

---

53. Crossan, *Four Other Gospels*, p. 183; Koester, *Ancient Christian Gospels*, p. 207. Now see the recent study by K. Erlemann, '*P. Egerton* 2: "Missing Link" zwischen synoptischer und johanneischer Tradition', *NTS* 42 (1996), pp. 12-34. Erlemann argues (p. 16) that *P. Egerton* 2 was produced as part of the apologetic efforts of a Jewish Christian group, that it is independent of the canonical Gospels, and that it presents a challenge to scholars concerned with the development of the Gospels and those concerned with the historical Jesus. Notwithstanding Erlemann's analysis and conclusions, which will be taken up at length in another publication, I remain unconvinced (cf. Charlesworth and Evans, 'Jesus in the Agrapha and Apocryphal Gospels', pp. 514-25). It is far more probable that *P. Egerton* 2 is nothing more than a second-century conflation of synoptic and Johannine traditions, with apocryphal touches.

a small portion of the Last Supper (Mk 14.27, 29-30), in which Jesus predicts the defection of his disciples and Peter's denials.[54]

Gnostic Gospels

The mysterious post-Easter Jesus, who makes luminous appearances on mountain tops, is the standard image one encounters in the gnostic Gospels.[55] With the exception of the *Gospel of Thomas*, whose gnostic qualities are secondary, the gnostic Gospels provide us with no useful information about the historical Jesus. Some scholars think they might help us understand better the origins of early Christology, but that is doubtful.

54. See Schneemelcher (ed.), *New Testament Apocrypha*, pp. 94-95, 100-102.

55. For selected studies, see E. Haenchen, 'Neutestamentliche und gnostische Evangelien', in W. Eltester (ed.), *Christentum und Gnosis* (BZNW, 37; Berlin: Töpelmann, 1969), pp. 19-45; J. Dart, *The Laughing Savior: The Discovery and Significance of the Nag Hammadi Gnostic Library* (New York: Harper & Row, 1976); H. Koester, 'Gnostic Writings as Witnesses for the Development of the Sayings Tradition', in B. Layton (ed.), *The Rediscovery of Gnosticism: Proceedings of the International Conference on Gnosticism at Yale, New Haven, Connecticut, March 28–31, 1978* (2 vols.; NumSup, 41; Leiden: Brill, 1980), I, pp. 238-61; E.H. Pagels, 'Gnostic and Orthodox Views of Christ's Passion: Paradigms for the Christian's Response to Persecution?', in Layton (ed.), *The Rediscovery of Gnosticism*, I, pp. 262-88; C.A. Evans, 'Jesus in Gnostic Literature', *Bib* 62 (1981), pp. 406-12; J.-M. Sevrin, 'Paroles et paraboles de Jésus dans des écrits gnostiques coptes', in Delobel (ed.), *Logia: Les Paroles de Jésus*, pp. 517-28; C.M. Tuckett, 'Synoptic Tradition in Some Nag Hammadi and Related Texts', *VC* 36 (1982), pp. 173-90; *idem, Nag Hammadi and the Gospel Tradition: Synoptic Tradition in the Nag Hammadi Library* (SNTW; Edinburgh: T. & T. Clark, 1986); E.M. Yamauchi, 'The Crucifixion and Docetic Christology', *CTQ* 46 (1982), pp. 1-20; C.W. Hedrick, 'Kingdom Sayings and Parables of Jesus in *The Apocryphon of James*: Tradition and Redaction', *NTS* 29 (1983), pp. 1-24; E. Segelberg, 'The Gospel of Philip and the New Testament', in A.H.B. Logan and A.J.M. Wedderburn (eds.), *The New Testament and Gnosis* (R.McL. Wilson Festschrift; Edinburgh: T. & T. Clark, 1983), pp. 204-12; R.D. Cameron, *Sayings Traditions in the 'Apocryphon of James'* (HTS, 34; Philadelphia: Fortress Press, 1984); J.M. Robinson (ed.), *The Nag Hammadi Library in English* (New York: Harper & Row, 3rd edn, 1988); H.-M. Schenke, 'Gospel of Philip', in Schneemelcher (ed.), *New Testament Apocrypha*, pp. 179-208; H.-C. Puech, 'Other Gnostic Gospels and Related Literature', rev. by B. Blatz, in Schneemelcher (ed.), *New Testament Apocrypha*, pp. 354-413; W. Schneemelcher *et al.*, 'Dialogues of the Redeemer', in Schneemelcher (ed.), *New Testament Apocrypha*, pp. 228-353; Rebell, *Neutestamentliche Apokryphen*, pp. 21-75.

The emphasis of these Gospels falls on the risen Christ, who transcends the earth and can disclose to his disciples the way of return to heaven. Descriptions of his appearance are reminiscent of the portrait of the risen Christ that we find in the Apocalypse. What Jesus had taught his disciples prior to his resurrection is relegated to insignificance, either because the risen Christ now has more to offer or because earlier his disciples lacked the capacity to appreciate his teaching.

'Orthodox' Apocryphal Gospels

In the 'Orthodox' Apocryphal Gospels pious imagination is given full rein.[56] We are met with an infant Jesus who performs miracles, usually through the intercession of his mother. We read of a child whose miraculous powers are sometimes used in a capricious manner. For example, Jesus humiliates his teacher, kills then resurrects the school-yard bully, claps his hands and brings to life clay pigeons, kills a poisonous viper by breathing on it (and at the same time restores to health his younger brother James), saves the lives of various ill and injured, and saves Joseph's reputation as a carpenter by stretching a plank of expensive cedar that had been cut too short.

We read of a young boy who is a prodigy, a master student, an athlete, an artist, and a carpenter of unequalled talents. The Jesus of these apocryphal Gospels advances no particular theology or line of interpretation. They are pious embellishments that attempt to fill in the 'silent' years of Jesus' life. What events took place in the birth and upbringing of Mary, Jesus' mother? What happened to the holy family during their sojourn in Egypt? What kind of boy was Jesus? These questions are answered with imagination and with little restraint. The resulting picture is not always flattering, for the youthful Jesus is sometimes dangerous and does not always show his elders and peers respect.

Other apocryphal Gospels tell of Jesus' correspondence with King Abgar, who has requested healing. The *Acts of Pilate* embellishes the

---

56. For selected studies, see M.R. James, *The Apocryphal New Testament* (Oxford: Clarendon Press, 1924), pp. 38-227; P. Vielhauer and G. Strecker, 'Jewish-Christian Gospels', in Schneemelcher (ed.), *New Testament Apocrypha*, pp. 135-78; O. Cullmann, 'Infancy Gospels', in Schneemelcher (ed.), *New Testament Apocrypha*, pp. 414-69; W.A. Bienert *et al.*, 'The Work and Sufferings of Jesus', in Schneemelcher (ed.), *New Testament Apocrypha*, pp. 489-60; Rebell, *Neutestamentliche Apokryphen*, pp. 87-136.

trial of Jesus, while *Christ's Descent into Hell* describes Jesus' discourses in hell and the raising up of various personages, such as Adam and the Patriarchs. A great number of other Gospels, many attributed to various apostles or arch-heretics, evidently related various stories and sayings designed in most cases to advance certain theologies or practices.

Although these documents have some value for the study of the history and ideas of the Early Church, they offer Jesus research virtually nothing of value.

Conclusion

The canonical and apocryphal Gospels present us with a rich assortment of images of Christ. Most are rooted in early, widespread tradition; all more or less emphasize certain aspects, to advance apologetic and/or paraenetic concerns. Common to all is the presupposition of the authority, even 'canonicity', of Jesus' teaching, experience, and person. The diversity and adaptability of the tradition is a testimony to the power and innovation of Jesus' message and his lifestyle.

It may prove disappointing to some, perhaps even to many, to conclude that the canonical Gospels, particularly the Synoptic Gospels, remain the only reliable sources for the historical Jesus. Some of the apocryphal Gospels and papyrus fragments may contain primitive elements, perhaps even an authentic saying or two not found in the canonical Gospels, but these are rare exceptions. The various portraits of Jesus in this vast assortment of Gospels are intriguing, but they add little reliable information beyond what can be recovered in the canonical Gospels. Indeed, in the canonical Gospels themselves there is a remarkably consistent picture of Jesus.

THE LIFE OF JESUS AS COMEDY:
PLOT STRUCTURE IN TWO CONTEMPORARY
HISTORICAL JESUS PORTRAITS

Susan Lochrie Graham

1. *Introduction*

It has been suggested that the text of the New Testament is a window on the past, a more or less transparent view into the first century; and that it is a mirror into which we peer and in which we see our own reflections. The mirror and window categories mask a problem with historical analysis: the window into the past is not transparent, and what is seen through the glass is overlaid with the contemporary context and the personality of the historian, so that the angle of vision affects the view of the past. This problem is sharply posed in studies of the historical Jesus. Since the end of the eighteenth century, biblical scholars have worked to create ever more sophisticated methods of literary and historical analysis, attempting to use these methods to draw accurate and authentic portraits of the historical Jesus. Two centuries of 'quests' have produced a variety of results, but no consensus has been reached as to the conclusions. Nevertheless, the study has continued, particularly in the past fifteen years, beginning with the creation of two working professional groups, the Historical Jesus Section of the Society of Biblical Literature, and the independent Jesus Seminar in 1985. Since then, the literature has proliferated at a surprising rate, and so much new work has been undertaken that we can now speak of a 'third quest'. Not only articles in scholarly journals, but monographs for the academic reader and popularizing books for the general public appear monthly. This social phenomenon is curious, and it invites critical scrutiny.

Scholars are beginning to produce critical summaries of the different portraits; recent examples include the work of Marcus J. Borg (1994) and Ben Witherington III (1995).[1] Witherington classifies the recent portraits according to their results: for some, Jesus is an 'itinerant cynic philosopher',[2] for others, a 'man of the spirit',[3] an 'eschatological prophet',[4] or a 'prophet of social change'.[5] Witherington himself sees Jesus as a 'sage',[6] but he reserves his highest praise for those who understand Jesus as a messianic figure.[7] It is immediately clear to the reader of the portraits that there is little agreement not only as to the interpretations but also as to the methods and the sources; and the critical studies of these portraits disagree on their evaluations as well. Such variety of opinion indicates that a new approach would be welcome.

Historians interested in theory have argued for at least thirty years that the meaning of historical writing is shaped in part by its form. The insight is not limited to historians, moreover; even mainstream biblical scholars have begun to think along these lines. For example, in a post to the 'Jesus at 2000' e-mail list by Luke Timothy Johnson, he poses this rhetorical question: 'Doesn't it make good sense of human experience, and make good historiographic method as well, to suppose that the memory of the basic story pattern... [preceded] the collection and organization of sayings and deeds?' He argues that the 'real' Jesus was the man whose character 'is found, not in the individual pericopes, but in the *narrative pattern of the compositions themselves*'.[8] From a literary point of view, he is concerned with characterization, but suggests here that the 'basic story pattern', what I am calling plot, precedes the data and functions intertextually to shape the way the data are collected. What is true for the writers of the first historical Jesus portraits in the Gospels is also true for contemporary writers. Rather than reading these portraits as repositories of 'facts' about the 'real' Jesus, they may be read as narrative structures in which the elements

1. Witherington, not surprisingly, evaluates the work of the Jesus Seminar scholars far more negatively than does Borg, who is a Fellow.
2. He discusses Crossan 1991, along with Mack 1988; cf. Mack 1995; and Downing 1988.
3. See particularly Borg 1984; Borg 1987; and Vermes 1973.
4. Discussing particularly Sanders 1985.
5. Most importantly, Theissen 1987; and Horsley 1987.
6. Along with Schüssler Fiorenza 1983 and 1994.
7. See Meier 1991; Meier 1994; Wright 1992.
8. 'Primary Message, Week 2 (Johnson)', Jesus2000@info.harpercollins.com (25 February 1996).

of plot and characterization, among others, work to establish meaning for historical events.

Northrop Frye's most complete statement of his archetypal theory is the third essay in *Anatomy of Criticism*, 'Archetypal Criticism: Theory of Myths' (1968: 131-239). It is at this level that I wish to begin, looking at the patterns of narrative in terms of these deep structures. Within the structures of mythic imagery, Frye begins by identifying the 'movement' of the plot: 'The downward movement is the tragic movement, the wheel of fortune falling toward hamartia, and from hamartia to catastrophe. The upward movement is the comic movement, from threatening complications to a happy ending and a general assumption of post-dated innocence in which everyone lives happily ever after.' Having identified these narrative movements, he classifies them in terms of the literary categories of the romantic, the tragic, the comic, and the ironic or satiric. These are the structures underlying all stories, whether fictional or not. They are, according to Frye, 'narrative categories of literature broader than, or logically prior to, the ordinary literary genres' (1968: 162).[9] The movement of comedy, for example, is inclusive, and focuses on the establishment of a new order of society; tragedy on the other hand is exclusive, and focuses on the isolation of an individual from society and the resultant effects on the social order. Historical Jesus portraits can be classified according to these types, depending on the sort of story the author thinks he or she is writing.

2. The Christ Myth and Jesus as a Romantic Hero

Mythmaking, as Burton Mack has seen,[10] is vital to the success of human social formations, and the various Jesus movements and Christ cults which arose after the death of Jesus produced a body of stories which taken together form the base of Christian tradition. To the extent that Jesus as Christ is understood as a divine figure, this story is myth

9. Frye has been criticized for the reductive nature of his system, and Hayden White agrees that it may be difficult to account for multi-layered literary works where the richness of meaning is produced by the simultaneous use of more than one type or mode. He comments, however, that since historians do not ordinarily think in terms of fictional structures, they tend to use more typical patterns. This does not preclude, as we will see, narratives composed of two separate modes operating simultaneously (White 1973: 8).

10. 'The Jesus Summit' (videotape; Trinity Church, NY: ECTN, 1994).

proper; but the life story of the human Jesus told in these early narratives places him in the realm of romance, one of the four 'archetypal' forms underlying all narrative, in Frye's terms. In romance, the land is ruled by an old king helpless to stop the ravages of a dragon, until the hero arrives. After passing through a series of adventures or tests, the hero finally kills the dragon, returns victorious, marries the king's daughter, and assumes the throne. This form, which is called the quest, has three phases: the perilous journey, the crucial struggle, and the exaltation of the hero (1968: 189). The canonical Gospels vary in their emphases, but taken together provide the details of all three phases. In the Christian symbolism which has grown out of these stories and their interpretations, Jesus as Christ kills the dragon Satan, supplants the impotent old king Adam, and takes the Church as his bride. Like all historical narratives, the Gospels shape past events into meaningful literary forms, based in this case on what Frye calls 'the mythos of summer': romance (1968: 186-206). While biblical critics have been hard at work for the past two centuries disintegrating the Gospels and distinguishing historical wheat from theological, not to say mythical, chaff, they have not paid attention to the form of the narrative itself. Clearly the characterization of Jesus as hero has changed, but in modern historical Jesus portraits, so has the plot.

3. *Genre: The Mythos of Comedy*

This paper explores the comic plot structure as it functions in two very different contemporary portraits of Jesus, those of Elisabeth Schüssler Fiorenza and of John Dominic Crossan. Because historians are not typically concerned with plot structures, one might say that their narratives are 'naive' from a literary perspective; that is, the structure more closely corresponds to the archetype than does that of a complex literary work, although this does not necessarily result in a simple plot. For the purposes of this study, I will focus primarily on the comic plot. It is not simply my contention that the concerns of the authors of historical narrative are reflected in their work,[11] but that the form of the

11. The observation invariably cited is from George Tyrell (1963 [1909]: 49): 'The Christ that Harnack sees [in *The Essence of Christianity*], looking back through nineteen centuries of Catholic darkness, is only the reflection of a liberal Protestant face, seen at the bottom of a deep well'. For a similar view, see also Schweitzer (1957 [1910]). It has become a truism in the history of New Testament research that

narrative itself has a significance which in these two cases reinforces the stated and implied purposes of the authors.[12]

Comedy has a socially subversive element to it, in the triumph of the younger hero over the established structures represented by the older opponents who are inappropriate rivals. However, the movement of comedy tends to be inclusive, so that at the end, even these blocking characters are reconciled to the new order and are included in the festivities. Frye comments that '[the] society emerging at the conclusion of comedy represents...a kind of moral norm, or pragmatically free society' (1968: 169). In comic plots, according to Frye, 'what normally happens is that a young man wants a young woman, that his desire is resisted by some opposition, usually paternal, and that near the end of the play some twist in the plot enables the hero to have his will' (1968: 163). The success of the hero and the emergence of the new society can only occur if the hero is strong enough to overcome the opposing forces of the old order. In ironic comedy, the new society may remain in embryo, or it may not prevail at all over the old order.[13] This is the case in the comic structures of the historical Jesus portraits we are discussing.

The ending which enables the formation of this new society is usually manipulated by a twist in the plot, often involving the revelation of mistaken identity, and sometimes also including metamorphosis

Schweitzer's book brought the first quest to an end. See, for example, Borg 1994: 4, and many others.

12. The longer study proposes to work out a literary taxonomy for classifying historical narrative and historical figures in narrative, and to place the contemporary historical Jesus work within this framework, in order to provide a basis for comparison among them, as well as to suggest how the form of the narrative shapes the historical explanations argued in them. Using the narrative forms of comedy, tragedy, and romance and their related modes of characterization of the hero, I will argue that the similarities in certain conclusions reached by very different methods have to do with similarities in the plot structure chosen to tell the story, while differences can be explained in terms of the mode of characterization, whether mythic, romantic, heroic, or ironic.

13. Hero and heroine are the terms Frye chooses to use in describing these plots, although such gendered terms should probably be replaced. Phaedre is doubtless the 'hero' of Racine's tragedy, in terms of her role in the plot structure. In the stories of Jesus, the hero or protagonist is male. But that in itself has caused problems among feminist theologians. Whether using the gendered terms, and for that matter, the 'archetypal' mythic structures themselves, renders this framework impossibly problematic from a feminist point of view remains to be seen.

of character, where a blocking character experiences a total change
that we are led to believe is permanent (1968: 170-71). In the generic
pattern of comedy identified by Frye:

> ...the movement of comedy is usually a movement from one kind of
> society to another. At the beginning of the play, the obstructing characters
> are in charge of the play's society, and the audience recognizes that they
> are usurpers. At the end of the play the device in the plot that brings hero
> and heroine together causes a new society to crystallize around the hero,
> and the moment when this crystallization occurs is the point of resolution
> in the action, the comic discovery (1968: 163).

Frye notes also that the appearance of the new society is usually marked
by some kind of festive ritual, which takes place at the end or immediately thereafter, and the audience is invited to recognize the comic
resolution and to participate in it by forming part of the comic society
in some way. This is in line with the structure of the Gospels, which
invite the hearer or reader to participate in the new order inaugurated
by Jesus. Frye concludes his general survey with the comment that
'[civilizations] which stress the desirable rather than the real, and the
religious as opposed to the scientific perspective, think of drama almost
entirely in terms of comedy' (1968: 171). If, then, it can be shown that
the plots of historical Jesus studies are comic, we would expect ethical
and theological ideas to be reflected in the plotting of the account, no
matter how 'objective' the method.

There is no doubt that a literary taxonomy of the sort proposed
here is helpful in understanding fictional narratives. But we are concerned with history. Paul Ricoeur addresses the question of the complex
relationship of history to fiction generally. In order to understand the
actions of human persons in the past, that is, to understand 'what
happened', it is necessary to place actions and events in context, as parts
of a meaningful whole (1978: 165). In historical writing, this understanding is mediated through the plot; events may be considered historical to the extent that they contribute to the development of the plot
(Ricoeur 1980: 171). Various plots suggest themselves to the historian
before any evaluation of the importance of single events; they become
important to the writer if they further one possible plot or another.
This can be verified by personal experience: we remember those events
in our own lives which can be understood as moments in a pattern that
enables us to give meaning to our existence. Hayden White comments,
'It is as if the plot were an entity in process of development prior to

the occurrence of any given event, and any given event could be endowed with historicality only to the extent that it could be shown to contribute to this process' (1987: 51). Understanding the plot structures and the modes of characterization that are available will help us to see how the 'facts' of historical events can be given different meanings depending on the historian's understanding of 'what really happened', that is to say, the narrative context.

4. *Elisabeth Schüssler Fiorenza's Comic Plot*

I want to turn now from this adumbration of comic structure to one of the specific portraits at hand, Elisabeth Schüssler Fiorenza's Jesus. Fiorenza has described the historical Jesus in two of her books. The first, *In Memory of Her*, appeared at the beginning of what we have called the third quest; the second, *Jesus: Miriam's Child, Sophia's Prophet*, was published in 1994. Neither book claims to provide a portrait of Jesus (1994: 4), but both in fact do. Schüssler Fiorenza's intent in writing is to create a historical reconstruction of Christian origins which focuses on the role of women; her reason for writing is to provide grounds for a feminist and liberationist dismantling of the kyriocentric theology which holds women, people of color, and the poor in bondage all over the world today. A classically trained biblical scholar, Schüssler Fiorenza relies on the methods of historical criticism, particularly redaction and form criticism, to do her own theological work. Unlike most biblical scholars, however, she does not attempt to be 'objective' in her historical analysis: her feminist ethics are foregrounded, and the historical work is in the service of her theological aims. It is probably this frank acknowledgment of bias that separates her work most clearly from that of other third quest writers. With this in mind then, I want to look at the structure of her implied narrative of Jesus in his first-century context.

Schüssler Fiorenza does not distinguish between the Jesus movement which grew up during the historical lifetime of Jesus from the post-Easter Jesus movement, nor does she attempt to delineate a historical Jesus apart from the movement. In narratological terms, this means that the emphasis in her narrative is on the setting and plot, rather than on characterization. Because of her insistence on a feminist perspective and her determination not to reinscribe a kyriarchal structure into her own christological work, she is at pains not to construct a heroic Jesus at the centre of her work. According to her, feminism must reject the methods of the third quest because 'kyriocentric scientific reconstructions reproduce not only androcentrism but also anti-Judaism in Christian historical-theological terms'. As a result, she rejects a narrative method of historical explanation centred on Jesus as the hero. Instead, the implied narrative traces some of Jesus' ideas but few of his actions: this is the story of the community grouped around Jesus, the child of Sophia sent by God/Sophia to bring about the *basileia* (kingdom) of God in a community of equals (1994: 87-88).

The significant action of the story is the growth of that community and its self-understanding, from its beginnings among the followers of Jesus to its fulfillment as the post-Easter Jesus movement. The action of the story follows the familiar lines of the Gospel: implied in Schüssler Fiorenza's account is the beginning of Jesus' ministry in the baptism by John, the teaching, healing, and table fellowship of the community during the days in Galilee, the trip to Jerusalem, the conflict with the authorities and Jesus' condemnation to death by the Romans. The death and burial in her narrative lead to the climax: the empty tomb, which she takes to be historical, is witnessed by the women who come in compassion to anoint the dead body of their friend; and the narrative ends with the suggestion that Jesus has gone ahead to Galilee where the women will find him.

In terms of the comic movement from blocking to freedom, the story of Jesus as Schüssler Fiorenza tells it begins with his baptism by John, clearly placing him in a social world which is governed by the laws of two obstructing societies: the world of Palestine under Roman rule, and the religious world of Judaism as it is represented by the establishment order. Jesus responds to the message of John the Baptist and is baptized by him, thus placing himself outside of the religious power structures of his time. Not only Jesus but many groups within Palestinian Judaism of the first century were convinced that 'God's intervention on behalf of Israel was immediate' (1983: 111). But this intervention was not necessarily an apocalyptic end of time; rather the expectations were those contained within the boundaries of the tensive symbol *basileia*. While John the Baptist expected and preached the eschatological restitution of Israel, Jesus preached that the 'eschatological salvation and wholeness of Israel as the elect people of God [was] already experientially available' (1983: 119), available according to Schüssler Fiorenza whenever Jesus 'casts out demons

(Lk. 11:20), heals the sick and the ritually unclean, tells stories about the lost who are found, of the uninvited, or of the last who will be first'. Thus Jesus' actions and words mediate the future kingdom 'into the structures and experiences of his own time and people' (1983: 120-21). His actions drew crowds of people anxious to share in this experience of the inbreaking kingdom in their midst.

Some of those crowds of people began to follow Jesus as his disciples, either traveling with him or providing food and lodging. Schüssler Fiorenza believes that the calling of the twelve male disciples is a later tradition; within the early Jesus movements an egalitarian mode of leadership obtained, with various people taking various leadership roles as needed. Because Jesus refused to define holiness in cultic terms, but rather redefined it as the wholeness intended in creation, and because he saw that wholeness as already available in his own ministry, his own practices were not ascetical. Jesus' ministry was characterized by 'festive table sharing'; and the parables which characterize his teaching provide 'ever-new images of a sumptuous, glorious banquet cele-bration' (1983: 119). This banquet, the central image of the kingdom, is, in Jesus' practice of inclusiveness, a symbol for God's inclusion of all people. Jesus' willingness to accept others without qualification was the root cause of the opposition of the religious authorities (1983: 120). The action of the plot focuses on the gathering of those people on the outside of the old society around a figure who promises to be at the centre of a new society of hope and freedom, a society symbolized as *basileia*.

The weight of the blocking characters in this narrative places Schüssler Fiorenza's plot in the realm of comic irony, where the new society will remain in embryo at the end of the action. But the comic expectation is that a romantic liaison, ordinarily embodied in a heroine, will produce the kernel around which the new society may develop. The Gospels of course provide no romantic interest for Jesus, although late traditions and apocryphal writings respond with stories centred on Jesus and Mary Magdalene. The desire for a couple who will provide the new family around whom the new comic society will grow marks Schüssler Fiorenza's comic structure. This element is displaced, but not entirely eliminated. In Schüssler Fiorenza's narrative, it is accom-plished by coupling Jesus with a mother-God figure: Sophia. This vision of God, ascribed to the earliest Jesus traditions, will allow Schüssler Fiorenza to present a God of gracious goodness in a woman's form as divine Sophia.[14] The female figure of Sophia functions here in the heroine's role, so that coupling Jesus with this female image provides a male–female pair around which the new society can emerge. In Schüssler Fiorenza's work, this is a theological interpretation made possible by certain historical data; but it is also a generic necessity.

Like other historical-Jesus critics, Schüssler Fiorenza is at pains to explain how the actions of Jesus could lead to his death, and how the Early Church could have developed from such inauspicious beginnings. She ascribes Jesus' execution to the political action of the Romans concerned with destroying any messianic pretenders who might threaten Roman rule. The Early Church then quickly moved to develop a theological rather than political explanation for Jesus' death, nearly effacing what she considers the real reason, and substituting the idea of atonement. In Schüssler Fiorenza's view, Jesus was not an innocent victim whose suffering and execution were in accordance with God's will; rather Jesus was *guilty* of the political charges against him. In a sense, his execution is the result of the success: 'Jesus' death is not willed by God but is the result of his all-inclusive praxis as Sophia's prophet' (1983: 135). She argues that theology cannot ignore the sociopolitical causes of Jesus' execution in focusing exclusively on the atoning results of his death; to do this is to continue 'the kyriarchal cycle of violence and victimization instead of empowering believers to resist and transform it' (1994: 106).

The climax of the story then is not the redemption of humankind through the sacrifice of Jesus on the cross, but instead the empty tomb and the resurrection experiences of the women disciples. She does not claim historicity for the resurrection, but instead treats whatever happened as 'visionary-ecstatic experiences' (1983: 139). When the women who had followed Jesus went to anoint his body, their experience at the empty tomb empowered them to keep the movement alive, and the Jesus movement continued to flourish in Galilee as a result. This is the new society toward which the plot moves, and which remains only partially realized at the end of the action. The ending which enables the formation of this new society, as we have seen, usually includes some twist in the plot, often involving the revelation of mistaken identity, and sometimes also including metamorphosis of

---

14. Using Lk. 7.35 (Q): 'The very old saying, "Sophia is justified [or vindicated] by all her children" probably had its setting in Jesus' table community with tax collectors, prostitutes, and sinners' (Schüssler Fiorenza 1983: 132).

character. In the case of the Gospels, the twist in the plot is no doubt the resurrection, where it is Jesus' identity which is revealed. For Schüssler Fiorenza, as a result, the disciples particularly experience a change of character from weak, disbelieving, and mistaken followers to the powerful and committed core of the Early Church. This change is usually given a theological interpretation, but it can also be seen as a generic requirement. Because such a change is appropriate in comic structure, it is believable.

In the larger narrative context of history, conflict continues and is characterized by a social system which is both hierarchical and andro-centric, what Fiorenza calls 'kyriocentric'.[15] But within this context, the egalitarian vision of Jesus continues to function as an alternative which if realized would lead to the creation of a new social order of justice and peace. Thus the entire movement of the history she con-structs is directed toward a future comic resolution, within which the story of Jesus and his first community is a microcosm of her vision of the whole.

In this analysis of Schüssler Fiorenza's work, I have tried to read the implicit narrative of Jesus' life as she presents it as if it were a fictional plot patterned on the comic genre. Understanding the plot structure can reveal how the 'facts' of historical events can be given different meanings depending on the historian's understanding of 'what really happened', that is to say, the narrative context. For Schüssler Fiorenza, 'what really happened' is the creation of an inclu-sive community, a discipleship of equals, centred around the figure of Jesus of Nazareth in his self-understanding as a child and prophet of Sophia. The kingdom of God which was partially realized in Jesus' actions remains to be realized in our own communities, centred around the risen Jesus, and is the source of our hope for the future. Of the historical data which she might have used, what count as 'facts' are those data which can help her build this meaning. And the comic plot, which is the structure of inclusivity and the creation of new community where human persons can flourish, underlies and rein-forces this view. Despite her denial that she was writing a historical portrait, she produced one in the only form her theological position can support, a comic plot which enables a feminist ethical stance.

---

15. A neologism introduced in Schüssler Fiorenza 1992. Cf. Schüssler Fiorenza 1994: 14.

5. *John Dominic Crossan's Ironic Hero in a Comic Plot*

John Dominic Crossan, in *The Historical Jesus*, on the other hand, is at
great pains to distinguish both Jesus and the movement which existed
during his lifetime from the post-Easter Jesus of the Early Church.
And unlike Schüssler Fiorenza, he attempts to delineate the character
of the historical Jesus, although Jesus remains firmly embedded in the
context of his historical community. He develops an elaborate system
for 'sifting' the evidence, pushing historical-critical method to the limits
and, some would say, beyond; his work has been subjected to numerous
critiques in this respect.[16] My concern here is not to evaluate the results
of his method, but rather to analyze the structure of the plot which
emerges from his narrative. In literary terms, Crossan's portrait of
Jesus emphasizes the characterization of the hero more than Schüssler
Fiorenza's does, but like Schüssler Fiorenza, Crossan provides a narrative for understanding Jesus' actions and words, his community, and
his death; he also sketches the relationship between the historical Jesus
and the movement which continued and grew after his death. Interestingly, the characterization of Jesus is cast in a tragic ironic form,
while the form of ironic comedy structures the events of his life. This
distinction is most clear in the more consciously fictional character
sketch in the prologue.

In the 'Overture', Crossan's portrait begins with Jesus' baptism by
John and his acceptance of John's apocalyptic message, but after John's
execution by Herod Antipas, when 'there was no apocalyptic consummation', Jesus 'began to speak of God not as imminent apocalypse but
as present healing'. He traveled from village to village exorcising and
healing, sharing meals with those whom he healed, and speaking of the
kingdom of God as experienced in the healing and the sharing. And then
he sent them out as 'healed healers' to take the kingdom to others. This
practice included both 'ecstatic vision and social program', based on
'principles of religious and economic egalitarianism', and it challenged
both purity regulations, and patriarchal structures and values, putting
Jesus in conflict with those in power. Jesus was executed as a result.
While the order of events leading up to his death is unclear, at some
point Jesus confronted and 'symbolically destroyed' the brokerage

---

16. The most virulent is probably that of Wright 1993. Cf. Johnson 1995; and
Hays 1994, who provides a less caustic assessment.

function of the Temple. If, as the accounts in the Synoptic Gospels would have us believe, this action took place during the Passover feast, it would have been 'quite enough to entail crucifixion by religiopolitical agreement' (Crossan 1991: xii). [17] The death of Jesus is not the end of the story, however, because the people who 'had originally experienced divine power through his vision and his example still continued to do so after his death', and Jesus' followers began to talk about their experience in terms of resurrection. The community of disciples lived on after his death and continued his ministry of healing and shared meals, preaching the kingdom (1991: xiii).

While none of these details contradicts the account in the historical narrative that follows, the character of Jesus outlined in the 'Overture' creates quite a different impression. Jesus is central, and he seems to move from village to village, healing those who needed healing and exorcising those who were possessed. He appears to act alone, sharing his vision and program with the people in the villages of Galilee and then moving on. When he leaves a village, he apparently goes alone, although some in the village 'ponder the possibility of catching up with Jesus before he gets too far' (1991: xi). This is the only notice of the disciples following Jesus, until the crucifixion, when they flee; the community of disciples, those who formed the early Christian movement, does not loom large in this story. And Jesus appears after the resurrection, in a story within the story which provides a metaphoric explanation for the development of the new society (1991: iii).

The emphasis on Jesus as a certain kind of hero, clearly distinguished from his society, moves from comedy into the world of tragic irony. Frye characterizes the phases of irony that parallel comedy as satiric; true irony has affinities with tragedy. Jesus comes into a village, as Crossan imagines the scene, and peasant villagers listen to him, at first from curiosity, then, after he performs an exorcism, with 'cupidity, fear, and embarrassment' (1991: xi), signs that while Jesus speaks of the kingdom of God, most of his audience is unreceptive.

17. Although historians may know what Jesus said and did with some degree of certainty, the chronology of Jesus' life is historically impossible to determine. Marcus Borg points out that 'no mainline scholar thinks the sequence of pericopes in the gospels corresponds to sequence in the life of Jesus', with the exception of the baptism by John, which belongs near the beginning, and the death and Easter stories, which belong near the end (M.J. Borg, 'Week 4: Response', Jesus2000@info.harpercollins.com [27 February 1996]).

This is not irony that satirizes the hero, irony in a comic mode, but rather irony that brings his 'all too human' characteristics to the fore.[18] This phase of irony, according to Frye, 'looks at tragedy...from the moral and realistic perspective of the state of experience. It stresses the humanity of its heroes.' Thus Jesus is seen through the 'cold, hard eyes' of the villagers, looking something like a beggar, but without the cringe, whine, or shuffle (Crossan 1991: xi). Moreover, unlike tragedy, irony stresses the 'social and psychological explanations for catastrophe' (Frye 1968: 237). What Jesus was doing was 'unacceptable' to the authorities, and they arranged to dispose of him with 'offhand brutality, anonymity, and indifference' (Crossan 1991: xii). There is no sense here of time out of joint, no 'ineluctable dialectic' that characterizes a tragic fall (Frye 1968: 217). This ironic account leaves Jesus a 'nobody', not a tragic hero; his vision and his social program should have brought freedom to the peasants of rural Galilee, but even those who believed he could do exorcisms feared him instead of following him. Nonetheless, after his death, he returns, at least figuratively speaking. The emphasis in his character type shifts then from the defeated ironic hero to the tragic. In Frye's terms, this is a third phase tragic hero, and it corresponds to the quest theme of romance; the emphasis is on the successful completion of the hero's task. In this case, Frye points out, there is 'the paradox of victory within tragedy', and 'the tragedy ends in triumph' (1968: 220-21). Thus during his lifetime, Jesus is shown as an ironic hero, while after his death, he becomes a tragic hero whose power and vision continue; yet in either case, his character functions as the hero of a comic plot.

From the historical perspective, the story of Jesus begins with his baptism by John. Initially Jesus accepted John's apocalyptic expectations, but he changed his mind.[19] Jesus rejected John's vision and his asceticism, hence the importance of the table and 'open commensality'. The open table was not an act of benefaction, as it would have been had he invited only outcasts; rather he invited 'anyone', negating the social function of the table. Crossan's Jesus does not make appropriate distinctions, which gives offense (1991: 261-63). This egalitarian attitude challenged the social hierarchy. Jesus' kingdom of nobodies is the

18. Frye 1968: 237. This distinguishes tragic irony from tragedy, in which the heroic aspects of the character are developed.

19. Crossan 1991: 237. Cf. a clearer presentation of the argument in Crossan 1994: 47-48.

new, free, comic society created through Jesus' practice. In Schüssler Fiorenza's narrative, a twist in the plot at the end, in which Jesus' identity is revealed, allows the new comic society to form. In Crossan's story, there is no twist at the end; rather the new society begins to form from the time when Jesus breaks with John and begins his own ministry. As a result, the comic society is more firmly in place at the end and the loss of Jesus as hero is less dramatically troubling.

Jesus and his disciples apparently traveled from house to house in the villages of Galilee, healing the sick, talking about the kingdom of God, and sharing meals with those they helped. While Crossan believes that some of the exorcisms and the healings, particularly the leper and the lame paralytic, are stories based on historical events, he argues that they are metaphorical condensations of many experiences over time. He understands the successful healing activity of the early Jesus movement in light of medical anthropology's distinction between disease and illness (1991: 336-37). Crossan does not argue for an understanding of Jesus' healing as miraculous cures of disease. But knowing what Jesus was doing is a central problem for him. 'Was he curing disease through an intervention in the physical world, or was he healing the illness through an intervention in the social world?', he asks. 'I presume that Jesus, who did not and could not cure that disease [leprosy] or any other one, healed the poor man's illness by refusing to accept the disease's ritual uncleanness and social ostracization' (1994: 82). Miracles, for Crossan, are historical occurrences implying changes in the social, not the physical, world.

In Crossan's telling, the development of the plot focuses on the activities of Jesus and the community that formed around him. As people experienced healing, they were sent out two by two as 'healed healers'. Since both men and women participated in this ministry, this way provided safety for female followers, who were paired as 'sister-wives' with men, a practice that Crossan feels 'might have been not only the best but the only way' to enable the women to do missionary work (1991: 335). Like Schüssler Fiorenza, Crossan rejects the historicity of the Twelve, but imagines rather that some people traveled with Jesus, while some welcomed him in their homes, and others traveled without him. Like John the Baptist's network of apocalyptic expectation, Jesus formed a network of shared healing (1994: 108-109). Thus the community of disciples grew, with missionary activity a constant both for Jesus and for his followers. They traveled without money and sandals, not to show self-sufficiency like the Cynics; they carried no bag for bread, and thus were dependent on those whom they healed for food. 'They share a miracle and a kingdom, and they receive in return a table and a house', Crossan summarizes. 'Here, I think, is the heart of the original Jesus movement, a shared egalitarianism of spiritual and material resources' (1991: 341). Jesus himself refused to settle in any one place so that his lifestyle could be a radical statement of 'unbrokered egalitarianism'. The political message is clear, and Jesus ran into difficulties as a result. Those difficulties come to a climax in his trip to Jerusalem and the Temple incident.

Crossan chronologically places the Temple incident just before Jesus' execution, and he argues that the action and saying 'involving the Temple's symbolic destruction' are authentic (1991: 159); but he has 'no plural attestation *linking* the Temple's symbolic destruction and Jesus' execution' (1991: 360). So while Jesus no doubt did something in the Temple that actualized his teaching, healing and open commensality, it is not certain that either the action or the saying is historical. Jesus functions as an opponent to the social order represented by the Temple whether or not the word or event is deemed historical (1991: 355). From the point of view of plot, Jesus created a new society, a community, by performing miracles and sharing with others, and in this he was 'an authoritative healing and purifying alternative to the Temple' (1991: 322). In these acts, he is opposed both by the political authorities and by the religious establishment. Whatever the historical details, at this point the blocking characters begin to reassert control and the result is Jesus' execution. But like John, Jesus had formed a 'discrete but united community'; also like John, the diffusion of the network made it possible only to strike down Jesus himself. The empowered community continued its work (1994: 43-44).

Crossan's story of Jesus follows the same lines as does that of Schüssler Fiorenza, although he ends his historical account with the desertion of the disciples, who then knew nothing about the details of his death (1991: 375). Jesus died under the gaze of soldiers whose task it was to prevent families and friends from coming to rescue the victims. After his death, according to Crossan, the soldiers probably buried the body, because 'ordinary families were probably too afraid or too powerless to get close to a crucified body even after death' (1991: 392). Thus no one could have known where the body was, and

Crossan speculates that it was thrown into a shallow grave, where wild dogs tore it apart (1994: 124). Jesus disappears entirely from the historical narrative at this point, although the community of disciples, because of their continued experience of power, grew and multiplied. For Crossan, because the accounts of the passion and the resurrection were created in order to explain the experience of the community, Jesus' identity is revealed in his practice, not in his death and resurrection, and the followers continued to experience his power in their own practice. They are not in need of the transformation which an atonement view of the death of Jesus provides, because it is their experience which ties the historical Jesus to the post-Easter Jesus.

As we have seen, even in ironic comedy, a female presence is felt to be necessary for the formation of the new society. In the more romantic phase of comedy which underlies Schüssler Fiorenza's work, a male–female couple is provided with the introduction of Sophia. In Crossan's account, this aspect is merely hinted at in his discussion of the servant leadership of Jesus. Arguing that the actions described in the Last Supper 'may well stem' from Jesus' own practice of open commensality, Crossan comments that two of the verbs, 'took' and 'blessed', refer to 'the actions of the master'; while the last two, 'broke' and 'gave', are the actions of a servant. More importantly, since Jesus' followers would have experienced being served by women rather than by slaves, 'Jesus took on himself the role not only of servant but of female. Jesus himself serves the meal, serves, like any housewife...' Crossan continues with the idea, drawn from Carolyn Walker Bynum, that 'just as the female both serves food and becomes food, so Jesus would both have served food here below and would become food hereafter. But long before Jesus was host, he was hostess' (1991: 404). That is, of course, a literary rather than a historical conclusion; nonetheless, for Crossan, Jesus is himself feminized by the narrative, and contains within himself the male and female elements around which the new society may develop.

Like Schüssler Fiorenza's, this story ends as a story of community, although Crossan's narrative of historical explanation begins by centring on Jesus. Because Crossan is not attempting to reconstruct the Jesus movement along gender lines, as is Schüssler Fiorenza, he is free to place Jesus at the centre of his narrative, and his Jesus is a more fully developed character than hers is. And while the community is inclusive and egalitarian in both accounts, women play a lesser role in

Crossan's narrative. They are not allowed to discover the empty tomb, because for Crossan it does not exist. Nonetheless, in his version of the story, as well as in Fiorenza's, what is important is the development of the community; Jesus as a hero increasingly merges with his community, until historically he disappears, and it is the community of followers that is emphasized.

Frye describes six phases of comedy of which Crossan's treatment corresponds to the most ironic first phase in part, and in part to the 'quixotic' second phase, in which 'a society is constructed by or around a hero, but proves not sufficiently real or strong to impose itself' (1968: 180). The action traces the clash of the heroic vision and 'a superior reality'. Crossan's plot gives Jesus a social vision which conflicts with the religiopolitical realities of his day, and historically speaking, Jesus is defeated, although his community survives and eventually flourishes. In this sort of ironic comedy, 'the demonic world is never far away', and 'the fear of a hideous death hangs over the central character to the end' when a potential tragedy is usually averted. Frye calls this moment 'the point of ritual death' (1968: 179), and in the historical narrative of Crossan, the hero does indeed die. Comic propriety is maintained in the Gospel narratives which recount resurrection appearances, but as these are impossible to verify historically, Crossan ends his story with the death of Jesus. The continued empowerment of his disciples displaces the resurrection, which cannot be told historically, and it provides the point of comic resolution. In this way Crossan explains the expansion of the Early Church, the new society which must eventually triumph. When the stories of the first disciples came to be told, they were 'the metaphoric condensation of the first years of Christian thought and practice into one parabolic afternoon. Emmaus never happened. Emmaus always happens' (1991: iii). But because 'Emmaus always happens', Crossan opens his narrative up to a larger comic vision of history, one like Schüssler Fiorenza's in which a future social order of justice, equality, and freedom is the goal, and in which the dignity of all human persons is affirmed.

Thus like Schüssler Fiorenza, who constructs her story of Jesus as an ironic comedy in order to reconstruct an egalitarian community in which contemporary Christian feminists can root both their faith and their political activity, Crossan also draws a comic portrait. What is at stake for him is the definition of facts about Jesus; 'we have', he claims, 'historical fact when everyone else has myth', and he is fighting a pitched battle to decide which incidents count as fact, and what sort of story can be told with those facts. As Crossan colourfully put it in a videotaped debate, his Jesus is not 'a sort of a transcendental mythic beast that kind of sucks like a black hole all power and dignity out of human beings and leaves them prostrate on their knees before him. I think that is obscene.' The crucial question for us now, he believes, is the pattern of leadership which emerges: 'Is it leadership that dominates or leadership that empowers?', he asks.[20] Empowerment, not domination, will provide the comic resolution of history by creating here and now the new society which Jesus called the Kingdom of God.

6. *Conclusions and Implications*

In the ternary movement of comedy as Hayden White describes it, a situation of order is disrupted by conflict involving a new vision, which is then resolved in a new social order. Within the historical context of both Crossan's and Schüssler Fiorenza's lives of Jesus, the pre-existent social order is characterized politically in terms of the Roman Empire and theologically in terms of Torah and Temple. With Jesus came a new vision of society as the kingdom of God and the establishment of a movement that grew into a new social order, at least in embryonic form. Placed within the larger historical context that includes the present, the Early Church struggled to impose one version or another of its vision, creating a situation of conflict which still continues today. The future is expected to bring the cosmic comic resolution, when the kingdom of God envisioned by Jesus will be fully realized. The struggle is part of the process, and maintaining a comic framework allows an optimistic mood to prevail; in theological terms, there is hope for the realization of God's kingdom. Thus the conflicts which arise and the partial solutions are a part of a greater whole toward which the movement of history tends. Both Schüssler Fiorenza and Crossan prefigure history synecdochically, in White's terms: 'The *mythos* of synecdoche is the dream of comedy, the apprehension of a world in which all struggle, strife, and conflict are dissolved in the realization of perfect harmony, in the attainment of a condition in which all crime, vice, and folly are finally revealed as the *means* to the establishment of the social order which is finally achieved...' (1973: 190). For Schüssler Fiorenza and Crossan, this new order is within the capacity of humanity to

20. 'The Jesus Summit' (videotape).

attain. For neither is that order presently realized, and for both it is a
theological and ethical ideal. It is not surprising that they both, with
different aims and methods, plotted their historical narratives as
comedy and provided an optimistic view of the future toward which
in their judgment we must strive.

For centuries, the Christian myth in its romantic telling has expressed
the goals of human life and human society. Romance is the generic
form through which the ruling social or intellectual classes have projected their ideals (Frye 1968: 186), and around which a consensus has
formed, at least in western society until recently. To change the form
is to attack those ideals and to undermine the social power of the myth
itself. In the televised debate with Crossan and Borg, Burton Mack
comments that 'we need to do our own mythmaking'.[21] As the contemporary historian need not repeat the same form in telling the
story, by telling the story in another form, he or she takes on this role
of new mythmaker. To the extent that a consensus grows to accept the
new version as reflective of contemporary ideals, real social and political changes can come about as a result. It is important to note that
feminist writers, including Schüssler Fiorenza, and the Jesus Seminar
scholars, including Crossan, are committed to popularizing their work,
a tactic that enables both groups to reach a wide public audience.
Crossan's *Revolutionary Biography* of Jesus and Schüssler Fiorenza's
Jesus, for example, not only describe the past, but do it in a way that

---

21. Indeed, that is precisely what they are doing, in much the same way that
Crossan imagines the Passion narrative was created: by searching in Scripture for
texts thematically related to the Passion generally, and by organizing those scriptural
connections into a coherent and sequential story, with an underlying generic framework. Details were added later in the interests of verisimilitude (1991: 375-76).
Contemporary historical-Jesus critics begin with an outline of events and sayings,
structured, I am arguing, by a generic intertext, search a wide variety of texts for
facts, analogies, and models, and then write a narrative history. Crossan sees his
own activity as analogous to that of the 'learned exegetes' of 'certain circles of the
Kingdom movement' of the 30s: you are 'very, very interested in studying the
scriptures to understand your past, reclaim your present, and envisage your future'
(1994: 146). And he understands this activity as one of the kinds of experience
through which the revelation of Jesus to his followers occurred in the earliest
Church, and presumably, today as well (1994: 169). In this regard, he writes himself
into his text: the peasants of the 'Overture' who looked at Jesus with 'cold, hard
eyes' (1991: xi) find their modern counterpoint in Crossan as critic, who looks with
the same 'cold, hard eyes' at the cruelty of human nature evidenced in the crucifixion
and in the events of the twentieth century as well (1994: 124).

may contribute to a profound social revolution in our own time.

BIBLIOGRAPHY

Borg, M.J.
1984   *Conflict, Holiness, and Politics in the Teachings of Jesus* (Studies in the Bible and Early Christianity; New York: Mellen).
1987   *Jesus: A New Vision* (San Francisco: HarperSanFrancisco).
1994   *Jesus in Contemporary Scholarship* (Valley Forge, PA: Trinity Press International).

Bynum, C.W.
1982   *Jesus as Mother: Studies in the Spirituality of the High Middle Ages* (Publications of the Center for Medieval and Renaissance Studies, UCLA, 16; Berkeley and Los Angeles: University of California Press).

Crossan, J.D.
1991   *The Historical Jesus: The Life of a Mediterranean Jewish Peasant* (San Francisco: Harper & Row).
1994   *Jesus: A Revolutionary Biography* (San Francisco: HarperSanFrancisco).

Downing, F.G.
1988   *Christ and the Cynics: Jesus and Other Radical Preachers in the First-Century Tradition* (JSOT Manuals, 4; Sheffield: Sheffield Academic Press).

Frye, N.
1968   *Anatomy of Criticism* (New York: Athaneum; orig. Princeton: Princeton University Press, 1957).

Hays, R.B.
1994   'The Corrected Jesus', *First Things* (May): 43-48.

Horsley, R.A.
1987   *Jesus and the Spiral of Violence: Popular Jewish Resistance in Roman Palestine* (San Francisco: Harper & Row).

Johnson, L.T.
1995   *The Real Jesus* (San Francisco: HarperSanFrancisco).

Mack, B.
1988   *A Myth of Innocence: Mark and Christian Origins* (Philadelphia: Fortress Press).
1995   *Who Wrote the New Testament? The Making of the Christian Myth* (San Francisco: HarperSanFrancisco).

Meier, J.P.
1991   *A Marginal Jew: Rethinking the Historical Jesus.* I. *The Roots of the Problem and the Person* (New York: Doubleday).
1994   *A Marginal Jew: Rethinking the Historical Jesus.* II. *Mentor, Message, Miracle* (New York: Doubleday).

Ricoeur, P.
1978   'Explanation and Understanding: On Some Remarkable Connections among the Theory of the Text, Theory of Action, and Theory of History', in C.E. Reagan and D. Stewart (eds.), *The Philosophy of Paul Ricoeur: An Anthology of his Work* (Boston: Beacon).

1980   'Narrative Time', *Critical Inquiry* 7.1: 169-90.
Sanders, E.P.
1985   *Jesus and Judaism* (Philadelphia: Fortress Press).
Schüssler Fiorenza, E.
1983   *In Memory of Her: A Feminist Theological Reconstruction of Christian Origins* (New York: Crossroad).
1992   *But She Said: Feminist Practices of Biblical Interpretation* (Boston: Beacon).
1994   *Jesus: Miriam's Child, Sophia's Prophet: Critical Issues in Feminist Christology* (New York: Continuum).
Schweitzer, A.
1957   *The Quest of the Historical Jesus: A Critical Study of its Progress from Reimarus to Wrede* (ed. W. Montgomery; New York: Macmillan [1910]).
Theissen, G.
1987   *The Shadow of the Galilean: The Quest of the Historical Jesus in Narrative Form* (Philadelphia: Fortress Press).
Tyrell, G.
1963   *Christianity at the Crossroads* (London: Longmans, Green, 1909; repr. G. Allen and Unwin).
Vermes, G.
1973   *Jesus the Jew: A Historian's Reading of the Gospels* (New York: Macmillan).
White, H.
1973   *Metahistory: The Historical Imagination in Nineteenth-Century Europe* (Baltimore: The Johns Hopkins University Press).
1987   'The Question of Narrative in Contemporary Historical Theory', in *The Content of the Form: Narrative Discourse and Historical Representation* (Baltimore: The Johns Hopkins University Press), pp. 26-57.
Witherington, B., III
1995   *The Jesus Quest: The Third Search for the Jew of Nazareth* (Downers Grove, IL: IVP).
Wright, N. T.
1992   *Christian Origins and the Question of God*. I. *The New Testament and the People of God* (Minneapolis: Fortress Press).
1993   'Taking the Text with her Pleasure: A Post-Post-Modernist Response to J. Dominic Crossan, *The Historical Jesus: The Life of a Mediterranean Jewish Peasant*', *Theol* 96: 455-61.

IMAGES OF CHRIST IN PAUL'S LETTERS

Stanley E. Porter

1. *Introduction*

Persistent misunderstanding continues to plague Pauline theology, especially in the area of what Paul thought about Jesus Christ. The use of the name Jesus Christ, however, is part of the problem itself, and provides one of the difficulties in coming to terms with this figure who looms so large in Paul's letters. So far as this paper and its relation to images of Christ is concerned, this misunderstanding falls into two major areas. The first is confusion regarding how Paul thought of the relationship of Jesus the man to the risen Christ, and of Jesus Christ to God. The second is how Paul formulated his thinking about Jesus Christ.

As we shall see, it is crucial that at least an attempt is made to keep these categories straight. For one, Paul is almost assuredly the earliest writer of any of the documents now in the New Testament (apart possibly from the letter of James), and hence he is the earliest inter-preter still accessible to us of the meaning and significance of Jesus Christ for a significant portion of early Christianity. Those involved in Gospels research might well wish to argue with me here, claiming that although the Gospels that we have are later than Paul (though Mark perhaps not much later than Paul's latest letters), there are sources used by the Gospels' writers, such as Q, that are at least as early as Paul's writings.[1] Here is not the place to discuss the nature of Q, its existence or the form or forms that it took, except to say that Q itself (if it was a document) is of course not found in the Gospels, only those portions of Q that the Gospel writers Matthew and Luke have

---

1. Even those of the Jesus Seminar in their optimism date the first edition of Q only to 50 CE. See R.J. Miller (ed.), *The Complete Gospels* (Sonoma, CA: Polebridge Press, 1992), p. 6.

chosen to use. Therefore, we do not necessarily have a complete or even coherent source. When that source is extrapolated from the Gospels what we find is essentially a sayings source purporting to record the words of Jesus, and only a few events. Therefore, Paul is still crucial to the discussion, since he is probably the earliest interpreter to whom we have direct access. Not only that, but he has arguably been the most important interpreter of Jesus Christ not only in the first century but throughout the history and development of Christianity. Even if one does not accept the statement by Wilhelm Wrede that Paul was 'the second founder of Christianity',[2] there are many who would argue that Paul was the Church's first and greatest theologian. Wrede meant, however, that although the life and teachings of Jesus may have been known to a small group of Palestinians near the midway point of the first century, it took someone like Paul—the preacher, church planter and missionary to the Gentiles—to establish the Church physically and intellectually within the context of the larger Graeco-Roman world, where it could take root and in fact thrive. Regardless of one's scenario for the emergence of early Christianity, whether it persisted as a part of Judaism until late in the century or whether it established its existence distinct from Judaism fairly early as Acts seems to indicate,[3] or whether from the beginning there was conflict between the Paulinists and the Petrines over the issue of law,[4] the fact of the matter is that Christianity essentially survived as Pauline Christianity, at least in the vast majority of places and certainly in the West. Pauline Christianity forms the heritage of western Christianity to this day, and therefore it is all the more important to understand as fully as possible Paul's conception of Jesus Christ. Or perhaps it is better to speak of conceptions of Jesus Christ.

In this study, I am not going to take the approach that attempts to establish and define statements about Jesus or Christ on the basis of the

2.   W. Wrede, *Paul* (London: Green, 1907), p. 179, cited in D. Wenham, *Paul: Follower of Jesus or Founder of Christianity?* (Grand Rapids: Eerdmans, 1995), pp. 2-3.

3.   See, for example, J.D.G. Dunn, *The Partings of the Ways: Between Christianity and Judaism and their Significance for the Character of Christianity* (London: SCM Press, 1991); A.E. Judge, 'Judaism and the Rise of Christianity: A Roman Perspective', *TynBul* 45.2 (1994), pp. 355-68.

4.   The Baur hypothesis, recently revived by M. Goulder, *A Tale of Two Missions* (London: SCM Press, 1994).

use of particular appellations or titles alone, although these will enter into the discussion from the beginning. I am instead going to distinguish by functional language, starting with the broad distinction between Jesus the man and the risen Christ. It is distinctions that Paul does and does not make regarding the earthly Jesus and the risen Christ that lead me to explore a number of Pauline conceptions of Christ. In anticipation of my conclusions, I think it is fair to say that my findings indicate a far more complex set of pictures than one might expect to find, but a series of pictures that point to a conclusion that has not always been fashionable in recent discussions of Paul.

2. *Jesus Christ as Man, Lord and God*

a. *Jesus the Man*

If the title of this conference had been 'Images of Jesus' this paper may well have had a completely different cast to it—at the least, it should have been significantly shorter according to the consensus of modern Pauline scholarship. It is almost a commonplace in Pauline studies today to state that Paul says very little about what the earthly Jesus did[5] and seems to know almost nothing of what he said.[6] It has been repeatedly pointed out that in Paul's account there are no references to Jesus' virginal conception, baptism, miracles, parables, disputes with the Pharisees, Transfiguration, cleansing of the Temple, setting of his ministry, or even the ministries themselves in Galilee or Jerusalem.[7] Whereas it has in the past been thought by some that Paul may have even seen Jesus in Jerusalem when he was on trial and crucified,[8] this is dismissed by most recent scholars.

5.   It must be pointed out, however, that even what is supposedly known has been subjected to critical analysis. See, for example, D. Seeley, *The Noble Death: Graeco-Roman Martyrology and Paul's Concept of Salvation* (JSNTSup, 28; Sheffield: JSOT Press, 1990).

6.   The best recent survey of a number of the issues is in A.J.M. Wedderburn (ed.), *Paul and Jesus: Collected Essays* (JSNTSup, 37; Sheffield: JSOT Press, 1989), especially V.P. Furnish, 'The Jesus–Paul Debate: From Baur to Bultmann', pp. 17-50, for a survey of the issues.

7.   J.M.G. Barclay, 'Jesus and Paul', in G.F. Hawthorne, R.P. Martin and D.G. Reid (eds.), *Dictionary of Paul and his Letters* (Leicester: InterVarsity Press, 1993), p. 498.

8.   See, for example, C.A. Anderson Scott, *Christianity according to St Paul* (Cambridge: Cambridge University Press, 1939), pp. 11-12; strongly opposed by

The concern today usually is not to find evidence for Paul's knowledge of the earthly Jesus but to explain the lack of references in his letters. Consequently, there have been many different explanations for Paul's apparent lack of interest. One of the most understandable perhaps is that he did not know any more about the life of the earthly Jesus, and hence could not have said more. Another is that although he may have known more, the death and resurrection—to which he refers on numerous occasions, even using them as examples of Jesus' meekness (2 Cor. 10.1), love (Gal. 2.20), obedience (Rom. 5.19), and poverty (2 Cor. 8.9)—were so overwhelming and all-consuming that the other events faded by comparison. A third explanation is that Paul was uninterested in these events because they were irrelevant for his proclamation of the gospel of the resurrection. A further explanation is that Paul may not have thought that the stories of the itinerant ministry of a Palestinian preacher were as relevant to his Hellenistic audience as the message of the significance of his death and resurrection. Or it may have been that some from the Jerusalem church were using these stories of Jesus as tools to oppose Paul in some way, so he avoided using them as much as possible. And a final suggestion is that Paul assumes that his audience already knew all of the facts about Jesus' life that they needed to know, although where they may have got these if Paul evangelized them is an item of some uncertainty. In any case, scholars are undecided on the reasons for the apparent lack of display of knowledge that Paul had of the earthly life of Jesus.

What, however, is it that Paul does seem to know about Jesus the man? Before we can fully appreciate what he says of the Christ we should take a look at exactly what he says of Jesus. What Paul appears to know about Jesus is that he was born as a human (Rom. 9.5) to a woman and under the law, that is, as a Jew (Gal. 4.4), that he was descended from David's line (Rom. 1.3; 15.12) though he was not like Adam (Rom. 5.15), that he had brothers, including one named James (1 Cor. 9.5; Gal. 1.19), that he had a meal on the night he was betrayed (1 Cor. 11.23-25), that he was crucified and died on a cross (Phil. 2.8; 1 Cor. 1.23; 8.11; 15.3; Rom. 4.25; 5.6, 8; 1 Thess. 2.15; 4.14, etc.), was buried (1 Cor. 15.4), and was raised three days later (1 Cor. 15.4;

C. Wolff, 'True Apostolic Knowledge of Christ: Exegetical Reflections on 2 Corinthians 5.14ff.', in Wedderburn (ed.), *Paul and Jesus*, pp. 81-98, although when he discusses grammatical issues he is at his least convincing.

Rom. 4.25; 8.34; 1 Thess. 4.14, etc.), and that afterwards he was seen by Peter, the disciples and others (1 Cor. 15.5-7). There have been efforts to draw out similarities in attitudes and events between the lives of Jesus and Paul as pointing to Paul's in some way knowing more of the life of Jesus,[9] but these efforts are highly circumstantial and speculative. It is better to confine ourselves to the above list, or one similar to it.

Confining our discussion to what is explicitly stated, even in what I have listed I have gone well beyond what most scholars would admit as events in the life of Jesus the man, because I have included reference to Jesus as the last Adam and to his resurrection and appearances. I have done so not because I have tried to conflate the two categories, but because Paul does.[10] The point is that Paul does not apparently know—or at least does not attempt to exploit—a difference between the earthly Jesus and the risen Christ. For example, in what is agreed to be one of the most important passages with regard to Paul's knowledge of the earthly Jesus, 1 Cor. 15.3-7, Paul begins with the important words that he is passing on what he first received. Most scholars think that Paul is referring here to tradition that he had received from other Christians, perhaps those who had known or seen the earthly Jesus.[11] He then states that 'Christ died for our sins according to the Scriptures, that he was buried, that he was raised on the third day according to the Scriptures, and that he appeared to Peter', etc. (1 Cor. 15.3-5). The images are clear: death, burial, resurrection and appearances. A similar pattern is found at Rom. 8.34, where Paul says that Christ Jesus died, was raised to life and is at the right hand of God interceding for us. Notice that Paul in these passages does not refer here merely to Jesus but to Christ or Christ Jesus and that he moves from earthly events such as death and burial to such things as resurrection, appearance and heavenly installation all in one chronological (and to him at least, logical) narrative motion.

9. See A.J.M. Wedderburn, 'Paul and Jesus: The Problem of Continuity', pp. 99-116 and 'Paul and Jesus: Similarity and Continuity', pp. 117-44, in Wedderburn (ed.), *Paul and Jesus*.

10. See M. Thompson, *Clothed with Christ: The Example and Teaching of Jesus in Romans 12.1–15.13* (JSNTSup, 59; Sheffield: JSOT Press, 1989), p. 26.

11. See G. Fee, *The First Epistle to the Corinthians* (NICNT; Grand Rapids: Eerdmans, 1987), pp. 718-19.

Other examples help to illustrate this more fully. In Rom. 4.24-25, Paul refers to Jesus our Lord as the one who was raised, having been delivered over to death for our sins and raised to life for our justification.[12] This is not untypical of Paul. In more than a few instances, events that are clearly ascribable to the earthly life of Jesus are described using such appellations as Christ Jesus or Jesus Christ, besides the simple use of Jesus. For example, Rom. 3.24-25 speaks of the redemption that came by Christ Jesus as a sacrifice involving blood, a clear reference to his death on the cross. Romans 6.3 speaks of Christians being baptized into Christ Jesus' death, with the baptismal motion of descent mirroring his descent. Romans 5.6-8 says twice that while humanity was sinful or powerless, Christ died for the ungodly. Romans 9.5 refers to the earthly ancestry of Christ. Romans 14.9 says Christ died and returned to life, and 14.15 speaks of concern for the brother for whom Christ died. In 1 Cor. 1.17, 23, as well as 8.11, Paul says that he preaches Christ crucified, what he labels a stumbling block to Jews and foolishness to Gentiles. Galatians 6.12 and 14 and Phil. 3.18 refer to the cross not of Jesus but of Christ. And Eph. 1.13-16 (which I take as authentically Pauline) speaks of the blood of Christ, his abolishing the law in his flesh, and the cross. Whereas in this large list of passages Paul uses Christ language to speak of what might be characterized as Jesus' earthly events, the reverse is also true—Paul refers to the events and activities of the resurrected and exalted figure by use of the name Jesus. For example, 1 Thess. 1.10 speaks of waiting for God's son from heaven, whom he raised from the dead, Jesus, and 4.14 says that Jesus died and rose again and that Paul believes that God will bring with Jesus, referring to his parousia or return, those who have fallen asleep. Thus in Paul it appears that images of Christ and images of Jesus are not as easily distinguishable as some would want them to be. To put it in more theological terms, for Paul Jesus clearly is the Christ.[13]

12. The use of the prepositions in this verse is recognizably difficult. See S.E. Porter, *Idioms of the Greek New Testament* (Biblical Languages: Greek, 2; Sheffield: JSOT Press, 2nd edn, 1994), pp. 150-51.

13. See M. Hengel, 'Erwägungen zum Sprachgebrauch von Χριστός bei Paulus und in der "vorpaulinischen" Überlieferung', in M.D. Hooker and S.G. Wilson (eds.), *Paul and Paulinism: Essays in Honour of C.K. Barrett* (London: SPCK, 1982), pp. 135-58.

b. *Jesus as Lord*

A similar pattern can be noted in reference to the supposed words of Jesus that Paul cites. Paul probably quotes words of Jesus at 1 Cor. 7.10 and 9.14, possibly at 1 Cor. 11.23-25, and may allude to his words at a few other places.[14] In all three passages where explicit quotation is made, Paul refers not to words of Jesus but to words or commands of *the Lord*. Whereas in the Gospels the term 'Lord' is ambiguous, sometimes being used simply as a form of respectful address and sometimes with more theological weight, in Paul the term is consistently used as a title, often in the form 'Lord Jesus Christ' or a variant of it.[15] Since the Septuagint's translation of Yahweh is almost exclusively 'Lord', and Paul cites a number of Old Testament passages with 'Lord', it is not surprising that Paul interprets several Old Testament passages as referring to God, even where the Old Testament text does not have the word God (e.g. Rom. 4.8 [Ps. 32.1-2]; 9.28-29 [Isa. 28.22; 1.9]; 10.16 [Isa. 53.1]; 11.3 [1 Kgs 19.1]; 11.34 [Isa. 40.13]; 12.19 [Deut. 32.35]; 15.11 [Ps. 117.1]; 1 Cor. 3.20 [Ps. 94.11]; 14.21 [Isa. 28.11]; 2 Cor. 6.17-18 [Isa. 52.11; 2 Sam. 7.14]). What is perhaps even more noteworthy, however, is that there are a number of passages where Paul appears to apply Old Testament passages referring to the Lord to the figure of Jesus Christ. Although the first two may not be as clear as the others, they probably reflect this pattern. In Rom. 14.11, in citing Isa. 45.23, Paul has just stated (v. 9) that Christ died and returned to life so that he might be the Lord of both the dead and the living, and then cites the Old Testament passage: '"As surely as I live", says the Lord, "every knee will bow before me; every tongue will confess to God"'. (When Phil. 2.6-11 is considered below, a passage that many scholars think reflects Isaiah 45, the evidence for the equation of Lord and Christ seems convincing.) In 1 Cor. 2.16 Paul also cites Isa. 45.23, 'For who has known the mind of the Lord that he may instruct him?', and follows this by saying that 'we have the mind of Christ'. Although these passages may be somewhat ambiguous, there are also several Old Testament passages where Paul clearly applies the use of 'Lord' to Christ. For example, in Rom. 10.13, after stating in v. 9 that, if one

14. See Wenham, *Paul*, p. 4. Cf. S. Kim, 'Jesus, Sayings of', in G.F. Hawthorne *et al.* (eds.), *Dictionary of Paul and his Letters*, pp. 474-92, who tries to argue for more clear allusions to Jesus' words.

15. See L. Hurtado, 'Lord', in Hawthorne *et al.* (eds.), *Dictionary of Paul and his Letters*, pp. 560-61.

confesses that 'Jesus is Lord' and believes that God raised him from the dead, one will be saved, Paul cites Joel 2.32, which states, 'Everyone who calls on the name of the Lord will be saved' (cf. also 1 Cor. 1.2).[16] In 1 Cor. 1.31, after speaking of being in Christ Jesus, Paul cites Jer. 9.24, 'Let him who boasts boast in the Lord'. The same quotation is used similarly in 2 Cor. 10.17. In 1 Cor. 10.26 Paul cites Ps. 24.1 of Christ, 'The earth is the Lord's, and everything in it'. And in 2 Tim. 2.19, the author[17] cites Num. 16.5 and a quotation that may be a paraphrase of one or more Old Testament passages (e.g. Num. 16.26; Isa. 26.13; 52.11; Ps. 6.8), stating that 'The Lord knows those who are his', and 'Everyone who confesses the name of the Lord must turn away from wickedness'.[18] In a number of places Paul also probably applies to Christ allusions to Old Testament passages using 'Lord' with reference to God (1 Cor. 10.21 [Mal. 1.7, 12]; 10.22 [Deut. 32.21]; 2 Cor. 3.16 [Exod. 34.34]; 1 Thess. 3.13 [Zech. 14.5]; 4.6 [Ps. 94.2]; 2 Thess. 1.7-8 [Isa. 66.15]; 1.9 [Isa. 2.10, 19, 21]; 1.12 [Isa. 66.5]).[19] Although it is much too strong to say that Paul conflates Christ with God so that he simply equates the two in an uncritical way, it is certainly true that for Paul there is a sense of close relationship, if not in essence or ontology at least in function.[20] It probably represents what Kreitzer calls 'conceptual overlap between Christ and God'.[21] In that sense

16. See C.J. Davis, *The Name and Way of the Lord: Old Testament Themes, New Testament Christology* (JSNTSup, 129; Sheffield: Sheffield Academic Press, 1996), pp. 103-40.

17. I believe that the author is Paul. For a discussion of issues related to this, see S.E. Porter, 'Pauline Authorship and the Pastoral Epistles: Implications for Canon', *BBR* 5 (1995), pp. 105-23.

18. For discussion of the above passages in detail, see D.B. Capes, *Old Testament Yahweh Texts in Paul's Christology* (WUNT, 2.47; Tübingen: Mohr–Siebeck, 1992), esp. pp. 115-49.

19. See Hurtado, 'Lord', in Hawthorne *et al.* (eds.), *Dictionary of Paul and his Letters*, p. 563, for discussion of most of the above passages, and a response, p. 564, to Capes. He rightly points out that Capes overextends the conclusions to be drawn. Capes's case may well have been helped, however, by recent publications from Cave 4 at Qumran, where there appear to be places where human and divine figures are interchanged. See, for example, 4Q521, and discussion in C.A. Evans, *Jesus and his Contemporaries: Comparative Studies* (AGJU, 25; Leiden: Brill, 1995), pp. 127-29.

20. See L. Hurtado, *One God, One Lord: Early Christian Devotion and Ancient Jewish Monotheism* (London: SCM Press, 1988), esp. pp. 93-124.

21. L.J. Kreitzer, *Jesus and God in Paul's Eschatology* (JSNTSup, 19; Sheffield: JSOT Press, 1987), p. 116.

images of Christ are for Paul also in some ways images of God.

This same pattern is found in another kind of imagery as well. One of the commonplace images of Jewish apocalyptic is the intervention of God in history. It has been increasingly well recognized in Pauline studies that Paul was an apocalyptic thinker,[22] and he looked forward to the wrath of God (Rom. 1.18; 2.5; 3.5; 5.9; 1 Thess. 1.10; Col. 3.6; Eph. 5.6) and his retributive judgment upon sin in the last day, that is, the Day of the Lord.[23] Paul shares the eschatological framework of the Old Testament, except that there is what Kreitzer calls a 'referential shift'[24] from Lord referring to God to its referring to Christ in a number of apocalyptic judgment passages. Besides Rom. 10.13 (see above) and Phil. 2.10-11 (see below), worth noting are Rom. 9.33 and 11.26, 1 Thess. 3.13, 4.15-18 and 5.8, and 2 Thess. 1.6-12, all of which utilize Old Testament passages but in terms of the return of Christ (see above). For example, in 2 Thess. 1.6-12, utilizing Isa. 66.4-6 and 15, Paul speaks of the Lord Jesus being revealed from heaven in blazing fire and with his powerful angels, punishing those who do not know God and obey the gospel with everlasting destruction.[25] As Kreitzer says, 'It appears clear that for Paul, the fact that Christology and eschatology are so closely linked is what determines his use of "Day of the Lord" texts from the Old Testament as a means of expressing his understanding of the Christian faith. For Paul, the Day of the Lord Yahweh has become the Day of the Lord Jesus Christ.'[26]

Whereas the imagery of the day of the Lord is redolent of the Old Testament, Paul also uses language of the Graeco-Roman world to convey his image of Christ. In Rom. 1.1, Paul refers to the 'good news' of God, which he defines in 1.2-4 as promised beforehand through his prophets regarding his son, who as to human descent was from David and who through spiritual descent was declared son of God by the resurrection from the dead, Jesus Christ our Lord. Not only does this language contain reference to the earthly Jesus' descent (1.3) but it

---

22. For a survey of recent work, see M. de Boer, *The Defeat of Death: Apocalyptic Eschatology in 1 Corinthians 15 and Romans 5* (JSNTSup, 22; Sheffield: JSOT Press, 1988), pp. 21-37.

23. See L. Morris, *The Apostolic Preaching of the Cross* (Grand Rapids: Eerdmans, 3rd edn, 1965), pp. 179-84, for a survey of the issues.

24. Kreitzer, *Jesus and God in Paul's Eschatology*, p. 113.

25. See Kreitzer, *Jesus and God in Paul's Eschatology*, pp. 113-28.

26. Kreitzer, *Jesus and God in Paul's Eschatology*, p. 129.

juxtaposes earthly and spiritual existence for 'Jesus Christ *our* Lord',
a personalized form of the full Pauline name of this figure. All of this
is to define what he calls the 'good news of God', which is here good
news from God concerning his son. This language resonates with two
other kinds of language in Paul regarding Jesus Christ. The first is
'son of God' language.[27] Though not frequent in Paul (there are four
explicit references [Rom. 1.4; 2 Cor. 1.19; Gal. 2.20; Eph. 4.13] and
several less specific references [Rom. 1.9; 5.10; 8.3, 29, 32; 1 Cor. 1.9;
15.28; Gal. 1.1; 4.4, 6; Col. 1.13; 1 Thess. 1.10]), it is significant terminology with regard to the close association established at least in
Paul's mind between Jesus Christ and God, so much so that Jesus Christ
can be called God's son.[28] In Rom. 1.2, the 'good news' of God (cf.
Rom. 15.16; 2 Cor. 11.7; 1 Thess. 2.2, 8, 9) is defined in terms of who
Jesus Christ is, which is specified in 1.9 as 'the good news of his son'.
This phrasing is used elsewhere in Paul as well (Rom. 15.19; 1 Cor.
9.12; 2 Cor. 2.12; 9.13; 10.14; Gal. 1.7; Phil. 1.27; 1 Thess. 3.2; 2
Thess. 1.8). Although the tendency is to dispute the Hellenistic and
endorse the Palestinian origins of the various Pauline christological
understandings (including Lord and son of God), to the contrary Paul
appears to be exploiting Hellenistic emperor cult language in this
terminology, especially at Rom. 1.2-4, where he brings together 'good
news' and 'son of God' language in terms of the events surrounding
the inception of a single figure.[29] Just as the Priene inscription (9 BCE)
proclaims the 'good news' of the birthday of the god (referring to
Augustus),[30] Paul appears here to be proclaiming the good news of
God—not the birth of the emperor but the birth of God's son, Jesus
Christ our Lord (cf. Rom. 10.9, where the significant confession is

27. See M. Hengel, *Son of God* (London: SCM Press, 1976), pp. 7-15.

28. That this language is also to be found in the surrounding Jewish world, see
C.A. Evans, 'The Historical Jesus and the Deified Christ: How Did the One Lead to
the Other?', in S.E. Porter (ed.), *The Nature of Religious Language: A Colloquium*
(RILP, 1; Sheffield: Sheffield Academic Press, 1995), pp. 47-67.

29. See O. Cullmann, *The Christology of the New Testament* (London: SCM
Press, 2nd edn, 1963), pp. 195-99.

30. For this and other inscriptions related to it, see L.R. Taylor, *The Divinity of
the Roman Emperor* (Middletown, CT: American Philological Association, 1931;
repr. Atlanta: Scholars Press, n.d.), esp. pp. 267-83, with p. 273 for the Priene
inscription (OGIS 458). See also V. Ehrenberg and A.H.M. Jones, *Documents
Illustrating the Reigns of Augustus and Tiberius* (Oxford: Clarendon Press, 1955),
pp. 81-97.

that 'Jesus is Lord'). Although it is open for debate what Romans may have thought about the divine characteristics of their emperors, Paul seems to have exploited Graeco-Roman categories that were compatible with Old Testament language of enthronement (e.g. Ps. 2.7; 2 Sam. 7.14) but has gone beyond it.[31] For Paul, Jesus Christ as God's son, according to Rom. 1.3-4, and elsewhere especially in Romans, encompasses not only an earthly character but a divine filial relation as well.

c. *Jesus Christ as God*
When one investigates the various ways that Paul speaks of this divine relation, especially in terms of the salvific work of God in the world, however, one encounters another set of images of Christ. Although the death and resurrection of Jesus are seen to be crucial to Paul's thinking, they are also often seen to be the means or instruments by which God works in the world. In other words, the Pauline focus in a vast number of passages may well be christological, but a Christology that is subordinate to Theology, as some of the passages above have already indicated (e.g. 2 Thess. 1.6-12). For Paul, Christ's death and resurrection are the means by which God works in the world. As a pious Jew, and a member of the religious group called the Pharisees, Paul not surprisingly reflects the monotheistic reverence for Yahweh that one would expect (cf. Gal. 3.20; Rom. 3.29-30; 1 Tim. 2.5; and 1 Cor. 8.6, discussed below). Although recently it has been debated whether Paul simply adopted, or transformed and developed traditional Jewish monotheism, this perhaps being occasioned by Paul's seeing Christ as God's agent in the world,[32] the point is that he begins his thinking with this relationship.[33]

31. See Cullmann, *Christology*, pp. 199-203.
32. See, for example, Hurtado, *One God, One Lord*, pp. 99-123, who speaks of the Christian mutation, and Capes, *Old Testament Yahweh Texts*, pp. 167-74, who finds no alteration in Jewish monotheism, but who must resort to the concept of corporate personality to do so. See S.E. Porter, 'Problems in the Language of the Bible: Misunderstandings that Continue to Plague Biblical Interpretation', in Porter (ed.), *The Nature of Religious Language*, pp. 33-36. Contra M. Casey, 'Chronology and the Development of Pauline Christology', in Hooker and Wilson (eds.), *Paul and Paulinism*, pp. 124-34.
33. Davis raises the issue of the chronological development of early deification language of Christ, examining the fact that Paul seems to use this language when addressing his letters even to churches he had never visited (such as at Rome). Davis sees this language dating to the earliest days of Christianity (*Name and Way of the*

Although some have thought that not enough attention has been given to Paul's language of God in recent times, recent work has devoted considerable attention to Paul's theistic references. Not only has the theological thread in much of Paul's discourse come to be appreciated—for example in such passages as Romans 9–11, 2 Cor. 1.18–3.23 and 2 Cor. 2.14–4.6[34]—but a number of the best-known Pauline themes are seen to relate primarily to God, with Christ depicted as accomplishing God's purposes. For example, the proclamation of the kingdom is in terms of its being 'the kingdom of God' (Rom. 14.17; 1 Cor. 4.20; 6.9, 10; 15.24, 50; Gal. 5.21; Eph. 5.5; Col. 1.13; 4.11; 1 Thess. 2.2; 2 Thess. 1.5 with the verb at Rom. 5.14, 17, 21; 6.12; 1 Cor. 4.8; 15.25).[35] It has been argued that 1 Cor. 15.20-28 is a Pauline conception of the kingdom of Christ, since in v. 24 Paul speaks of Christ turning the kingdom over to God, having destroyed all other powers.[36] Nevertheless, although Christ is said to reign (v. 25), all of what he does is in terms of a God who first has put everything under Christ, obviously excluding himself (v. 27), since the son is himself subject to God (v. 28). Although this passage may have prepared the way for Col. 1.13 and Eph. 5.5, which refer to the kingdom of Christ, even in these passages this kingdom is also God's kingdom. Adoption terminology is for Paul adoption as 'sons of God' (Gal. 4.5; Rom. 8.15, 23; 9.4; Eph. 1.5),[37] a provocative image that may well imply an extension of Christ-imagery as in Rom. 1.2-4 to Christian believers. The concept of redemption, although it involves for Paul faith in Jesus Christ or is accomplished through his blood, is effected by God (Rom. 3.24-25; 8.23; 1 Cor. 1.30; Eph. 1.7, 14; 4.30; Col. 1.14). Although Christ Jesus is seen by Paul as a sacrifice of atonement by

Lord, pp. 134-36). I think that Davis is undoubtedly correct that much of this thought dates to the earliest days of Christianity, even if Paul may have been the first to formulate some (though certainly not all) of the language.

34. See N. Richardson, *Paul's Language about God* (JSNTSup, 99; Sheffield: Sheffield Academic Press, 1994), a book devoted to the topic and exposition of the passages noted above.

35. See Kreitzer, *Jesus and God in Paul's Eschatology*, pp. 132-34, although he goes on to discuss 1 Cor. 15.24-25.

36. See Kreitzer, *Jesus and God in Paul's Eschatology*, pp. 132-54. Cf. de Boer, *Defeat of Death*, pp. 114-18.

37. J.M. Scott, *Adoption as Sons of God: An Exegetical Investigation into the Background of ΥΙΟΘΕΣΙΑ in the Pauline Corpus* (WUNT, 2.48; Tübingen: Mohr–Siebeck, 1992).

blood, it is God who presents him as such in order to demonstrate his justice (Rom. 3.25).[38] Although accomplished through or by Jesus Christ, it is God who reconciles the world to himself in 2 Cor. 5.18 and 19, Rom. 5.10 and Col. 1.20. However, in Col. 1.22 and Eph. 2.16 it appears to be Christ who is the agent of reconciliation.[39] The passage in Colossians may evidence the conceptual complexity mentioned above, in this case one in which Christ's instrumentality becomes agency. The 'hymnic' Col. 1.15-20 describes Christ, though subordinate to God (v. 19), in terms of divine functions, such as preeminence (v. 15), creation (v. 16), and dominion (vv. 17-18).[40] The attribution of these divine functions to Christ makes it only a short step to Christ himself being seen as divine reconciler. Lastly, and perhaps most importantly, one of Paul's most significant concepts, justification or righteousness, that is, God's righteous character (Rom. 1.17; 3.5, 21, 22, 25, 26; 10.3; 2 Cor. 5.21; Phil. 3.9) demanding and effecting human righteousness (Rom. 4.3, 5, 6, 22; 5.17; 6.16),[41] is an act of God, though accomplished through Jesus Christ (Rom. 5.1). Although Jesus Christ's death may be instrumental, it is God who is effective.

It is nevertheless Christ who is the means by which God's work is accomplished. The phrase 'through Jesus Christ/Christ Jesus' is relatively frequent in the Pauline letters (e.g. Rom. 1.8; 2.16; 5.11, 17, 21; 7.25; 15.30; 1 Cor. 15.37; Eph. 1.5).[42] It is conceptually closely related to the very frequent phrase 'in Christ'. Although there have been various attempts to see a physical sense to this phrase, it is probably best seen in terms of a spherical use, in which Christians are said to be within the sphere of Christ's authority and power (Rom 6.11, 23; 8.1, 2,

---

38. See Morris, *Apostolic Preaching*, pp. 179-250.

39. See S.E. Porter, *Καταλλάσσω in Ancient Greek Literature, with Reference to the Pauline Writings* (Estudios de Filología Neotestamentaria, 5; Córdoba, Spain: Ediciones El Almendro, 1994), pp. 125-89, on the Pauline passages.

40. On so-called hymns in early Christianity, see S. Fowl, *The Story of Christ in the Ethics of Paul: An Analysis of the Function of the Hymnic Material in the Pauline Corpus* (JSNTSup, 36; Sheffield: JSOT Press, 1992), pp. 31-45.

41. See J. Ziesler, *The Meaning of Righteousness in Paul: A Linguistic and Theological Enquiry* (SNTSMS, 20; Cambridge: Cambridge University Press, 1972), esp. pp. 186-209; Morris, *Apostolic Preaching*, pp. 251-98; and M. Seifrid, *Justification by Faith: The Origin and Development of a Central Pauline Theme* (NovTSup, 68; Leiden: Brill, 1992), esp. pp. 182-257.

42. See D.R. de Lacey, 'Jesus as Mediator', *JSNT* 29 (1987), pp. 101-21, esp. pp. 101-102.

39; 9.1; 12.5; 15.17; 16.7, 9, 10; 1 Cor. 1.2, 4, 30; 3.1; 4.10, 15, 17; 15.18, 19; 2 Cor. 2.14, 17; 3.14; 5.17, 19; 12.2, 19; Gal. 2.4; 3.28; 5.6; Eph. 1.3, 10, 12, 20; 2.7, 13; 3.11, 21; 4.32; Phil. 1.1, 13, 26; 2.1, 5; 4.7, 19, 21; Col. 1.2, 4; 1 Thess. 1.1; 2.14; 4.16; 5.18; 2 Thess. 1.1; 3.12; Phlm. 8, 23).[43] Somewhat similar is language of accompaniment, where things are done 'with Christ', such as dying and rising with Christ or being raised with Christ (Rom. 6.8; 8.32; 2 Cor. 4.14; 13.4; Phil. 1.23; Col. 2.13, 20; 3.3, 4; 1 Thess. 4.14, 17; 5.10).

What has been said above perhaps makes more understandable three passages in Paul that would otherwise look more perplexing. The first is 1 Cor. 8.6, one of Paul's clear affirmations of monotheism.[44] But it is more than that. In this provocative passage, after stating that there are many gods and many lords, Paul juxtaposes parallel statements regarding God the Father and the Lord, Jesus Christ (perhaps reflecting Deut. 6.4, the shema: 'Hear, O Israel, the Lord our God is one Lord', with similar language to 1 Cor. 8.6 in the Septuagint). The passage has been called 'binitarian', since it seems to treat God and Christ in parallel ways. The passage is still subordinationist, however, in that proclamation of Christ is made in terms of God the Father (see below), and a distinction is maintained in how God and Jesus Christ function. By a careful use of prepositions, God is proclaimed here as the ultimate origin (ἐκ, out of, from) and goal (εἰς, towards) of all things, but Jesus Christ is seen as the one through whom the Father works to create (διά, through whom all things came) and to sustain existence (διά, through whom we live). Although this has many characteristics of a credal affirmation, and may well reflect a wisdom Christology (or a refutation of it), some consider it a unique and significant contribution by Paul to images of Christ.[45] As Fee says of Paul, 'In the same breath that he can assert that there is only one God, he equally asserts that the designation "Lord", which in the OT belongs to the one God, is the

---

43. See Porter, *Idioms of the Greek New Testament*, p. 159. Cf. K. Grayston, *Dying, We Live: A New Enquiry into the Death of Christ in the New Testament* (London: Darton, Longman and Todd, 1990), pp. 382-94; A.J.M. Wedderburn, 'Some Observations on Paul's Use of the Phrases "in Christ" and "with Christ"', *JSNT* 25 (1985), pp. 83-97.

44. See Fee, *First Corinthians*, pp. 373-76.

45. See D.R. de Lacey, '"One Lord" in Pauline Christology', in H.H. Rowley (ed.), *Christ the Lord: Studies in Christology Presented to Donald Guthrie* (Downers Grove, IL: InterVarsity Press, 1982), p. 202.

proper designation of the divine Son. One should note especially that Paul feels no tension between the affirmation of monotheism and the clear distinction between the two persons of Father and Jesus Christ.'[46]

A second Pauline instance is Rom. 9.5, also a highly controversial passage. The major bone of contention is whether this is a direct affirmation that Christ is God ('Christ, who is God over all') or not (e.g. 'Christ who is over all. God be blessed'). Unfortunately, much discussion has been plagued by far too many theological presupposi-tions influencing exegesis. One of the major reasons for not taking this passage as a clear affirmation by Paul of Christ as God is that such an explicit statement is said not to be found elsewhere in the undisputed Pauline writings (but cf. Titus 2.13, where Jesus Christ is called our great God and saviour). In the light of what has already been said regarding Paul's use of christological terminology, and its potential Graeco-Roman background, although such an explicit statement is not found elsewhere, there are certainly enough other statements where the divine function is attributed to Christ that such a statement as Rom. 9.5 is not as surprising as it may at first sound. As Harris has recently shown in the most exhaustive treatment of the verse, the matter is essentially one of how the verse is punctuated in the critical editions and translations (of course, there was little or no punctuation in the original texts), as well as how the grammar is understood. These are decided on a number of grounds, including the interpreta-tion of the word of blessing or praise, which is probably not a dox-ology proper, the interpretation of the articular participle ('the one who is') as attributive and modifying 'Christ', and the phrase 'above all things' being linked with the participle. In the light of usage else-where in the New Testament, and what we have observed above regarding Paul's christological understanding, it is most likely that Paul is stating that Christ not only traces his human ancestry from the patriarchs but is God over all as well.[47]

The kind of christological imagery and understanding that I am speaking of is perhaps best seen in Phil. 2.6-11, a passage that combines many of the images and ideas that we have been discussing. Although

46. Fee, *First Corinthians*, p. 375.

47. See M.J. Harris, *Jesus as God: The New Testament Use of Theos in Reference to Jesus* (Grand Rapids: Baker, 1992), pp. 143-72; J.A. Fitzmyer, *Romans* (AB, 33; New York: Doubleday, 1993), p. 549.

much exegesis of this passage has been bedeviled by form- and source-critical disputes over whether it was a pre-existent credal or hymnic passage, and whether its origins are in some proto-gnostic or other background,[48] recent work by Fowl has shown that these questions have diverted attention from the major issue.[49] The major issue is the movement of ideas, and the role that this played in Pauline thought (both his and his community's). The passage is full of provocative christological imagery and bears brief recounting.

The passage begins with Christ Jesus in an exalted position. It says that he was in the 'form' (μορφή) of God. This language has been highly debated. Whereas many recent scholars have wanted to equate μορφή and εἰκών ('image'), on the supposed basis of similar usage in the Septuagint, nowhere in the Septuagint are these terms seen as synonymous or interchangeable.[50] Never is μορφή used in the Septuagint to speak about humanity in the image of God. This severs the link between Phil. 2.6 and Gen. 1.26. Instead, on the basis of Hellenistic usage (e.g. *Corp. Herm.* 1.12, 14), μορφή seems to indicate the visible and perceptible appearance of something, in this case God. Rather than taking advantage of being in appearance God, in the second stage of the passage, Christ Jesus is said not to have retained this status[51] but to have changed positions, taking that of a servant. This change of status (what kenosis probably means in Paul) is conveyed by Paul using several provocative images. One is that of a servant, an image that Paul uses frequently to describe not only Christ's incarnation in the human realm but his and other Christians' relations to Christ (e.g. Rom. 14.18; 15.16; Gal. 2.27). Servant language provides a stark contrast to the language of exaltation and being in the appearance of God. But Paul goes further when he states that Christ Jesus was found as a man who humiliated himself and became obedient to the point of death on a cross. Crucifixion was designed not only to kill in an

48. For a summary of these kinds of issues, see R.P. Martin, *Carmen Christi: Philippians 2:5-11 in Recent Interpretation and in the Setting of Early Christian Worship* (SNTSMS, 4; Cambridge: Cambridge University Press, 1967; repr. Grand Rapids: Eerdmans, 1983).

49. See Fowl, *Story of Christ*, pp. 49-75. See also G.D. Fee, 'Philippians 2.5-11: Hymn or Exalted Pauline Prose?', *BBR* 2 (1992), pp. 29-46.

50. Fowl, *Story of Christ*, p. 51. See also D. Steenburg, 'The Case against the Synonymity of *Morphē* and *Eikōn*', *JSNT* 34 (1988), pp. 77-86.

51. There has been much confusion over this phrasing, but see R.W. Hoover, 'The Harpagmos Enigma: A Philological Solution', *HTR* 64 (1971), pp. 95-119.

exceptionally prolonged and painful way but to subject the one crucified to humiliation and indignity.[52] The fact that crucifixion was a common means of executing slaves is coordinate with the servant and humiliation language. As Fowl labels v. 8, it reflects 'ultimate humiliation'.[53] There have been a variety of opinions regarding Christ's obedience. Although the text does not say to whom he was obedient, it appears to be God (cf. Rom. 5.18). The third stage of the passage involves another reversal of fortune, this one growing directly out of humiliation and obedience (although the text does not say how). In language that probably reflects Isaiah 45 or 51–52,[54] Christ Jesus is said to be exalted by God to the highest position and given the name above every name. Although many scholars note that the name is not specified, it would appear, as Fowl says, that 'the highest name would be the name of God, and would correspond to the universal acclamation of Christ as Kurios in v. 11'.[55] At this name all creatures bow and proclaim that the Lord, that is God, is Jesus Christ.[56]

In recent discussion, it has been argued, for example by Dunn, that Phil. 2.6-11 reflects not a three-stage but a two-stage Adam Christology. In other words, the passage begins with an equation of Christ and Adam and it is the last Adam who is exalted.[57] Although the last Adam is clearly a Pauline image (cf. Rom. 5.12-21), the equation here is probably inaccurate. Dunn's argument depends on an equation of μορφή and εἰκών, shown by Fowl to be mistaken. Without this kind of linkage, the case collapses, especially since there is no substantive evidence for linking the idea of taking the form of a servant with Adam's condition after the fall. (Dunn's endorsement of

---

52. M. Hengel, *Crucifixion* (London: SCM Press, 1977), p. 24.

53. Fowl, *Story of Christ*, p. 61.

54. Cf. Fowl, *Story of Christ*, p. 17; Kreitzer, *Jesus and God in Paul's Eschatology*, p. 116.

55. Fowl, *Story of Christ*, p. 65.

56. Most take this as 'Jesus Christ is Lord', but word-order in Greek in verbless equative clauses tends to indicate that the first element is the subject and the second the predicate, in statements such as this with neither being articular. Contra Fowl, *Story of Christ*, p. 68.

57. See J.D.G. Dunn, *Christology in the Making: A New Testament Inquiry into the Origins of the Doctrine of the Incarnation* (Philadelphia: Westminster Press, 1980), pp. 113-21.

the idea that Jesus refused to grasp at unattained equality with God has also been shown to be mistaken.)

In summarizing this passage, we can see that several of the Pauline christological images are maintained. He uses the composite name, Christ Jesus, to describe both earthly and exalted status and events, with the figure moving between them. Although he is seen to be in the appearance of God, and equal with him in some way, Jesus Christ also is subordinate to him, being obedient to the point of death and consequently being exalted by him to a position of preeminence in the universe. Along the way other important christological images are also reiterated. As Fowl concludes of this and similar passages, these passages are hymns in the very general sense of poetic accounts of the nature and/or activity of a divine figure,[58] in this case Paul's Christ Jesus.

3. *Conclusion*

What appears clear from this evidence is that the distinction between Jesus the man and the risen Christ that some Pauline researchers are concerned to make is more a modern scholarly differentiation than a Pauline one. As valuable as it may be in modern theological discussion, it does not appear to be a valid Pauline category. One might be tempted in the light of this to think that Paul saw all events, even those of the earthly realm, as merely spiritual events, re-reading the resurrection and exaltation into the earthly events of death and burial. Even though some later interpreters of Paul have indeed thought this, the passages that I have cited, however, do not seem to indicate such a perspective. One might likewise be tempted to conclude that underlying the Pauline language of exaltation are a number of simple historical events, taken by Paul and re-interpreted in the light of his own spiritual experience into something other than they originally were. Even though here again many later interpreters of Paul have indeed thought this, the passages that we have cited, however, do not seem to indicate such a transformation. Instead they seem to begin with a very real recognition of the earthly events in the life of Jesus and proceed without hesitation to resurrection and exaltation in one unbroken line—both of them independently and together constitute Pauline images of Christ.

58. Fowl, *Story of Christ*, p. 45.

NURSING MOTHER, ANCIENT SHEPHERD, ATHLETIC COACH? SOME IMAGES OF CHRIST IN THE EARLY CHURCH

Isobel H. Combes

There can hardly be a better way to outrage a church or to get your words splashed across the tabloids than to suggest the use of a controversial image of the divine—speak of God as a female or Christ as a customer in a gay bar and you will undoubtedly bring wrath, if not notoriety down upon you. Suggest something inelegant or modern and laughter will probably be your reward. Outside the fairly limited scope of biblically approved metaphors, new descriptions of God or Christ seem, these days, to be controversial at best, derided at worst.

We like to appeal to tradition—the 'proper' ways of speaking about God and Christ—as if there were some sort of dictionary laid out already detailing what language is acceptable, to go on the bookshelf along with the New Testament and *Hymns Ancient and Modern* as the guide to how we are to see the interaction between Christ and the world.

But how valid is such an appeal to tradition, and was there ever a universally accepted criterion for religious language to guide Christian writers? The writings that make up the canon of the Old and New Testaments present certain images of Christ and, to a large extent, these are still in use today, having gained this official seal of approval. But as we look further into the literature that succeeded the New Testament, as the Church began to establish its foothold in the world, we can see that although these original images provide a foundation for what is subsequently written about Christ, they also act for many writers as a springboard, inspiring a rich and varied religious language, which although very occasionally grotesque or bizarre to modern ears, shows a lively imagination and willingness to take risks with traditional ideas. Anyone, for instance, who scoffs at the famous Seventies hymn *Dropkick me Christ, through the Goalposts of Life* should perhaps consider the first-century letter of Ignatius to the Ephesians:

> You are the stones of the temple... hoisted up on high by the crane of Jesus Christ, that is his cross, using the Holy Spirit as a rope, your faith is your windlass and love is the road that leads you up to God.[1]

Or his exhortation to his readers to

> Be salted with him [Christ] so that no one of you may be spoiled, for you will be convicted by the smell.[2]

In this paper I would like to discuss three images of Christ that can be found in the writings of the Patristic era—Christ as Mother, Christ as Shepherd, and Christ as an athlete's coach. These three different images sum up different aspects of Christ which were of importance in this era, namely Christ as nourisher and nourishment, Christ as leader and master, and Christ as supporter and friend.

The first of these images—that of Christ as a nursing mother—enjoyed a more widespread use than one might at first imagine. In its most direct form, it occurs in a small number of hymns, reflecting the intensity of the poets' emotional outpouring. The third-century Clement of Alexandria, in his *Hymn to Christ the Saviour* speaks of Christ as

> celestial milk poured out from the sweet breasts of a young bride... [Christ's] little children, with their tender mouths, are nourished by those incorporeal nipples.[3]

A similar theme is found in Ephrem's *Hymns on the Nativity*:

> Though the Most High, yet he sucked the milk of Mary, and of his goodness all creatures suck! He is the Breast of Life and the Breath of Life: the dead suck from his life and revive. [4]

In the *Odes of Solomon,* the whole of the Trinity is included:

> A cup of milk was offered me
> And I drank it in the sweetness of the Lord's kindness

---

1. *Ign. Eph.* 9 (*PG* 5.652). Trans. in J.B. Lightfoot and J.R. Harmer, *The Apostolic Fathers* (rev. M.W. Holmes; Grand Rapids: Eerdmans, 2nd edn, 1989), p. 89.

2. *Ign. Eph.* 10.2 (*PG* 5.672). Trans. in Lightfoot, *Apostolic Fathers*, p. 96.

3. Clement of Alexandria, *The Teacher* 3.12 (*PG* 8.684 A). Trans. in A. Hamman (ed.), *Early Christian Prayers* (trans. W. Mitchell; Chicago: University of Chicago Press, 1961), p. 39.

4. Ephrem, *Hymn on the Nativity* 3. Trans. in *A Select Library of Nicene and Post-Nicene Fathers of the Christian Church* (Oxford: Oxford University Press), VIII, p. 233.

The Son is the cup
And the Father is He who is milked
And the Holy Spirit is She who milked him;

Because his breasts were full
And it was undesirable that his milk should be ineffectually released.

The Holy Spirit opened Her bosom
And mixed the milk of the two breasts of the Father

Then She gave the mixture to the generation without their knowing.
And those who have received it are in the perfection of the right hand.[5]

What appears at first sight to have gnostic or even proto-feminist implications turns out to be of a more orthodox pedigree when considered within its theological and liturgical context. When we turn to the baptismal liturgies of the early centuries, we find included in the ceremony the offering of a cup of milk and honey to the newly baptized. This drink was taken to symbolize the entry of the believer into the promised land and also his or her status as a spiritual 'infant'.[6] Thus, the description of baptism found in *The Apostolic Tradition* of Hippolytus tells us that the newly baptized are given

> milk and honey mingled together in fulfilment of the promise which was made to the Fathers, wherein He said I will give you a land flowing with milk and honey; which Christ indeed gave, even His Flesh, whereby they who believe are nourished like little children, making the bitterness of the human heart sweet by the sweetness of His word.[7]

The idea of milk for those who are, in the spiritual sense, infants,[8]

---

5. *Odes* 19.1-5. Trans. in J.H. Charlesworth (ed.), *The Old Testament Pseudepigrapha* (London: Darton, Longman & Todd, 1985), II, p. 752.

6. Further on this, see J. Crehan, *Early Christian Baptism and the Creed: A Study in Anti-Nicene Theology* (London: Burns, Oates & Washbourne, 1950), pp. 171-75.

7. Hippolytus, *The Apostolic Tradition* 23.2. Trans. in E. Yarnold, *The Awe-Inspiring Rites of Initiation: Baptismal Homilies of the Fourth Century* (Slough: St Paul Publications, 1971), p. 269; Sources chrétiennes (SC), XI, pp. 53-54.

8. 'Bernard... has gathered impressive evidence that "the representation of the Word as Milk, and the interpretation of Milk as the Flesh of the Word were current in the second and third centuries"... In contrast to the patristic quotations presented by Bernard, however, the Odist's imagery is more subtle and lacks the sacramental dimension of the Fathers. There is no reason therefore, why the imagery could not have its roots in the first century: indeed there is evidence that in the Early Church "milk" and "word" had been linked conceptually. Paul wrote that he had fed the

dates back of course to the New Testament, where 1 Peter makes a similar point:

> Like the new-born infants you are, you must crave for pure milk (spiritual milk, I mean), so that you may thrive upon it to your souls' health. Surely you have tasted that the Lord is good (1 Pet. 2.2-3 [NEB]).

Paul in 1 Corinthians states: 'And so I gave you milk to drink, instead of solid food, for which you were not yet ready' (1 Cor. 3.2 [NEB]).

The use to which other writers put images of milk and breast makes evident the other scriptural antecedent for this language—the erotic imagery of the Song of Solomon. This opens with the words of a bride speaking to her bridegroom:

> Let him kiss me with the kisses of his mouth; for your breasts are sweeter than wine and the smell of your ointment is beyond all spices.[9]

Ambrose associates this passage with Christ, saying,

> 'Because your breasts are better than wine': that is, your thoughts, your sacraments are better than wine: which in spite of the sweetness, the happiness, the joy it gives, is still a worldly joy; but in you there is also a spiritual joy.[10]

Similarly in Gregory of Nyssa,

> ... Thy breasts are sweeter than wine and the odor of thy ointments above all ointments... in this comparison which shows how far superior is the milk we draw from the divine breast to the joy we derive from wine, we learn that all human wisdom or the exercise of the imagination cannot be compared with the simple nourishment we derive from divine revelation.[11]

Thirdly, looking back again at the words of Hippolytus, 'which Christ indeed gave, even His Flesh, whereby they who believe are

members of the Corinthian Church with milk... as if they were "babes in Christ"' (Charlesworth, *Old Testament Pseudepigrapha*, II, p. 44 n. 17).

9.   Song 1.2-3. While 'breasts' is used in the LXX, a number of English translations (such as the NEB and the NRSV) render this as 'love'.

10.   Ambrose, *Homilies on the Sacraments* 5.8. Trans. in Yarnold, *The Awe-Inspiring Rites of Initiation*, p. 145; SC, XXV, p. 124.

11.   Gregory of Nyssa, *Commentary on the Canticle* 1 (*PG* 44.781A-B). Trans. in H.A. Musurillo (ed.), *From Glory to Glory: Texts from Gregory of Nyssa's Mystical Writings* (New York and London: John Murray, 1992), p. 157.

nourished like little children', there is a clear link between the image of Christ as milk and nourisher and the Eucharist itself. Theodore of Mopsuestia thus says that Christ, in the Eucharist,

> ...with a love like that of a natural mother devised a way to feed us with his own body.[12]

Similarly, even Augustine speaks of his heart suckling on Christ's name, during his infancy,[13]

> for the Word was made flesh so that your Wisdom, by which you created all things, might be milk to suckle us in infancy.[14]

Here we see that this image is being used in a more complex way—the breast and milk not referring to the Eucharist as such, but to the Incarnation. As Ireneaus says,

> Thus, as if we were infants, the perfect Bread of the Father is given us in the form of milk—that is, his coming as man—so that, nourished, so to speak, by the breast of his flesh and made fit by that suckling to eat and drink the word of God, we are able to hold within ourselves the bread of immortality, which is the Spirit of the Father.[15]

The two uses of the image of Christ as milk—in baptism and in eucharist—are evoked in the account of the *Martyrdom of Perpetua*, a young North African martyr of the early third century. Perpetua, while she is under arrest, has several visions. The following occurs shortly after her baptism:

> Then I saw an immense garden, and in it a grey-haired man sat in shepherd's garb; tall he was, and milking sheep. And standing around him were many thousands of people clad in white garments. He raised his head, looked at me, and said: 'I am glad you have come, my child'.
>
> He called me over to him and gave me, as it were, a mouthful of the milk he was drawing; and I took it into my cupped hands and consumed

---

12. Theodore of Mopsuestia 5.25. Trans. in Yarnold. See also homily 4.6 (p. 124) and 5.23 (p. 214).

13. Augustine, *Confessions* 3.4 (*PL* 32.686). Trans. in R.S. Pine-Coffin, *Saint Augustine's Confessions* (London: Penguin, 1978), p. 59. See also 4.1 (p. 71).

14. Augustine, *Confessions* 7.18 (*PL* 32.745). Trans. in Pine-Coffin, *Confessions*, p. 152.

15. Irenaeus, *Against the Heresies* 38.1.23-29L (SC, C). Trans. in A. Roberts and J. Donaldson (eds.), *Anti-Nicene Christian Library* (Edinburgh: T. & T. Clark, 1869), p. 42.

> it. And all those who stood around said: 'Amen!' At the sound of this
> word I came to, with the taste of something sweet still in my mouth.[16]

The gift of the milk and the 'taste of something sweet', possibly honey
in the milk, is a clear reference to the cup of milk taken after baptism,
while her receiving of the milk in 'cupped hands' as the early
Christian manuals dictated that the eucharist should be received, and
the chorus of 'Amen' from those around her, surely gives this image
an added eucharistic significance.

The fact that the donor of this milk is an elderly shepherd leads us
conveniently into the second image that this paper set out to discuss—
the image of Christ as a shepherd.

The association between Christ and shepherd has proved enormously
popular in the Judaeo-Christian tradition and in the societies from
which it emerged. We find shepherd kings and gods in the Greek tradition, shepherd gods among the Mesopotamians,[17] while the Old
Testament, to give only one example, gives us one of the most
phenomenally enduring and popular images of God—'The Lord is my
shepherd, I shall not want' (Ps. 23.1).

It is hardly necessary to point out how important the image of the
good shepherd was in the New Testament, and it went on to become the
most common pictorial representation of Christ in early Christian art,
consistently chosen in preference to images of crucifixion or kingship.
The use of the image of shepherd for Christ was widespread throughout
the writings of the Early Church. Ephrem, for example, says,

> This is the flock bought with the blood
> of that Chief Shepherd.
> Call and review the sheep by name
> for this is the flock whose name is written
> And whose reckoning is in the Book of Life.[18]

Augustine consistently uses shepherd, along with king and master,

---

16. *Martyrdom of Saints Perpetua and Felicitas* 4. Trans. in Musurillo (ed.), *The
Acts of the Christian Martyrs* (Oxford: Clarendon Press, 1972), pp. 110-12.

17. 'Both En-lil and Tammuz… were addressed as shepherd, the hero Gilgamesh
is the shepherd of Uruk while Ur called itself the sheepfold of the gods' (R. Murray,
Symbols of Church and Kingdom: A Study in Early Syriac Tradition [London:
Cambridge University Press, 1975], p. 187).

18. *Nisibene Hymns* 20.3. Trans. in Murray, *Symbols of Church and Kingdom*,
p. 189.

when he addresses Christ, and he frequently refers to the community of the faithful as Christ's 'meek flock'.

We can find a more lively use of this image when we turn again to the liturgies of baptism. One vital part of the baptism liturgy was the imposition of a seal—the sign of the cross traced in holy oil—on the forehead of the baptized, a mark that was intended to identify its recipient forever as being under the ownership of Christ. This gives rise to many vivid descriptions on the part of the writers, one of which is the idea that the newly baptized is being branded in the same way as a sheep receives the mark of its owner.[19] Theodore of Mopsuestia reminds his audience that

> The seal that you receive at this point marks you out forever as the sheep of Christ, the soldier of the King of Heaven. As soon as a sheep is bought, it is given a mark to identify its owner; it feeds in the same pasture and lives in the same fold with the other sheep that bear the same owner's mark.[20]

Cyril of Jerusalem makes a similar point:

> Come for the mystical seal, that ye may be easily recognised by the Master; be ye numbered among the holy and spiritual flock of Christ, to be set apart on the right hand, and inherit the life prepared for you.[21]

Although it is common to examine the historical reality of shepherding in order to better understand the metaphor, I would argue that the popularity of the shepherd imagery lay not in its association with common or day to day experience—for then one would expect it to be less used among urbanized Christians—but that it was an expression of one very simple idea, that of authority. It is a clear picture of the relationship between benevolent authority and meek obedience, and as a result it becomes, if anything, more popular, as its original social roots recede. Where writers are concerned with instilling a hierarchical

19. 'Absolutely fundamental in the Syrian tradition of the *rushma* (anointing) is the idea that it provides a mark of ownership, and by far the most frequent image is that of the newly baptized being branded as a sheep' (S. Brock, *The Holy Spirit in Syrian Baptismal Tradition* [Bronx, NY: Syrian Churches, 1979], p. 96).

20. Theodore of Mopsuestia, *Baptismal Homily* 2.17 (trans. in Yarnold, *The Awe-Inspiring Rites of Initiation*, pp. 186-87) referring to the first anointing before baptism.

21. Cyril of Jerusalem, *Catechetical Lecture* 1.2 (SC, CXXVI). Trans. in *Select Library*, VII, p. 6. See also Clement of Alexandria, '... and the dumb animals show through a seal whose property each is, and from the seal they are claimed' (*Excerpta ex Theodoto* [SC, XX, p. 111] 4.86.1-3.

notion of theology and Church order, the shepherd motif comes easily to the fore, so that not only is Christ the shepherd of the flock, the leader and the protector, but he also has undershepherds, who care for the flock in his place and under his authority. Thus, the metaphor extends gracefully to include the virtues of the bishops, as we see, for example, in Chrysostom's words:

> What is this I see? The shepherd is not here and still his sheep show a well disciplined attitude. And this marks the pastoral success and virtue of the shepherd when, whether he is present or away, his flocks display complete earnestness and attention.[22]

To return to the *Martyrdom of Perpetua*—in the last of her visions she describes herself as participating in a wrestling match with Christ as the referee. Her extraordinary vision is worth quoting in full. In a vision, she is taken by one of the deacons to an amphitheatre,

> Then out came an Egyptian against me, of vicious appearance, together with his seconds, to fight with me. There also came up to me some handsome young men to be my seconds and assistants.
>
> My clothes were stripped off, and suddenly I was a man. My seconds began to rub me down with oil (as they are wont to do before a contest). Then I saw the Egyptian on the other side rolling in the dust. Next there came forth a man of marvellous stature, such that he rose above the amphitheatre. He was clad in a beltless purple tunic with two stripes (one on either side) running down the middle of his chest. He wore sandals that were wondrously made of gold and silver, and he carried a wand like an athletic trainer and a green branch on which there were golden apples.
>
> And he asked for silence and said: 'If this Egyptian defeats her he will slay her with the sword. But if she defeats him, she will receive this branch.' Then he withdrew.
>
> We drew close to one another and began to let our fists fly. My opponent tried to get hold of my feet, but I kept striking him in the face with the heels of my feet. Then I was raised up into the air and I began to pummel him without as it were touching the ground. Then when I noticed there was a lull, I put my two hands together linking the fingers of one hand with those of the other and thus I got hold of his head. He fell flat on his face and I stepped on his head.
>
> The crowd began to shout and my assistants started to sing psalms. Then I walked up to the trainer and took the branch. He kissed me and said to me: 'Peace be with you, my daughter!' I began to walk in triumph

22. Chrysostom, *On the Incomprehensible Nature of God* 1.1. Trans. in R.A. Krupp, *Shepherding the Flock of God: The Pastoral Theology of John Chrysostom* (New York: Peter Lang, 1991), p. 117; SC, XXVIII, p. 72.

towards the Gate of Life. Then I awoke. I realized that it was not with wild animals that I would fight but with the Devil, but I knew that I would win the victory.[23]

The athletic arena with its massive audiences, its judges and the competitors struggling to earn the crowns given out to the victors or, in the case of gladiators, fighting for their lives, provides a ready source of images of Christ and the believer. The idea of the believer as a competitor struggling to earn the prize given by Christ can be found as early as the New Testament where Paul presses 'towards the goal to win the prize' (Phil. 3.14) and urges Timothy to 'run the great race of faith' (1 Tim. 6.12).

The use of this metaphor in conjunction with martyrdom (as in the passage from the *Martyrdom of Perpetua*, above) is, perhaps surprisingly, rare. In his work on the Martyrdom of St Ignatius, Chrysostom uses the athletic metaphor in conjunction with martyrdom in the arena:

> ... in the case of the heathen contests, since the tasks are bodily, men alone are, with reason, admitted. But here, since the contest is wholly concerning the soul, the lists are open to each sex, for each kind, the theatre is arranged.[24]

It is, however, to the baptismal liturgies that we must look in order to find any real development of the idea of the spiritual life as a contest against the devil with Christ as supporter and judge.

Cyril of Jerusalem, in his lectures to those seeking baptism, describes the Christian as an athlete and urges him to 'run with reverence the race of godliness'.[25] He also assure them that, as wrestlers against the devil, God will give them the strength they need to attain victory.

Ambrose compares the anointing in baptism with the anointing of the athlete:

> You were rubbed with oil, like an athlete, Christ's athlete, as though in preparation for an earthly wrestling match, and you agreed to take on your opponent. The wrestler has something to hope for: every contest has its trophy. You wrestle in the world, but it is Christ's trophy you receive—

23. *Martyrdom of Saints Perpetua and Felicitas* 10. Trans. in Musurillo, *The Acts of the Christian Martyrs*, pp. 116-18.

24. Chrysostom, *Martyrdom of St Ignatius* 1 (*PG* 50.587). Trans. in *Select Library*, IX, p. 135.

25. Cyril of Jerusalem, *Catechetical Lectures* 2.13 (SC, CXXVI). Trans. in *Select Library*, VII, p. 6.

the prize for your struggles in the world. And even though the prize is awarded in heaven, the right to the prize is achieved here below.[26]

These images are even more well developed in Chrysostom's Catechetical lectures, where the catechumen is the wrestler in training[27] and Christ appears as a judge—a judge who so favours one side over the other that he takes on more the quality of a coach or supporter, hence

> In the Olympic combats, the judge stands impartially aloof from the contestants, favouring neither the one or the other... Christ does not stand aloof, but is entirely on our side.[28]

The prebaptismal anointing of the candidates with oil before they approached the water, a ritual part of baptism during this time, lent itself very well to an association with the athletic arena where contestants, too, were anointed before the contest. Chrysostom draws this parallel, associating it also with the metaphor of Christ as bridegroom:

> ...through the chrism the cross is stamped upon you. The chrism is a mixture of olive oil and unguent; the unguent is for the bride, the oil for the athlete.[29]

Finally, we can also find instances of Christ himself described as athlete. Having struggled himself, he is thus able to sympathize with the struggle of Christians, as may be seen in the words of Theodore of Mopsuestia:

> When our Lord was praying in fear of the approaching passion, St Luke tells us 'there appeared to him an angel from heaven, strengthening him'. Like spectators who shout to encourage athletes, the angel anointed him to help him bear his sufferings, encouraging him to endure, and reminding him that the passion was short in comparison with the benefits it would produce; for he would gain great glory immediately after his passion and

26. Ambrose, *On the Sacraments* 1.4 (SC, XXV). Trans. in Yarnold, *The Awe-Inspiring Rites of Initiation*, p. 101.

27. See, for example, Chrysostom, *Catechetical Instruction* 9.28 (*PG* 49.228). Trans. in P.W. Harkins (ed.), *Baptismal Instructions* (Westminster, MD: Newman Press, 1963), p. 140.

28. *Catechetical Instruction* 3.9 (SC, L). Trans. in Harkins, *Baptismal Instructions*, p. 58. See also *Instruction* 12.35 (*PG* 49.236). Trans. in Harkins, *Baptismal Instructions*, p. 185.

29. *Catechetical Instruction* 11.27. Trans. in Harkins, *Baptismal Instructions*, p. 169. See A. Papadopoulos-Kerameus, *Catechesis ultima ad baptizandos* (Series prima, varia Graeca Sacra; St Petersburg: n.p., 1909), p. 173.

death and would be the source of many benefits, not only for mankind, but also for the whole creation.[30]

In the early fourth century, the emperor Constantine converted to Christianity and the Church found itself not only tolerated but established as the state religion. The stress of persecution now has evolved seamlessly into the stress of theological controversy and the wolves that prey upon the flock of Christ are not the wolves of paganism, but the wolves of heresy. The image of Christ as shepherd retains its popularity, and the Good Shepherd who laid down his life for his sheep now keeps his flock safe from taint and leads them in the paths of orthodoxy for his name's sake. The bishops and deacons play their part as undershepherds in keeping the flocks placid and obedient in the face of hysteria and controversy. This image of Christ is one that necessitates a corporate view of the faithful community. It is an image which discourages an individualistic approach to Christ, emphasizing instead the ideals of conformity and obedience.

In contrast, the association of Christ with the athletic arena creates an essentially individualistic image of the believer. To see Christ as an athletic coach or a judge at the games places the emphasis on individual endeavour, and although this is appropriate in the context of the personal suffering of the martyr or the struggle of the catechumen for his or her own soul, the athletic image finds little role in the corporate theological battles of the time.

Breast and nourishment imagery is similarily individualistic, an expression of the intimacy between the believer and the nourishing Christ. It associates itself well with the ongoing personal elements of faith, such as learning and baptism and, indeed, in the central nourishing motif of Christianity—the Eucharist. Unlike athletics, it is a passive metaphor where Christ gives and the believer receives and thus it has more in common with the shepherd motif, which may account for its regular, though sparse, appearances in the literature throughout the era we have been considering.

In this discussion of the metaphors of Christ, I have set out to show in each case how the image was designed to play a certain role within a specific theological context, and how the growing prevalence of one theological concern, namely that of the hierarchical Church, helped to

---

30. Theodore of Mopsuestia, *Baptismal Homily* 4.25. Trans. in Yarnold, *The Awe-Inspiring Rites of Initiation*, p. 227.

ensure the continued use of one particular metaphor for Christ, that of the Good Shepherd.

It is all too easy to ignore the context of images of Christ when searching the tradition for appropriate language. One must always beware of assuming that the metaphor comes with its full meaning neatly packaged within itself. To take another example from the Early Church: when Jesus calls his disciples salt, the emphasis is on the flavour of salt and its usefulness in that context, but when the martyr Ignatius warns his readers to be 'salted with Christ' it is the preserving properties of the salt that concern him, and he warns that if one is not so 'salted' one will become putrid and condemned for one's decaying smell.

In theological language, where images and metaphors have such a vital role to play in our understanding of the divine, it must never be forgotten that the metaphors only make complete sense within their own, limited context.

The danger of plucking the metaphor out of that context is that, unrestrained by the knowledge that Christ (or God) is only X within the context and limitations of Y, one may begin to consult X alone for further information about Christ (or God). The most obvious example of this, one that has caused the most pain and alienation in Christian language, is the *God is Father* metaphor. Instead of using the metaphor properly, that is, *God is Father* in the context of say, divine love and concern, the tendency of history has been to turn to *Father* in order to draw out attributes not necessarily intended by the original user— masculinity, patriarchalism, authority and so on.

This error has also led to great limitations in the language available to us, so that the religious imagination which should be a source of ever changing and vivid imagery, forever runs the risk of leaving Christ petrified into an effete long-haired shepherd in a nightgown. By losing hold of the fact that we *can* say that Christ is X in the context of Y we run the risk that by focusing again on the details of X we are denied a whole range of language simply because X may have other connotations beyond the context of Y which might be found offensive or silly. Why should Christ not be referred to as mother, breast, milk or even a crane, except that the misuse of metaphor allows irrelevant attributes of the image to be brought in against it?

It is only when both writer and reader are able to obey the disciplines of the proper contextual use of metaphor that literature is truly set free to do its theological task, to present the divine in language that is truly alive and vivid and speaks to the soul of the reader.

Because this is an historical essay, I shall leave the last words to Basil, speaking in the late fourth century:

> Scripture denotes him [Christ] by innumerable other titles, calling him Shepherd, King, Physician, Bridegroom, Way, Door, Fountain, Bread, Axe and Rock. And these titles do not set forth his nature... but the variety of effectual working which out of his kindness to his creation he bestows upon them that need according to each one's individual necessity.[31]

---

31. Basil, *On the Holy Spirit* 8.17 (SC, XVII, p. 97). Trans. in *Select Library*, VIII, p. 11.

Part II

THEOLOGY

IMAGES OF JESUS AND MODERN THEOLOGY

Gerald O'Collins, SJ

There is always a tension between reality and our representations, betweeen the way things (and people) exist and the way our minds, affected by our desires, shape and re-create them. Whether we are dealing with verbal or visual images of Jesus or anyone else, sooner or later we will become aware of the gap between being and wanting— between the (mysterious) way people are and the way we perceive them and want them to be. At the end of my paper, I will come back to the question of this gap.

Verbal images of Christ coincide, by and large, with titles for him: as Good Shepherd, Divine Lord, Saviour, Suffering Servant, Son of man, Word of God, Eschatological Prophet, Lamb of God, and the rest. These perceptions or versions of him relate to the visual images that we see on the walls of catacombs, high on the ceilings of churches, in homes, along the corridors of some schools, and in many art galleries. The earliest Christians pictured him in their catacombs as a beardless, curly-haired youth, the Good Shepherd who rescues his persecuted flock from the devouring wolves. After the conversion of the Emperor Constantine, Christians won their liberty and Jesus acquired an imperial nimbus or halo. As the Divine Lord in majesty he stands in heavenly glory or sits enthroned to judge all peoples. A mosaic in the Basilica of Saints Cosmas and Damian, which guards the entrance to the Roman forum, depicts such a majestic Christ in Judgment.[1] It took Christians a thousand years to find the courage to represent more directly the mystery of his crucifixion and resurrection. The utter shamefulness of Calvary inhibited them when creating images of the Crucified One. Like the anonymous artist who carved the crucifixion

1. This mosaic supplied the illustration for the cover of my *Christology: A Biblical, Historical, and Systematic Study of Jesus* (Oxford: Oxford University Press, 1995).

on a door of the fifth-century Basilica of Santa Sabina in Rome, for centuries Christians depicted Jesus as untouched by pain, bypassing death, and already reigning in triumph from the cross. Once they began to portray him as truly dying on the cross in agony, they could also face the task of trying to provide some images for the resurrection. At least in Western Europe, no artist has provided a more compelling vision of the Suffering Servant of God than Matthias Grünewald (d. 1528), whose Isenheim altarpiece shows Jesus crowned with horrendous thorns, his body flayed with wounds, and his livid mouth opened in a rictus of pain. The last and most important of Gothic painters in Germany, Grünewald expressed deep emotion and the almost terrifying religious intensity of the Reformation period. On his Isenheim altarpiece he has also left a panel representing Christ luminously transformed by the resurrection and rising into the sun—one of the most brilliant versions of the resurrection in all western art and in some ways more successful than Piero della Francesca's masterpiece at San Sepolcro. Grünewald's images face the truth of the first Good Friday and Easter Sunday.

Such visual images of Christ, like our verbal ones, do not belong just to scholars or merely to the educationally privileged; they do much more than simply articulate the Christology of the theologically elite. Mental representations and the verbal images that correspond to them give life and substance to hymns, devotional books, liturgical texts, Sunday sermons, and media messages of all kinds. We can recall here the poignant words sung three times at the unveiling of the crucifix on Good Friday: 'Behold the wood of the cross, on which hung the Saviour of the world'. The verbal image, 'the Saviour of the world', comes through powerfully. One can think also of such images from well-loved, traditional hymns as 'O come, O come Emmanuel': 'O come now, Wisdom from on high, who orders all things mightily'— the images of Emmanuel and Wisdom from on high work so well in that Advent hymn. One could mention also '*Love divine*, all loves excelling', 'Soul of *my Saviour*', 'Jesus, my *Lord*, my *God*, my all', and '*Christ the Lord* is risen today'. Visual images of Christ turn up constantly in film, drama, dance, sculpture, and painting—not to mention pictures mass-produced for cards and calendars. Beyond question, there is more to Christian faith in Jesus and theological reflection on him than verbal and visual images. But images contribute to our understanding and interpretation of him, by providing some access to the mystery of his person. They belong to everyone. My mother used to sum up her faith in Jesus by calling him 'Son of God' and 'Son of man'; for her the first image expressed Jesus' divinity, the second his humanity.

Faith is a kind of visual perception; it has its eyes. It brings a new way of seeing, that 'enlightening of the eyes of the heart' (Eph. 1.18; see Phil. 1.9; Col. 1.9), which perceives Jesus in a different manner and articulates its perceptions through a range of images.

Apropos of christological titles, Jacques Dupuis has commented on their meaning and cautioned against exaggerating their importance. [2] I have done much the same,[3] insisting that I did not intend to endorse a merely titular Christology. What we both glossed over was the way titles are verbal images that have often been translated into visual images. To echo, adapt, and extend Paul Ricoeur's classic dictum about symbols, images give rise to thought, action, and worship—a theme to which I will return later. In what we wrote, Dupuis and I underestimated the power and impact of titles: from the fifty or so to be found in the New Testament right down to 'Jesus the Evangelizer' (a title drawn a little strangely from Pope Paul VI's 1975 *Evangelii nuntiandi*[4]) and 'Jesus the Spirit Person' of some recent exegetes.

The problem to be faced is that of sheer abundance. Nowadays we can at times feel overwhelmed by the words and images of consumer society, as a tidal wave of pictures and perceptions flows over us from the television, the radio, and the press. Or else we may feel anaesthetized against visual and verbal images. Media journalism tends to give every event the maximum impact. If all things and all images are equal in their mega-importance, then none of them really counts for us. The late twentieth century poses this fresh challenge for those who wish to appropriate and reflect on images of Christ. Keeping in mind

2.   J. Dupuis, *Who Do You Say I Am? Introduction to Christology* (Maryknoll, NY: Orbis Books, 1994), pp. 19-20.

3.   O'Collins, *Christology*, pp. 114-15.

4.   In the Latin text of this apostolic exhortation (n. 7; see n. 8) Paul VI in fact called Jesus 'the first and greatest herald or preacher (*praeco*)', not 'the first evangelizer (*evangelizator*)'. For some reason the official translations into English, Italian, and Spanish translated *praeco* as 'evangelizer', added a section heading (not found in the Latin original) that named Christ 'the first Evangelizer', and launched this christological title. It was taken up by the final document of the 1992 CELAM Conference of Santo Domingo (n. 28) and by Pope John Paul II in his allocution of 5 January 1995 to the delegates at the 34th General Congregation of the Society of Jesus (n. 7).

this challenge, let me first develop some thoughts on current images and then take a position on their functions in theology and beyond.

I

From among the images or titles used for Jesus in the New Testament some have always more or less held their own, while others have been revived. The classical triad, 'Christ (or Messiah), Lord, and Son of God', moved ahead in the aftermath of the First Council of Nicaea (325) and enjoys its central place in the Nicene-Constantinopolitan Creed. By and large, the previously popular 'the Word of God' or 'God the Word', based on the prologue of John, tended to retreat in common usage, even if it did make an appearance in the Chalcedonian definition of 451. As recently as the common christological declaration, signed in November 1994 by Mar Dinkha IV (the Patriarch of the Assyrian Church of the East) and Pope John Paul II, the traditional three titles, 'Christ, Lord, and Son of God', bulked large in the text, although it also named Jesus once as 'the Word of God' and once as 'God the Word'.[5]

Raymond Brown, for his masterly studies on the birth and death of Jesus,[6] chose the title 'Messiah'—a tribute to the popularity of that title. A current work in Christology, Jacques Dupuis's *Who Do You Say I Am?*, uses frequently the titles 'Christ' (or 'Messiah') and 'Son of God' but hardly ever introduces the title 'Lord'. Another recent christological work, Jürgen Moltmann's *The Way of Jesus Christ: Christology in Messianic Dimensions*, studies very thoroughly what calling Jesus 'Christ/Messiah' involves in terms of his mission, person, suffering, resurrection, relation to the cosmos, and coming parousia. Some attention is paid to Jesus as 'Son' or 'Child' of God, but very little notice is taken of Jesus as 'Lord'.[7] Walter Kasper's now classic *Jesus the Christ* (German original 1974) allots much space to the titles/images

5. The text is to be found in the *Osservatore Romano*, 12 November 1994, p. 1; and in *Istina* 40 (1995), pp. 232-39 (in several language versions).

6. R.E. Brown, *The Birth of the Messiah* (London: Geoffrey Chapman, 2nd edn, 1993); *The Death of the Messiah* (2 vols.; London: Geoffrey Chapman, 1994).

7. J. Moltmann, *The Way of Jesus Christ: Christology in Messianic Dimensions* (London: SCM Press, 1990), pp. 142-45, 149, 165-67 on 'Son' or 'Child' of God, but only pp. 322-29 on 'Lord'.

of 'Messiah' and 'Son of God',[8] but has little at all to say about Jesus as 'Lord'. *The Catechism of the Catholic Church*[9] likewise favours the first two titles over the third. To be sure, when dealing with faith in 'Jesus Christ, his only Son, our Lord' (nn. 430-55), the *Catechism* attends to 'Lord' (nn. 446-51, 455). Otherwise, apart from one occurrence of 'Lord' (n. 1090) in a paragraph quoted from Vatican II's *Sacrosanctum Concilium*, the *Catechism* ignores that image/title, while making many references to 'Christ' and a good number to 'the Son of God'.[10] A similar linguistic preference shows up in a very different, non-traditional work, John Hick's *The Metaphor of God Incarnate: Christology in a Pluralistic Age*.[11] Hick spends pages on 'Christ' or 'Messiah' and 'the Son of God' or 'God the Son'. But he simply bypasses the Pauline and pre-Pauline attribution to Jesus of the title 'Lord'. It could be that Martin Hengel's magisterial study, *The Son of God*,[12] helped to focus attention on the title—both for those who agreed with him and for those who disagreed with him. But should attention to 'Son of God' encourage a neglect of 'Lord'?

Around 230 times and right from his first letter (1 Thessalonians), Paul gives Jesus the title of 'Kyrios' or 'Lord', doing so sometimes in passages that derive from a pre-Pauline tradition (e.g. Rom. 10.9; 1 Cor. 12.3; Phil. 2.11). For Paul, the mark of a Christian is the confession of Jesus as 'Lord'. The apostle even splits the Jewish confession of monotheism (Deut. 6.4-5) by glossing 'God' with 'Father' and 'Lord' with 'Jesus Christ' to put Jesus as Lord right alongside God the

8.   W. Kasper, *Jesus the Christ* (London: Burns & Oates, 1976), pp. 104-11, 163-96.

9.   *The Catechism of the Catholic Church* (London: Geoffrey Chapman, 1994).

10.   Here the *Catechism* differs markedly from the documents of Vatican II (1962–65). While 'Christ' is easily the most frequent title or name for Jesus in the conciliar texts and 'Son of God' turns up frequently, 'Lord *(Dominus)*' is applied to Jesus in thirteen of the sixteen documents: from the first *(Sacrosanctum concilium)* to the last *(Gaudium et spes)*. This title is used often in the Dogmatic Constitution on the Church *(Lumen gentium)* and in the Decree on the Ministry and Life of Priests *(Presbyterorum ordinis)*, and enters the title of the Decree on the Pastoral Office of Bishops in the Church *(Christus Dominus)*.

11.   J. Hick, *The Metaphor of God Incarnate: Christology in a Pluralistic Age* (London: SCM Press, 1993).

12.   M. Hengel, *The Son of God* (trans. J. Bowden; London: SCM Press, 1976 [German original 1975]), repr. with other works in M. Hengel, *The Cross of the Son of God* (London: SCM Press, 1986).

Father and present him also as (divine) agent of creation: 'for us there is one God, the Father, from whom are all things and for whom we exist, and one Lord, Jesus Christ, through whom are all things and through whom we exist' (1 Cor. 8.6). Paul's standard greeting to his correspondents goes as follows: 'Grace to you and peace from God our Father and the Lord Jesus Christ' (e.g. Rom. 1.7). Here the apostle put 'the Lord Jesus Christ' on a par with 'God our Father' as the joint source of 'grace and peace'—that is to say, of integral salvation. Paul's practice has supplied an alternative greeting in the Order of Mass: 'The grace and peace of God our Father and the Lord Jesus Christ be with you'. The obvious (if often ignored) importance of 'Lord' in Paul's letters and in pre-Pauline traditions encouraged me to dedicate pages to that title in my own *Christology*.[13]

What we also need here would be a full-length study of how the title functions in current liturgical texts and hymns. Jan Struther's popular hymn, 'Lord of all hopefulness', illustrates how the image of 'Lord' articulates not so much a sense of majestic divinity but the constant and compassionate caring of the risen Jesus towards everyone. He is the 'Lord of all hopefulness, joy, eagerness, faith, kindliness, grace, gentleness, and calm', ready to put 'bliss, strength, love, and peace in our hearts'. In the refrain of Sydney Carter's 'I danced in the morning', Jesus is 'the Lord of the dance'. Once again the term is the same, but the verbal image of 'Lord', as used by Jan Struther and Sydney Carter, conveys something rather different from, let us say, the eastern representations of Christ as sovereign Lord of the universe or *Pantocrator*.

Recent years have seen the revival of a range of images which normally express aspects of Jesus' authentic humanity and human activity: he is hailed as the Second/Last/New Adam, the (Cynic) Sage, the Eschatological Prophet. Talk of Jesus as the New Adam has its background in Judaism, seems to have been developed by Paul (Romans 5 and 1 Corinthians 15), flourished in the writings of St Irenaeus, was taken up in John Henry Newman's *Dream of Gerontius*, entered into the last and longest document from the Second Vatican Council (*Gaudium et spes*, n. 22), and has surfaced in the teachings of Pope John Paul II (e.g. in his 1979 encyclical *Redemptor hominis*, n. 8).

In *Jesus Christ in Modern Thought*, John Macquarrie makes exaggerated claims for this title, calling Paul's Adam Christology 'the earliest written witness to Jesus Christ'. This Christology appeals to

13. O'Collins, *Christology*, pp. 136-43.

Macquarrie, inasmuch as it does not suggest anything superhuman about Jesus, who as the New Adam is contrasted with the first Adam and with his failure to attain appropriate human status.[14] In Adam Christology Macquarrie finds

> a theology of his [Jesus'] person which can serve as a model for our post-Enlightenment mentality two thousand years later. For, put at its simplest, the career of Jesus Christ is seen as a rerun of the programme that came to grief in Adam but has now achieved its purpose in Christ and with those who are joined with him in the Christ-event.[15]

Hence Macquarrie hopes that a renewed Adam Christology will recognize unambiguously 'the complete humanity of Christ' and rescue Christology from the pervasive tendency to docetism under which it has long suffered.[16]

In developing his Adam Christology, Macquarrie relies heavily upon one exegete, James Dunn, and his work, *Christology in the Making*.[17] Macquarrie summarizes as follows Dunn's position (with particular reference to the Christ-hymn in Phil. 2.6-11):

> Paul's christological teaching turns on a contrast between Adam and Christ, or between the sinful humanity of the fallen human race and the new humanity that came into being in Christ. Adam was made in the image or form of God (Dunn says that the words *eikon* and *morphe* are virtually synonymous) but grasped at something more—to take God's place, we may suppose; through this grasping he lost the likeness that was already within his reach. Jesus Christ, by contrast, faced the same archetypal choice that confronted Adam, but chose *not* as Adam had chosen (to grasp equality with God). Instead, he chose to empty himself of Adam's glory and to embrace Adam's lot.[18]

Macquarrie goes on to make two problematic claims: that Adam Christology (1) formed 'the mainstream of Paul's christological reflection', and (2) seems 'to have been current even before Paul' and so 'must be considered the most ancient christology of all'.[19]

---

14. J. Macquarrie, *Jesus Christ in Modern Thought* (London: SCM Press, 1990), pp. 63, 359.

15. Macquarrie, *Jesus Christ*, p. 59.

16. Macquarrie, *Jesus Christ*, pp. 343, 359.

17. J.D.G. Dunn, *Christology in the Making* (London: SCM Press, 2nd edn, 1989).

18. Macquarrie, *Jesus Christ*, p. 57.

19. Macquarrie, *Jesus Christ*, p. 59.

Macquarrie seems unaware of the strong criticisms brought against Dunn's particular exegesis of Phil. 2.6-11 by various scholars, including some like N.T. Wright who also detect an Adam reference in this hymn.[20] In particular, the totally 'Adamic' or merely human interpretation of the hymn that Macquarrie argues for does not command general agreement. In *An Introduction to New Testament Christology*,[21] Raymond Brown comments that

> most scholars...would understand Phil. 2.6-7 to mean that Jesus did not consider being equal to God something to be *clung* to. In this interpretation, unlike Adam who, as a creature was not equal to God but sought to be, Jesus was already equal to God but was willing to empty himself to accept the form of a servant by *becoming* a human being. Those who support this interpretation argue correctly that a more normal understanding of the Greek in Phil. 2.7-8 would have the Son becoming a human being.[22]

Two years after Macquarrie published *Jesus Christ in Modern Thought* Dunn himself acknowledged that 'the majority of scholars' would hardly agree with him in finding an expression of Adam Christology in Phil. 2.7.[23] Secondly, the assertion that Adam Christology formed 'the mainstream of Paul's christological reflection' runs up against the fact that scholars remain in dispute as to where Adam references should be acknowledged in Paul's letters outside Romans 5 and 1 Corinthians 15.[24] Major Pauline commentators make only modest claims about the extent and significance of Adam Christology for Paul. Thus J.A. Fitzmyer in *According to Paul*[25] refers merely in passing to Adam, and at no point suggests that Adam Christology enjoys the importance for Paul that Macquarrie (and Dunn) propose. In *Paul*,[26] C.K. Barrett briefly discusses Paul's Adam Christology, but does not highlight its significance for the apostle. Three other titles, 'Christ/Messiah, Lord and Son of God', point rather to the heart of Pauline Christology.

20. See N. Coll, *Some Anglican Interpretations of Christ's Pre-Existence: A Study of L.S. Thornton, E.L. Mascall, J.A.T. Robinson and J. Macquarrie* (doctoral thesis, Gregorian University Rome, 1995), pp. 194-97; O'Collins, *Christology*, pp. 35-37.

21. R. Brown, *An Introduction to New Testament Christology* (London: Geoffrey Chapman, 1994).

22. Brown, *Introduction*, p. 135.

23. J.D.G. Dunn, 'Christology (NT)', *ABD* 1 (1992), pp. 979-91, at p. 983.

24. See O'Collins, *Christology*, pp. 31-37.

25. J.A. Fitzmyer, *According to Paul* (New York: Paulist Press, 1993), pp. 10, 15, 26.

26. C.K. Barrett, *Paul* (London: Geoffrey Chapman, 1994), pp. 109-12.

Martin Hengel, for instance, has maintained that 'Son of God', though used somewhat rarely (only fifteen times) by Paul, 'is the real *content of his gospel*' (italics Hengel's). Thus the veteran German scholar can say that this title 'has become an established, unalienable metaphor of Christian theology, expressing both the origin of Jesus Christ in God's being...and his true humanity'.[27] Thirdly, one can reasonably challenge Macquarrie's claim about the antiquity of Adam Christology. It is most likely a Pauline introduction and not pre-Pauline, let alone 'the most ancient Christology of all'. Paul seems to have drawn on Jewish traditions and the Hebrew Scriptures to develop in his own striking way the Adam Christology to be found in 1 Corinthians 15 and Romans 5. Fitzmyer produces evidence to show that 'the incorporation of all human beings in Adam' is an idea which 'seems to appear for the first time in 1 Cor. 15:22'. He likewise offers evidence that allows him to qualify as 'novel teaching' Paul's argument about the way Adam's sin had a 'maleficent influence' on all human beings.[28]

I have dwelt on Macquarrie's recent attempt to renew Christology by making much of the title/image of the New Adam. Undoubtedly this image has solid biblical and traditional credentials, expresses significantly the authentic humanity of Jesus, is implied by such a central liturgical text as the *Exultet* (or Easter Proclamation sung during the Easter Vigil), and is wonderfully represented in some icons used by the official liturgy of the eastern Christian tradition and in the decoration of its churches. This iconographic tradition illustrates the theological value of the Adam image by linking creation (which reached its climax at the creation of the first Adam and Eve) and the redemption (effected by the Last Adam, who releases the first Adam, Eve and the others in the *limbus patrum* from their long bondage). Some enduring legends also helped to relate creation and redemption. The tree from which Adam and Eve took the forbidden fruit was identified with the tree of Calvary on which Christ hung and died to save us. Without going as far as identifying them, a Good Friday hymn by Venantius Fortunatus, 'Crux fidelis', linked the two trees in the whole drama of creation, fall, and redemption. According to another legend Calvary was the place where Adam's skull was buried, and Christian art has frequently represented that skull in paintings of

27. Hengel, *The Cross of the Son of God*, pp. 7, 8, 89-90.
28. J.A. Fitzmyer, *Romans* (AB, 33; New York: Doubleday, 1993), pp. 412, 136, 406.

the crucifixion. In connecting Adam and Christ no work of literature has surpassed John Donne's 'Hymn to God my God, in my Sickness':

> We think that Paradise and Calvary,
>> Christ's Cross, and Adam's tree, stood in one place;
> Look Lord, and find both Adams met in me;
>> As the first Adam's sweat surrounds my face,
>> May the Last Adam's blood my soul embrace.

Unfortunately, the way the Adam image has been used in art, literature, legend and liturgical traditions to hold together creation and redemption is not brought out fully and clearly by Macquarrie. A renewed use of this image could be mounted much more successfully and on a sounder biblical basis.

Something similar should be said about certain recent proposals to construct an image of Jesus as Sage or even as Cynic Philosopher, a figure that often comes across as non-messianic, non-eschatological, and much more Hellenistic than Jewish. The extreme reconstruction here has to be Burton Mack's image of Jesus as a Cynic-like Sage, a counter-cultural figure whose aphoristic speech and parables ridiculed conventional concerns that preoccupied the society of his time. No Jewish prophet or other such traditional figure within Judaism, Jesus did not think of himself in messianic, eschatological terms. Rather he was a wandering and witty teacher of wisdom, whose alternate vision of human life became subsequently overlaid with apocalyptic themes of judgment to come, claims to personal and prophetic authority he never made historically, and a fictionalized theology of his death and resurrection.[29] In *The Lost Gospel: Q and Christian Origins*,[30] Mack went on to 'explain' the literary history of Q or a source containing the sayings of Jesus. The earliest layers, made up of sapiential sayings, put us in touch with the real Jesus, who confronted the conventions of his culture and challenged his hearers to see things differently. The prophetic and apocalyptic layers in Q, which spoke of the end of the world and the Son of man coming in judgment, were developed and added later. This image of Jesus as a subversive Cynic Sage who was later transformed into a prophet uttering eschatological warnings has been vigorously challenged—both in the form coming from Mack and

29. See B.L. Mack, *A Myth of Innocence: Mark and Christian Origins* (Philadelphia: Fortress Press, 1988).

30. B.L. Mack, *The Lost Gospel: Q and Christian Origins* (London: HarperCollins, 1993).

in those coming from others.[31] In the second volume of *A Marginal Jew: Rethinking the Historical Jesus*,[32] John Meier rightly warns against the extraordinarily tenuous conclusions reached by those like Mack who turn their creative fantasies loose on the Q hypothesis. We are dealing with fanciful speculations about the literary history of a document we do not have as such.

Those who de-eschatologize Jesus, playing down—if not completely dismissing—any talk of God's imminent rule as a later accretion coming from the Christian community, and developing an image of Jesus as a travelling sage who preaches wisdom and makes no claims for himself, do not necessarily go quite as far as Mack. R.W. Funk, R.W. Hoover and other members of the Jesus Seminar in *The Five Gospels: The Search for the Authentic Words of Jesus*[33] plead for the attractiveness of the Jesus-as-sage image: it is the objective 'truth about Jesus', and not 'held captive' by traditional doctrines or a 'smothering cloud of historical creeds'. Marcus Borg, himself listed in the roster of Jesus Seminar fellows, offers a complex profile of Jesus, one made up of four images: not only that of wisdom teacher, but also those of Spirit person (= the traditional type of Jewish holy man), social prophet and movement founder.[34]

As with Macquarrie's refurbishing of the image of the Last Adam, some things get misrepresented in this renewed interest in a sapiential approach to Jesus and some things are largely missing. In *Images of Jesus Today* James Charlesworth notes how Borg fails to situate Jesus

31. See D.C. Allison, 'A Plea for Thoroughgoing Eschatology', *JBL* 113 (1994), pp. 651-68, at pp. 661-63; H.-D. Betz, 'Jesus and the Cynics: Survey and Analysis of a Hypothesis', *JR* 74 (1994), pp. 453-75; J.H. Charlesworth, 'Jesus Research Expands with Chaotic Creativity', in J.H. Charlesworth and W.P. Weaver (eds.), *Images of Jesus Today* (Valley Forge, PA: Trinity Press International, 1994), pp. 1-41 (16-19); P. Eddy, 'Jesus as Cynic Sage?', to appear in *Journal of Biblical Literature*; R. Horsley, 'Jesus, Itinerant Cynic or Israelite Prophet', in Charlesworth and Weaver (eds.), *Images of Jesus Today*, pp. 68-97 (70-74); and B. Witherington III, *Jesus the Sage: The Pilgrimage of Wisdom* (Minneapolis: Fortress Press, 1994), esp. pp. 117-45.

32. J. Meier, *A Marginal Jew: Rethinking the Historical Jesus* (New York: Doubleday, 1994), pp. 177-81.

33. R.W. Funk, R.W. Hoover *et al.*, *The Five Gospels: The Search for the Authentic Words of Jesus* (London: Maxwell Macmillan, 1993), pp. 2, 5, 7.

34. M. Borg, 'Jesus and Eschatology: A Reassessment', in Charlesworth and Weaver (eds.), *Images of Jesus Today*, pp. 42-67 (55-56).

in the cosmology and eschatology of his Jewish contemporaries. Furthermore, 'Borg's Jesus seems so inoffensive and familiar', not the preacher of a message that could lead to his crucifixion.[35] As regards *The Five Gospels*, reviews have been little short of devastating.[36] Against all the solid evidence recalled by Betz, Charlesworth, and others that Cynic philosophers were simply not there in Jesus' environment, the Jesus Seminar gratuitously speaks of 'the Cynic philosophers who plied their trade in Galilee in Jesus' day'.[37] One may talk in a facile fashion of how the people in Nazareth 'benefited from supposedly Graeco-Roman culture' of nearby Sepphoris: 'they could attend Greek plays, listen to Greek philosophers, and generally acquire cosmopolitan polish'. Ed Sanders shows how such a reconstruction of the situation in which Jesus grew up is 'exceptionally improbable'.[38] It is also very doubtful to credit Jesus with a sociopolitical message (with aphorisms and parables forming the earliest layer in an historically reliable sapiential tradition), while discounting end-of-the-world sayings as much later, or at least as post-Easter, apocalyptic accretions. In volume two of *A Marginal Jew* John Meier argues persuasively that Jesus proclaimed and inaugurated God's final entry into world history, the divine rule that would bring to an end the present world order. This preaching of the future kingdom was also reflected in the parables of Jesus,[39] who as God's final envoy expected to be personally vindicated. By reviving long-discredited assertions about Paul introducing from Hellenistic mystery religions belief in Jesus as a dying and rising god,[40] the Jesus Seminar tip-toes around the truth witnessed by John 1 and 6, 1 Corinthians 1–2, Hebrews 1 and other New Testament passages: the crucified and risen Jesus is now manifested as divine Wisdom in person, the creative and revealing Wisdom of God prefigured in the Old Testament's sapiential writings.

---

35. Charlesworth, 'Jesus Research', pp. 21-23.
36. See D. Catchpole, *Theol* 97 (1994), pp. 457-64; R. Hays, *First Things* 43 (1994), pp. 43-48; G. O'Collins, *Tablet* (17 September 1994), p. 1170; M.L. Soards, *TTod* 52 (1995), pp. 270-72; C.M. Tuckett, *JTS* 46 (1995), pp. 250-53. See also B. Witherington III, *The Jesus Quest: The Third Search for the Jew of Nazareth* (Downers Grove, IL: InterVarsity Press, 1995), pp. 42-57.
37. Funk *et al.*, *The Five Gospels*, p. 33.
38. E.P. Sanders, *The Historical Figure of Jesus* (London: Penguin Press, 1993), p. 104.
39. Meier, *Marginal Jew*, pp. 349, 149.
40. Funk *et al.*, *The Five Gospels*, p. 7.

The manifestation of Jesus' identity as divine Wisdom in person should be, but often is not, the heart of a Christology in the sapiential mode. Among the Latin Fathers no one excelled Leo the Great in maintaining the full and authentic status both of Jesus' humanity *and* his divinity. The same Leo pictured the unborn Jesus in Mary's womb as 'Wisdom building a house for herself' (*Epistola* 31.2-3).

Before leaving Wisdom Christology let me pay tribute to the help available from Ben Witherington's *Jesus the Sage*. Arguing that a sapiential way of looking at Jesus goes back to Jesus himself, Witherington shows how Jesus not only used wisdom speech (as well as prophetic and apocalyptic modes of speech) but also presented himself as the embodiment of divine Wisdom. Jesus identified himself as God's Wisdom in person. Witherington's contribution has four further advantages, the first two being clearly recognized by him. This sapiential approach appreciates Jesus' Jewish roots; it meshes with contemporary feminist concerns; it helps in dialogue with other cultures and religions;[41] it can be applied ecologically.[42]

Thus far we have looked at the classical triad, 'Christ/Messiah, Lord, and Son of God', noting the lack of attention to 'Lord' in some christological and other texts. In examining the two images at the heart of recent Adam and Wisdom Christologies, I expressed both dissatisfaction at some current misuse of these images along with sincere appreciation for their rich possibilities. This paper has sampled only a few of the christological images that turn up in twentieth-century theological writing. Many more could be cited and scrutinized: Jesus the Jew, the Man for Others, the (Charismatic) Healer, the Teacher (Mk 9.17, 38; 10.17), the Rabbi (Mk 9.5; 11.21), the Eschatological Prophet, the Victim, the Suffering Servant, the Liberator, the Beautiful One, the Cosmic Christ, my/our Brother, my/our Friend, our Mother, and so forth. Such images are solidly based in the record and reflection provided by the New Testament. It is important for the apostle Paul that Jesus was born a Jew (Rom. 9.5; Gal. 3.16) and of the house of David (Rom. 1.3). The Man for Others, Jesus 'did not please himself' (Rom. 15.3) but 'went about doing good' (Acts 10.38). Jesus' ministry of healing bulks large in the Synoptic Gospels and provides the frame for

41. See O'Collins, *Christology*, pp. 303-305.
42. See D. Edwards, *Jesus the Wisdom of God: An Ecological Theology* (Maryknoll, NY: Orbis Books, 1995).

his remark about being the 'physician' come for the sick and sinful (Mk 2.17 parr.). The parable of the last judgment identifies Jesus the Victim with the homeless, prisoners, refugees, and other victims of our world (Mt. 25.31-46). The liberating power exercised by Jesus in his earthly ministry (e.g. Mk 3.27) and already at work in his risen power and glory (e.g. 2 Cor. 12.9; 13.4; Rev. 19.11-16) more than justifies the image of Liberator. The titles of Jesus my Brother and Friend enjoy their warrant from the Scriptures (e.g. Mk 3.31-35 parr.; Jn 15.13-15; Rom. 8.29), as well as from such witnesses of tradition as St Richard of Chichester (d. 1253), to whom I return shortly. Being 'the radiance of God's glory' (Heb. 1.3), Jesus is the infinitely Beautiful One, an image that the wisdom literature fills out wonderfully (e.g. Wis. 7.25-26). His picture of himself as a hen with her chickens (Lk. 13.34 par.) helps to provide homely backing for those who style Jesus 'our Mother'. The christological hymn which represents Jesus as creator and conserver of the universe (Col. 1.15-17) supports the image of the Cosmic Christ, which can also be maintained for other reasons. In his *Jesus and the Cosmos*,[43] Denis Edwards appeals, among other things, to Karl Rahner's theology of death and reflections on the coming of the cosmos to consciousness when proposing the image.[44]

II

At the start of this paper I noted the way our projective desires help to re-create or at least shape our images of people. Albert Schweitzer offered the classic warning against picturing Jesus in the light of our personal and cultural interests and presuppositions. Summing up decades of attempts to write the life of Jesus, he declared: 'it was not only each epoch that found its reflection in Jesus; each individual created Him in accordance with his own character'.[45] Almost a century later than Schweitzer's classic study, we should be aware of the ways in which we can use Jesus to personify ourselves and our values, whether religious or (even more broadly) cultural. All theologians and

---

43. D. Edwards, *Jesus and the Cosmos* (New York: Paulist Press, 1991), pp. 27-31, 100-102.

44. See J.A. Lyons, *The Cosmic Christ in Origen and Teilhard de Chardin: A Comparative Study* (Oxford: Oxford University Press, 1982).

45. A. Schweitzer, *The Quest of the Historical Jesus* (London: A. & C. Black, 2nd edn, 1936), p. 4.

exegetes bear the imprint of their own time and place; we can be painfully aware of the ways our desires shape our picture of Jesus. But I want to finish on a positive note, by acknowledging some valuable aspects of our christological titles and images.

We betray our deepest hopes and fears in our images of Jesus. We express our religious feelings about him, and what we want him to be not only in himself (*in se*) but also for us (*pro nobis*). In disclosing our desires for salvation, the titles we give him inevitably bulk large in our liturgical texts. Along with this petitionary function, the christological images coming from believers, right from the early representations of the Good Shepherd and the Divine Lord, have also articulated and confessed their faith and hope in Jesus. As visual and verbal images available for others, these images have gone on inviting and encouraging the spread of faith and hope in him. Since they openly express what our loyalty to him means for us, our Jesus-images inevitably enjoy this public function of calling on others to respond to him in an imaginative, worshipping, and committed fashion.

Here I wish to dwell above all on three roles involved in our christological images, which link up with our search for beauty, goodness, and truth. Our minds search for truth, our wills are drawn to do what is good, and our imaginations take in and fashion what is beautiful. Our images come out of a search to know Jesus; they galvanize and shape our Christian discipleship; they feed the prayerful and imaginative contemplation of the infinitely Beautiful One, who fills us with the joy of being in his presence. Right from the New Testament, christological images have expressed and shaped Christian worship, life, and knowledge of Jesus. Could it be that a renewed appreciation of the range of functions for images could serve to renew Christology as we move towards the new millennium? We could do worse than take a cue from the New Testament. There worship is paid to Jesus the Lord (e.g. Phil. 2.9-11); discipleship entails following the Son of man 'on the road' (Mk 10.52); scholarly research can be inspired by the wide investigation and 'orderly' way St Luke went about providing 'authentic knowledge' of Jesus, with help from 'eye witnesses and ministers of the Word' (Lk. 1.1-4). The triple desire to worship, follow, and know comes through the famous prayer which St Richard of Chichester built around five christological images or titles: 'Thanks be thee, my Lord Jesus Christ for all the benefits which thou hast given me—for all the pains and insults thou hast borne for me. O most merciful Redeemer,

Friend and Brother, may I know thee more clearly, love thee more dearly, and follow thee more nearly'.

By putting images into sequence we offer a scheme for studying the dramatic stages of Jesus' pre-existence, birth, life, death, and resurrection. He begins as the eternal Word or Wisdom; he is incarnated as the Baby Jesus (if I am allowed to use 'Bambin Gesù' which means so much to those who have let me make Italy my second home). He is born as Jesus the Jew. Through acting as the Healer, Evangelizer, Good Shepherd, and new Moses, he becomes the Suffering Servant, the Victim, the crucified Son of man, and the High Priest. He rises in glory to act as the Son of God with power and prove himself the Brother and Friend to all. As the Alpha and Omega, he will be manifested at the end as the Lord of lords and the Spouse for the community of the redeemed. These and other images tell us who he is, what he has done, and what he will do. Put together in a logical and chronological order, they make up a narrative Christology.[46] Titles and images have a clear narrative function.

In short, there may well be room for a renewed titular Christology, one that appreciates the overlap of titles and images, sees how they can create a narrative Christology, and recognizes how the images of Jesus reveal answers to the human quest for truth, goodness, and beauty. Christological images belong to all believers, being so closely intertwined with their worship, discipleship, and knowledge of Jesus. They emerge from and then give life to their thought, action and worship.

---

46. This proposal about using a sequence of images to tell the Jesus story and produce a narrative Christology differs from the way Sydney Carter exploited one image ('the Lord of the dance') to tell the whole story: from creation till the eternal life that will 'never, never die'.

THE MAGI FROM BENGAL AND THEIR JESUS:
INDIAN CONSTRUALS OF CHRIST DURING COLONIAL TIMES

R.S. Sugirtharajah

Recently literary scholars, historians and anthropologists have been remapping their disciplines scouring their own fields for colonial motifs. Such investigations have given rise to what are known as post-colonial theories and discourse. What this paper intends to do is to utilize some aspects of this post-colonial discourse in order to appraise some of the christological constructions which emerged in India during colonial days. The paper has three interrelated objectives. First, it tracks how some Indians freed themselves from the hegemonic images of Jesus propagated by missionaries during the days of the Empire—images which denigrated their culture and history—and also tracks how some Indians came up with their own sketches of Jesus. Secondly, by reinvoking these colonial encounters, it challenges the notion that the colonialized were only ever docile, incoherent, mute and hapless consumers of imperialized interpretations. Thirdly, it uses the christological controversy as a template for providing an early example of de-colonization.

Unlike perhaps other faith traditions, Indian Hindus have worked out elaborate and varied images of Jesus. The Hindus who were at the forefront of fashioning a christological discourse during the nineteenth century were three upper-caste, urbanized Bengali Brahmins—the magi from Bengal, as I should like to call them—Raja Rammohun Roy (1772?–1833), Keshub Chunder Sen (1838–1884), and P.C. Mozoomdar (1840–1905). They were, to borrow a phrase from Salman Rushdie, the original 'Macaulay's Minute men'[1]—the ideal colonized subject envisaged by Thomas Macaulay in his famous minute of 1835: 'a class of persons, Indian in blood and colour, but English in taste, in

---

1. S. Rushdie, *The Moor's Last Sigh* (London: Jonathan Cape, 1995), p. 165.

opinions, in morals and in intellect'.[2] In other words, they were the products of the colonial system and its cosmopolitanism. All three belonged to the Hindu ethical and reform group called the Brahmo Samaj (Society of God). These men mapped out their understanding of Jesus in response to the missionaries' essentialist, and biased, view of Hindus, but they never lost their admiration and affection for Jesus and his teachings. Compared to the then prevalent European images of Jesus worked out by H.S. Reimarus (1694–1768), D.F. Strauss (1808–1874) and Ernest Renan (1832–1892), which were marked by skepticism, and an anti-Christian slant, and projected Jesus as a sad, mistaken and failed reformer, the portrayals by these Indians were, by contrast, enthusiastic and positive and projected a person worthy to be followed and emulated. Keshub Chunder Sen, in one of his lectures, entitled 'India asks, "Who is Christ?"', said: 'I am thankful to say I never read anti-Christian books with delight, and never had to wage war with my Christ' (Sen 1901: 391). He went on to urge India to receive Christ as her bridegroom:

> Oh, the bridegroom is coming; there is no knowing when he cometh. Let India, beloved India, be decked out in all her jewellery—those 'sparkling oriental gems' for which the land is famous, so that at the time of the wedding we may find her a really happy and glorious bride. The bridegroom is coming. Let India be ready in due season (Sen 1901: 392).

First let me bring out the images of Jesus these men fashioned, as a response to the dominant Christologies of the missionaries.

1. *Asiatic Jesus, Oriental Christ*

Rammohun Roy: Jesus as a Moral Teacher

Rammohun Roy, who was himself at the forefront of reinventing his own Hindu tradition by de-centring its idolatrous and polytheistic elements, found the Jesus of the missionaries, immersed in evangelical doctrines of atonement and Trinity, unacceptable. The metaphysical and miraculous dimensions in which Jesus was presented did not appeal to Rammohun Roy, a beneficiary of the Enlightenment and its values, and he was keen to stress and elevate the moral and rational dimensions. Dissatisfied with a Jesus embedded in evangelical dogma,

---

2. T.B. Macaulay, *Speeches by Lord Macaulay with his Minute on Indian Education* (ed. G.M. Young; London: Oxford University Press, 1935), p. 359.

Rammohun Roy went on to do to Christian texts what he did with his own Hindu texts—he stripped away the doctrinal accretions which had gathered over the years. He was looking for a Jesus who was an Asiatic moral teacher, and wanted to locate him within the Eastern spiritual tradition. He textualized his quest in *The Precepts of Jesus: The Guide to Peace and Happiness. Extracted from the Books of the New Testament, Ascribed to the Four Evangelists* (1820). This was even before Strauss had started his lives of Jesus project in Europe. The *Precepts* is a compilation of synoptic materials, minus genealogies, miracles, historical incidents and doctrinal references. He saw his task as to 'free the originally pure, simple and practical religion of Christ from the heathenish doctrines and absurd notions' (1978 [1906]: 921). In the introduction to the *Precepts of Jesus*, he reiterates his hermeneutical position. His aim was to present the essence of the gospel, which for him lay not in the doctrines, as the missionaries claimed, but in the moral teachings of Jesus. He also sought to purge the Gospel narratives of their miracles, which he called 'heathen notions', because he believed that anyone who was rational enough to reject Hindu mythologies would find them ridiculous and unhelpful. What in effect the *Precepts of Jesus* did was to wrest Jesus from his place as the focal point of the missionary preaching, and to reframe him as a moral teacher and a true guide to God. In other words, such a portrayal called in question the powerful pillars of evangelical Christianity—belief in the atonement, the doctrine of the Trinity and the divinity of Jesus, and the self-sufficiency of the Christian Scriptures. His objective was to present the essence of the gospel, which he considered to be contained in the moral teachings of Jesus, not in doctrines, as the Baptist missionaries at Serampore insisted. During the height of the controversy generated by the *Precepts of Jesus*, Rammohun summed up his position in a letter to a friend:

> I regret only that the followers of Jesus, in general, should have paid much greater attention to inquiries after his nature than to the observance of his commandments, when we are well aware that no human acquirements can ever discover the nature even of the most common and visible things, and, moreover, that such inquiries are not enjoined by the divine revelation (1978: 919).

He saw his task as rescuing Jesus from the imperial portrayals, which he regarded as a travesty. The implication was that he could do a better job in presenting Jesus than the missionaries, because they were obsessed with their evangelical theology. He went on to say, 'I hope to God these Missionaries may at length have their eyes opened to see their own errors' (1978: 922).

Keshub Chunder Sen: Jesus as an Asiatic

Before the European colonization, India had been introduced by the persecuted Nestorians to a Jesus who showed solidarity with their cause. Keshub Chunder Sen and his contemporaries, however, were brought up on images of Jesus which identified him with the European race and its sentiments. It was against this aggressive and muscular christo-logical landscape that Keshub Chunder Sen engaged in his christological quest. He used oration as a mode of communicating his vision of Jesus. The four open lectures he delivered, in front of an audience composed mainly of middle-class educated Hindus, colonial officials and a mixed group of missionaries, encapsulated his views of Jesus. In these lectures he set out to do three things. First, he wanted to revalorize Indian values and traditions which, as he put it, had been 'Europeanised' (Sen 1904: 52) and slaughtered by European invasion:

> Alas! Before the formidable artillery of Europe's aggressive civilization, the scriptures and prophets, the language and literature of the East, nay her customs and manne, her social and domestic institutions, and her very industries have undergone a cruel slaughter (Sen 1904: 51).

Secondly, he wanted to make it clear to Indians that the Jesus whom the missionaries were parading was not an Englishman, but an Asian, with whom Indians could easily feel at home, for he had similar manners, instincts and sentiments. In a lecture entitled 'Asia's Message to Europe', he asked,

> For England has sent unto us, after all, a Western Christ. This is indeed to be regretted. Our countrymen find that in this Christ, sent by England, there is something that is not quite congenial to the native mind, not quite acceptable to the genius of the nation. It seems that the Christ that has come to us is an Englishman, with English manners and customs about him, and with the temper and spirit of an Englishman in him... But why should you Hindus go to England to learn Jesus Christ? Is not his native land nearer to India than England? Is he not, and are not his apostles and immediate followers more akin to Indian nationality than an Englishman?... Gentlemen, go to the rising Sun in the East, not to the setting Sun in the West, if you wish to see Christ in the plenitude of his glory and in the fullness and freshness of his divine life... Recall to your minds, gentlemen, the true Asiatic Christ, divested of all Western

appendages, carrying on his work of redemption among his own people.
Behold he cometh to us in his loose-flowing garment, his dress and
features altogether Oriental, a perfect Asiatic in everything… Surely Jesus
is our Jesus (Sen 1901: 363-65).

And thirdly, Keshub Chunder Sen wanted to re-claim Jesus for Asia. He
saw in the coming of the missionaries an indication of their returning
Christ to his rightful home:

It is not the Christ of the Baptists, nor the Christ of the Methodists, but
the Christ sent by God, the Christ of love and meekness, of truth and self-
sacrifice, whom the world delights to honour. If you say we must renounce
our nationality, and all the purity and devotion of Eastern faith, for sectarian
and western Christianity, we shall say most emphatically, No. It is *our*
Christ, *Asia's* Christ, you have come to return to us. The East gratefully and
lovingly welcomes back her Christ (Slater 1884: 101 [emphasis original]).

Keshub Chunder Sen was relentless in telling his audience that all the
great religious figures of the world were of Asian origin, and that Asia
was the birth place of the major religions. He situated Jesus as one
among many on-going, revealing instances of God, along with earlier
manifestations who had come before him, such as: Sakya Muni,
Confucius, Zoroaster, and Moses, and those like Chaitanya and Kabir
who followed him. Though he regarded Jesus as the 'Prince of
Prophets', and reiterated that he deserved 'the profoundest reverence',
Sen went on to say yet again that 'we must not neglect that chain, or
any single link in that chain of prophets, that preceded him, and prepared the world for him; nor must we refuse honour to those who,
coming after him, have carried on the blessed work of human regen-
eration for which he lived and died' (Slater 1884: 10).

P.C. Mozoomdar: Orientalizing Christ

Mozoomdar's hermeneutical concern, as the title of his book *The
Oriental Christ* indicates, is to orientalize Christ. In a lengthy introduction, where he acknowledges his theological debt to his friend and
mentor Keshub Chunder Sen, Mozoomdar juxtaposes two competing
figures of Jesus—the stern, exclusive, historical, doctrinal, figure
of western muscular Christianity, and the homely, poetic, loving,
sweet Jesus of the Galilean lake (1933 [1833]: 40). In his reckoning,
the Eastern Christ is 'the incarnation of unbounded love and grace',
and 'the Western Christ is the incarnation of theology, formalism,
ethical and physical force' (1933: 41). Mozoomdar's construals of Jesus

resemble those of Hindu adherents in relation to their chosen deity, where closeness to the deity is expressed not necessarily through abstract images but through intimate ritualistic acts. His portrayals of Jesus as the bathing, fasting, weeping, pilgrimaging, dying and reigning Christ fall within this category.

In concluding this section, we need to note that these formulations of Jesus, as a moral teacher, an Asiatic ascetic and an Oriental guru, did not go down well with the missionaries. In fact, these Bengalis had to battle on two fronts: on the one hand, there were the missionaries, who wanted to thrust forward their own form of evangelical Christianity; and on the other, there were their own Hindu pundits, who wanted to assert the superiority and sufficiency of Hindu religious texts and ritual practices in the face of the militant and jaundiced view of the missionaries. What in effect these portrayals did was to invalidate one of the pillars of evangelical Christianity—the divinity and the atoning power of Jesus. They wrested Jesus from his place at the focal point of missionary preaching, and reframed him as a moral teacher, a great man and a true guide to God. The missionaries were the products of an evangelical revival and piety and could not envisage Jesus without his sacrificial death. In Rammohun Roy, Keshub Chunder Sen and Mozoomdar, the missionaries faced an unexpected enemy. In England, as dissenters, they faced the strong theological arm of high-church Anglicanism, whereas in India they came up against opponents who, from a different cultural, religious and linguistic position, not only threatened their cherished doctrines, but far worse, de-centred Jesus and made him look like a culturally relative figure. The following words of Rammohun Roy typify the position of the Bengalis:

> If the manifestation of God in the flesh is possible, such possibility cannot reasonably be confined to Judea or Ayodhya, for God has undoubtedly the power of manifesting himself in either country and of assuming any colour or name he pleases (1978: 980).

It would be presumptuous on my part to say that I have done justice to the powerful and often complex portrayals of Jesus worked out by these men. Nor can I claim that I have attempted to situate their christological constructions over against the philosophical and religious backdrop which influenced and informed their articulations. There are many studies which address these issues.[3] Some of these tend to evaluate the

3.   See, for instance, M.M. Thomas, *The Acknowledged Christ of the Indian*

works of these men from the perspective of Christian theology, for their failure to measure up to it. Others try to rehabilitate them within the Hindu philosophical and religious fold. As I indicated earlier, I have a different hermeneutical agenda. My main objective is to foreground colonialism as the site in which the Christologies of these men were worked out, and to detect in their work marks of an early instance of post-coloniality, which the present-day post-colonial theorists speak about.

2. *Marks of Cultural De-Colonization*

Culture and the Hermeneutics of Power

Post-colonial theorists talk about three forms of decolonization: political, economic and cultural.[4] Political decolonization points to territorial freedom, which has been largely achieved. Various forms of development strategy are seen as a form of economic decolonization; and transition from western hegemonic cultural control is seen as intellectual decolonization.

These Bengali Christologies are early instances of cultural decolonization. They emerged as a response to an active confrontation with a dominant system of thought, and their Bengali authors were pioneers in addressing the relationship between interpretation, culture and power. Now, nearly one hundred and fifty years later, we are witnessing a similar unmasking of the dominant Christologies. This time it is being done through the work of the Latin American, feminist and African theologians who are uncovering concealed biases in these Christologies. The three Bengalis were the first to expose and call in question the acceptability of a Christ who was couched in European terms and arrived in India with colonial power. In their view, these were not christological formulations in the genuine sense, but assertions of power, or as Rammohun Roy himself put it, they were undertaken by

Renaissance (London: SCM Press, 1969); R. Boyd, *An Introduction to Indian Christian Theology* (Madras: The Christian Literature Society, 1969); D.C. Scott, *Keshub Chunder Sen* (Madras: The Christian Literature Society, 1979); H. Staffner, *Jesus and the Hindu Community: Is a Synthesis of Hinduism and Christianity Possible?* (Anand: Gujarat Sahitya Prakash, 1987).

4.   J. Nederveen Pieterse and B. Parekh, 'Shifting Imaginaries: Decolonization, Internal Decolonization, Postcoloniality', in *idem* (eds.), *The Decolonization of Imagination: Culture, Knowledge and Power* (London: Zed Books, 1995), pp. 1-19.

'men possessed of wealth and power' (1978: 212), and their interpretations were 'elevated by virtue of power' (1978: 201). Such an
image they looked upon as oppressive and unacceptable. Being high-
caste Hindus, Jesus for them was a *mlecha*, an outsider, but admitted
into India along with the imperialists. To quote Mozoomdar: He [Jesus]
is a mlecha to Hindus, a kaffir to Mohammedans...he is tolerated only
because he carries with him the imperial prestige of a conquering
race. Can this be the Christ that will save India?' (1933: 34). Their
way of de-Europeanizing Christ is to retrieve the Jesus of the Gospels,
and to place him within his own continent and situate him along with
the long line of Asia's illustrious religious figures. In the words of
Keshub Chunder Sen,

> Let all people in this country who bear the Christian name remember that it
> is not by presenting a western Christ to our countrymen that they will be
> able to regenerate India. If you like, present the English side of Christ's
> many-sided character to the English nation. If you wish, present a German
> Christ to Germans, and an American Christ to the American people. But if
> you wish to regenerate us Hindus, present Christ to us in his Hindu
> character. When you bring Christ to us, bring him to us, not as a civilized
> European, but as an Asiatic ascetic whose wealth is communion, and
> whose riches prayers (1901: 390).

Colonial racialization and stereotypes also played a key role in their
christological debate. The imperial discourse generated the image of
the Englishman as manly, strong and brave, and the Indian/Bengali as
effeminate, weak and cowardly. This racialization created stereotypical
images of the other—of Asians, as an inferior race.[5] In one of his
lectures, Keshub Chunder Sen captured the mood of the colonialists at
that time:

> They say, Asia is a vile woman, full of impurity and uncleanliness. Her
> Scriptures tell lies; her prophets are all imposters; her people—men,
> women and children—are unfaithful and deceitful. There is neither light
> nor purity in Asia. The entire continent is given to ignorance and bar-
> barism and heathenism; and nothing good, it is said, can come out of this
> accursed land (Sen 1904: 50).

Mozoomdar, too, records that Europeans often treated 'Hindus as a
primitive Eastern race' (1933: 14).

---

5. M. Sinha, *Colonial Masculinity: The 'Manly Englishman' and the 'Effeminate
Bengali' in the Late Nineteenth Century* (Manchester: Manchester University Press,
1995).

The answer of these Bengalis to the missionaries' description of the degradation and decline of Asia was to reinstall Asia as the site of everything that is best in religion, science and literature. Rammohun Roy went on to claim that for science, literature or religion, the world was indebted to '*our ancestors* for the first dawn of knowledge which sprang up in the East, and thanks to the Goddess of Wisdom, we have still a philosophical and copious language of our own, which distinguishes us from other nations who cannot express scientific or abstract ideas without borrowing the language of foreigners' (1978: 906 [italics in the original]). They were reinvoking, to use the phrase of Keshub Chunder Sen, the 'glory of our Asiatic home' (1904: 55). Thus Asia became the ground for rehabilitation, and Jesus was reinstated as an Asiatic endowed with various imagined Asian qualities. They pointed out everything that was good in India: her spirituality, her religious leaders, literature, art, music were completely Asian in origin. They re-valorized Asia as the site, not only for the birth of Christianity, but also for all the major faith traditions in the world. In a letter to the editor of *Bengal Hurkaru*, Rammohun Roy wrote,

> Before 'A Christian' indulged in a tirade about persons being degraded by '*Asiatic* effeminacy', he should have recollected that almost all the ancient prophets and patriarchs venerated by Christians, nay even Christ himself, a Divine Incarnation and the *founder* of Christian Faith, were ASIATICS. So if a Christian thinks it degrading to be born or to reside in *Asia*, he directly reflects upon them (1978: 906 [italics and capitals in the original]).

Keshub Chunder Sen was equally enthusiastic about re-asserting his Asianness. He asked: 'Shall we not magnify our race by proclaiming Christ Jesus as a fellow-Asiatic? Surely, the fact that Christ and other masters all belong to our nationality, and are all of Asiatic blood, causes a thrill of pride in every Eastern heart' (Sen 1904: 55-56). He said in another lecture,

> I rejoice, yea, I am proud, that I am Asiatic. And was not Jesus Christ Asiatic? [Deafening applause] Yes, and his disciples were Asiatic, and all the agencies primarily employed for the propagation of the Gospel were Asiatic. In fact, Christianity was founded and developed by Asiatics, in Asia. When I reflect on this, my love for Jesus becomes a hundredfold intensified; I feel him nearer my heart, and deeper in my national sympathies. Why should I then feel ashamed to acknowledge that nationality which he acknowledged? (1901: 33).

As a way of legitimizing European intervention, colonizers were actively involved in producing images which reinscribed the cultural and religious differences between the imperialists and the imperialized natives. One interesting aspect of the debate generated by the *Precepts of Jesus* was the deployment of the term 'heathen', both by the colonizer and the colonized. Joshua Marshman, the Baptist missionary, in his debate with Rammohun, kept on referring to the latter as 'heathen'. By using a term which was part of the imperial vocabulary of the time, he was denying the possibility that a native was capable of intelligent articulation. His was the rhetorical strategy of debasing the 'other', and making the arguments of the native unworthy. It was insensitive and injudicious on the part of Marshman to call Rammohun Roy a heathen, for he was well aware of him as a formidable scholar and a religious reformer who was at the forefront of emancipating his own Hindu tradition. Rammohun Roy considered the use of the term 'unchristian'. He appealed to the public to judge whether the compiler of the *Precepts of Jesus* was a believer or a heathen, based on the evidence of the text. He went further and claimed that it was the missionaries' presentation of Jesus which was imbued with heathen notions. Rammohun Roy was not a passive assimilator of colonial categories. He reappropriated the word initially mobilized by the missionaries, and recast it and turned it against them. In his case, it was an ironic reversal, and a good example of what Homi Bhabha would call the mimicry and mockery of authority.

Cultural Transactions: Hybridity and Cross-Culturality
The other characteristic features of post-coloniality are hybridity and cross-culturality. One of the significant marks of colonialism is the mixing of races and cultures. Cross-culturality and hybridity occur when an invading power tries to obliterate or assimilate the native cultures. Cultural studies view the hybridized nature of post-colonial writing not as a sign of weakness but of strength:

> Such writing focuses on the fact that the transaction of the post-colonial world is not a one-way process in which oppression obliterates the oppressed, or the coloniser silences the colonised in absolute terms. In practice it rather stresses the mutuality of the process. It lays emphasis on the survival, even under the most potent oppression, of the distinctive aspects of the culture of the oppressed and shows how these become an integral part of the new formulations which arise from the clash of cultures characteristic of imperialism (Ashcroft *et al.* 1995: 183).

These men saw their task as revitalizing Hinduism and modernizing Indian civilization by borrowing, infusing, and mixing them with

whatever was good in western tradition and Christianity. Rammohun
Roy saw a future in which the Vedanta would be amalgamated with
western scientific methods, and Indian moral values with western
political values. Similarly Keshub Chunder Sen wanted to synthesize
ancient wisdom with modern western enterprise.[6] Keshub Chunder's
New Dispensation Church had all the hallmarks of harmonizing and
synthesizing. Sen celebrated this 'critical synthesis' (Bikhu Parekh's
phrase) thus:

> All great religions are mine. Mine too is the mountain on which Christ
> Jesus preached his famous sermon. Mine also the Himalayas on which
> Aryan devotees lost themselves in contemplation. Mine likewise is the
> memorable Bo tree under whose shade the great Buddha attained final
> Beatitude. Sinai is mine, saith Asia, and the Jordan is mine, and the great
> Ganges is mine. The Vedas and the Bible are mine, the cross and crescent
> are mine (1904: 57).

In a lecture Keshub Chunder Sen gave in Calcutta, he put it thus:

> Thus shall we put on the new man, and say, the Lord Jesus is my will,
> Socrates is my head, Chaitanya my heart, the Hindu Rishi my soul, and
> the philanthropic Howard my right hand. And thus transformed into the
> new man, let each of us bear witness unto the new gospel. Let many-
> sided truth, incarnate in saints and prophets, come down from heaven and
> dwell in you, that you may have that blessed harmony of character, in
> which is the eternal life and salvation (1881: 28).

Seen generally from the Christian polemical point of view, such a
mixing and fusing is condemned as syncretistic, inauthentic and a
watering down of the gospel. But seen from the perspective of colonialism, it has an affirmative purpose. It is a sign of resistance and
survival, and an act of validation in the face of colonial hegemony.

3. *Some Concluding Observations*

Jesus who is the centre of Christian faith was now in the hands of
people who did not accept him on conventional Christian terms nor
perceive him through traditional biblical categories. These men were
able to incorporate Jesus into the Hindu framework without feeling
any need to give up their own religious tradition. For them, the gospel

---

6.   B. Parekh, *Colonialism, Tradition and Reform: An Analysis of Gandhi's
Political Discourse* (New Delhi: Sage Publications, 1989), p. 60.

of Jesus did not offer anything dramatically new or different from the teachings of their seers or their own sacred texts. In Jesus, or in his teachings, they did not see a new testament or fresh good news but the re-appearance or re-statement or re-localization of the eternal dharma. Jesus was, in essence, restating anew some overlooked aspects of the perennial message. Mozoomdar put it thus: '...each prophet has his personal surroundings, his peculiarities of time and circumstance. There is about him the local, the personal, the historical, as well as the universal... Those who leave these out of consideration can never understand the true character of the man whom they view as their exemplar' (1933: 16).

The thrust of their christological construction was that they had the innate capacity, denied to the missionaries, to refigure a Jesus appropriate to Indian context. They thought that they had a natural gift of spirituality, the power of discernment, and possessed the necessary cultural, national and spiritual ability to articulate who Jesus was better than the missionaries could. Being Brahmins, they believed that they had the inherent, divine gift of teaching others. Mozoomdar encapsulates their mood:

> It is the fact that the greatest religions of the world have sprung from Asia. It has, with some accuracy, been said, therefore, that it is an Asiatic only who can teach religion to Asia... But the efforts of European agencies, suggestive and helpful as they are, do not go far enough, do not go deep enough, but still float on the surface, and affect the merest externals of human life. It is a national ideal only that can touch the undercurrents of national trust and aspiration. And let us assure our European friends that, in religion at least, Hindus have a powerful national life, which remains all but utterly uninfluenced by foreign preaching (1933: 14).

At a time when missionaries were using Jesus to expose the deficiencies of Hindus, the Bengalis took it as their task to show how the ancient Asiatic tradition can elucidate their experience of Jesus. In confronting the negative European depictions, the colonized used the language and the technique provided by the colonizer. These were the anglicized Bengali gentry, who benefitted most from colonial rule. They even welcomed the British presence and never aimed for the physical removal of the British. Keshub Chunder Sen was seen among his own followers as a 'semi-Europeanized young innovator'.[7] He even

7.   D.G. Dalton, *Indian Idea of Freedom* (Gurgaon: The Academic Press, 1982), p. 40.

went so far as to say that the British nation had been 'brought here by the hand of Providence' (1904: 436). These Bengalis accepted the paradigm of representation manufactured by the colonizer. In the nineteenth century, there were two schools of thought which were influential in shaping the colonial cultural map—the Anglicists and the Orientalists. The former saw their task as vitalizing the moribund Indian culture by injecting western values, whereas the latter saw their task as sanctifying and elevating the ancient Hindu courtly culture as a way of preserving India. Inspired by these schools, these Bengalis sought to shape the Indian to meet the hostilities of the missionaries and their imperial demands. Though occupying distinctly different terrains, the imperialized and the imperializer were interwoven and locked together according to the parameters set by the dominant force.

It is paradoxical that for the restoration of self-confidence and pride in their national heritage, they drew on and transformed the landmark instances supplied mainly by the work of European scholars, who fabricated for them a monumentalized India. They exploited to the full the binary types generated by colonialism—Asia as spiritual, eternal, intuitive and ascetic—and transformed them to their own advantage in order to resist and survive. Negatively they were reinforcing further the image of the East as the alluring other. Positively they made use of the work of the Orientalists to make their own people realize that their culture was ancient and one of which they could be justifiably proud. They never spelt out what this 'Asianness' or 'Indianness' was that they were trying to recover. Though they reacted to the missionaries from the West, they themselves were missionaries, but missionaries with a difference, missionaries in the sense of negotiating a new sense and a new purpose for their own people whose lives were being dramatically re-shaped by colonial demands.

In reinvoking, mobilizing, and directing their attention to illustrious characteristics of Vedic and Sanskritic tradition, they not only over-looked the hierarchical features of ancient Indian courtly tradition, but also in the process erased the aspirations of Muslims, Dalits, the indigenous peoples and the rural poor, from their hermeneutical con-siderations. As Sumanta Banerjee put it, 'For them these lower orders still remained an invisible mass, their actual problem beyond the com-prehension of the educated Bengalis...' (1989: 640). How these sub-alterns have engaged in their internal decolonization and tried to recover their self-identity is another story.

One final comment. These Bengalis in a way set the trend for mobilizing ethnicity as a site for christological construction. Under colonial pressure, it was natural for them to turn inward and rebuild their wounded self image, by emphasizing Indianness, and infusing Jesus with worthwhile and distinctive Asian racial characteristics. In perceiving him as an Asiatic, or Oriental, what in effect they did was to ethnocize Jesus. Now, in a changed post-colonial context, to reiterate ethnic, racial and nationalistic traits will sound like racist exclusivism. Currently we witness an emergence of many an ethnocized Jesus—Jesus as Black, Native Indian, Hispanic, Chinese, etc. In the Fanonian hermeneutical schedule these ethnocized Christologies fall within the second phase, that of self-discovery and national pride.[8] As a way of repairing the lost dignity of the victims of imperialism, these constructions were a historical necessity. But Christology should go beyond the role of simply being a defensive ideology. At a time when one operates with multiple frames of reference and the maps of what it means to be an Asian or African are being redrawn, to reinvent Jesus with cultural traits may be a way of avoiding our present reality. If we persist with such a hermeneutical approach, we will be like the man in the Buddha's story who was so excited with the raft when crossing the river that he carried it with him wherever he went and was unwilling to part with it. As the Buddha would have said, an ethnocized Christology, or for that matter any Christology, is like a raft—it is for crossing over and not for clutching onto forever.

BIBLIOGRAPHY

Ashcroft, B., G. Griffiths and H. Tiffin (eds.)
1995   *The Post-Colonial Studies Reader* (London: Routledge).
Banerjee, S.
1989   *The Parlour and the Street: Elite and Popular Culture in Nineteenth Century Calcutta* (Calcutta: Seagull Books).
Mozoomdar, P.C.
1933   *The Oriental Christ* (Calcutta: Navavidhan Publication Committee [1833]).
Roy, R.
1978   *The English Works of Raja Rammohun Roy with an English Translation of Tuhfatul Muwahhiddin* (New York: AMS Press [1906]).

8.   Fanon's three phases are imitation, self-discovery and resistance. See his *The Wretched of the Earth* (Harmondsworth: Penguin Books, 1990 [1967]), pp. 178-79.

Sen, K.C.
    1881   'We Apostles of the New Dispensation' (pamphlet) (Calcutta: Navavidhan Publication Society).
    1901   *Keshub Chunder Sen's Lectures in India* (London: Cassell).
    1904   *Keshub Chunder Sen's Lectures in India* (London: Cassell).
Slater, T.E.
    1884   *Keshub Chunder Sen and the Brahma Samaj: Being a Brief Review of Indian Theism from 1830–1884 together with Selections from Mr Sen's Work* (Madras: Society for Promoting Christian Knowledge).

THE IMAGE OF CHRIST IN ISLAM: SCRIPTURE AND SENTIMENT

Mona Siddiqui

In an age of religious pluralism and an increasing emphasis on Muslim–Christian 'dialogue', there nevertheless remains in Muslim society an attitude of mistrust towards those outside the faith who wish to understand Islam. Aside from academic research by European scholars which quite often takes a critical view of some of the most fundamental areas of Muslim belief such as the Divine revelation of the Qur'an, and development and authenticity of Prophetic Traditions (*hadith*),[1] mistrust usually arises in response to a selective Christian appreciation of the role of the Prophet Muhammad and the ambivalent attitude towards the nature of his prophecy. Muslims regard criticism of the Prophet as a direct attack on their faith and are anxious to point out that though the Christian approach to Muhammad is sceptical at best, Islam has no difficulty in accepting Jesus as an eminent prophet and messenger of God and that, furthermore, he holds a special place in the Muslim religious and eschatological tradition. This comparison between the two messengers is erroneous to some extent and it reflects more the approach and prejudice of popular piety as opposed to the actual position that each messenger holds within the doctrines of his religion and the role he played in representing and conveying the Divine to his people.

In Christian theology, perhaps the one issue that has generated the most controversy is that of Christology. Speaking coherently of the divinity and humanity of Jesus is not only an issue that has occupied

---

1. See J. Burton, *The Collection of the Qur'an* (Cambridge: Cambridge University Press, 1977). The overall conclusion is that the Qur'an was 'edited' and 'checked' by the Prophet himself. Also the works of I. Goldziher, *Muhammedanische Studien* (Halle, 1890), II, pp. 1-274, a pioneering work in European scholarship on Islam bringing into question the authenticity of Prophetic Traditions by asserting that the majority do not belong to the time of the Prophet.

theologians and academics of religion, but it is also central to making the faith understood and accepted. Thus, it may be a matter of debate whether the use of a particularly Christian concept such as Christology, and all the issues associated with it, can be applied in the Islamic context. But in using this term even in an Islamic vision, all that is being discussed is the nature and person of Jesus; it does not imply an affirmation of any particular Christian perception. The position of Jesus is being observed within a specifically Muslim framework and the image that is presented is one that is largely dependent on the Qur'anic Revelation.

The belief that the Qur'an[2] is the very word of God and that Muhammad, chosen to be the last Prophet, was the recipient of this final divine Revelation, is the reality upon which the Muslim faith is based and developed. The descent of the Qur'an is God's intercession in human history. Revealed to Muhammad through the medium of the archangel Gabriel over a period of twenty years, the Qur'an is believed to be the Scripture that confirmed but superseded the previous Scriptures including the Torah and the Bible. The Qur'an fulfills what is missing or what has been distorted or misinterpreted from these earlier Scriptures. The concept of 'misinterpretation' implies either a misunderstanding of the earlier texts or inaccuracies in compiling earlier Revelation into the written form. It is in this wider context that the Qur'an must be appreciated though the criticism of this Muslim view of the Qur'an is that it accords the Qur'an an unfounded superiority. This is because while confirmation of the Bible and the Torah implies recognition of previous divine Scriptures, the status of the Qur'an as the last Revelation sets it apart as God's final Word in which Islam, the primordial religion, is restored.

There are many passages in the Qur'an which affirm the legitimacy of past revelations:

> Say, We believe in Allah and that which is revealed unto us and that which was revealed unto Abraham and Ishmael, and Isaac and Jacob and the tribes and that which Moses and Jesus received and that which the Prophets received from their Lord. We make no distinction between any of them (2.136).[3]

2. The word Qur'an literally means 'recitation'; the first Revelation to the Prophet began with the words 'Recite in the name of your Lord...'

3. I have generally relied on the English translation of the Qur'an by M. Pickthall. This particular edition is M. Pickthall, *Holy Quran* (Karachi: Taj, 1982). However,

These passages complement verses such as

> Verily We sent messengers before thee, among them those of whom We
> have told thee, and some of whom We have not told thee (40.78);

> Lo! those who believe, and those who are Jews and Sabaeans and
> Christians—whosoever believeth in Allah and the Last Day and doth
> right—there shall come no fear upon them neither shall they grieve (5.69).

There is running through verses such as these a sense of both unity
and continuity binding all Revelations. Furthermore, this is reinforced
in the Muslim tradition by the belief that all Scriptures belong to a
Heavenly Archetype, the 'Mother of Books'. The prophet Muhammad
is made to say in the Qur'an: 'I believe in any and every Book that
God has revealed' (42.15). Indeed the term 'Book' in the Qur'an is
often used not to denote any specific Scripture but as a generic term
for the totality of revealed Scriptures.[4] Though each has had an
exclusive manifestation, they are all emanating from the same divine
source. This has an interesting consequence for the Muslim for he can
feel assured though not complacent that his Scripture is a path to his
salvation as well as affording an embracing generosity to those of
other monotheistic traditions. It is after all God's will that there should
be a multiplicity of ways:

> For each We have appointed a divine law and a traced-out way. Had Allah
> willed, He could have made you one community. But that he may try you
> by that which He hath given you (He has made you as ye are) (5.48).

It is recognized of course that the situation is more complex than this,
that the real tension amongst people of different faiths lies in the
concept of religious exclusivity, an implicit belief or quite often a need
to 'prove' that their way is the *only* route to salvation, that all other
faiths are at best shadows of the One truth that they follow. The difficulty lies in reconciling God's universal love as an axiom of faith, with
the believer's conviction that truth and form are inseparable in religion.

If we examine this issue in the light of Muslim–Christian polemics,
it is reasonable to state that both faiths meet and part with the discussions on Jesus. While the figure of Jesus is doctrinally more central to
Christianity than to Islam, it is the differing perception of his status

where I have substituted my own translation, I have given Pickthall's in the footnotes.

4.   F. Rahman, *Major Themes of the Qur'an* (Minneapolis: Bibliotheca Islamica,
1980), p. 137.

upon which both faiths ultimately reject each other's message. From the Christian perspective, the popular expression of this rejection often includes the reductionist view of the Prophet Muhammad who is used as a comparison with Jesus and whose mission as a messenger is denied precisely as a result of this comparison. This is usually the result irrespective of the extent of the Christian's own veneration of Jesus, so that whether he interprets the language of Jesus' own divinity literally or metaphorically is of little significance. Before we embark upon this problem, we will briefly examine the image of Jesus that emerges from various verses in the Qur'an.

View of Jesus in the Qur'an

The proper name of Jesus in the Qur'an is 'Isa. There is some dispute as to the form of the name but it is generally accepted that 'Isa came from the Syriac Yeshu' which derived it from the Hebrew Yeshua.[5] The name 'Isa occurs 25 times in the Qur'an. In addition, reference to him as the Messiah and son of Mary means that he is spoken of on 35 occasions. Examples are

> We gave unto Jesus, son of Mary clear proofs...and We supported him with the holy Spirit (2.87).

> When the angels said, Oh Mary! Lo! Allah giveth thee glad tidings of a word from Him, whose name is the Messiah, Jesus son of Mary, illustrious in the world and the Hereafter and one of those brought near (unto Allah) (3.45).

> When Allah said, Oh Jesus! Lo! I am going to bring thy term in this world to an end and raise thee to myself. And I am cleansing thee of those who disbelieve (3.55).[6]

> Oh people of the Book, Do not exaggerate in your religion nor utter anything concerning Allah save the truth. The Messiah, Jesus, son of Mary was only a messsenger of Allah and His word which he cast upon Mary[7] and a spirit from Him. So believe in Allah and His messengers and do not

---

5. See G. Parrinder, *Jesus in the Qur'an* (Oxford: Oneworld Publications, 1995), p. 16. Professor Parrinder's listing of Qur'anic verses pertaining to Jesus has been of invaluable help in this paper.

6. Pickthall's translation of the first part of this verse reads, 'I am gathering thee and causing thee to ascend unto Me'.

7. Pickthall uses the phrase, 'conveyed unto Mary'.

say 'Three—Cease!' it is better for you!—Allah is Only one God. Far is it removed from His transcendant majesty that He should have a son (4.171).

We sent Jesus after them and gave Jesus, son of Mary the Gospel (57.27).

And when Jesus son of Mary said, Oh children of Israel! Lo! I am the messenger of Allah unto you, confirming that which was revealed before me in the Torah and bringing good tidings of a messenger who is to come after me whose name is the Praised one (61.6).

From this select referencing of Jesus' name in the Qur'an it will be seen that one of the commonest titles for him is 'son of Mary' or, in Arabic, 'Ibn Maryam'. Parrinder points out that this metonymic occurs 23 times in the Qur'an, sixteen times as 'Jesus, son of Mary' and seven times as 'son of Mary' alone or with some other title. In the Bible, 'son of Mary' occurs only once in the New Testament, Mk 6.3: 'Is not this, the carpenter, the son of Mary?'.[8] However, neither in the Qur'an nor in the Bible is she specifically referred to as the Virgin Mary though the Qur'an explicitly mentions her chastity:

And Mary, the daughter of Imran, who kept her virginity intact, We breathed into her of our spirit; and she believed in the words of her Lord and in His books and was of those who are resigned (66.12).

Both Islam and Christianity are agreed that Jesus had no human father but the Qur'an refers to this sublime status by speaking of him as 'son of Mary' and levelling the holiness of the son with the sanctity of the mother. Schuon explains that in the Islamic description Mary is seen as a devoted and obedient servant of God who believes sincerely in his revelations:

(Qanitin): the Arabic term implies the meaning not only of constant sub-mission to God, but also of absorption in prayer and invocation (qunut), meanings which coincide with the image of Mary spending her childhood in front of the prayer-niche and thus personifying contemplative prayer.[9]

There are many theories as to why this epithet should have been used. The use of the term 'Ibn Mariam' may be emphasizing Jesus' mortality like the other prophets of God, that Jesus like any human being was born of a woman. Or perhaps it draws attention to the miracle of Jesus' birth, that he was born without a father. What is established is

8.   Parrinder, *Jesus in the Qur'an*, p. 22.
9.   F. Schuon, *Dimensions of Islam* (London: George Allen & Unwin, 1970), p. 95.

that the Qur'an gives Mary an extremely honourable status. Muslim scholarship asserts that one of the reproaches made by Islam against the Jews is in their casting aspersions on Mary's character and chastity. The Qur'an categorically rejects any shame or stigma on Mary's part since she is the bearer of a messenger, she is the reminder to humanity of God's divine grace. Her purity is never in doubt, on the contrary it is exalted for indeed she is the 'most saintly' (5.75) and the one to whom the angel says,

> Allah has chosen thee and made thee pure, and hath preferred thee above all the women of creation (3.42).

This honorific description of Mary complements the status of Jesus who though a prophet is special by the very nature of his birth. Indeed when Mary is reproached for having given birth and thus of improper behaviour, the child himself speaks on her behalf from the cradle:

> I am the slave of Allah. He hath given me the Scripture and hath appointed me a Prophet (19.30).

Jesus is many things in the Qur'an. He is a sign to the world (19.21), a parable or example to the Children of Israel (43.59), a mercy from God (19.21), illustrious in this world and the hereafter (3.45), prophet and messsenger of God as well as spirit and word of God, *ruh* and *kalima* respectively.[10] It is these last two concepts around which there is controversy and a variety of interpretation. Jesus is said to be a spirit from God and the word of God (4.171). 'Jesus, son of Mary is…His word which He cast upon Mary and a spirit from Him. Oh Mary, Allah gives thee tidings of a word from Himself, whose name is the Messiah, Jesus' (3.40, 45). Though the nature of both these terms is controversial, nevertheless interpretations of Qur'anic verses such as this do not ascribe any sense of divinity to Jesus. Jesus is a spirit from God but he is a created spirit. Along with this concept, he is the word of God as being the word that was cast into Mary, the product of his divine will and command. This creative command is associated in the Qur'an both with the birth of Jesus and the creation of Adam. Both are events that came about with God's creative *kalima*, 'Be!' or '*kun!*' in Arabic:

> Lo! The likeness of Jesus with Allah is as the likeness of Adam. He created him from dust, then He said unto him, Be! and he is (3.59).

10. See Parrinder, *Jesus in the Qur'an*, for a comprehensive study of the different epithets describing him.

The absolute unity of God[11] is the central tenet of Islam and the believer is reminded of this constantly in the Qur'an. Note the short chapter, *sura* 112:[12]

> Say, He is One, Allah, the One! Allah the eternal; he hath neither brought forth nor hath he been brought forth; equal with him hath there been no-one.[13]

This sura may have been revealed as an attack on the polytheism of Arabia and the rejection of pagan deities. For it must be borne in mind that nascent Islam grew amidst a pagan people and idolatrous society. However, there are also direct references to the Christian concept of Jesus being the 'son' of God and the idea of association whereby God is said to have 'acquired' offspring:

> The Messiah, Jesus, son of Mary was only the messenger of Allah... Far is it removed from His transcendant Majesty that He should have a son (4.171).

> The Christians say that the Messiah is the son of Allah, that is what they say with their mouths conforming to what was formerly said by those who disbelieved. Allah Himself fights against them! How they are involved in falsehood (9.30).[14]

Apart from the verse 'They surely disbelieve who say: Lo! Allah is the third of three; when there is no God save the One God' (5.73), the Qur'an does not explicitly criticize any concepts of the Trinity as in the Christian sense. But in Muslim interpretation, the identification of God with Jesus, the Incarnation and the concept of the Trinity, admittedly a later development in Christianity's defense of God's unity (the Gospels mention Father, Son, and Holy Spirit, not Trinity), are all violations not expressions of the unity of God; this is because union with God rather than unity of God becomes the more apparent message of Christianity, thus widening the theological gap between the two religions. These concepts are based on association with God, the Absolute with the relative and may even be condemned as being *shirk*,

---

11. The word *tawhid* in Arabic denotes the Islamic belief in the essential unity of God.

12. A *sura* from the Qur'an is usually translated as a chapter.

13. Pickthall: 'Say: He is Allah, the One! Allah the eternally besought of all! He begetteth not nor was begotten. And there is none comparable unto Him.'

14. Pickthall uses the word 'imitate' instead of 'conforming' and ends with, 'How perverse are they!'

that is, associating partners with God, the gravest of all sins in Islam. As Eaton puts it, 'Islam cannot perceive of God descending in any form into the human matrix'.[15] No doubt Christians would deny that the Trinity amounts to tritheism and argue that theirs is as much a mono-theistic faith as Islam. For the Christian, frustration lies with the attitude of the Muslim who ultimately cannot appreciate the true nature of God's self-revelation in Jesus, so that the concept 'son of God' is devoid of any vulgar sense of physical procreation. Nevertheless, the problematic nature of the Trinity or at least its language of expression is viewed by Muslims as compromising the divine transcendence. Schuon states,

> For the Christians, to say that God is one means nothing if one does not add that God is three; for the Muslim, to say that He is three amounts to denying that He is one.[16]

For the Muslim, that the Qur'an accords Jesus a sublime status and that his birth was a miracle in itself does not pose a problem for Jesus' humanity and his rank within the prophetic line. God has chosen to create in this particular way but this creation is quite simply a mani-festation of his powers and does not encroach in any way upon his own transcendence.

Lastly it should be noted that the crucifixion of Jesus is important in the Qur'an as an event that did not lead to Jesus' death:

> They (the Jews) slew him not nor crucified him, but it appeared so unto them; and Lo! those who disagree concerning it are in doubt thereof; they have no knowledge thereof save pursuit of a conjecture; they slew him not for certain: But Allah took him up unto himself. Allah was ever Mighty, Wise. There is not one of the People of the Scripture but will believe in him before his death and on the Day of Resurrection, he will be a witness against them (4.157–159).

Muslim commentators have offered varying explanations of a substi-tute dying in place of Jesus, that Jesus did not die but was raised by God. What is controversial is that traditional Muslim belief views Jesus as an eschatological figure, who will return to earth in a second advent although many Muslim commentators have argued that the death of

15. G. Eaton, *Islam and the Destiny of Man* (London: George Allen & Unwin, 1985), p. 45.

16. F. Schuon, *From the Divine to the Human* (Indiana: World Wisdom Books, 1981), p. 42.

Jesus is implied in the verse, 'Allah took him up unto Himself'. He did not die on the cross but his term in this life ended when God raised him to himself. What this shows is that there are themes concerning Jesus in the Qur'an which from the Christian perspective appear even more problematic precisely because there are no explanations for these issues within the Islamic tradition. What has to be understood though is that, within the Muslim context, this type of speculation is not central to its theology, and that, furthermore, the supernatural events concerning Jesus' life are one of the many manifestations of God's supreme powers; the Qur'an is a reminder that the status of Jesus remains firmly within the human domain and that he is a human prophet in a long line of prophets who came with a book and a mission.

What has been said so far reflects the significance if not the centrality of the figure of Jesus within Muslim thought. It is perhaps worth finishing this section by reference to our opening passages that Islam is obliged to admit the prophecy of Jesus even though his message may not be viewed as the final revelation. The denial of even one of the messengers or messages is tantamount to a denial of all the messengers and messages including ultimately the Qur'an itself. In fact a well-known credal statement attributed to one of the most eminent theologians and jurists within Islam says,

> Whosoever believes all that he is bound to believe, except for saying, 'I do not know whether Moses or Jesus, peace be upon them, are or are not among the messengers of Allah', he is an infidel.[17]

The Prophecy of Muhammad

It was established at the outset that the Qur'an is viewed by Muslims as the final Revelation, the very speech of God and that the recipient of this message, Muhammad, is the last in the line of prophets chosen by God. There is no mystery or miracle surrounding the events of his birth; the miracle lies in the Revelation of the Qur'an which he received through the medium of the angel Gabriel. The Prophet's task was to spread God's words according to the directions given to him by God. The importance of the human element in the revelation of the Qur'an lies with the persona of the Prophet. As the revealer of God's sacred law, obedience to Muhammad and acceptance of his exalted position is

17. Eaton, *Islam and the Destiny of Man*, p. 19.

the nucleus of the Muslim faith. The bipartite statement of the shahada, the credo of the Muslim faith, 'I bear witness that there is no God but God and that Muhammad is the Messenger of God', is a testimony to the Prophet's exalted position. There is no doubt that Muslim piety is very often centred on the veneration of the Prophet, he is seen as the link to God. Love of the Prophet constitutes a fundamental element in Islamic spirituality as Muslims see in the person and role of the Prophet the prototype of the ideal man, the embodiment of all virtues but always mortal, devoid from any sense of divine essence.

Therefore, criticism of the Prophet is tantamount to rejection of Islam for it is generally accepted among pious Muslims that the Prophet was living Islam; he represents the Message that is Islam. Perhaps the severest reproach against many eminent non-Muslim scholars lies in their unspoken assumption that Muhammad was the 'author' of the Qur'an. Without wishing to reject the view outright that Islam is based on some form of revelation or inspiration, though it is important to distinguish the supremacy of revelation over inspiration, they limit the miracle of the Qur'an by defining it as the product of either Muhammad's mental genius or his mental degeneration. He is called a sorceror, one possessed with an evil spirit, a madman, a poet, and a soothsayer. The Qur'an itself refutes the allegations of authorship which were made upon him during his life:

> Those who disbelieve say: This is naught but a lie that he hath invented, and other folk have helped him with it, so that they have produced a slander and a lie. And they say: fables of the old men which he hath had written down so that they are dictated to him morn and evening. Say (unto them O Muhammad): He who knoweth the secrets of the heavens and the earth, hath revealed it. Lo! He is ever Forgiving, Merciful (25.4-6).

But many non-Muslim Islamicists see the foundation of his claim to prophecy as resting upon these very refutations. Verses from the Bible itself which are used by the Muslim scholars as indications of Muhammad's advent are dismissed as naive and ignorant and not worthy of serious consideration by most Christian theologians. Perhaps this is the real problem within interfaith dialogue that any scriptural cross-referencing is regarded as inventive nonsense. Since most religious traditions look for the sacred in the written word, interpretation of religious texts from outside the faith is regarded with caution or dismissed. This poses a particular problem for Islam because, though the third of the monotheistic Semitic faiths, it is not regarded as a unique confirmation of the Judaeo-Christian tradition. Thus, neither its Scripture nor its prophet is seen as a confirmation of what preceded or a prophecy that was foretold. An example of this has been quoted by Martin Lings who refers to an argument put forward by Schuon concerning the following verses:

> I have yet many things to say unto you but you cannot bear them now. Howbeit when he, the Spirit of truth, is come, he will guide you into all truth (Jn 16.12-13).

Schuon states that the Christian identification of these promises with the miracle of Pentecost does not mean that they cannot also and above all refer to the Revelation of Islam, for sacred utterances can generally be taken in more ways than one. 'If Muhammad is a true Prophet, the passages referring to the Paraclete must inevitably concern him—not exclusively but eminently—for it is inconceivable that Christ, when speaking of the future, should have passed over in silence a mani-festation of such magnitude.'[18]

This is precisely the problem—'if Muhammad is a true Prophet'. This touches not only upon the persona of the Prophet as a true and sincere person, but as God's final messenger; accepting the existence of Muhammad and showering him with favourable magnanimous epithets mean nothing unless his prophecy is also acknowledged.

The other issue pertaining to the origin of the Qur'an lies in the views insisting that its historical antecedents are either the Jewish or Christian Scriptures. Exactly what is meant by this is unclear mainly because the criticisms range from Muhammad having written the Qur'an himself after hearing the stories from the Judaeo-Christian traditions, to Islam being no more than a form of Christian heresy. Islamic thought does not generally deny that there was widespread diffusion of Jewish and Christian ideas which would have influenced the traditions of the emerging community, but to stretch this argument to the point where Islam is reduced to being no more than a byproduct of the Judaeo-Christian tradition is to destroy the divine nature of the Qur'an and dismiss Islam altogether. Again what is brought into doubt is the prophecy of Muhammad so that the Revelation of the Qur'an is reduced to Muhammad's own 'ideas'. Even under the guise of a sym-pathetic conclusion, Montgomery Watt states of Muhammad,

18. M. Lings, *Symbol and Archetype, A Study of the Meaning of Existence* (Cambridge: Quinta Essentia, 1991), pp. 39-40.

> Not all the ideas that he proclaimed are true and sound, but by God's grace he had been able to provide men with a better religion than they had before.[19]

One assumes that the 'before' refers not to Christianity as Professor Watt is himself a Christian, but most probably paganism. But as Gai Eaton argues,

> Transpose this to the Christian context and it might reasonably be asked how a believing Christian would respond to the statement that 'not all Jesus' ideas were true and sound', but that Christianity represented an advance on Greek and Roman religion.[20]

The notion that Islam has elements that are socially and morally good, but that it cannot either historically or theologically represent the Truth lies at the root of Christian rejection of the religion and its Prophet. But it is not only Muhammad's relationship vis-a-vis revelation that is questioned. Perhaps even more offensive to the Muslim psyche is the non-Muslim's particular understanding of his personality. This stems from comparing Muhammad with Jesus and concluding that Muhammad was too human, and that too great a part of his life centred upon the fulfilment of earthly duties and the satisfaction of earthly pleasures. References to the plurality of wives and fondness for perfume are seen as reflections of a voluptuous nature, devoid of any spiritual reality. What is ignored is that both messengers had a completely different role in the scheme of things ordained by God. Whereas Jesus' life exemplified self-denial, love and sacrifice for humanity, all aspects of a suffering God, that of Muhammad was based on the fulfilment of an earthly as well as a spiritual life. The primary aim was to show how man could live God's will and law in every aspect of life, that is, worshipping, eating, drinking, marriage, business ethics, etc. This meant actively partaking in all the different areas of life for all was a reflection of the religion; the secular does not exist.

Observance of the law in Islam amounts to obedience to God; it permeates every aspect of earthly life as well as being the key to salvation. In the implementation of personal and social duties in accordance with the law of Islam, man is constantly remembering God and living God's will. Invocation through prayer is perhaps the most conscious way of drawing nearer to God in all religions, but in Islam,

19. Cf. Eaton, *Islam and the Destiny of Man*, p. 10.
20. Eaton, *Islam and the Destiny of Man*, p. 10.

to live according to God's will is regarded as the utmost challenge. Muhammad's mission was not only to reveal God's warnings and extol his mercy but to exemplify the totality of life in its earthly manifestation as well as its spiritual dimensions. The Prophet combined his duties towards his family and community with a life of austerity and relative asceticism. This included night-time vigil and prayers, supplication to God in the privacy of his own chambers as well as in the public arena of the mosque. This should not be interpreted as an apologetic defense of the Prophet but quite simply as the depiction of the twin realities of his life.

It should be noted that although the concept of a pious ascetism is within Islamic culture, any form of celibacy or monasticism in enclosed communities in the Christian sense is deplored. But far from seeing this as a perfection of life, constructive and all-embracing, critics of Muhammad view it as an inadequacy in prophethood. It does not reflect moral excellence or purity. Muhammad's ethos on life is contrasted with that of Jesus who from the Christian perspective symbolizes love and sacrifice and only through whom man can achieve salvation in the hereafter. What is ignored is that in Muhammad's life, it is God's will which is realized through Muhammad, but that it is God not the Prophet whose mercy will ultimately reward humanity.

The accusation that Muhammad was too involved in all that was sensual is an incongruous comparison with the life of Jesus whose teachings were basically life-denying. In reply to the Christian objection that there is in Islam a tendency towards the sensual in life, the Muslim argument is that Islam's perception of sensual pleasures is that they are earthly projections of the paradisal archetypes, not a rejection of spirituality. As Schuon states,

> Christianity distinguishes between the carnal in itself and the spiritual in itself, and is logical in maintaining this alternative in the hereafter; Paradise is by definition spiritual, therefore it excludes the carnal. Islam which distinguishes between the carnal that is gross and the carnal that is sanctified, is just as logical in admitting the latter into its paradise.[21]

To conclude I would say that in order to understand the nature of Muhammad's prophecy, it should perhaps be realized that the Muslim develops his sense of Islam through the words and actions of the

---

21. F. Schuon, *Islam and the Perennial Philosophy* (World of Islam Festival Publishing Company Ltd, 1976), p. 19.

Prophet. They are the directive force behind his piety and thus to diminish them or ridicule any motives is abhorrent to his sensibilities. Thus, if the Christian can accuse the Muslim of rejecting salvation by not understanding the love and humility represented in Christ, the Muslim argues that the Christian starts with rejection, that is, the denial that the Qur'an is divine Revelation. If the reality of the Divine is denied, then the messenger loses his significance as the conveyor of God's will. We are then left with a Christian prophet who is revered as God incarnate and a Muslim messenger who is reduced to the status of a false prophet.

LIBERATING CHRISTOLOGY:
IMAGES OF CHRIST IN THE WORK OF ALOYSIUS PIERIS*

David Tombs

Aloysius Pieris is a Sri Lankan Jesuit who has devoted his working
life to inter-faith dialogue and grass-root social activism. The distinctive Asian liberation theology that he draws from these experiences
presents profound challenges to traditional western theology. This
paper explores the key elements in his theology and relates them to his
understanding of Christ's baptism and crucifixion. His interpretation
of these two events is shown to provide the liberating images of Christ
that are central to his daily work. To appreciate Pieris's use of these
images it is first necessary to describe the context of his work (part 1)
and his principal theological concerns (part 2). It will then be possible
to consider his understanding of the images in more detail (part 3), and
to interpret them in terms of a 'liberating Christology', which is to
say, both a 'liberation of Christology' and a 'Christology of liberation'.

1. The Life and Work of Aloysius Pieris[1]

Pieris has been a visiting lecturer at many western academic institutions and lectures annually in the Philipines as Visiting Professor at

* My interest in the work of Aloysius Pieris first arose during a year I spent as
an Ecumenical Fellow at Union Theological Seminary, New York, where Pieris was
Visiting Professor in Spring 1988. Further research for this paper was carried out
during a four-week study visit to Sri Lanka, based at Tulana Dialogue Centre, in the
summer of 1994. I am greatly indebted to all at Tulana who contributed to my stay in
different ways and wish to thank my home institution, Roehampton Institute London,
for the research grant that supported the trip.
    1. For further biographical information, see D.W. Ferm, *Profiles in Liberation:
Thirty Six Portraits of Third World Theologians* (Mystic, CN: Twenty Third
Publications, 1988), pp. 96-101. Regrettably there is little secondary literature on
Pieris's work. Ulrich Dornberg's general account of Sri Lankan contextual theologies

the East Asian Pastoral Institute in Manila.[2] However, the primary focus of his work is determined by his pastoral work in his local context. Pieris is founder, and current director, of the Tulana Dialogue Centre at Gonawala-Kelaniya, just outside the Sri Lankan capital Colombo. His work at Tulana has a profound influence on his theology and his daily involvement with the religious and social challenges of Sri Lankan society determines both the style and the substance of his writing.[3]

Pieris was born in 1934 and grew up in a Christian family close to the Jesuit seminary in Kandy.[4] During his adolescence he was a frequent

---

(*Searching through the Crisis: Christians, Contextual Theology and Social Change in Sri Lanka in the 1970s and 1980s* [Logos, 31; Colombo: Centre for Society and Religion, 1992]) is an invaluable work for anyone interested in contextual theology in Sri Lanka and has an excellent bibliography. However, Dornberg's material specific to Pieris is relatively brief and only permits an overview of his main ideas. N. Abeysingha is useful in the same way but has even less on Pieris (*The Radical Tradition: The Changing Shape of Theological Reflection in Sri Lanka* [Colombo: The Ecumenical Institute, 1985], see pp. 127-32), and D.W. Ferm is even briefer (*Third World Theologians: An Introduction* [Maryknoll, NY: Orbis Books, 1986], pp. 86-87).

    2.   For example, in Rome at the Gregorian University, in the United Kingdom at Oxford and Cambridge Universities, and in the United Stat at the Graduate Theological Union (Berkeley), Washington Theological Union (Washington, DC), Union Theological Seminary (New York) and Vanderbilt University (Nashville, TN).

    3.   In view of his theological priorities and working environment it is hardly surprising that Pieris's publications in English take the form of numerous journal articles and conference papers rather than full-length books. He has served as editor of the Sri Lankan journal *Dialogue* for many years, and his many articles and editorials are essential reading for anyone seriously interested in his writing. Another Sri Lankan journal, *Outlook*, offers interesting examples of his very early work, often in a light-hearted and satirical style (see *Outlook* 2-6, 1969-73).

    Perhaps one of the reasons that his work has not attracted more secondary literature is that it is only recently that convenient collections of his writings have been available in book form. Many of his significant works up to the late 1980s have been published as *An Asian Theology of Liberation* (Faith Meets Faith Series; Maryknoll, NY: Orbis Books; Edinburgh: T. & T. Clark, 1988) and *Love Meets Wisdom: A Christian Experience of Buddhism* (Faith Meets Faith Series; Maryknoll, NY: Orbis Books, 1988). A third collection, including his more recent work, is currently in press: *Fire and Water: Basic Issues in Asian Buddhism and Christianity* (Maryknoll, NY: Orbis Books, 1996).

    4.   Kandy has been the centre of Sinhalese Buddhist cultural identity since colonial

visitor to the seminary and when he was nineteen years old he started his Jesuit training. He was trained first in India (Sacred Heart College, Shembaganur, LPh 1959) before completing an external BA degree in Sanskrit and Pali from the University of London (1961) and an STL degree from the Pontifical Theological Faculty in Naples (1966). His ordination, in 1965, came at a time of great change in the Church. The Second Vatican Council (1962–65) inaugurated a new spirit of Catholic openness to the world that profoundly influenced his sense of vocation in an Asian context.[5] Pieris has taken up the direction indicated by the Council in two key areas that mark his theology: inter-faith dialogue and concern for the poor and oppressed.

After completing his theological studies in Naples, Pieris had the opportunity to further his understanding of Buddhism and the other non-Christian religions of his native Sri Lanka. He taught Asian religions at the Gregorian University in Rome for a year and explored possibilities for a doctorate in Buddhist Studies at a western university. However, he decided instead to return to Sri Lanka for his PhD because he wished to encounter Buddhism at an everyday level, as well as making an academic study of Pali texts. This was to prove a decisive turning point. Pieris's proposal faced initial resistance from the Buddhist monk who was to be his supervisor and he had to demonstrate both the seriousness of his quest and his humility in undertaking it before he could begin.[6] It was some time before he gained the respect and trust of the monk but he learnt much about Christian–Buddhist relations in the process and in 1972 he was the first Christian to gain a doctorate in Buddhist studies awarded by the University of

times. The independent Kandyan kingdom successfully resisted both Portuguese and Dutch colonialists in the seventeenth and eighteenth centuries. On the history of the Kandyan kingdom and its relations to the European colonial powers, see K.M. de Silva, *A History of Sri Lanka* (London: C. Hurst; Berkeley and Los Angeles: University of California Press, 1981), pp. 113-235.

5.   Pieris (*An Asian Theology of Liberation*, p. xv) writes: 'The Second Vatican Council was for me a point of departure rather than a point of arrival, as I joined my Asian colleagues over twenty years ago in the challenging task of applying the conciliar teachings to our Asian context and of trying to give concrete Asian form to the spirit of the Council'.

6.   Pieris describes how he gained the trust of his supervisor and the reasons for initial suspicions over the proposal in 'Two Encounters in My Theological Journey', in R.S. Sugirtharajah (ed.), *Frontiers in Asian Christian Theology: Emerging Trends* (Maryknoll, NY: Orbis Books, 1988), pp. 141-46 (141-43).

Sri Lanka.[7] This 'double formation', Christian and Buddhist, and the attitude it requires, has a profound influence on his theological work. Pieris claims that it is common for Sri Lankan Buddhist monks to have this double formation but much rarer for Christians to be in the same position. Describing his theological vocation he says,

> ...having received my theological education in Europe and a Buddhist education in Asia, I feel obliged in conscience to exercise a ministry of reconciliation whereby the *implicit judgement of the non-Christian East is brought to the threshold of Western theology.*[8]

The other major determinant in Pieris's work is his concern for the poor and oppressed. Pieris's commitment to liberation and social justice is the basis for the common ground between his work and that of other Third World liberation theologies that have developed since Vatican II. While Pieris was completing his doctorate in Sri Lanka the first works of liberation theology were being published in Latin America. However, Pieris has always sought a distinctively Asian approach to liberation especially in relation to poverty. In some of his most important works he has been critical of the way that some aspects of Latin American liberation theology have been applied, or as he would see it misapplied, to the Asian context. The most significant difference, for Pieris, is that the Asian context is characterized not only by a need for liberation but also by the fact that Christianity is a minority religion.[9] An Asian liberation theology cannot address one at the expense of the other. Pieris's work is to be understood as his response to both challenges posed by his Asian context.

---

7.   Pieris retains a keen interest in Sanskrit and Pali studies in addition to his theological writing. According to Dornberg (*Searching through the Crisis*, p. 140), he even prefers to be known as an Indologist and does not apply the term 'theologian' to himself.

8.   Pieris, *Love Meets Wisdom*, p. 18.

9.   See especially his influential keynote speeches at Ecumenical Association of Third World Theologians Conferences in 1979 (in Wennappuwa, Sri Lanka) and 1981 (in New Delhi, India). Both his papers ('Towards an Asian Theology of Religion: Some Religio-Cultural Guidelines', in V. Fabella [ed.], *Asia's Struggle for Full Humanity* [Maryknoll, NY: Orbis Books, 1981] and 'The Place of Non-Christian Religions and Cultures in the Evolution of Third World Theology', in V. Fabella and S. Torres [eds.], *Irruption of the Third World* [Maryknoll, NY: Orbis Books, 1983]) address the need for an Asian liberation theology to be worked out with regard for other major world religions. Both papers are republished in Pieris, *An Asian Theology of Liberation*, pp. 69-86 and 87-110.

2. *The Twin Poles of Pieris's Theology*

Pieris offers his work as a response to what he calls 'the twin poles' of Asian reality, that is to say: Asian religiosity and Asian poverty. Asian religiosity creates a challenge for dialogue; Asian poverty creates a challenge for liberation. According to Pieris neither pole of Asian reality should be addressed without simultaneous reference to the other. Pieris sees the commitment to dialogue and the commitment to liberation as inseparable.

a. *Asian Religiosity and the Commitment to Dialogue*
Christians comprise only about 7.5% of the 17 million total population in Sri Lanka.[10] By contrast about 70% of Sri Lankans are Buddhist, 15% are Hindus and 7.5% are Muslims.[11] Pieris is keenly aware that Christianity is a minority religion and that during the colonial period Christianity was a privileged religion and a religion of the privileged. He argues that the legacy of hostilities from these times has been disastrous. Christian relations with other faiths, especially Buddhism, are severely affected by this colonial heritage.[12] During the nineteenth century Christianity was intimately linked to the political and cultural imperialism of the British. Protests against colonialism were also against Christianity.[13] Buddhism, the single most important

10. The Christian minority is strongly Catholic (approximately 90%) rather than Protestant.

11. The divide between Buddhists and Hindus is rooted and reinforced along ethnic and linguistic lines. The Buddhist majority are Sinhalese (about three-quarters of the population) and the Hindus are Tamil (about one-fifth of the population). For a detailed description of ethnic tension in the late 1980s, see M. Ram, *Sri Lanka: The Fractured Island* (Harmondsworth: Penguin Books, 1989).

12. Pieris, *Love Meets Wisdom*, pp. 83-88.

13. Pieris (*Love Meets Wisdom*, p. 130) cites the great Buddhist revivalist Anagarika Dharmapala as an example of this: 'Dharmapala, took delight in making odious comparisons between the two founders. The "Nazarene Carpenter", as he referred to Jesus with disdain, had no sublime teachings to offer and understandably so, because his parables not only reveal a limited mind but they also impart immoral lessons and impractical ethics.' See A. Dharmapala, *Return to Righteousness: A Collection of Speeches, Essays and Letters of the Anagarika Dharmapala* (ed. A. Gurugue; Colombo: Government Press, 1965), pp. 447-76.

For a detailed study of the relationship between Christian missionaries and Sri Lankan Buddhists in the nineteenth century, see E. Harris, *Crises, Competition and*

element in Sinhalese nationalist heritage, played a leading role in this struggle. As a result Buddhist–Christian relations have been marked by continuous suspicion and tension. It is against this historical back-drop that Pieris's work for a new Buddhist–Christian relationship in Sri-Lanka should be understood.

Pieris sees Christianity and Buddhism as compatible partners rather than opposed competitors. He claims that serious misunderstandings on both sides have contributed to the hostile competition between them. A new approach to dialogue is required that recognizes the differences between them as mutually complementary rather than mutually exclusive.[14]

Pieris's argument is that Buddhism and Christianity are best understood as emphasizing alternative 'idioms of salvation'. Pieris claims that Buddhism and Christianity share a liberating core which can and should provide the basis for Christians and Buddhists to work together *for human liberation*. However, the liberating core is expressed according to the different 'idiom' emphasized in each religion. The idiom emphasized in Buddhism is *gnosis* or *wisdom* and the idiom stressed in Christianity is *agape* or *love*. By 'idiom' Pieris means the underlying orientation, or expressive key, of the language framework. He argues that both Buddhism and Christianity should be understood as rooted in alternative language frameworks: liberative knowledge and redemptive love. He therefore cautions members of either religion against making simplistic and reductionist judgments about the other. Proper understanding of the relation between Christianity and Buddhism rests on the recognition that their primary differences arise from their alternative idiomatic emphases rather than an unbridgeable conflict of truth. Pieris writes,

Conversion: The British Encounter with Buddhism in Nineteenth Century Sri Lanka (Unpublished PhD thesis, Postgraduate Institute of Pali and Buddhist Studies, University of Kelaniya, Sri Lanka, 1993).

14. For example, one of the differences that Pieris specifically rejects as mis-leading is a geographical contrast between Buddhism and Christianity as 'eastern' and 'western'. Pieris writes (*Love Meets Wisdom*, pp. 10-11): 'First of all, one is astounded by the way the Sino-Indian religions are labelled "Eastern"; for it implies that the Judeo-Christian heritage with which they are contrasted is Western! In fact there is no surviving major world religion that is not Eastern. The basis on which religions are divided into "Eastern" and "Western" cannot, therefore, be geographical.'

We are dealing here with *two language games*, each having its own set of rules. One game should not be judged/played according to the rules of the other. Thus, the Christian mystic speaks in terms of 'sin and grace', but the gnostic vocabulary of the Buddhist arahant knows only of 'ignorance and knowledge'. The gnostic process of realizing an 'Impersonal I' and the agapeic encounter with a 'personal Thou' imply two modes of religious discourse, each having its own logic and its own grammar and syntax.[15]

Furthermore, Pieris views the two idioms as 'complementary' alternatives not only because they are equally valid and *compatible* with each other but because they are *necessary* to each other. As he puts it,

They are certainly not soteriological alternatives or optional paths to human liberation. They are two mystical moods that can alternate according to the spiritual fluctuations of individuals, groups, and even of entire cultures, without either of them allowing itself to be totally submerged by the other... They are, in other words, two irreducibly distinct languages of the spirit, each incapable, unless aided and complemented by the other, of mediating and adequately expressing the human encounter with the ultimate.[16]

Gnosis and agape are mutually dependent, neither is sufficient on its own:

... both gnosis and agape are necessary precisely because each in itself is *inadequate* as a medium, not only for experiencing but also for expressing our intimate moments with the Ultimate Source of Liberation. They are, in other words, complementary idioms that need each other to mediate the self-transcending experience called 'salvation'.[17]

Pieris makes clear that, although he sees each religion as having a dominant idiom, both religions are influenced by the other idiom to some extent. Pieris's distinction between Christianity and Buddhism in terms of agape and gnosis is a distinction of emphasis. Neither idiom is exclusive to either religion. It would therefore be wrong to typify either religion exclusively in terms of one or the other. An idiom may, at times, be submerged, but it is never entirely absent. Pieris points to gnostic traditions in Christianity and agapeic influences in Buddhism. For example, Pieris cites Christian mystics, in particular Teresa of Avila, as an example of the Christian gnostic tradition.[18] Pieris

15. Pieris, *Love Meets Wisdom*, p. 85.
16. Pieris, *Love Meets Wisdom*, pp. 9-10.
17. Pieris, *Love Meets Wisdom*, p. 111.
18. Pieris, *Love Meets Wisdom*, p. 85. On the 'gnostic agape of Christians' and

concludes that 'Any valid spirituality, Christian or otherwise, *must* and, as history shows, *does* retain both poles of religious experience'.[19]

In the encounter of Buddhist gnosis and Christian agape both religions can learn from engagement with the idiom emphasized by the other. Each religion comes to a more complete understanding of itself as it rediscovers its own submerged idiom. Pieris argues that 'today more than ever, we Christians should be made aware that gnosis and agape are the two eyes of the soul'.[20] Buddhism prompts Christians to recognize that another legitimate way of seeing and interpreting reality exists.[21] For Pieris, therefore, authentic inter-religious dialogue offers three different types of insight: first, greater understanding of another religion; secondly, deeper understanding of one's own religion; and finally, fuller understanding of the ultimate reality that all religions strive to express. However, Pieris's radical openness to Asian religiosity, shown in his attitude to Buddhism, is only one part of his response to Asian reality. It would be wrong to draw any conclusions on Pieris's attitude to Asian religiosity without considering his engagement with Asian poverty. His attitude to Asian religiosity and the commitment to dialogue cannot be separated from his attitude to Asian poverty and his commitment to liberation.

b. *Asian Poverty and the Commitment to Liberation*
Sri Lanka, or Ceylon as it was until 1972, was under the influence of European powers for approximately four hundred years: the Portuguese from the mid-sixteenth century to 1658, the Dutch from 1658–1796 and the British from 1796 until independence in February 1948. At independence it inherited many of the typical problems of post-colonial Third World countries: an economy that was overdepen-

the 'agapeic gnosis of Buddhism', see pp. 114-19. Pieris is careful to distance valid 'Christian gnosticism' from the gnostic movement of the second century that was judged as heretical.

19. Pieris, *Love Meets Wisdom*, p. 10.

20. Pieris, *Love Meets Wisdom*, p. 86.

21. It should be emphasized that Pieris does not see dialogue as an academic luxury but an urgent necessity for many global concerns. For example, Pieris (*Love Meets Wisdom*, p. 86) links the need for dialogue with the current ecological crisis: 'As with God-experience, so also with regard to the external world, we can adopt *two postures*; that of the Christian who delights in it and that of the Buddhist who keeps a critical distance from it. Each attitude has its own danger: stark consumerism and stoic indifferentism, respectively.'

dent on agricultural export (especially tea) and a social structure marked by a wide gap between the powerful rich and the powerless poor. Since the mid-1980s the situation in Sri Lanka has become particularly tragic.[22] The explosion of ethnic tensions in 1983 eventually resulted in a bitter civil war. On one side, the Sinhala dominated government, on the other side, the Liberation Tigers of Tamil Eelam and other militant Tamil separatists in the north and east. The intervention of an Indian Peacekeeping Force (1987–90) failed to resolve the war and despite brief periods of hope during the 1990s the fierce ethnic conflict continues. Over one million Tamils have become refugees as a result.

On top of this, from 1987–89 a Sinhala youth uprising against the government brought chaos and terror to much of the rest of the island, especially to the south.[23] The organization behind the insurgency was the Janatha Vimukhti Peramuna (JVP or People's Liberation Front) which had emerged in the 1960s and had been at the forefront of a youth uprising in April 1971.[24] The ferocity of the second rebellion convulsed much of the island and the brutality of government repression that followed compounded the horror. Retaliation against the JVP and their alleged supporters left an estimated 30,000 Sinhala youth dead or 'disappeared' at the hands of government death-squads.[25] Against the background of these recent tragedies the Asian human rights 'Asia Watch' describes the situation in Sri Lanka as

22. For an accessible introduction to recent Sri Lankan history by a western journalist, see W. McGowan, *Only Man is Vile: The Tragedy of Sri Lanka* (New York: Farrar, Strauss & Giroux; London: Picador, 1993). For more detailed information and analysis the so-called 'pink pages' of the Sri Lankan *Christian Worker* are indispensable. This widely-respected journal, published quarterly by the Christian Workers Fellowship, offers excellent coverage of the economic, political, social, ethnic and religious problems that have beset Sri Lanka in recent years.

23. See C.A. Chandraprema, *Sri Lanka: The Years of Terror—The JVP Uprising 1987–1989* (Colombo: Lake House Bookshop, 1991); R. Gunaratna, *Sri Lanka: A Lost Revolution? The Inside Story of the JVP* (Colombo: Institute of Fundamental Studies, 1990).

24. For a bibliography on the first JVP uprising, see H.A.I. Goonetileke, 'The Sri Lanka Insurrection of 1971: A Select Bibliographical Commentary', in B.L. Smith (ed.), *Religion and the Legitimation of Power in South Asia* (International Studies in Sociology and Social Anthropology, 25; Leiden: Brill, 1978), pp. 134-83.

25. See McGowan, *Only Man is Vile*, p. 376.

'human suffering on an almost incalculable scale'.[26]

1. *The struggle for liberation from forced poverty.* The poor and powerless, both Sinhalese and Tamil, have borne the brunt of Sri Lanka's economic and social problems. The peasants and the workers, the vast majority of the Sri Lankan people, continue to face a life of intense hardship.[27] It is their experiences that form the second pole of Pieris's thought. Pieris is committed to the fundamental principle of liberation theology: God is on the side of the poor and oppressed.[28] As an influential member of the Ecumenical Association of Third World Theologians during its early years, Pieris shared his colleagues' insistence that the struggle for the liberation of the oppressed should be a fundamental theme within Christian theology. Pieris affirms the preferential option for the poor advocated by Latin American liberation theologians and describes the concern for the poor as the most fundamental of biblical themes:

> The Ecumenical Association of Third World Theologians (EATWOT) has made repeated appeals to the universal church to focus its attention on the plight of the poor as the pole of reference in its theology, and to make the poor both the point of departure and the point of arrival of its spirituality inasmuch as God's concern for the poor is the axial theme of the Bible as a whole.[29]

Pieris recognizes that Christianity has often been, and in many ways

26. Cited in McGowan, *Only Man is Vile*, p. 377. As McGowan notes it is tragically ironic that the island was once called 'Serendip' by Arab traders, for its apparently happy good fortunes.

27. The average per capita income for Sri Lanka in 1992 was $540 (c. £360). This is to be compared with the $17,790 (£11,860) average per capita income for the United Kingdom in 1992. See R.R. Bissio (ed.), *A Third World Guide 1995/96* (Oxford: Oxfam, Instituto del Tercer Mundo, 1995), p. 513.

Furthermore, per capita income figures can give a misleading impression of the situation of the poor, especially in Third World countries. The marked gap between the rich and the poor in Sri Lanka disguises the real hardship faced by rural peasants and urban workers. The disproportionate wealth of the elite means that many Sri Lankans are below the per capita average.

28. Of the many passages in which this is stated, see for example Pieris, *An Asian Theology of Liberation*, p. 22: '...within God's partiality to the oppressed... we have a God who assumes the struggle *of* the poor as God's own so that it becomes the divine struggle *for* the poor, the struggle God launched against the proud, the powerful, and the rich (Luke 1.51-53)'.

29. Pieris, *An Asian Theology of Liberation*, p. 15.

continues to be, an oppressive rather than a liberating force. He believes that, in the same way, all religions have both a positive and a negative history. He does not ignore the fact that all religions, including Buddhism, can enslave rather than liberate people. In calling for a radical engagement with Buddhism he is not encouraging an uncritical acceptance of it. He advocates an approach to inter-religious dialogue in which concern for religion is inseparable from a concern for liberation.

Pieris argues that both Christianity and Buddhism must be tested against the option for the poor and the liberation of the oppressed. Any religious teaching or practice that perpetuates the exploitation and enslavement of the poor is to be challenged. However, the direction of judgment is not just one way. Pieris seeks to interpret and judge Christian and Buddhist ideas from the perspective of the poor but he also seeks to interpret and judge poverty from a perspective that is influenced by both Buddhism and Christianity. To determine the right attitude to Asian poverty, Pieris wishes to do more than repeat other Christian liberation theologians in their emphasis on the struggle against forced poverty. Buddhist perspectives point to what Pieris calls the struggle for 'voluntary poverty'.

2. *The struggle for submission to voluntary poverty.* The distinction between 'forced poverty' and 'voluntary poverty' is of crucial importance for understanding Pieris's theology. According to Pieris the Bible represents *mammon* as the great enemy of God.[30] Mammon is an enslaving force that competes for a person's soul, driving him or her to be 'the rich fool'.[31] An inner struggle *for voluntary poverty* is required for liberation from the power of mammon, that is to say from greed, acquisitiveness and the false gods of materialism. Pieris sees this as being as important to a holistic Asian liberation theology as the social struggle *against forced poverty* which is required for liberation from oppression.

It should, however, be emphasized that the 'voluntary poverty' that Pieris has in mind is moderation not destitution. It requires a genuine rejection of consumerist cravings and a radical reorientation of values away from materialism. The fruits of the earth are to be enjoyed but they must not be indulged in to excess. The central principle in

30. See Pieris, *An Asian Theology of Liberation*, pp. 15-23.
31. Pieris, *An Asian Theology of Liberation*, p. 16.

'voluntary poverty' is that earthly goods must be relativized to truly human needs and shared fairly. Pieris sees the appreciation of such moderation as a central truth of Buddhism and a necessary component of full liberation. He claims that the same teaching is to be found in Christianity but it has usually been ignored or underemphasized. By drawing attention to the critical importance of voluntary poverty for both religions he highlights a significant link between them. He argues that the renunciation of wealth so important in the example of the Buddha is paralleled in the self-giving of Christ's incarnation and life in solidarity with the oppressed.[32]

Pieris is critical of any attempt to address material poverty which does not recognize the positive value of voluntary poverty. This includes economic development theories based on either Capitalist or Marxist ideologies. He claims that any approach that fails to value voluntary poverty is alien to the Asian cultural ethos. This criticism even extends to Christians in Asia who, under the influence of early writings in Latin American liberation theology, have an arrogant and disparaging attitude to Asian religions and Asian traditions of renunciation and voluntary poverty. Pieris argues that this approach oversimplifies the attitude to poverty demanded by the Bible and is as inappropriate to the Asian context as any other western approach.

However, Pieris argues it is not enough to embrace voluntary poverty if this is divorced from service to the oppressed and struggle against poverty's structural causes. Pieris is, therefore, also critical of those that embrace voluntary poverty without confronting the forced poverty of those around them. For example, he condemns the type of Christian ashram that provides a tranquil haven for its affluent members to experiment with Asian meditation while completely ignoring the injustices and suffering outside the ashram's gate. He argues that Christians must base themselves on Jesus' example, which was equally a struggle to be poor and a struggle for the poor. Pieris sees this as reflected in EATWOT's understanding of Christian spirituality:

32. See, for example, Pieris, *Love Meets Wisdom*, p. 87: 'The only meeting point of the gnostic and the agapeic models of spirituality is the belief that *voluntary poverty* constitutes a salvific experience. Hence Jesus, as God's own kenosis and as the proof and sign of God's eternal enmity with mammon, is an endorsement of the Buddhist ascesis of renunciation. *The struggle to be poor* is one of the two dimensions of Christian discipleship, and it coincides with the Buddha's path of *interior* liberation—namely, liberation from possessions as well as from greed for possessions.'

The EATWOT thesis on spirituality can be contracted into a three-point formula: a Christian is a person who has made an irrevocable option *to follow* Jesus; this option necessarily coincides with the option to be poor; but the 'option to be poor' becomes a true 'following of Jesus' only to the extent that it is also an option *for the poor*. Christian discipleship or 'spirituality', therefore, is a coincidence of all these three options.[33]

To sum up, Pieris's theology rests on a dialogical approach to Asian religiosity combined with a liberationist approach to Asian poverty.[34] He interprets Asian religions and Asian poverty as both having liberating and enslaving dimensions. The challenge for Christians is to work out a right relationship to Asian religions and Asian poverty rather than uncritically embrace, or reject, either in their entirety. In this process Asian Christians will need to constantly reevaluate inherited practices and doctrines as they define the elements of an authentic theology for themselves.

3. *Images for Liberating Christology*

Pieris is adamant that an authentic Asian liberation theology can only arise from the experiences and reflections of grass-root communities. In Sri Lanka this happens in what Pieris calls 'human base communities' made up by activists, workers and peasants. These communities cross ethnic and religious boundaries and are open to all.[35] In the discussions

33. Pieris, *An Asian Theology of Liberation*, p. 15.

34. An emphatic statement on the great significance of Pieris's work in this regard is provided by Paul Knitter in his Foreword to Pieris, *An Asian Liberation Theology* (p. xi): 'Herein lies the creativity and the challenge of Pieris' thought—in the way he argues, from a variety of perspectives, that Christians will not adequately address the problem of Asian poverty unless they do so within the context of dialogue with Asian religions, and that they will not carry on an authentic and successful interreligious encounter unless they base that dialogue on a concern for the poor. Asian theology of liberation will take shape out of a Christian dialogue with Asian religion. Dialogue and liberation call out to each other.'

35. For Pieris's views on the role of such communities, see 'Inter-Religious Dialogue and Theology of Religions: An Asian Paradigm', *Voices from the Third World* 15 (1992), pp. 176-88; reprinted *The Month* NS 26 (1993), pp. 129-34; first published (in Dutch) in *Qoholet* 2.6 (1992), pp. 3-7. However, at present such groups are rare and their theological impact has been extremely limited. Dornberg's study of the emergence of contextual Christian theology in Sri Lanka (*Searching through the Crisis*) provides an excellent survey of the various groups that Pieris identifies as Human Base Communities.

of such communities an inter-faith dialogue guided by an option for the poor can emerge 'from below' as ordinary men and women seek to find a liberating understanding of their faith in response to the struggles of their lives.

Pieris is conscious that much academic discussion of theology is irrelevant or inaccessible to many of the participants in human base communities. If theology is to serve its proper role in a Christian engagement with Asian reality it needs to be liberated from what Pieris sees as a one sided 'pastoral magisterium' (ecclesial control) or 'academic magisterium' (scholarly control). It needs to become responsive to a 'third magisterium': 'the magisterium of the poor'.[36] To *be liberating*, for the poor and oppressed, theology must *be liberated*, from ecclesial and academic dominance.

Pieris's involvement with a number of Sri Lankan human base communities has challenged him to communicate his theology in simple and memorable ways and to avoid complex abstractions. He begins with events in the Gospel narratives to create concrete images that express his thinking in a clearer and more powerful way. There are two particularly significant christological images that Pieris draws upon to represent and express the theological themes of the preceding section: *baptism* in the Jordan of Asian religiosity and *crucifixion* on the cross of Asian poverty. Pieris liberates these images to convey the key points of his thought and to relate his work, in a simple but profound way, to its christological foundation—the example of Christ.

a. *Baptism in the Jordan of Asian Religions*[37]
As has been seen, Pieris suggests that Asian Christians should engage more openly with other Asian religions. He claims that Christian faith is not lost or weakened by opening oneself up to Asian culture and Asian religions. On the contrary, a radical openness to other religions is the way, at least in Asia, for Christians to rediscover their true identity and faith. He appeals to the image of Christ's baptism to support this and calls Asian Christians to 'baptism in the Jordan of Asian religiosity'.

Pieris argues that the example of Jesus' encounter with John the Baptist reveals a crucial lesson that the Church has long ignored. Christ's baptism is a form of self-giving or ascesis. Jesus did not seek

---

36. See Pieris, 'Inter-Religious Dialogue', pp. 179-81.
37. See, for example, Pieris, *An Asian Theology of Liberation*, pp. 45-48.

to baptize John but to *be baptized* by John. Pieris argues that the Church's priority in Asia should not be to convert but to *be converted*. For Pieris, it is only when the Asian Church is willing to do this, to lose its current form and identity in a new religious baptism, that it will find its true Christian identity. The encounter with Asian religiosity offers an opportunity for a renewed sense of its own original mission; a renewed dedication to the kingdom of God. A visitor to the Tulana Dialogue Centre will see a remarkable mural representing the story of Jesus in the Temple when he was twelve years old (Lk. 2.41-51). For Pieris this biblical passage is a model of the Church's task. Pieris notes that Jesus was sitting among the teachers 'listening to them and asking them questions' (Lk. 2.46), not holding forth in a sermon to his religious elders. In Pieris's eyes this provides a biblical precedent by which the Asian Church should judge itself.[38]

b. *The Calvary of Asian Poverty*[39]

The second image that Pieris identifies as essential to liberating Christology is the image of Christ's cross. Pieris presents Jesus' life and death as revealing both God's *contradiction of mammon* and God's *covenant with the oppressed*.[40] The liberating praxis of Jesus, in rejecting mammon and siding with the oppressed, resulted in his confrontation with worldly powers and ultimately in his crucifixion. The cross is therefore like a 'second baptism' in which Christ's self-giving at Calvary matches his earlier self-giving at the Jordan. The cross is a constant reminder that in confronting 'the Calvaries of Asian poverty' a Christian is called to a struggle that may lead to suffering and even death. Understood in this light, the cross is an image of potential suffering but also the way of authentic spirituality orientated to self-liberation and social liberation.

1. *Contradiction of mammon.* As representative of voluntary poverty the cross demonstrates Jesus' freedom from worldly concerns in his self-giving for others. Viewed from the perspective of voluntary poverty, the central symbols of Buddhism and Christianity coincide in

38. The various works of art at Tulana, and their theological interpretations, are described in Pieris, 'Inculturation in Asia: A Theological Reflection on Experience', *Concilium* 6 (1994), pp. 70-79.

39. See, for example, Pieris, *An Asian Theology of Liberation*, pp. 48-50.

40. See A. Pieris, 'Universality of Christianity?', *Vidyajyoti* 57 (1993), pp. 591-95 (595); 'Whither New Evangelism', *Pacifica* 6 (1993), pp. 327-34 (329).

their emphasis on inner liberation as the foundation for the struggle against mammon. The image of Buddha, seated under the tree of wisdom, symbolizes the inner liberation offered by the self-less sage. The image of Christ, hanging on the tree of love, symbolizes the same inner liberation offered by the self-giving prophet.

2. *Covenant with the oppressed.* Christ, as a true representative of voluntary poverty, was also the victim of forced poverty. The cross is the consequence of the covenant with the oppressed. Jesus was crucified by sinful and unjust structures, in solidarity with all victims of forced poverty. For Pieris the cross is an image of both submission and protest. In terms of the covenant with the oppressed, the cross is an image of judgment on worldly power. It represents rejection and condemnation of all sinful human structures that bring suffering and premature death. When seen in the image of the cross, Christ is simultaneously the innocent *victim* and the ultimate *judge* of the sinfulness of oppression and forced poverty. Christ on the cross is an evocative image for all who are victims of human injustices. Christ suffers in solidarity with the oppressed. Christ risen from the cross is the other side of this image. Christ stands in judgment on all human sin. The empty cross signifies that oppression does not have the final say. The resurrection sets Christ over all oppressors.

4. Conclusion

The images of Christ's baptism and crucifixion draw together many of the different threads in Pieris's theological thought. To be properly understood they must be seen against the background of his twin theological interests, Asian religiosity and Asian poverty. The 'many religions of Asia' challenge Christians to follow the image of Christ's self-giving—his baptism in the Jordan of Asian religiosity. The 'many poor of Asia' challenge Christians to recognize a second and equally important image of liberating self-sacrifice—Christ's death and resurrection viewed from the Calvary of Asian poverty.

Pieris's Sri Lankan context requires a genuine openness to Asian religions and an acceptance of the magisterium of the poor. These are central to Pieris's work and determine the challenges that his writings present to more traditional western Christologies. Pieris's liberating theological praxis rests on his Christology of liberation and reflects his radical liberation of Christology.

WHO DO YOU SAY THAT I AM?
IMAGES OF CHRIST IN FEMINIST LIBERATION THEOLOGY

Mary Grey

1. *Introduction*

The great christological question 'And who do *you* say that I am?',
which in the Synoptic Gospels is addressed to Peter,[1] in the Fourth
Gospel is posed to Martha of Bethany, in her grief at the death of
Lazarus:

> Jesus said to her, 'I am the Resurrection and the life; he who believes in
> me, though he die, yet shall he live, and whoever lives and believes in me
> shall never die. Do you believe this?' She said to him, 'Yes Lord, I believe
> that you are the Christ, the Son of God, he who is coming into the world'
> (Jn 11.25-27).

I take the significance of Martha's confession of faith—lost in the
dominant western tradition—as inspiration and starting point for a
feminist liberational reflection on images of Christ. Martha's leadership and authority have been lost to a tradition of ambiguity which, on
the one hand, despised her for being obsessed with housework, yet on
the other hand needed her as a model of women's essential role as
servant. The significance of her confession is that she is articulating
faith in the risen Jesus from all the grief and the poverty of her context in first-century Palestine. That is the vital connection which all
Liberation Theologies today make with the New Testament context.
Poor communities of faith are empowered by Jesus' response to the
desperation of marginalized peoples of his time. (Yes, there were
levels of desperation, levels of poverty, but poverty—with economic,
social, racial and gender dimensions—was the backdrop to Jesus'
ministry.)[2] Martha's confession is echoed today by poor women from

---

1. See Mt. 16.16; Mk 8.29; Lk. 9.20.
2. I am influenced in this argument by the German liberation theologian, Luise

Asia, Africa, Latin America and the Caribbean, Eastern Europe—as well as by their less impoverished, yet sisters-in-solidarity from Euro-America.

If solidarity in the struggle for justice for poor women is the point of connection between all these images, this in no way diminishes the diversity, the distinctness of the social context from which the images emerge. But the difficulty in freeing a Jesus who can speak to the suffering of contemporary women in the diversity of their contexts is the first stumbling block. It is depicted sharply by both Rosemary Ruether's article, 'Can Christology be Liberated from Patriarchy?',[3] and by Alice Walker's arresting story, 'The Welcome Table'.[4] Ruether shows how, even if church authorities have yielded to that fact that women are human beings too, and, notionally at least, a kind of egalitarianism is espoused, yet in practice Christology continues to underpin a patriarchal anthropology, where real authority is denied women.

Alice Walker's story illustrates the difficulty of rescuing Jesus from a racist, Euro-American ideology. She tells of a poor woman trying to be part of a white church congregation in the United States. It is the rich wives who will not tolerate her presence:

> God, mother, country, earth, Church. It involved all that and well they knew it. Leather bagged and shoed, with good calfskin gloves to keep out the cold, they looked with contempt at the bloodless, gray, arthritic hands of the old woman... Could their husbands expect them to sit up in Church with that...? No, no, the husbands were quick to answer and even quicker to do their duty.[5]

The poor woman, rejected and ejected from the church, stumbles along the road, and, who should she meet, but Jesus:

> He was wearing an immaculate, white, long dress trimmed in gold...[6]

She recognized him, of course, and had learnt to love him through the

Schottroff, *Lydia's Impatient Sisters* (trans. J. Bowden; London, SCM Press, 1995 [1994]).

    3.   R.R. Ruether, 'Can Christology be Liberated from Patriarchy?', in M. Stevens (ed.), *Reconstructing the Christ Symbol: Essays in Feminist Christology* (New York: Paulist Press, 1993), pp. 7-29.

    4.   See A. Walker, 'The Welcome Table', in *In Love and Trouble* (London: The Women's Press, 1984).

    5.   Walker, 'The Welcome Table', p. 84.

    6.   Walker, 'The Welcome Table', p. 85.

picture in a white lady's Bible. This white, blue-eyed Jesus accompanies her—but we are never told if their encounter is truly redemptive or not, or if Jesus can be disentangled from the pages of the white slave owner's Bible. Her body is found by the road the next day.

So, if the first hermeneutical point is that Jesus is imaged from out of the concreteness of women's struggle for justice, or (according to Elisabeth Schüssler Fiorenza) the ongoing struggle against *kyriarchy*, the rule of the lord and master, in all its diversity of context; the second point is to redeem Jesus himself from patriarchal and eurocentric constructions. As Rita Nakashima Brock wrote,

> We redeem Christ when we recognize the images of Jesus that reflect our hunger for healing and wholeness and claim these images as resources for hope because we belong to a community of transformation and empowerment... Christ is an image of shared power that works and is increased only in the sharing.[7]

What are these images of Christ which provide resources of hope which work for transformation? I begin with an image which is ancient, but has been reclaimed in many contexts: it is Christ as Christa, in whom I see the image of my crucified sister...

2. *Christa, My Crucified Sister...*

The 'Christa' image of Edwina Sandys was brought to the Bay area in the United States by Stanford University and was displayed at Stanford Memorial Chapel from October to December 1984.[8] Christ as Christa immediately became the centre of a theological storm—evoking both enthusiastic lectures by theologians and art historians, deeply moving testimonies and prayers by violated and abused women who found identifying with this Christa a healing experience, as well as outraged cries and expressions of hatred. The reactions to Christa—Christ crucified as a woman—are still pouring in. Before arguing theologically about this, rather than launching immediately into theological refutation relying on a narrow orthodoxy and before I put this Christa image into an art-historical and theological context—and there exists

7. R. Brock, 'The Feminist Redemption of Christ', in J.L. Weidman (ed.), *Christian Feminism: Visions of a New Humanity* (San Francisco: Harper & Row, 1984), p. 74.

8. The following information is from E. Hunter (ed.), 'Reflections on the Christa', *JWR* 4.2 (1985).

now a constellation of Christa images—I suggest that we spend a moment reflecting on deep personal experiences which these images touch and evoke. To do this, I present two reactions to the healing power of the Christa. The first is a simple prayer:

> Christa, you are the beautiful embodiment of the universal suffering of humankind. Just as Jesus was neither male nor female, you also are the personification of the balance of the masculine and the feminine energies within us.[9]

The second passage is a testimony of a wounding personal experience and used by the writer, whose own experience it is, as inspiration for a book on boundaries in pastoral care:

> O God,
> through the image of a woman
> crucified on the cross
> I understand at last...
>
> In the warmth, peace and sunlight of your presence
> I was able to uncurl the tightly clenched fists.
> For the first time
> I felt your suffering presence with me
> in that event.
> I have known you as a vulnerable baby,
> as a brother, and as a father.
> Now I know you as a woman.
> You were there with me
> as the violated girl
> caught in helpless suffering.[10]

Now I pose the question: are these witnesses to the healing power of

---

9.   In Hunter, 'Reflections', p. 9. It is interesting to note the parallels with the Toronto Christa. This was donated by an artist to Bloor St United Church, Toronto in the Memorial Chapel. This Christa caused heated discussion within Victoria University; so much so that it was decided to place the suffering woman in the backyard of Emmanuel College, Toronto (part of Victoria University). However, after the Université de Montréal massacre in 1989, when eleven women were gunned down, an annual memorial for the victims has been held in her presence. So the statue is now linked directly to that event and has come to symbolize it on campus. I am grateful for this information to Michel Desjardins, Wilfrid Laurier University, Waterloo, Ontario.

10.   C. Doehring, *Taking Care: Monitoring Power Dynamics and Relational Boundaries in Pastoral Care and Counselling* (New York: Abingdon Press, 1995), Introduction, p. 1.

the Christa rooted at all in the Christian tradition? Art-historian Jo Milgrom of the Center for Judaic Studies at the Graduate Theological Union, Berkeley, puts the Mother Jesus strand firmly within Jewish and Christian tradition, in a line from the androgynous Adam and Moses as a nursing father.[11] For example, there is an image of the crucified Christ—at the Cooper Union Museum in New York—a drawing from 1657 of *Christus Iudex, Christ the Judge.* Christ as a woman is here the ruler of the world, holding the scales of justice and the sword with which to enforce peace. Another example is of the martyrdom of St Eulalia, sculpted by Emilio Francheschi (1839–1890)—7'4^{1/2}" high, in white marble, and housed at the Galleria d'Arte Moderna, Turin. Eulalia lived in fourth-century Merida and was martyred at the age of 12. Eulalia is clearly not Christ, but the identification in the mind of the sculptor is clear. A third image, found in a church in Santa Fe, Mexico, is of a bearded Christ in a female gown. Of all the theological inferences two stand out clearly—that Christ identifies with the suffering of women, and that the gender of Christ is fluid and flexible. He is a man in such a way as not to block out representation as a woman.

So the first theme calls us back to an ancient motif of early Christianity—that there was a deep identification and union between Jesus and the Christian who was persecuted and suffering for the faith. And more: that this suffering Christian—man or woman—was affirmed and recognized by the community as a figure of the crucified Jesus. The earliest witness—that we know about, at least—comes from the Acts of the Martyrs of Lyon and Vienne in 177 CE: it is one story of the persecuted Christians, from Lugdunum, in Roman Gaul, thrown to the lions. Among them in this particular story was a woman, Blandina:

> Blandina was hung on a post and exposed as bait for the wild animals that were let loose on her. She seemed to hang there in the form of a cross, and by her fervent prayer she aroused intense enthusiasm in those who were undergoing their ordeal, for in their torment with their physical eyes they saw in the person of their sister him who was crucified for them, that he might convince all who believe in him that all who suffer for Christ's glory will have eternal fellowhip with the living God.[12]

11. J. Milgrom, 'Reflections on the Christa from an Art-Historian', *JWR* 4.2 (1985), pp. 6-21.

12. H. Musurillo, *Acts of the Christian Martyrs* (Oxford: Clarendon Press, 1972), p. 75.

This profound theme of the identification of Jesus with the suffering woman as witness to faith is seen too in another early document, roughly contemporary (Perpetua died in 203 CE), *The Passion of Perpetua*. Here Perpetua's slave, Felicity, is forced to give birth to her baby in prison and is taunted by the gaoler. 'If you scream now', he mocks her, 'what will you do when thrown to the beasts?' To this, Felicity's courageous response is,[13]

> Now it is I who suffer, but then another shall be in me, since I am suffering for him.

Not only is the theme of Christ's identification with the suffering woman evident in a strikingly physical way—and this is the very root of the doctrine of the *Church as the body of Christ*—but the theme of Christ as Mother is present (a theme developed later in this paper). The suffering mother theme as archetypal for all human suffering is also taken up by a contemporary Jewish writer, Chaim Potok. Although I think he is wrong in denying an effective iconography of suffering to his own Jewish tradition, yet what he gives us, a young Jewish boy, Asher Lev, from the conservative Hasidic tradition, who paints his mother on a cross, is an astonishing link between Christ, Christa and the mother as encapsulating the persecution of the Jews, and all the tragedy of the world.

It is his mother who mediates in Asher Lev's battle with the male authorities of the community to advance his career as a painter. In the exhibition which crowns his career yet marks his expulsion from the Jewish community he paints this picture of 'ultimate anguish and torment':

> I drew my mother in her housecoat, with her arms extended along the horizontal of the blind, her wrists tied to it with the cords of the blind, her legs tied at the ankles to the vertical of the inner frame with another section of the cord of the blind... I split my mother's head into... segments, one looking at me, one looking at my father, one looking upward. The torment, the searing anguish I felt in her, I put in her mouth, into the twisting curve of her head, the arching of her slight body, the clenching of her small fists... I painted in a strange nerveless frenzy of energy: 'for all the torment of your past and future years, my mama... for all the anguish this picture of pain will cause you... for the unspeakable

13. See 'The Martyrdom of Perpetua: A Protest Account of Early Christianity', in P. Wilson-Kastner *et al.* (eds.), *A Lost Tradition: Women Writers of the Early Church* (Washington, DC: University Press of America, 1981), pp. 1-32 (27).

mystery that brings good fathers and sons into the world and lets a mother
watch them tear at each other's throats. For the Master of the Universe,
whose suffering world I do not comprehend...'[14]

So Christ as Christa liberates not by condoning the suffering of abused
women, or proclaiming that there is an innate redemptive quality in it;
but by being present with and sharing in the brokenness, identifying
this as the priority for God's healing love, Christ gives hope, empowers
and enables the process of resistance. Secondly, Christ as Christa is
embodied in the community, Christa community. Just as Jesus of
Nazareth was nurtured by messianic community in its poverty, its hopes
and dreams, these images of Christa—the liberating Christ today—
emerge from specific communities of women and men, whose focus
is *Christic living, Christopraxis*—the healing, redemptive flow of
reciprocal energy which resists injustice and oppression, enables and
embodies a different lifestyle. I now turn to another embodiment of
Christa community—*Christ the Tree of Life,* which in this instance is
an Asian image, expressing the Christology of Asian women, together
with an image from Zimbabwe, from the Shona people.

3. *Christ the Tree of Life in Asian and African Contexts*

When we speak of Asian Women's theology, it is vital in some way to
reflect the diversity of that continent, as what is referred to is the
theology of the women of India, Korea, the Philippines, Thailand, Hong
Kong, Japan, China, Nepal, Pakistan, Sri Lanka, Vietnam, Indonesia
and so on. There is a whole painful history of Asian women trying
to make their voices heard even at the gatherings of Liberation
Theologians of Asia itself.[15] Yet within this cultural diversity there is
a tragic similarity in the oppression from which most Asian women
suffer:

> In all spheres of Asian society, women are dominated, de-humanised, and
> de-womanised; they are discriminated against, exploited, harassed, sexually
> abused, and viewed as inferior beings, who must always subordinate
> themselves to the so-called male supremacy. In the home, church, law,

14. C. Potok, *My Name is Asher Lev* (New York: Knopf, 1972), pp. 212-13.
Also cited in Milgrom, 'Reflections', pp. 19-20.
15. See V. Fabella, *Beyond Bonding: A Third World Woman's Theological
Journey* (Manila: Ecumenical Association of Third World Theologians and Institute
of Women's Studies, 1993).

education and media, women have been treated with bias and condescension. In Asia and all over the world, the myth of the subservient,
servile Asian woman is blatantly peddled to reinforce the dominant male
stereotype image.[16]

The Korean theologian Chung Hyun Kyung describes this oppression,
in all its pain and sorrow, as the starting point for Asian women's
journey to know their place in the world and the meaning of their
whole existence. It is truly an *epistemology of the broken body, a
broken body longing for wholeness and healing.*[17] The double consciousness of the chains of oppression and yet their own collusion
through the sin of the oppressed—which they see as ignorance, as
internalized self-hate caused by many forms of colonialism and
patriarchy—means that, according to Chung:

> They cannot endure meaningless suffering if they do not dream of a world
> defined by wholeness, justice and peace. They... know they will perish
> without a vision of life in its fullness and in its deepest beauty.[18]

Let me depict two images from India that carry a visionary, dreaming
quality. They envision a Christ who addresses the concrete situation of
Indian women—a Christology which both takes old themes and gives
new meanings, and also develops new themes arising from Asian contexts. The first image is Christ, Christa, the Tree of Life, painted by
the Indian artist Lucy de Souza, who draws on both Christian and
Hindu traditions. (Some will know the Misereor Hunger Cloth on
biblical women which she painted, imaged from an Indian perspective.) But here Christ/Christa as Tree of Life has a deep cosmic and
ecological significance.[19] For around the Tree are the four elements of
life—earth, water, fire, spirit. Each panel recalls a text from both
Hindu and Christian traditions. For example, the top right panel is
Mary of Bethany/the goddess Sita playing the sitar. She represents
spirit—and is a union of the contemplative and active dimensions. The
Swan—symbol of the Spirit in Hinduism—is behind her. At the feet of
Christ/Christa is Mary his mother—a contrast with the oceanic feel of

16. 'Final Statement: Asian Women Speak' (Manila, Philippines, November
21–30, 1985), in V. Fabella and M.A. Oduyoye, *With Passion and Compassion:
Third World Women doing Theology* (Maryknoll, NY: Orbis Books, 1988), p. 119.

17. H.K. Chung, *Struggle to be the Sun Again: Introducing Asian Women's
Theology* (Maryknoll, NY: Orbis Books, 1990), p. 39.

18. Chung, *Struggle to be the Sun Again*, p. 39.

19. This is my own reflection on the Christ as Tree of Life picture.

the bottom left panel where she cradles the infant. We have the strong impression that here is birth agony—the arms of Christ/Christa are the very branches of the tree, extending into the cosmos, re-vitalizing earth, sky, spirit, water, represented by the women. Secondly, we are given an iconic expression of co-creation—the women are drawn into the activity of giving birth to the re-vitalized creation, drawing its life from the Sacred Tree, where Christ in an agony of love pours forth the energy which the cosmos needs. But, notice the group around the Tree—this is Christa community, almost as if the messianic community collectively gives birth to new creation. Several theological points are important.

(1) For Indian Christians the gender of Christ is not the stumbling block as it has been in the west, where Christ being male continues to block not only the priesthood of women but also the question of the meaning of the incarnation for women. There is here a much more fluid concept of gender—as there was in early Christianity. (We have seen how Blandina was a witness to this.) It is the same thing in Latin America and Africa. Jesus as suffering brother in the struggle is a *uniting factor, not a stumbling block.*

(2) Following this, it seems what is vitally important in this freedom of imaging Jesus as male or female is not that divinity is being reduced to humanity—and female humanity at that—but that women are part of the symbolism of mediating sacred power. Divine sacred power which is healing and redemptive. Here *Christology is soteriology* which is itself part of divine creative love. A new symbolic nexus can be created in which the Christ/Christa community embody and become the channels of redemptive love.

(3) The focus is not so much the man Jesus, but the life praxis of the Jesus community, Christic living or Christo-praxis, as I said. Jesus as person becomes an interpersonal reality—and is not that what Paul meant by the Body of Christ, vulnerable to the Christ/community? This is in no way to minimize what happened in the life and person of Jesus, but to throw the focus back to the liberating, reconciling dynamic he opened up. *Christic community did not stop with Jesus.* Power-in-liberation, in power-in-relation, goes on.

Two further images emphasize these points. One is by an English artist Caroline Mackenzie, who has lived for many years in India in the same Ashram for artists as Lucy de Souza. She has re-imagined the Good Samaritan parable. In her depiction, the Samaritan is a woman—

is there any reason why she should not be? Also, the Samaritan's horse is drawn into the picture. The whole forms a mandala—a sacred circle— and gives the impression that the three are caught up in a movement of compassionate love. The red of the woman's dress is the colour of life and vitality: the blue of the wounded man encaptures the desperate landless, emaciated poor of India's cities. Reclaiming the compassion of Jesus means for Indian women not a passive acceptance of suffering, and blind obedience to the dictates of patriarchy—which for Asian women mean bride burnings, being sold into prostitution—but the courage to resist, and to develop a notion of active suffering, performing acts of solidarity and active participation in the struggle for justice.

An image from the Shona people in Zimbabwe illustrates the same idea of the flexibility of the gender of Jesus. He is a man—he has a beard. Yet he has breasts and is feeding a baby on his back—just like African mothers who have to work in the fields. Not only is Christ feeding the baby—he is also the redemptive Christ who struggles against evil. The serpent is at his feet. So he is a nurturing mother who struggles for justice for his people. And he represents the ongoing vitality of life—for the tree is a generation Tree, carved by the Shona people from one block of wood. Motherhood, responsibility for ongoing generations, icon of suffering, link with cosmic growth— all these are themes of this Christ, Christa-mother.

Christ the tree of life is of course an ancient symbol for Christianity. It is eucharistic, redemptive and connected both with the Tree of the Garden of Eden and the Tree of reconciliation in the Book of Revelation:

> And the leaves of the tree were for the healing of the nations (Rev. 22.2).

It is also a popular symbol in folk-lore, as the Christmas Carol 'Jesus Christ the Apple Tree' shows. And of course Jesus used tree symbolism as an image of the kingdom of God:

> What is the Kingdom of God like? And to what shall I compare it? It is like a grain of mustard seed which a man took and sowed in his garden; and it grew and became a tree and the birds of the air made nests in its branches (Lk. 13.18-19).

But what does it mean for feminist liberation, linked to the communities from which this symbol springs?

Christ, Christa, tree of life, evokes not a romantic connection between women and nature, but the very real way that poor women depend on the earth for sheer survival. (In fact, everyone does, but it is poor women who live the closest to life and death.) When the drought comes, it is women's work to walk miles into the desert for water, to collect the twigs—all that are left in a de-forested region—for cooking, feeding the animals and keeping warm. That women know the preciousness of trees is illustrated by the Chipko story. When the Maharajah's soldiers came to chop down trees to build a palace, it was the women who hugged the trees—Chipko means *tree-hugging*—in an effort to save them. They were felled with the trees. But today there are many Chipko movements as communities realize the significance of trees for the bio-region.[20]

Secondly, Christ/Christa, tree of life and mother evokes not only the Christ our mother tradition we know from Anselm and Julian of Norwich, not only the theme of the *suffering mother* which was mentioned earlier, but more the *need for Christology to be grounded in the material reality of poor communities. Christus Mater*, the theologian Mark Kline Taylor tells us, is a constant reminder that *matter matters*.[21] He wants Christology to be grounded in what he calls *maternalization,* as one element in the broader task of emancipation. *Maternalization* invokes two movements—that of revaluing women's reproductive powers and that of relocating society's maternal functions. By this is meant that it is no use calling for a revaluing of women's reproductive powers without undergoing a thoroughgoing social reform. I can endorse much of his very movingly-written argument. Here in Britain, for example, it would be making a genuine commitment to the poverty of single mothers, the long hours worked by Asian mothers as office cleaners, the many Nigerian mothers in prison with or without their babies. This Christic revaluing would root itself, for example, in the attention which the earthly Jesus gave to the vulnerability of the small girl—the raising to life of Jairus's daughter—and the breaking of taboos around the woman with the flow of blood.[22]

20. See V. Shive, *Staying Alive* (London: Zed Books, 1989).

21. M.K. Taylor, *Remembering Esperanza: A Cultural Political Theology of North American Praxis* (Maryknoll, NY: Orbis Books, 1993), chapter 6.

22. The crucial significance of this last passage as a locus of hope for Latin American women is discussed in M. Althaus-Reid in 'Do not Stop the Flow of my Blood: A Critical Christology of Hope amongst Latin American Women', *Studies of World Christianity* 1.2 (1995), pp. 143-59.

Within the commitment of Christa community to liberation and reconciliation, and out of the commitment to this process of maternalization,
Taylor argues that the multi-layered, interlocking oppressions begin
to break down.

It is now time to draw the threads together. Yet many voices have not
been heard, in particular the voices of women calling for the Black
Christ: in other words, 'the challenge of the darker sister'. [23] I will use
this last image as a starting point for a contextual reflection, asking
what kind of liberation Christology is necessary for a European
context, where Europe is part of the colonizing and oppressing context
from which the Two-Thirds World continues to suffer.

4. *Seeking a New Starting Point*

The images we have been discussing have been revealing commonalities and differences. The commonalities stressed the need to begin
with the contextuality of the situations of women in all their diversity.
There has been a tendency to shift from the person of Christ, to the
redeeming dynamic of what happened in Christ, to the healing relationships of Christa community and to the praxis of Christic living.
The figure of Christ as mother has brought the poverty and suffering
of mothers globally to the centre of the search for Christic images as
starting point for the transformed society. Christ as mother stands at
the fulcrum of the birth of a new society—but it is the Christic community itself that is the agent of the new birth. The diversity revealed
stems from the tragic legacy of imperialist history: poor people from
the Two-Thirds World have had the white Christ thrust upon them as
the stabilizing core of oppressive régimes, as was shown in the story
by Alice Walker. Hence from the Christology of African women, of
Latina/Hispanic women and of Womanist theology[24] come messages
that conflict with the idea that the idea of Christ as male is problematic.

23. This is the title of one of the chapters of J. Grant's book, *White Women's
Christ and Black Women's Jesus: Feminist Christology and Womanist Response*
(Atlanta: Scholars Press, 1989).

24. This is the theology of black women in the United States. It includes J. Grant's
book, *White Women's Christ*; K.B. Douglas, *The Black Christ* (Maryknoll, NY: Orbis
Books, 1994); E.M. Townes (ed.), *A Troubling in my Soul: Womanist Perspectives
on Evil and Suffering* (Maryknoll, NY: Orbis Books, 1993), and is a significant and
growing field.

Rather, Christ is suffering brother, co-sufferer. Suffering with Jesus brings closeness to God. He is equalizer and liberator.[25] As equalizer black women find Jesus helps them hold their head high not just within the white community but in front of black men. Jesus as liberator is best illustrated by the life of Sojourner Truth. When asked by a preacher if her source for preaching was the Bible, she replied, 'No honey, can't preach from the Bible—can't read a letter'. Then she explained, 'When I preaches, I has jest one text to preach from, an' I always preaches from this one. My text is, "when I found Jesus!".' But this is far from being an individualist narrative. Jacquelyn Grant writes,

> In this sermon Sojourner Truth talks about her life, from the time her parents were brought from Africa and sold, to the time that she met Jesus in the context of her struggles for dignity and liberation for black people and women.[26]

Jesus as fellow-struggler is also reflected in the Christology of African women. Furthermore—as Mercy Oduyoye makes clear—whereas western feminist Christology seems to collapse the divinity of Jesus into his humanity, embodiment being the key category, African women's Christology has no problem with Jesus' divinity. [27] In fact Jesus as mediating between the two worlds connects effectively with the world of the ancestors. Jesus himself is seen as in equal need of liberation—from the white Church, from the privileged classes, and from both a vicious form of racism and a debilitating language of servanthood which continues to oppress the black community, women and men.

But if I take as starting point the *praxis* of poor women—which is stressed in the theology coming from the Latina and Hispanic community, known as *mujerista* theology,[28] the question of starting point raises its head. According to the research of Ada Maria Isasi-Diaz, the great christological question on which this paper is based, 'And who

25. These four points are taken from J. Grant, '"Come to my Help, Lord, For I'm in Trouble": Womanist Jesus and the Mutual Struggle for Liberation', in M. Stevens (ed.), *Reconstructing the Christ Symbol* (New York: Paulist Press, 1993), pp. 54-71.

26. Grant, *White Women's Christ*, p. 69.

27. See E. Amoah and M.A. Oduyoye, 'The Christ for African Women', in Fabella and Oduyoye, *With Passion and Compassion*, pp. 35-46.

28. See especially the research of A.M. Isasi-Diaz, *En La Lucha (In the Struggle)* (Minneapolis: Fortress Press, 1993).

do *you* say that I am?', does not arise among these women—all women of faith and deeply religious. Existential questions like how to find food for the baby, and whether it is right to steal in order just to keep the baby alive—these are burning issues. And God is present in community, as a God of justice, for example, in one social worker's struggle to keep an old lady living in her own apartment. Isasi-Diaz relates how this same woman organized an agape in the Church Hall. She said,

> The people really shared what the eucharist means for them. . . and then since not everyone had talked, I said, 'Now we will go around and let us hear in just one word what the Eucharist means for you'. And the people started to shout 'Joy, hope, resurrection, love. . .' I was crying and if you had been there you would have been crying.[29]

Mujerista theology insists on asking *new* questions, like 'Why is it that Hispanic women do not relate to Jesus?' It insists on refusing the answers given by traditional theology before it is even clear what the questions are. It is very clear that, submerged as *mujerista* women are, as a sub-culture in the United States, Christology is being used to keep them subservient to the dominant classes. By remaining true to lived experience, they hope to affirm their own world-view and construct a liberating praxis.

What then does this mean for a western feminist Christology which wants to be in solidarity with our sisters globally, and yet is implicated in the world systems that continue to oppress them?

Like all liberation Christologies we start with our context—but with the difference that we are not necessarily the victims. Nor is it so simple that we admit that there are poor and abused women in western society, and reclaim the 'suffering, rejected Christ figure' with whom they can be identified. We all admire the Abbé Pierre-type figures, those who discover the face of Christ in the homeless—but do we join them? Rather, we avoid confronting the systems.[30]

The social and political context today is one where rampant individualism and greed for wealth seem to have won. If there is a dominant Christology here today it is one where Christ comforts, consoles and enables us to live with the system and still be Christian. The rich can

29. Isasi-Diaz, *En La Lucha*, p. 128.

30. Mark Kline Taylor did not reclaim the Christ-as-mother figure to make a point about the gender of Jesus, but to transform the whole social reality of women as mothers.

amass wealth and still be his disciples. What a feminist liberation Christology calls for is a Christ who de-stabilizes these unjust systems. The Jesus who knocks, unheard, on the door of the churches seeks to de-stabilize individualism and challenge us to discover liberating relational notions of being human. We need a Christology that de-stabilizes kyriarchy with its complex web of racism, sexism, classism, militarism. A Christology that disowns the hero-concept. (When, in his earthly life, did Jesus give a crumb of encouragement to his being made a hero?) Such a Christology will issue from the many Christ/Christa communities which must be *prophetic* in their denunciation of injustice, *mystical* in their stress on silence, contemplation and discernment of where God's Spirit is leading them, *embodied* or rooted in real groups of people committed to the praxis of justice among people and the earth, and *faithful* to these communities and their lived realities. And, dare I say it, *learning to be sacrificing communities!* By this I mean that it could be the only chance for that peace and justice in the world for which we all long, that people of faith make sacrifices—change their lifestyle, live frugally to save resources. But more still: I have an intuition that Christ may be knocking on other doors—the doors of people of other faiths, and people of goodwill in secular communities—because Christians cannot give up on their own superiority. To 'lose your life in order to find it' is one of the most profound notions of Christianity. We cheapen it when we see it merely as giving up chocolate for Lent, or despising physical goods. Perhaps the Spirit who discovers the cracks in the finely-woven seam of our selfish culture is actually saying that the Christology relevant for our times is not the re-discovery of the universal Christ, but the European renunciation of the life-style which accompanied the imperial Christ in order that all may have life to the full, and the renunciation of assumed superiority of Christianity so as to listen to the presence of the sacred in other groups of people in our midst. Let the solidarity of Christa communities and christic transforming praxis lead the way!

Part III

LITERATURE

IMAGES OF CHRIST IN CORPUS CHRISTI
MEDIEVAL MYSTERY PLAY CYCLES

Deane E.D. Downey

The ends of all, who for the scene do write,
Are, or should be, to profit and delight.[1]

In a 1986 article reviewing a National Theatre production called *The Mysteries,* based largely on one of the four existing medieval biblical play cycles—the York version—critic Darryll Grantley complained that the show had largely ignored 'the serious and didactic qualities of the medieval religious cycles' it was purporting to be reviving. He continued: 'In its insistence on quaintness and "merrie England" jolliness the production implicitly restates ideas about medieval drama which have for some time been outdated: that it was rather simple-minded drama performed by unsophisticated men'. Grantley concluded that the production amounted to a parody of medieval biblical drama, for although producer Bill Bryden had seemed to be attempting to popularize and make accessible to modern audiences this material, in the final analysis he had succumbed to 'the temptation to cheap tricks and glitter instead of trust in the text'.[2]

Back in 1961, critic Eleanor Prosser masterfully exposed the anti-religious bias of much modern criticism of medieval biblical drama.[3] For example, one critic had held that the mysteries, from a literary viewpoint, were crude in workmanship and 'insipid'.[4] Another had

1.   B. Jonson, 'Prologue' to *Epicoene,* in *Ben Jonson's Plays and Masques* (ed. R.M. Adams; New York: Norton, 1979), p. 99.

2.   'The National Theatre's Production of *The Mysteries*: Some Observations', *Theatre Notebook* 40.2 (1986), p. 73.

3.   E. Prosser, *Drama and Religion in the English Mystery Plays: A Re-Evaluation* (Stanford, CA: Stanford University Press, 1961).

4.   A.P. Rossiter, *English Drama from Early Times to the Elizabethans: Its*

suggested that because such drama had originated, or so he thought, in the medieval church, there was little thought of dramatic effect, so that when these plays passed into the hands of simple people they were inevitably naive. Thus any serious attention to these plays would be merely a waste of time.[5] Prosser concludes, 'Inevitably, the early plays are [considered] conventional, didactic, dull'.[6] The assumption was that only when comedy was added did the plays became dramatically interesting and worth studying. As a result, she notes, most scholars of medieval drama turned to the study of external facts—sources, borrowings, dates, verse forms, guild records, etc.—rather than to the plays themselves. Most such critics seemed to unquestioningly assume that any didactic content inevitably spoiled the play's dramatic effect, completely ignoring in the process the time-honoured tradition dating at least back to Horace's *Ars Poetica* and captured in the passage from Ben Jonson's *Epicoene* quoted above that great literature could teach and delight simultaneously.[7] Such critics' main problem is that they had established no clear criteria to ascertain whether didacticism spoils a play or not, or whether, for that matter, humour is always good. Prosser concluded that these critics were really attempting to justify their own personal likes or dislikes.[8]

Background, Origins and Developments (London: Hutchinson, 1950), p. 66 in Prosser, *Drama and Religion*, p. 7.

   5.   H. Craig, *English Religious Drama of the Middle Ages* (Oxford: Oxford University Press, 1955), in Prosser, *Drama and Religion*, p. 7.

   6.   Prosser, *Drama and Religion*, p. 7.

   7.   See H.M. Whall, *To Instruct and Delight: Didactic Method in Five Tudor Dramas* (New York: Garland Publishing, 1988) for a succinct critique of this modern critical inadequacy. She asserts: 'In the post-romantic world of literary criticism, the term "didactic" is normally used to summon negative connotations which range from "utilitarian" to "tyrannical". The phenomenon of didacticism, acknowledged as a dominant force in English literature of the Middle Ages, the early Rennaissance and the eighteenth century, has been considered alternately as a childhood illness from which great artists have had to recover or as a proto-puritanical obsession thwarting the development of great art itself. Such a view is, to say the least, unhistorical' (p. 1).

   8.   E.K. Chambers (*English Literature at the Close of the Middle Ages* [Oxford: Oxford University Press, 1947], pp. 36-37) evaluated the plays in terms of their verse. Others evaluated the plays in terms of their comic element; others, in terms of whether the play handled the sordid or grisly 'realistically'. But Prosser captures the biggest problem beautifully: 'the unconscious rationale' that 'the religious plays are judged good by the degree to which they are not religious' (p. 9). Tucker Brooke (*The Tudor Drama* [Hamden, CT: Archon Books, 1939], p. 15), for example, 'saw

This paper shares the contention of Prosser and others,[9] then, that for a medieval audience, didactic intent did not necessarily detract from dramatic impact or effectiveness in these biblical dramas. I maintain that the origin of the material in the biblical record did not impede the artistry or the creativity of either the dramatists themselves or the lay actors who performed these plays. I contend that it therefore behooves us as twentieth-century students of medieval biblical drama to focus upon the content of the plays themselves in order to assess their probable dramatic impact. The view that biblical stories were mere folktales and myths of a naive people is simply indefensible and invalid historically. Medieval people saw the Bible as a record of true historical experiences, not mere myths. As with many of the plays based on historical figures written by Shakespeare and his contemporaries, we can legitimately pose many of the questions regularly asked by drama critics of any age: Does the play have a core of meaning or a significant insight about the human condition? Does the play present a conflict resolved? Does it have an identifiable pattern or plot? Does the characterization serve the play's purpose(s)? Does the play engage our emotions in some way? And does it give the audience a sense of closure by the end?

A number of recent studies of the four extant biblical drama cycles have focused on the *texts* of these plays, attempting to recover a sense of how medieval audiences might have responded over the initial two

---

any growth of independence from the religious frame as an advance in freedom and consequently a growth in absolute value' (Prosser, *Drama and Religion*, p. 9).

9.　　Other critics have also protested against the above-outlined bias against medieval biblical drama: (a) H.C. Gardiner (*Mysteries End: An Investigation of the Last Days of the Medieval Stage* [Yale Studies in English Series, 103; New Haven: Yale University Press, 1946]) said that medieval drama died because of the hostility of the Reformation, not because the plays were poor drama or the medieval man was primitive and unenlightened. (b) H. Craig (*English Religious Drama of the Middle Ages*) said medieval drama scholarship up to that point had been preoccupied with largely irrelevant issues—especially the plays' secular elements. He argued that the life-blood of such drama was religion and that it was designed to arouse strong religious feeling in its audience. (c) F.M. Salter (*Medieval Drama in Chester* [Toronto: University of Toronto Press, 1955]) attacked the view that medieval dramatists and their audiences were naive and thus incapable of artistic discrimination. He argued that we need to try to imagine the experience of the plays as they were originally produced. (d) G. Wickham (*Early English Stages: 1300 to 1660* [London: Routledge & Kegan Paul, 1959]) did much to advance Salter's agenda (Prosser, *Drama and Religion*, p. 9).

hundred years of their fourteenth- to sixteenth-century performance history.[10] As I have indicated, it is a critical commonplace to acknowledge that these vernacular dramas were designed not just to entertain but also to teach redemptive virtue and promote piety as the medieval playwrights, many if not all of them no doubt clerics themselves, depicted the key biblical episodes in the salvation history of God's dealings with humans from the Creation to the Last Judgment. What is not nearly as consensual is the question of whether such unapologetically didactic intentions served as a liability or an asset in terms of these cycles' power and effectiveness as drama. In my view it is critically important (the pun is intentional) to avoid a largely twentieth-century propensity to see such a dichotomy between the sacred and the secular that a play's dramatic effect would be deemed to be somehow diluted the more evident its didactic intention.

Without question the central focus of these mystery play cycles' depiction of key biblical episodes in God's dealings with humans was upon those events dealing with the birth, life, and death of Christ. These pageants were designed to portray the Christian doctrine of the simultaneously human and divine natures of Christ, thereby fostering greater understanding of orthodox Christian beliefs about sin, salvation, and the promise of future bliss for the devout believer. In keeping with the theme of this volume, I propose to look at how Christ is portrayed in one play from each of the four extant mystery play cycles: 'The Annunciation' play from the Towneley or Wakefield Cycle; 'The Woman Taken in Adultery' play from the N. Town or mistakenly-named *Ludus Coventriae* Cycle (an early speculation that this cycle had been performed in Coventry was later proven inaccurate when fragments of another very different and authentically Coventry cycle were discovered); 'The Crucifixion' play from the York cycle; and the 'Christ's Ascension' play from the Chester cycle. I shall attempt to

10. Two that I have found particularly helpful are J.W. Robinson's *Studies in Fifteenth-Century Stagecraft* (Kalamazoo: Western Michigan University, 1991) and C. Richardson and J. Johnston's *Medieval Drama* (London: Macmillan, 1991). The former examines several plays from the Towneley/Wakefield cycle by the so-called Wakefield Master and several others from the York cycle by the so-called York Realist. Richardson and Johnston's book discusses one representative play from each of the four extant complete—or nearly complete—cycles, chosen from what is probably the most popular or at least widely-used contemporary textbook of such plays, A.C. Cawley's *Everyman and Medieval Miracle Plays* (London: J.M. Dent, 1956).

demonstrate that these medieval biblical plays, chosen partly because they depict a broad range of key events in Christ's earthly life from his birth, ministry, crucifixion, and ascension to heaven, effectively reinforce doctrinal orthodoxy about Christ's Incarnation, God's plan of redemption for humankind, and the personal responsibility of people to live lives pleasing to God because of—not in spite of—their power as drama.

I need first of all to briefly explain the term 'mystery play' for the benefit of those who may be unfamiliar with this early form of creative endeavour in medieval England. The word 'mystery' is misleading for many. It was apparently first applied to these cycles by an eighteenth-century editor, Robert Dodsley, in 1744, on the analogy of the French *mystere*, a scriptural play. Most critics use the term 'mystery play' in this sense, but some modern editors such as Cawley prefer the term 'miracle play', although most prefer to apply the latter term solely to plays of the same period based on the legend of some extra-biblical saint or sacred object, very few of which survive.

Contemporary records suggest that while these plays may have initially been presented in churches around either Christmas or Easter, by the first half of the fourteenth century they were being performed outdoors, each pageant by a specific community craft guild either in conjunction with the Corpus Christi festival in June, first established by Pope Urban VI in 1311 to celebrate the doctrine of transubstantiation, or at Whitsuntide, fifty days after Easter (and thus normally in June also). In York we know it was customary to perform all 48 pageants in the cycle within a single day, starting around 4.30 am and finishing about 9.00 at night. In many cases each play would be repeatedly performed on its own pageant wagon at from twelve to sixteen different sites in the town. In other towns somewhat more fixed sites for the performances may have been employed.

The Wakefield (the town in which it was performed) or Towneley (the name of the nineteenth-century Lancashire squire who owned the single existing manuscript) cycle consisted of thirty-two plays. Six of these, because of their high degree of sophisticated poetic style as well as their dramatic artistry, are attributed to a single playwright, the so-called Wakefield Master, who flourished around 1430.

The N. Town (for *nomen* or name) cycle was made up of forty-two plays. Many critics favour Lincoln as the probable site at which these plays were performed. A performance of the York cycle, consisting of at least forty-eight plays, is recorded as taking place in 1378, but some scholars speculate it may have been around as early as 1340.

The Chester cycle, made up of twenty-four plays, is normally considered the earliest extant mystery play cycle, dated with a high degree of certainty around 1375 but possibly performed as early as 1328. It is thus probably the earliest of the existing mystery play cycles. Unlike the other cycles noted above, which exist in a single text only, this one has five texts.

Contemporary municipal records mention the existence of at least twelve mystery play cycles, but only these four exist in relatively full form. In addition, there are four other single mystery plays and one fragment.[11]

We turn now to an examination of the way four plays about key events in the life of Christ from the four extant cycles manage both to reinforce orthodox Christian belief and yet also to serve as effective works of drama.

Wakefield Cycle: 'The Annunciation' (No. 10)[12]

The actor playing God, speaking at the opening of this play, outlines the divine plan for Adam's redemption (and, by implication, all of humankind's). He explains that Adam has suffered sufficiently for his sin, both on earth and in hell, '[f]or these five thousand yers and more...' (p. 175). He goes on to say that his Son 'shall take on human form' (p. 176), affirming

> My son shall by a maid be born,
> The fiend of hell to hold in scorn...
> Both God and man shall he be,
> And both mother and maiden she... (p. 176).

Note how succinctly the playwright conveys the following essentials of orthodox Christian belief about the person of Christ:

11. A.M. Kinghorn, *Medieval Drama* (London: Evans Brothers, 1968), p. 64.

12. M. Rose (ed.), *The Wakefield Mystery Plays* (Garden City, NY: Doubleday, 1963), pp. 175-85 (page numbers are cited in the text). I have chosen to use either a modern 'translation' of the four plays under discussion here or to provide an in-text 'translation' of the more obscure passages. In my judgment the best scholarly edition of the Wakefield/Towneley plays, for example, is M. Stevens and A.C. Cawley (eds.), *The Towneley Plays*, I (Oxford: Oxford University Press, 1994). This play, entitled 'Incipit Annunciacio' originally, is on pp. 92-103.

1.   The divine nature and pre-birth existence of the Son;
2.   The mystery of the dual nature of the incarnated Son, being simultaneously human and divine. Just a few lines later God reiterates this point—that Mary 'shall of her body bear / God and man...' (p. 177);
3.   The doctrine of the virgin birth—that Mary would be both maiden and mother;
4.   The essential purpose of the incarnation of Christ: to provide a solution for humankind's estrangement from God—that is, to provide for their salvation.

By means of this opening soliloquy by God, the playwright makes explicit divine intentionality regarding Christ's incarnation that is largely implicit in the account recorded in the Gospel of Luke ch. 1.

The ensuing speech to Mary by the archangel Gabriel follows quite closely the biblical text in Lk. 1.28-37 save for one additional didactic element: Jesus' role in releasing humankind from their servitude to sin:

For thou hast found, without a doubt,   When he is come, that is thy son,
The grace of God that has gone out   He shall take circumcision,
    For Adam's plight.   Call him Jesus.
This is the grace that gives thee bloom   God's son shall men him call
Thou shalt conceive within thy womb   Who comes to free the thrall
    A child of might.   Within us (p. 177).

(Note the angel's identification, by the way, with humanity, by his word 'us'. It is as if the identity of the speaker as human actor eclipses his assumed persona as angel.)

In response to Mary's query about how it will be possible to give birth to a child without having slept with a man, Gabriel reiterates the miracle of Christ's virgin birth earlier announced in God's introductory speech about her being both mother and maiden:

Lady, this secret hear of me;
The holy ghost shall come to thee,
    And in his virtue
Thee enshroud and so infuse,
Yet thou thy maidhood shall not lose,
    But ay be new.

The child that thou shalt bear, madame,
Shall God's son be called by name... (p. 178).

Immediately after the angel Gabriel's departure, the Wakefield playwright telescopes time by presenting Joseph in a state of shocked disbelief at the fact that his beloved Mary is in the full bloom of pregnancy. (The person playing the role of Mary would be obliged to effect some quick changes in her appearance during Joseph's speech—from wondering maiden to a mature woman in the advanced stages of pregnancy.) The playwright, in his desire to present a convincing characterization of Joseph, adopts the convention not even implicit in the biblical record that Joseph was much older than Mary. Joseph's attempt to explain Mary's apparent unfaithfulness during his nine-month absence (another realistic circumstantial detail not in any of the scriptural records) focuses on this age differential. For example, he rues,

I am irked full sore with my life,	I am old, indeed to say
That ever I wed so young a wife,	And passed the pleasures of love's play,
Repent I of that plan;	Those games from me are gone.
To me it was a doleful deed,	Youth and age are poorly paired;
I might have known the wench had need	That know I well, since ill I fared,
To love a younger man.	Some other she dotes on (p. 179).

Accordingly, in Joseph's ensuing encounter with Mary, he immediately challenges her to name the father of her child. She responds that the child is 'God's and yours' (p. 180), insisting that she has done nothing amiss.

Joseph continues to realistically struggle with his own feelings of inferiority because of his age. Mary having temporarily withdrawn, Joseph takes the audience into his confidence by explaining to them how he had been selected by temple authorities, of all the eligible bachelors, for Mary's hand. He is certainly being compellingly portrayed as the epitome of the reluctant bridegroom:

> I was full sorry to be thus caught,
> My age put marriage past my thought
> For us to share a tether;
> Her youth would find my age no use,
> But they would hear of no excuse,
> But wed us thus together (p. 182).

At the end of his soliloquy, Joseph, feeling unworthy to live with the mother of God's son, resolves to secretly flee away to the wilderness and never see Mary again.

At this point the angel Gabriel appears to Joseph in the wilderness and directs him to return to his wife again, for '…she is without

stain, / Nor ever was defiled' (p. 184). Joseph reassumes his role as
the voice of the playwright's doctrinal teaching in this play by immediately acknowledging the privilege of serving as a caregiver to the
Son of God and repenting of his misconceptions about his wife's purity:

<table>
<tr><td>Ah, Lord, I love thee above all,</td><td>Repent I now what I have said</td></tr>
<tr><td>For so great boon as may befall</td><td>Against her matchless maidenhead,</td></tr>
<tr><td>That I should tend this stripling:</td><td>For she is pure in deed;</td></tr>
<tr><td>I that so ungracious were</td><td>Therefore to her now will I go</td></tr>
<tr><td>To cast on her the slightest slur,</td><td>And pray her be my friend not foe,</td></tr>
<tr><td>Mary, my dear darling.</td><td>And her forgiveness plead (p. 184).</td></tr>
</table>

The play ends with a brief exchange between Joseph and Mary in which
he repents of his wrongful accusation and she affirms that both she and
God forgive him. He concludes with the following prayer:

> He that can quench all grief
> And every wrong amend,
> Lend me grace, power, and might
> My wife and her sweet son of light
> To keep to my life's end (p. 185).

In short, what the Wakefield playwright is underlining for his
medieval audience is the Christian doctrine of the Virgin Birth as the
crux of Christ's identity as both God and man. In the process he has
portrayed the growth of a very plausible Mary and Joseph as they
move from incredulity to not just understanding but also acceptance of
their own divinely-ordained, crucial roles in God's plan of redemption through Christ. The play more than adequately fulfils the principal religious purpose of these mystery play cycles, as affirmed as late
as the sixteenth century by William Newhall (concerning the Chester
cycle):

> Forasmuch as of old time, not only for the augmentation of the holy and
> catholic faith of our Saviour, Jesu Christ, and to exhort the minds of the
> common people to good devotion and wholesome doctrine thereof, but
> also for the commonwealth and prosperity of this City, a play and decla-
> ration of divers stories of the Bible, beginning with the Creation and Fall
> of Lucifer, and ending with the general judgment of the world, to be
> declared and played in the Whitsun week... [13]

---

13. Cawley (ed.), *Everyman and Medieval Miracle Plays*, p. ix.

The N. Town Cycle: 'The Woman Taken in Adultery'[14]

This episode in Christ's ministry, described in St John's Gospel 8.3-11, is treated in three[15] of the four extant English Corpus Christi cycles, largely, according to Robert Potter, because it effectively—and ironically—prefigures the Last Judgment.[16] Cawley explains that he prefers this N. Town version because the playwright 'shows greater skill both in dramatizing the scene of the adultery and in heightening the excitement of the battle of wits between Christ and the Pharisees. The action is vividly presented', he continues, 'and the dialogue rings true... But while the human interest of the episode is exploited to the full, its Christian meaning—the quality of divine mercy—is also made plain.'[17]

I believe Potter is correct in pointing out that this pageant depicts a power struggle 'between antithetical notions of justice: the letter and the spirit; vengeance versus forgiveness, the Old Law and the New'.[18] This two-pronged emphasis—the relation between God's mercy and his justice—is the essential thread tying together virtually all of the pageants making up these mystery play cycles. No play examines this seemingly paradoxical doctrine more fully than does this one. In the process the playwright adds considerably to the rather sketchy details of the original narrative: he creates a character called 'Accuser' in addition to the representative Scribe and Pharisee (both offices were pluralized in the original text); he adds a planning session among the three representatives of the existing power structure, with a strong suggestion that the voyeuristic motives of the three are just as strong as their desire to place Jesus in a difficult interpretative dilemma; he also invents a scene depicting the actual arrest of the woman, complete with the half-dressed 'john' of the day threatening to kill anyone that would have the audacity to lay hands on him, and the harlot pleading with her captors, when they ignore first her request for mercy, and then her offer of a bribe, to execute her on the spot so that she might

---

14. Cawley (ed.), *Everyman and Medieval Miracle Plays*, pp. 131-42. Because of the presence of line references in this edition, page references have not been included. Translation of difficult words is presented within square brackets.

15. The York and the Chester cycles besides this N. Town one.

16. R. Potter, 'Divine and Human Justice', in P. Neuss (ed.), *Aspects of Early English Drama* (Cambridge: D.S. Brewer, 1983), p. 138.

17. Cawley (ed.), *Everyman and Medieval Miracle Plays*, p. 131.

18. Potter, 'Divine and Human Justice', p. 139.

avoid being shamed and slandered before all her friends. The much
fuller realization of the Woman's character is also accomplished by her
explicit admission of her guilt to Christ, her expression of repentance,
and her plea for mercy, elements not present in the biblical account:

> Now, holy prophet, be merciable [merciful]!
> Upon me, wretch, take no vengeance.
> For my sins abominable,
> In heart I have great repentance.
> I am well worthy to have mischance,
> Both bodily death and worldly shame;
> But, gracious prophet, of succurrance [help]
> This time pray you, for God's name (ll. 209-16).

The necessity of the Woman's plea to Christ for mercy is established
for the audience at the very beginning of the play, where Christ, in a
speech five octaves (40 lines) long affirms his identity as not only the
dispenser but the means of God's mercy. No fewer than thirteen times
is the word 'mercy' (or in one instance its cognate 'merciable') used,
with Christ urging his auditors not only to ask God's mercy for
themselves but also in turn to practice mercy in their interaction with
others. The didactic point cannot be evaded, as the fifth of these octaves
reveals:

> Each man to other be merciable [merciful],
> And mercy he shall have at need;
> What[ever] man of mercy is not treatable [inclined],
> When he asketh mercy he shall not speed.
> Mercy to grant I come indeed:
> Whoso ask mercy he shall have grace;
> Let no man doubt [fear] for his misdeed,
> But ever ask mercy while he hath space [time] (ll. 33-40).

The Pharisee confirms the identity of Christ as merciful in the
ensuing plotting scene when he contrives to set that mercy up in
conflict with Mosaic law, which declared that such a woman should be
executed by stoning:

> Of grace and mercy ever he doth preach,
> And that no man should be vengeable [vengeful].
> Against the woman if he say wreak [i.e., she should be punished],
> Then of his preaching he is unstable;
> And if we find him variable [changeable],
> Of his preaching that he hath taught,

Then have we cause, both just and able,
For a false man that he be caught [arrested] (ll. 89-96).

As he does a number of times in several of the later passion play sequences, when challenged by the high priest or King Herod or Pilate, Jesus does not at first respond when the three accusers hale the Woman before him, demanding that he decide whether she should be stoned, in accordance with Moses' law, or be set free. During their recital of the litany of allegations against the Woman Jesus, as in the biblical text, silently writes on the ground. Finally he succinctly challenges them, in a single quatrain:

> Look which of you that never sin wrought,
> *But is of life cleaner than she* [my emphasis];
> Cast at her stones, and spare her nought,
> Clean out of [Entirely free from] sin if that ye be (ll. 229-32).

In a fascinating elaboration of the original text (where Jesus had simply said, in Jn 8.7, 'He that is without sin among you, let him cast a stone at her'), Jesus is lowering the criterion for their participation in her punishment from a claim of sinlessness to a profession of being merely less sinful than she! The Pharisee, Accuser, and Scribe proceed in turn to make explicit what the scriptural account does not concerning the basis for their embarrassed withdrawal, one by one, from the scene: Jesus has recorded the particulars of their sins for all to see. When Jesus invites the Woman to explain where her foes have gone, her understanding of the situation is impeccable: 'Because they could not themselves excuse, / With shame they fled hence every one' (ll. 267-68).

Accordingly, when Christ observes that she cannot be condemned now because the prosecution has abandoned her case, he also grants her his divine pardon:

> For me thou shalt not condemned be;
> Go home again and walk at large:
> Look that thou live in honesty,
> And will no more to sin, I thee charge (ll. 277-80).

Clearly it is not an inconsequential granting of mercy, then. An accompanying expectation stipulates that the exonerated person abandon her former sordid lifestyle. With repentance, the playwright is making abundantly clear, comes the requirement of reformation. Lest this important spiritual principle be lost on a less than attentive audience, the playwright twice reinforces the point, first by having the Woman affirm her resolve to reform:

> I thank you highly, holy prophet,
> Of this great grace ye have me grant;
> All my lewd life I shall down let [forsake],
> And fond [try] to be God's true servant (ll. 281-84).

Secondly, the playwright has the character playing Jesus suspend, it would seem, his role as the central historical figure in this episode to express what amounts to a parish priest's admonition:

> When man is contrite and hath won grace,
> God will not keep old wrath in mind;
> But better love to them he has,
> Very contrite when he them find.
> Now God, *that died for all mankind* [emphasis mine],
> Save all these people both night and day [i.e., always];
> And [may] of our sins he us unbind [deliver],
> High Lord of heaven that best may [i.e., is best able to do so]. Amen (ll. 289-96).

His reference in the third person to the death of God for all mankind— that is, his own death—confirms this concluding change of persona.

This play, therefore, as most good drama, is replete with conflict, suspense, intrigue, colourful characters, climax, and satisfying resolution. Interestingly, it effectively undercuts masculine hegemony by portraying the Woman as superior in every meaningful respect to the male villains of the piece. At the same time, the action illuminates a powerful spiritual principle central, as intimated earlier, to all mystery play cycles: the nature of God and his redemptive purpose for humankind as revealed both in his dealings with individuals, starting with Adam and Eve, but particularly in the life, death, resurrection, and ascension of Jesus Christ.

The York Cycle: 'The Crucifixion'[19]

The play depicting the crucifixion of Christ is portrayed with considerable restraint in the Chester and N. Town cycles, but the York and Towneley pageants make 'a direct assault on the feelings of the

---

19. Cawley (ed.), *Everyman and Medieval Miracle Plays*, pp. 143-55. All quotations will be identified by line numbers. Translation of difficult words is presented within square brackets.

audience'; here the dramatist displays 'his flair for realistic presentation of the physically horrible...where the business of the Crucifixion is mercilessly drawn out...'[20]

The four soldiers who serve as Christ's executioners are portrayed as grimly competent in their work. They exhibit no compassion whatsoever for their victim; for example,

1 Soldier calls him 'this dote [fool]' (l. 5).
4 Soldier suggests, 'Let[s] ding [knock] him down! Then he is done. /
    He shall not dere [harm] us with his din' (ll. 17-18).
4 Soldier: 'Come on, let[s] kill this traitor strong' (l. 32).
2 Soldier: 'For all his fare [boasting] he shall be flayed [terrified]:
    That on essay [trial] soon shall ye see' (ll. 43-44).
3 Soldier: 'Come forth, thou cursed knave,
    Thy comfort soon shall keel [grow cold]' (ll. 45-46).

The image of Christ in this play is conveyed largely in terms of the cruel treatment he receives at the hands of these executioners, not in terms of what he himself says. In fact, the playwright gives him only two twelve-line speeches. In the first of these, in the form of a prayer to God the Father, Christ affirms his willingness to suffer the tortures of crucifixion in order to effect humankind's salvation:

Almighty God, my Father free [noble],
Let these matters be marked in mind:
Thou bade that I should buxom [ready] be,
For Adam's plight to be pined [tortured].
Here to death I oblige me [pledge myself],
From that sin for to save mankind,
And sovereignly [above all] beseech I thee
That they for me may favour find;
And from the fiend them fend [defend],
So that their souls be safe
In wealth [happiness] withouten end;
I keep not else to crave [I have no wish to ask for anything else] (ll. 49-60).

The grisly cruelty portrayed in this play is therefore by no means gratuitous spectacle. The playwright, in keeping with these Corpus Christi mystery play cycles' overall purpose, is attempting to foster in his lay audience piety, devotion, and thanksgiving to Christ for his sacrificial death on the cross to pay the penalty for human sin.

In his second speech, near the end of the play, Jesus first confirms the

---

20. Cawley (ed.), *Everyman and Medieval Miracle Plays*, p. 143.

extent of his suffering but then extends his mercy to the soldiers that
have so cruelly abused him by imploring his Father to forgive them:

> All men that walk by way or street
> Take tent [care] ye shall no travail tine [waste];
> Behold my head, my hands, my feet,
> And fully feel now, ere ye fine [stop],
> If any mourning may be meet [fitting],
> Or mischief [misfortune] measured unto mine.
> My Father, that all bales may beet [ills may remedy],
> Forgive these men that do me pine [inflict suffering on me].
> What they work wot [know] they nought;
> Therefore, my Father, I crave,
> Let never their sins be sought [examined],
> But see their souls to save [But see that their souls are saved] (ll. 253-64).

After his first prayer, the soldiers think him mad for thinking about
Adam's race rather than himself. They assume that he is insufficiently
afraid of the suffering he is about to endure and say he should be
repentant of his wicked works and words. They then order him to lie
down on the cross, and incredibly, much to their amazement, he
wordlessly complies. The fourth soldier remarks,

> Behold, himself has laid him down,
> In length and breadth as he should be (ll. 75-76).

Jesus is symbolically portraying the important truth of his voluntary
submission to the ignominious indignities of crucifixion as outlined in
Jn 10.17-18: 'Therefore doth my Father love me, because I lay down
my life, that I might take it again. No man taketh it from me, but I lay
it down of myself. I have power to lay it down, and I have power to
take it again.'

The playwright proceeds to depict in chilling detail the callous
cruelty of the four soldiers as they nail Jesus to his cross. Unlike any
of the other extant Crucifixion pageants, these executioners are obliged
to stretch and pull Jesus' body to reach the incorrectly-bored nail holes.
(Cawley points out the interesting possibility that the use of cords by
the actors to ostensibly stretch Jesus limbs to fit the boreholes might
have been a practical means of justifying the use of necessary cords to
attach to the cross the actor playing the part of Jesus.)[21] They describe
their actions in chillingly explicit detail as they are performed; for
example:

21. Cawley (ed.), *Everyman and Medieval Miracle Plays*, p. 143.

4 Soldier	I hope [think] that mark amiss be bored.
2 Soldier	Then must he bide in bitter bale [torment].
3 Soldier	In faith, it was over-scantily scored [i.e., put in the wrong place]; That makes it foully for to fail [i.e., That's why it is so badly out].
1 Soldier	(Obviously the straw boss) Why carp ye so? Fast [fasten] on a cord, And tug him to [the holes], by top [head] and tail [feet] (ll. 109-14).

They proceed to pull Jesus this way and that, noting the possibility that his sinews will split asunder, until finally they successfully nail him to the cross. The completion of their cruel task is confirmed by this summative exchange:

1 Soldier	These cords have evil [severely] increased his pains, Ere he were till the borings [bore-holes] brought.
2 Soldier	Yea, asunder are both sinews and veins On ilka [each] side, so have we sought [so far as we have looked] (ll. 145-48).

Just when it appears that the limits of a medieval audience's emotional tolerance level would have been reached in this prolonged portrayal of callous cruelty inflicted on Christ, the playwright extends the painful scene even further by introducing another complication: 1 Soldier announces that the authorities have ordered Jesus' cross to be raised into an upright position 'that men might see' (l. 156). (Up to this point their victim has remained fastened to the cross as it lay on the ground.) Amidst much complaining about the cross's weight and awkwardness—including their having to put it down temporarily for fear of breaking their backs—they finally manage to carry it to 'yon hill' (l. 172) and drop it like a dead weight into its mortice. Of course—one could almost have predicted this—the hole is too big for the cross, so the soldiers are obliged to hammer in wedges to stabilize it. This whole process is described with agonizing particularity, without a single word from Jesus until his response to the following taunting jibes from two of the soldiers:

1 Soldier [to Christ]	Say, sir, how likes you now This work that we have wrought?
4 Soldier	We pray you say us how Ye feel, or faint ye aught (ll. 249-52).

In the reply already commented on above, Jesus says not a word of castigation against his tormentors but rather asks his Father to forgive them, because '[w]hat they work wot [know] they nought...' (l. 261).

This Crucifixion pageant concludes with the soldiers first verbally abusing Jesus for claiming to be God's Son and saying that he would destroy the temple and rebuild it in three days (from Mk 14.58 and Jn 2.19) and then deciding on the disposition of Christ's mantle. The three subordinates suggest that they draw lots, but the supervising soldier pulls rank by taking it for himself.

It seems clear that the principal point of this extended portrayal of the crucifixion of Christ is to convey to the medieval audience the excruciating suffering that the Son of God endured to pay the penalty for the sins of humanity. One critic comments on the 'unparalleled emotional intensity' of this pageant as follows:

> It is sometimes difficult for a modern sensibility to appreciate how any spiritual end could be served by scenes as brutal in their detail as the Crucifixion plays of the York or Towneley cycle... But that unsparing assault is precisely the aim of the scenes...[22]

Furthermore, the essential elements of Christ's overwhelming love for humankind are conveyed as much by what he doesn't say as by what he does. Clearly the 'image' of Christ projected in this play transcends, in importance, his words.

Chester Cycle: 'Christ's Ascension'[23]

This pageant, following, as it does, the play about Christ's resurrection, furthers the portrayal of Christ as the risen Savior who has conquered death and the grave. Not unexpectedly, the playwright depicts four of the disciples (Peter, Andrew, John, and James) as understandably dubious about whether they can trust what they are seeing. Obviously much about Christ has changed. For one thing, he appears in their midst without the inconvenience of having to gain admittance via the door. The Chester playwright addresses the difficulty of presenting such a miraculous phenomenon on stage by opening this pageant with Christ reassuring his followers:

22. R.J. Collier, *Poetry and Drama in the York Corpus Christi Play* (Hamden, CT: The Shoe String Press, 1977), p. 120.
23. M. Hussey, *The Chester Mystery Plays: Sixteen Pageant Plays from the Chester Craft Cycle adapted into Modern English* (London: Heinemann, 1957), pp. 117-21. There being no line numbers indicated, quotations from this play will be cited by page number.

My brethren that sit in company,
I greet you in peace full heartfeltly;
I am He that shall stand by thee:
Fear you for nothing (p. 117).

He goes on to say that he understands their wonderment about whether in fact he had actually risen from the dead, inviting them to touch his wounded hands and feet and asserting that 'ghosts have neither flesh nor bone...' The playwright is clearly following rather closely the biblical record contained in Lk. 24.36-53 in this respect.

But then the playwright fashions a most interesting exchange between the four disciples that is pure invention, as they debate among themselves whether this is really Jesus they are seeing. The discussion proceeds as if Jesus was not even there:

Peter: Ah, what is this that stands us by?
          A Ghost he seems to be verily;
          Methinks lightened much am I
          This spirit for to see.
Andrew: Peter, I tell thee secretly,
          I dread me yet full greatly
          That Jesu should show such mystery
          And whether that this be he.
John: Brethren, good is it to think ever more,
          What words he spake the day before
          He died on cross, he had not gone for evermore
          And we should steadfast aye.
James: Ah, John, that leaves us in fear
          That he will as he please appear,
          And when we most wish to have him here
          Then will he be away (pp. 117-18).

Such uncertainty about his identity elicits gentle chiding from Jesus about their lack of faith—a return, indeed, to the biblical source. He does two more things to reassure them: first, he asks to participate in their meal with them, and secondly, he reminds them of how he was explicitly fulfilling what had been predicted in the writings of Moses and the Psalms about him. He also reaffirms his divine role as the Savior of all humankind, a message that his disciples were to proclaim throughout the world:

My sweet brethren, dearest so dear,
To Me is granted fullest power
In Heaven and earth, both far and near,

> For My Godhead is most.
> To teach all men now go ye,
> That in the world will followed be,
> In the name of My father and of Me
> And of the Holy Ghost (p. 119).

In the compass of this very brief play, then, the playwright has once again portrayed both the human and divine natures of Christ—his corporeal identity and his deep concern and love for these human followers, and yet his deity and omnipotence as a member of the triune Godhead.

This latter aspect of Christ's identity is affirmed by the next exchange between Jesus and three angels who are welcoming Jesus back to heaven. The stage direction indicates that Jesus 'ascends', so it is likely that this extrabiblical exchange occurs on an upper stage. The angels remark that Jesus has freed souls from the world of sin and the grip of hell and that a number of saints are accompanying him. Jesus again confirms his majesty and power in his response:

> I that speak righteousness
> Have brought man out of distress;
> For Buyer [= Redeemer?] I am called and was
> Of all mankind through grace.
> My people that were from Me reft
> Through sin and through the devil's craft
> To heaven I bring and not one left
> All that in Hell there was (p. 119).

When the third angel asks him about his bloodstained body and head, as well as about the graveclothes he is wearing, Jesus explains:

> These drops now, with good intent,
> To my Father I will present
> That good men that to earth be lent
> Shall know certainly,
> How graciously that I them bought
> And for good works that they wrought
> The everlasting bliss they have sought
> I proved the good worthy.
> For this cause, believe you Me,
> The drops I shed on the rood tree
> All fresh shall reserved be
> Ever till the last day (p. 120).

It is interesting how the dramatist has moved from a portrayal of Jesus' warm and affirming relationship with his disciples to a depiction of Christ as redeemer of all humankind. This play anticipates the Last Judgment play, where a definite distinction will be made between the redeemed and the damned. Christ's mercy is extended to all, but not all will choose to accept that provision for their soul's salvation.

The play concludes by briefly depicting the scene described in the Book of Acts 1.10-12. The stage direction states that the angels 'descend' to the apostles to assure them that Jesus will '[r]ight so again come… / Even as you saw him go' (p. 120). Peter and Andrew resolve to return to Jerusalem forthwith to await the coming of the Holy Spirit, who will empower them to fulfil Christ's commandment to spread the gospel worldwide. Peter concludes the play by directly addressing the audience:

> Jesus, that from us now went
> Save all this company. Amen (p. 121).

In just two lines, the playwright has brought the historical past and the dramatic present together. The essence of God's redemptive plan through Christ has been tellingly and persuasively conveyed, made accessible to both medieval and modern audiences alike by means of the dramatist's art and the actor's craft.

Conclusion

In these four plays from the four existing mystery play cycles, then, we can observe what I believe to be a very successful imaging of Christ as both human and divine—as God incarnated in human form, without question the central doctrine of the Christian faith. Each play presents both conflict and resolution. Each play portrays complexities of characterization that both reinforce and enhance the biblical originals. Each play attempts to come to grips with the miraculous nature of Christ's identity—from his being born of the virgin Mary in 'The Annunciation' to his omniscient knowledge of his accusers' past in 'The Woman Taken in Adultery' to his divine capacity to forgive his executioners in 'The Crucifixion' to his ascension to heaven in 'The Ascension'. Interestingly, a common thread running through all four plays is the expression of doubt about Jesus' divine identity—by friend as well as by foe. In 'The Annunciation' play, Joseph expresses doubt about Mary's supernaturally induced pregnancy; in 'The Woman Taken in Adultery', Christ's accusers doubt his ability to respond adequately to the dilemma they face him with—whether to apply the rules of Mosaic law to the woman's crime or to extend mercy to her; in 'The Crucifixion', the disbelief is expressed by Jesus' executioners about his identity as one who could destroy the temple and rebuild it in three days; in 'Christ's Ascension' his own disciples debate whether it is really he that is standing before them. The presence of doubt, in short, constitutes a conflict that each play must resolve.

Each play's didactic purpose is readily identifiable, but I believe the dramatic power of each has unquestionably enhanced that purpose.

THE IMAGE OF CHRIST IN THE WRITINGS OF TWO SEVENTEENTH-CENTURY ENGLISH COUNTRY PARSONS: GEORGE HERBERT AND THOMAS TRAHERNE

Pat Pinsent

George Herbert and Thomas Traherne are probably among the seventeenth-century English writers regarded today with the greatest degree of affection as well as respect. Superficially they may seem to us to have a great deal in common. The centre of life for both of them was their relationship with God and it is scarcely surprising that both of them make very frequent references, in their poetry and prose, to Christ as Saviour, particularly to his cross and passion, emphasizing the virtue of his redeeming blood. Despite their absence from the public scene, both of them are clearly well aware of contemporary thought and events; influences from other seventeenth-century writers, especially poets, theologians and philosophers, can be detected in their work. Both have what today would be seen as a very didactic view of the need for the Christian writer to influence readers to 'right' beliefs and good behaviour. Even the appearance of their poems on the page, with apparently irregular patterns of rhyme and line length, is superficially similar.

Similarities go beyond their works. Both writers led short lives and their combined ages barely add up to a respectable life span; Herbert died in 1633 at forty and Traherne in 1674 at thirty-seven. These dates immediately reveal to us something of how their lives were affected by the turbulent events of the seventeenth century. Neither poet had in his lifetime the fame which posterity has afforded him, but Traherne waited a great deal longer for his fame than Herbert did. After the publication of Herbert's poetry soon after his death, his work went on to become esteemed and imitated by a range of lesser seventeenth-century poets. The manuscripts of the most significant of Traherne's prose and all his poetry, however, had to wait until the late nineteenth and the twentieth century for discovery and publication. Even more recently, his work is beginning to receive the acclaim that it deserves.

These writers then had much in common, yet in some respects these resemblances are skewed. Herbert was born of a noble family, had a distinguished university career and the prospects of a future at Court, yet left the glittering prizes for the country parish of Bemerton, close to Wilton House and near to Salisbury. Traherne was probably the son of a Hereford tradesman and after university and ordination spent a few years as vicar of Credenhill, near Hereford, before coming to the metropolis as chaplain to Sir Orlando Bridgeman in Teddington, Surrey.

In their works, too, the apparent similarities between subjects and devotions sometimes mask significant differences. Most germane to our theme, I want to suggest that while both writers remain well within the bounds of orthodoxy, they present in their poetry and in their prose surprisingly different images of Christ. Some of their dissimilarities in theology, devotion and expression probably result from disparity in temperament and background; others may well reflect the fact that while Herbert died some years before the English Civil War, Traherne grew up in the midst of it.

One fairly obvious difference, which may relate to talent and audience as much as to period, is the fact that Herbert's poetry, in his major work, *The Temple*, which was published posthumously by his friend Nicholas Ferrar, is much more intense than his prose treatise, *A Priest to the Temple Or The Countrey* [sic] *Parson his Character and Rule of Holy Life*. On the other hand, it has often been suggested that Traherne's prose, in his *Centuries of Meditation,* is more impassioned than his poetry. Louis Martz claims that his full power 'is not displayed in his poetry, which too often consists primarily in versified statement, assertion or exclamation' (1964: 80). This implied inferiority could well be true if the best pieces of prose are compared with some of the weaker poems, but may nevertheless be too sweeping a judgment overall. Of the two poets, Herbert is of course very much the more conscious literary artist, often creating a persona whose stance ironically expresses views which need to be put into question, a technique much less common in Traherne, whose 'wit' is of a different cast. I will illustrate some of the other ways in which these two writers differ, by reference to examples which are particularly relevant to the kind of image of Christ which they present.

I would claim that Herbert's Christology is to a considerable extent integral to the drama of religious experience he presents in his poems and that in his prose it provides the basis of his pragmatic advice. Traherne's theology and his depiction of Christ seem to me, however, to display a greater degree of separation from his presentation of his own personal religious and mystical experience, even though the theological perspectives appear to be the result of later reflection on this experience.

I do not of course intend to imply that Herbert did not reflect on *his* experience but rather that he does not present the theologizing separate from the account of the experience, as Traherne often seems to do.

It is also notable that Herbert tends to make more use of traditional typology in writing about Christ and other aspects of religion than Traherne does. This often has a medieval origin, as in the dependence of Herbert's poem 'The Sacrifice' on the liturgical Reproaches, the *Improperia*. Traherne on the other hand shows more explicit concern with fashionable (though not contemporary) philosophy, such as Pico del Mirandola and Hermes Trismegistus, who are referred to explicitly in *Centuries* (IV, 74). This could of course be simply an aspect of chronology, but I think it is rather to be seen as indicative of a dichotomy in approach between the two writers.

In order to exemplify these and some of the other differences between Herbert and Traherne, I propose now to concentrate particularly on some examples of their writing: 'Redemption', 'Longing' and 'Love III' by Herbert, and two of Traherne's *Centuries* (I, 62 and 86), as well as part of one of his poems, 'The World'. Throughout their work, of which these pieces are fairly typical examples, there seems to be a striking difference between the ways that these two orthodox and devoutly Christian writers address and portray Christ.

Although it would be easy to demonstrate, largely from his prose, that Herbert accepts without question the belief in the Trinity, it is quite difficult to discover in his poetry any evidence of distinction between the attributes of the three persons of the Godhead. During the course of a single poem, or indeed of a single stanza, he abruptly changes focus from describing God as Creator to seeing God as Redeemer. In 'Longing', for example, he addresses the Lord, from whom 'all pity flows', whose book is the world, and whose 'dust' the persona of the poem is. All of these images would seem to signify Creatorhood, yet the following lines which clearly address Christ seem

to be a continuum addressed to the same Lord as the earlier section of
the poem:

> Lord Jesus, thou didst bow
> Thy dying head upon the tree:
> O be not now
> More dead to me!
> Lord, hear! Shall he that made the ear
> Not hear? (stanza 6).

Christ on the cross is thus explicitly identified with the God of
creation. A similar identification occurs in 'Love III', where Love
claims responsibility for both creation, 'Who made the eyes but I?',
and redemption, 'And know you not, says Love, who bore the blame?'
Complex intertextual allusions to both the Eucharist and to Psalm 23
complete the rich ambivalence.

A more extended and complex situation occurs in the little story told
in Herbert's 'Redemption', where the tenant (surely to be seen as both
collective humanity and a slightly obtuse individual voice) searches for
the 'Rich Lord' who owns the Manorial rights (Creatorhood), only to
find that he has 'gone/About some land…on earth'. There is no hint
that a greater Lord, God the Father, still remains behind in heaven. On
earth, the reader, guided by the ironic implications of the words 'great
birth' and knowledge of the Gospel account of the Magi seeking Christ,
is well ahead of the persona and is not really surprised to find the
Lord dying on Calvary, hence pointing to the several levels of
meaning in the poem's title. Thus there seems in Herbert's poetry to
be a single Lord, who is both Creator and Redeemer; to attempt to
distinguish between the Father and the Son, or between the divinity
and the humanity of Christ is, as so often in Herbert's poems, not
merely impossible but also perverse.

Herbert therefore seems to want to have God as an undivided subject,
sometimes a singular addressee, possessing all the qualities that are
traditionally attributed to different persons of the Trinity: creator,
redeemer and sanctifier. I suspect that as well as this being more aesthetically satisfying, it is also one of the reasons for the appeal of
Herbert's poetry to many people without any religious affiliation. His
work is strongly concerned with relationship to God but does not
demand that in order to appreciate the poem the reader be explicitly
aware of the theological aspects of that relationship or about the nature

of God and of salvation. A knowledge of the theological or scriptural aspects however is likely to deepen the reading.

Traherne, on the other hand, generally makes explicit a difference between God as Creator and Christ as Redeemer, and seems frequently to address a different aspect of God from Herbert's. His God, as generally addressed, is Creator, revealed in his works; his Christ is indeed the Divine Son. He speaks to him as 'Image of Thine Eternal Father' (*Centuries of Meditation*, I, 86), who 'didst suffer the wrath of GOD for me' (*Centuries*, I, 62). Many of his *Centuries* are very explicit about the Passion of Christ and the motive it supplies for gratitude to God. His invocation to the crucified Christ,

> I beseech Thee let those trickling drops of blood that ran down Thy flesh drop on me. O let Thy love enflame me (I, 62),

is as fervent as either the baroque counter-Reformation intensity of Crashaw on the one hand or the enthusiasm revealed in the hymns of eighteenth-century Methodists and Evangelicals such as Wesley, Cowper and Newton on the other. Lines like these, however, do not remind me of the work of most seventeenth-century Anglican writers of either poetry or prose.[1]

Generally Herbert's frequent references to the redeeming blood of Christ are far more restrained than Traherne's. The economy of 'and died' ('Redemption'), 'bore the blame' ('Love III') and the lines quoted above from 'Longing' could equally be exemplified from a variety of Herbert's poems. Even his most explicit and detailed treatment of the passion of Christ, in 'The Sacrifice', makes intellectual rather than overtly emotional demands on the reader:

> Then with a scarlet robe they me aray;
> Which shews my bloud to be the only way,

---

1.   In a research project on the work of over 200 seventeenth-century minor poets, only about 11 per cent of whom were Catholic, it was found that a very high proportion of those writing on the passion of Christ in terms which seemed most influenced by the Continental Baroque were in fact Catholic. The poets in whom this seemed most notable were: Joseph Beaumont (Anglican), Patrick Carey (Catholic), Richard Crashaw (Catholic), Arthur Crowther and Thomas Sadler (Catholics, joint authors), Eldred Revett (religion unknown), Sir Edward Sherburne (Catholic), Thomas Stanley (Catholic connections), Edward Thimelby (Catholic). For further details, see P.A. Pinsent, 'Religious Verse of English Recusant Poets', *Recusant History* (October 1995), pp. 491-500.

> And cordiall left to repair mans decay:
> > Was ever grief like mine?
>
> Then on my head a crown of thorns I wear:
> For these are all the grapes Sion doth bear,
> Though I my vine planted and watred there:
> > Was ever grief like mine? (ll. 157-64).

The use of Old Testament antitype, the adaptation of the complaint tradition into paradox and double meaning, even the implicit link with the Eucharist ('cordiall' with a two-fold allusion to both drink and the heart, 'grapes' and 'vine' with all their associations)—all these aspects unite to make even these few lines extraordinarily complex. Traherne's prose quoted above, which could be paralleled by a number of similarly purple passages, while visually extravagant, has nothing like the same intertextuality. This is the result of the differing modes and aims of the poets. Herbert's readers are expected to be led to make deductions about their share in the human responsibility for Christ's death and, resultant upon this, they should be helped to realize that the effects of his passion should be made their own. Traherne's readers are encouraged to *feel* sympathy and sorrow for Christ's sufferings as a man.

This difference between the intellectual and the affective modes of meditation has frequently been commented on in distinctions drawn between Donne and Crashaw (see Martz 1962 and Low 1978), but it is equally notable here between Herbert and Traherne. The first mode might be described as concentric, drawing readers to a concentrated appreciation of the spiritual significance of what is often a short anecdote, with the hope of intensifying and deepening their relationship with God. All the parts neatly fit into a whole. Though the technique depends on the intellect, the intention is through this to influence the will, a process which may of course incidentally involve the emotions. On the other hand, the affective mode, which is more peripheral in its tendency to follow a kind of stream-of-consciousness approach, is directly aimed at arousing emotional heat through descriptions aimed at the senses. The language used differs too, Traherne's meditations on the passion of Christ being characterized by both a kind of synaesthesia, including touch, and an exclamatory tone: 'O my life and my all' (I, 62). Repetition is far less out of place in this kind of meditation than it would be in Herbert's, of which economy and restraint are more characteristic.

Although repetition and heightened emotion are to be found throughout Traherne's *Centuries*, the effect seems a little less emphatic and more spontaneous in his meditations upon nature and creation than in those upon the passion of Christ. It could be argued that Traherne is writing in this affective manner as a direct result of his intended reader being a woman, probably Mrs Susanna Hopton.[2] As noted by Low (1993: 247) in a study of Crashaw, women were thought to be drawn particularly to 'sensible affection', and spiritual directors, of whom Traherne clearly is one, would have written to excite such emotions. My own feeling, however, is that in encouraging his reader to gaze intently on the person of the crucified Christ, Traherne is also admonishing himself. His natural instinct seems to be to perceive God in nature, so that he feels the need consciously to bring himself to concentrate on the explicitly Christocentric element of religion. Herbert's gaze needs no such direction; it is already totally integrated with his theology.

Traherne seems however to need little self-admonition to attend to Christ's injunction to recognize him in others: 'Whatever you do to the least of my brethren, that you do unto me'. At many points in the *Centuries* he shows his awareness of Christ as the means by which he, and all humanity, can be described as 'sole heirs' of all the greatness of creation (*Centuries* I, 29). The doctrine which was so important to St Paul (see 1 Cor. 12) and to Gerard Manley Hopkins (as in 'For Christ plays in ten thousand places... To the Father through the features of men's faces', from 'As kingfishers catch fire') pervades, for instance, *Centuries* I, 86:

---

2.   The author's inscription on the first leaf of *Centuries of Meditation* is:

> This book unto the friend of my best friend
> As of the wisest Love a mark I send,
> That she may write my Maker's prais therin
> And make her self therby a Cherubin.

The dedicatee may well have been Mrs Susanna Hopton, a friend who possessed some of his manuscripts and was at one stage attributed with some of his writings (cf. A. Bradford [ed.], *Thomas Traherne: Selected Poems and Prose* [Harmondsworth: Penguin, 1991]). M. Bottrall, however (*Celebrating Traherne* [Hereford: Traherne Press, 1991]), finds this attribution unlikely, since Mrs Hopton was older than Traherne and his social superior.

> Thou wholly communicatest Thyself to every soul in all kingdoms and art
> wholly seen in every saint, and wholly fed upon by every Christian. It is
> my privilege that I can enter with Thee into every soul...

This sense of being one in Christ with all other Christians does not seem to me to be a particularly conspicuous aspect of Herbert's poetry, though it could be argued that it underpins much of his practical advice in prose to the Country Parson. The Christ of his poems is always omnipotent and omniscient and ever at hand in a close personal relationship with the persona of the poem.

It has sometimes been suggested that Herbert's Christ has female attributes; Pearlman (1983) claims that Herbert's relationship with God cannot be divorced from his relationship with his mother, whose death in 1627 seems to have been the prelude to his period of greatest poetic activity. Certainly in 'Longing' he addresses to God these lines:

> Mothers are kind, because thou art,
> And dost dispose
> To them a part:
> Their infants them; and they suck thee
> More free.

The tradition of the Motherhood of God can of course be recognized in both Testaments of the Bible; it was exploited freely by St Anselm and St Bernard (see Jantzen 1987: 117), though the best known linking of motherhood with Christ is to be found in Julian of Norwich (Jantzen 1987: 120-23). While it is clearly possible that at least the first two of these writers were known to Herbert, it is equally likely that the theme results from his own spiritual experience, dependent as that no doubt was on his personal psychological biography. Elsewhere there can no doubt be detected a gender ambivalence in the aspect of God to whom the persona relates. In 'Love III' the Host is gracious, offers a meal, and is addressed by the guest as 'My dear'. In an extended discussion of sexuality in *The Temple*, Schoenfeldt suggests that this poem

> exploits... a conflation of the imagery of eating and of sexual intercourse.
> In offering himself to all at each celebration of the Eucharist, Christ is like
> a desirable and desiring lover, promiscuously permitting suitors to
> possess him again and again (1990: 289).

This only implies the portrayal of a specifically female Host if we adhere to a strict polarization of gender attributes. It could be argued

that the eroticism of the relationship, which is also frequently emphasized by Herbert's employment of sacred parody, as in the final stanza
of 'Longing'—

> My love, my sweetness, hear!
> By these thy feet, at which my heart
> Lies all the year,
> Pluck out thy dart,
> And heal my troubled breast which cries,
> Which dies.

—is merely an instance of the very long-standing mystical tradition of
the soul, of a man as well as that of a woman, being seen as female,
the 'anima', before God. We might compare the concluding lines of
Donne's Holy Sonnet, 'Batter my heart': 'I / Except you enthral me,
never shall be free, / Nor ever chaste, except you ravish me'.

A reference to this same tradition is also to be found in Traherne's
Centuries IV, 77, where he provides a traditional exegesis of Psalm 45:

> The Psalmist here singeth an Epithalamium upon the Marriage between
> Christ and His Church... evry Child of this Bride, is if a Male a Prince over
> all the Earth; if a Female Bride to the King of Heaven. And every Soul that
> is a Spous of Jesus Christ, esteemth all the Saints her own Children and
> her own Bowels.

The male/female role dichotomy in the penultimate sentence seems
strange here, and its effect appears to be negated by the final sentence. It
is almost as if Traherne is resisting the logic of the older tradition yet
capitulating to it after all. It may be relevant to recall that the intended
first reader of the *Centuries* was probably a woman.

A convenient way of summarizing the differences between these two
writers is to suggest that whereas Herbert's God is *indoors*, in all senses
of the word, Traherne's is *outdoors*. Herbert finds God both in ordinary
indoor activities, and, most notably, in the Eucharist and within the
heart. The way he finds Christ recalls very much the dawning recognition of the two disciples on the road to Emmaus; he often hears a
voice and recognizes it as his *Master*'s—as Nicholas Ferrar's prefatory
address to the reader of Herbert's poems makes clear, this was his
favourite title for Christ. The whole controlling image of the collection
The Temple is that God is dwelling within the heart—a theme made
explicit at many points, including the initial poem of the 'Church'
section, 'The Altar', and later in 'The Church-floore':

Blest be the *Architect*, whose art
Could build so strong in a weak heart.

The presence of Christ in the Eucharist is a natural concomitant to this; in addition to the plethora of images relating to this theme in his poetry, Chapter 22 of his prose work, entitled 'The Parson in Sacraments', makes his belief clear:

Especially at Communion times he is in a great confusion, as being not only to receive God, but to break, and administer him.

Traherne, however, seems to give very little attention to the Eucharist in his poems or prose. It is true that in *Centuries* I, 86 he talks about Christ being 'fed upon by every Christian', but in the absence of anything in the context that suggests Holy Communion, I would regard this as a much more generalized kind of indwelling. Even in his long 'Thanksgiving for God's Providence', a prose-poem where he runs through all the causes for gratitude that he has as a Christian, there is no explicit reference to Holy Communion, and the word 'Sacrament' is in the midst of a long list starting with 'Our Ministers, Bishops, Pastors, Churches, Sacraments, Liturgy, Sabbaths...' which finishes with 'Quires where they sing his praises'. The lack of emphasis on the Eucharist could of course be related to the different situation of the Anglican church experienced by the two writers; whereas Herbert in the early part of the reign of Charles I is conducting his ministry in a period of renewed stress on the sacraments, Traherne was actually appointed to Credenhill initially under the Commonwealth, though he was not ordained until the Restoration of the monarchy. This would suggest that his views on the sacrament may have been less 'Catholic' than Herbert's, and in any case more similar to the trend of the post-Restoration church and the spirituality of the Cambridge Platonists such as Henry More (1614–87).

In seeing Traherne's focus as 'outdoors', I am not implying that he ignores the indwelling presence of God, but rather that he relates this to God as the milieu in which everyone lives, instead of Herbert's awareness of God's particular personal presence. Most of Traherne's writing can be seen as a commentary on his early mystical experience of perceiving God in creation, detailed most famously in *Centuries* III, 3: 'The Corn was Orient and Immortal Wheat...' Reference to this experience occurs in much of his prose and many of his poems, while explicit references to the life, and even the passion, of Christ (so common in his prose) are few in his poems; only seven out of about one hundred poems could be judged to have explicit allusions to Christ as such. Of these, 'The World' is fairly typical. A few lines are given to Adam's sin and the effect of 'my Savior's precious Blood / Sprinkled...', but six stanzas relate to God in creation and allude to the poet's childhood experience:

> For so when first I in the Summer-fields
>> Saw golden Corn
>> The Earth adorn,
> (This day that Sight its Pleasure yields)
> No Rubies could more take mine Ey;
>> Nor Pearls of price...
>
> The choicest Colors, Yellow, Green and Blew
>> Did on this Court
>> In comly sort
> A mixt variety bestrew;
>> As if my God
>> From his Abode
> By these intended to be seen.
> And so He was: I Him descry'd
>> In's Works, the surest Guide
> Dame Nature yields; His Lov, His Life doth there
>> For evermore appear.

Thus the ways in which Herbert and Traherne image Christ in their writings seem to me to relate very closely to the differences between their works, and indeed their lives, in more general terms. Herbert, who retired from the stage of the Court and the university to the tiny church of Bemerton, apprehends within the heart a Christ who is closely integrated with the Father; he expresses this insight in highly concentrated, tightly structured, verse. Each poem focuses on a renewed encounter with Christ in prayer, and the working out of the relationship in dramatic terms is one that communicates easily to any reader familiar with human relationships—that is, to everyone. The whole work, *The Temple*, itself gives the impression of structure and it is difficult to see how it could have been any longer, though no doubt the poet might have organized it differently had he lived longer.

Traherne, who went from the tiny church of Credenhill to the wider world of Sir Orlando Bridgeman's Surrey mansion, is continually exploring the implications of his childhood experience of God, which in itself has little that is distinctively Christian. Although his poems and the most popular of his prose writings show a much greater concern with God's creation and humanity's inheritance as heirs of it, he nevertheless devotes a good deal of attention in his prose to affective meditations on the passion, focusing on Christ the man. Though he never loses sight of Christ's eternal Sonship, Traherne's emphasis is on the whole of humanity being raised to what appears to be a similar level to Christ in the glory of heaven. No doubt both perspectives are needed, but I think for the contemporary reader, Herbert's poems of relationship, rather than his *Country Parson*, and Traherne's raptures about creation rather than his detailed imaginings of the crucifixion, will be the reason why we reread the work of these two seventeenth-century Anglican parsons.

BIBLIOGRAPHY

Primary Sources
Herbert, G.
  1970   *Remains* (A Scolar Press facsimile, Menston [1652]).
Patrides, C.A. (ed.)
  1974   *The English Poems of George Herbert* (London: Dent).
Ridler, A. (ed.)
  1966   *Thomas Traherne: Poems, Centuries and Three Thanksgivings* (London: Oxford University Press).

Secondary Sources
Jantzen, G.
  1987   *Julian of Norwich* (London: SPCK).
Low, A.
  1978   *Love's Architecture* (New York: New York University Press).
  1993   'Richard Crashaw', in T.N. Corns (ed.), *The Cambridge Companion to English Poetry: Donne to Marvell* (Cambridge: Cambridge University Press).
Martz, L.L.
  1962   *The Poetry of Meditation* (New Haven and London: Yale University Press, rev. edn).
  1964   *The Paradise Within: Studies in Vaughan, Traherne & Milton* (New Haven: Yale University Press).
Pearlman, E.
  1983   'George Herbert's God', *ELR* 13.1, pp. 88-112.
Schoenfeldt, M.C.
  1990   ' "That Ancient Heat": Sexuality and Spirituality in *The Temple*', in E.D. Harvey and K.E. Maus (eds.), *Soliciting Interpretation: Literary Theory and English Poetry* (Chicago: University of Chicago Press).

IMAGES OF CHRIST IN EAST AFRICAN LITERATURE:
THE NOVELS OF NGUGI WA THIONG'O

John Anonby

Introduction

Most critics of African literature would acknowledge that Ngugi wa Thiong'o is 'Kenya's best-known writer', as Killam states in *An Introduction to the Writings of Ngugi*.[1] A playwright, essayist, and novelist who has lived in self-imposed exile in England until his more recent move to the United States, Ngugi has focused his literary skills on the Kenyan political scene over the last half century. His novels display his talents at their best, and they range from his lyrical work, *The River Between* (his first novel, though it was not published until 1965, the year after the appearance of *Weep Not, Child*) to his most daring novel, *Devil on the Cross* (1982), a work initially written and published in Ngugi's native Gikuyu before Ngugi himself translated it into English. His latest novel, *Matigari*, a satiric novel on more recent events in Kenya, appeared in an English translation from Gikuyu by Wangui wa Goro in 1989 but was censored for several years in Kenya. Of all Ngugi's novels, the most widely admired has probably been *A Grain of Wheat* (1967), though his *Petals of Blood* (1977) is also a richly imagistic work.

Ngugi's personal and vicarious experiences have been incorporated into much of his work. Anglican and Presbyterian missionaries were particularly active among the Kikuyu (one of the largest of Kenya's forty-six major tribes), and they founded many primary and secondary schools. Subsequent to his education in such missionary schools, Ngugi took further studies at Makerere University College in Kampala, Uganda and Leeds University in England. In 1968 he received an

---

1.   G.D. Killam, *An Introduction to the Writings of Ngugi* (London: Heinemann, 1980), p. 1.

appointment as lecturer in the Department of English, University College, Nairobi, which later became the University of Nairobi. After an interval of study and teaching in the United States, Ngugi eventually took the Chair of the Department of Literature at the University of Nairobi, but he lost this position while being detained without trial from 1977–78 by the authority of Kenyatta's post-colonial government, which was unsympathetic to Ngugi's Marxist leanings. (His *Petals of Blood*, for example, had been completed in Russia in 1975.)

It was, however, Ngugi's early experiences that began to shape all of the subsequent decisions of his life. Ngugi was still in primary school when clashes between European colonial settlers and the increasingly displaced Kikuyu began to intensify. Reports of chilling incidents and sporadic killings associated with the Mau Mau freedom fighters appeared in the newspapers of the western world. In his assessment of the tension-ridden decade of 1952–62, Ngugi writes in his prison diary these grim words:

> These were the ten years when the sword and the bullet held unmitigated sway over every Kenyan. It was a period of mass trials, mass murder and mass torture of Kenyans. So brutal were the workings of this culture that even some democratic-minded British were shocked into protest against its anti-human character.[2]

The protagonist of Ngugi's *Weep Not, Child*,[3] Njoroge (a name unmistakably similar to 'Ngugi'), embodies the trauma of the Kikuyu children, whose education had been provided by the white foreigners who were now increasingly regarded as oppressors. The despair of the Kikuyu people, who dominated the Kenyan national resistance towards colonialism, is epitomized in Njoroge's attempted suicide after the loss of his educational opportunities, his family, and his Christian faith. The first novel we will scrutinize in detail, *The River Between*,[4] though published after Kenya's acquisition of independence in 1963, focuses primarily on the period prior to the dark years referred to by Ngugi, and it illuminates some of the issues emanating from the acceptance of Christianity by some of the Kikuyu clans, while other clans from the

---

2. Ngugi wa Thiong'o, *Detained: A Writer's Prison Diary* (Nairobi: Heinemann, 1981), p. 38.

3. Ngugi wa Thiong'o, *Weep Not, Child* (Nairobi: Heinemann, 1964).

4. Ngugi wa Thiong'o, *The River Between* (Nairobi: Heinemann, 1965). Page numbers are cited in the text.

same tribe rejected Christianity because it was perceived as a threat to their cultural survival.

Although generally unsympathetic towards the Christianization of Kenya, Ngugi's novels are nevertheless permeated with diverse imagistic biblical patterns. Four of these novels employ Christ imagery in particularly fascinating ways: *The River Between*, *A Grain of Wheat*, *Devil on the Cross*, and *Matigari*. In *The River Between*, Ngugi's protagonist, Waiyaki, is depicted as an embodiment of a messianic vision emanating out of the aspirations of the Kikuyu tribe. *A Grain of Wheat*, a resonant novel portraying Kenya's painful struggle for independence, encapsulates Johannine and Pauline metaphors in its characterization of Kihika as a self-sacrificing Christ-figure. A rather bizarre work, *Devil on the Cross* employs techniques of inversion and parody in its biblical and Bunyanesque imagery, while *Matigari* symbolizes, in christological motifs, the irrepressibility of the spirit of truth and justice.

The River Between

The geographical setting of *The River Between* is a significant feature of the novel. Kikuyuland is a generally fertile area in central Kenya, dominated by the ice-flanked spires of Mt Kenya (5199 m. or 17,058') to the north-east, and the Aberdare Mountains and a series of ridges to the west and south-west of the Nyeri plains. Kikuyu towns such as Kiambu, Limuru (Ngugi's home town), and Nyeri dot the landscape north of Nairobi, which historically bordered the areas claimed by the nomadic Masai tribes further south and west. Ngugi's descriptive skills surface in the very first paragraph of *The River Between*, bringing the setting to life:

> The two ridges lay side by side. One was Kameno, the other was Makuyu. Between them was a valley. It was called the valley of life. Behind Kameno and Makuyu were many more valleys and ridges, lying without any discernible plan. They were like sleeping lions which never woke. They just slept, the big deep sleep of their Creator... A river flowed through the valley of life... (p. 1).

This serene setting is framed by 'Kerinyaga [Mt Kenya]...the mountain of He-who-shines-in Holiness', Murungu, the creator, who made Gikuyu and Mumbi, the ancestral parents of the Kikuyu people; this took place 'in the beginning of things' (pp. 17-18). This region was bequeathed by Murungu to Gikuyu and Mumbi, and to 'their children and the children of the children...world without end' (p. 18). As glimpses of the Kikuyu heritage are transmitted to the youthful protagonist of the novel, Waiyaki, by his aging father, Chege, a prophecy of a famous ancestral seer is introduced: 'There shall come a people with clothes like butterflies' (p. 19), but 'salvation shall come from the hills' (p. 20). This backdrop to the major events of the novel intimates that, for Ngugi, the arrival of foreigners in Kikuyuland resulted in the 'loss of Eden' (if we may borrow a phrase from Milton's *Paradise Lost*).[5]

Ngugi's handling of plot in this early novel is a foretaste of the intricate variety that would appear in his later works. The basic story seems straightforward enough, but it becomes increasingly permeated with irony as events unfold. The two Kikuyu clans featured in the novel live on the adjacent ridges of Kameno and Makuyu, separated by a small but perpetually flowing 'river of life' (p. 1), the Honia. Chege and Waiyaki live on Kameno and assiduously maintain their traditional manner of living. The leader of Makuyu is Joshua, an iron-willed man who has embraced the teachings of a Christian missionary, Mr Livingstone, who had founded a primary school at Siriana. While it is not completely accurate that Joshua, a preacher, draws 'all of his examples and allusions...from the Old Testament', as Palmer affirms,[6] his determination 'to enter the new Jerusalem' is indeed bolstered by a rigid predilection toward the legalism of the Old Testament rather than the New Testament's message of mercy, forgiveness, and love. His distorted Christianity begins to alienate even some of his converts, such as his former friend, Kabonyi, who abandons Christianity and makes the preservation of the Kikuyu tribal customs his supreme goal in life. The difficulties Joshua faces are, ironically, augmented by both of his own daughters, who attempt to combine their Christian teaching with their traditional culture. His younger daughter, Muthoni, eager 'to be initiated into womanhood' (p. 26), escapes to her aunt in Kameno to be circumcised, thereby incurring the implacable wrath of Joshua, who repudiates her as a daughter. Tragically, the trauma of these developments is too much for Muthoni to bear, and she is taken by Waiyaki to the hospital at the Siriana Missionary Centre, where she dies.

5. J. Milton, *Paradise Lost* (1667) (Book I; ed. M.Y. Hughes; New York: Odyssey Press, 1957), l. 4.
6. E. Palmer, *An Introduction to the African Novel* (Nairobi: Heinemann, 1972), p. 14.

The unfolding of events on the other ridge, Kameno, also demonstrates an ironic twist. Concerned with the threat posed by the white missionaries and settlers, Chege concludes that he must send Waiyaki, his only son, to the school at Siriana to learn 'the white man's magic' (p. 21). His hope is that Waiyaki will become the prophesied saviour of the hills, an ambition that Waiyaki also hopes to achieve by attempting to unify the two clans. His vision of unity coincides with his increasing attraction to Joshua's remaining daughter, Nyambura, but his love for her incurs both the wrath of Joshua, who regards him as a pagan, and that of his own tribal elders, as well as the fury of Kabonyi, who regards Waiyaki's attachment to the uncircumcised Nyambura as a polluting influence on the purity of the tribe. Kabonyi forms a secret organization, the Kiama (a fictional equivalent to the Mau Mau), who capture Waiyaki and Nyambura and subjugate them to public denunciation; the reader is spared the presumed execution of these African Romeo and Juliet counterparts by the timely ending of the novel.

Even if we concede that Killam is accurate in his view that Ngugi is 'exploiting similarities between the role [Waiyaki] is assigned to play as saviour with that of the biblical Christ, against a legendary history which reveals a strong association between the Gikuyu and the Christian creation myths',[7] many of these parallels are handled in subtle and fascinating ways. We have already noted the Edenic aura of the land given by the Creator to Gikuyu and Mumbi who, of course, typify the Genesis figures of Adam and Eve. Less obvious, however, is the similarity between Kerinyaga, 'the mountain of He-who-shines-in-Holiness' (p. 17), and the poetic glimpse of Eden depicted, not in Genesis, but in Ezek. 28.13-14 as 'the holy mountain of God'. The three great patriarchal ancestors of Christ in Genesis—Abraham, Isaac, and Jacob—find counterparts in 'the select few sent by Murungu' in the Kikuyu ancestral line: 'Mugo, the great seer; Wachiori, the glorious warrior; Kamiri, the powerful magician' (p. 3). The first of these, Mugo, resembles Abraham, who was given a divine revelation that his seed would be multiplied as the stars of the heavens and the sands of the seashore (Gen. 22.17); Mugo saw, as 'the future unfolded before his eyes', an invasion of 'people with clothes like butterflies...disrupting the peace and ordained life of the country' (pp. 18-19). This solemn traditional history is communicated to Waiyaki by his aging father, Chege, after a distant journey to a high hill marked by a sacred tree,

7.   Killam, *An Introduction*, p. 33.

'thick and mysterious' (p. 15), somewhat paralleling the journey of Abraham and Isaac to the top of Mt Moriah, where a ram caught in a thicket was sacrificed (Gen. 22.2, 13). This sacred tree can also be viewed as an imagistic link to the burning bush in Exodus 3, where Moses is given a divine mandate to deliver the children of Israel from their bondage to the Egyptians. Like Moses, whose sepulchre was never found, Mugo had died on a high hill but, as Chege reports, 'our fathers do not know where his grave is. But some say he was carried up by Murungu' (p. 19). Ngugi's literary montane landscape is traced even further as 'Chege seemed to gain in stature and appearance, so that Waiyaki thought him transfigured' (p. 18), parallel to the transfiguration of Christ—accompanied by Moses and Elijah—before Peter, James, and John on a 'high mountain', prior to his crucifixion, as recorded in Mt. 17.1-8.

It is not Chege, however, but Waiyaki who is 'the last in the line of that great seer who had prophesied of a black messiah from the hills' (p. 38). As a brilliant educator of his people, Waiyaki enjoys a period of great popularity, and schools are established throughout Kikuyuland. Chege's hope that his son will be the long-awaited saviour of his people seems likely to be fulfilled, even though Chege dies midway through the novel. Meanwhile, antagonistic forces are gathering momentum, and traces of imagery relating to Christ's passion prefigure Waiyaki's tragic end as well as the rejection of his vision of tribal unity and wholeness. One of his childhood companions, Kamau, who discovers to his great chagrin that his romantic attraction to Nyambura has been thwarted by the mutual love of Nyambura and Waiyaki, arrives on a dark night and escorts him to his enemies in the Kiama, paralleling Judas's betrayal of Christ. Waiyaki's life-long friend, Kinuthia, attempts to assist and advise him during the rising tension, even declaring firmly, 'whatever the others do, I will be with you all the way' (p. 139). When the hostile Kiama leaders, in the presence of all the people, call an assembly to decide Waiyaki's fate, however, Kinuthia tries to lose himself in the crowd, even though 'he cried and blamed himself because he had failed Waiyaki' (p. 145), echoing Peter's denial of Christ. The assembly is presided over by Kabonyi, whose ambitions for his son, Kamau, correlate to those of Chege for Waiyaki. Kabonyi's public denunciation of Waiyaki's presumed guilt, as 'evidenced' by Waiyaki's declaration of his love for the uncircumcised Nyambura, who stands with him, hardly qualifies

Kabonyi as a neutral Pilate counterpart. Nevertheless, the people's final rejection of their 'black messiah' (p. 38) reinforces Ngugi's depiction of Waiyaki as a Christ figure whose vision could have saved the tribe from further disunity and fragmentation.

A Grain of Wheat

A Grain of Wheat,[8] a novel that focuses on the preparations for the celebration of Uhuru in 1963, is Ngugi's masterful tribute to those who had risked or sacrificed their lives for the national cause. More intricate and complex than the earlier novels, *A Grain of Wheat* interweaves the motifs of suffering and hope within two imagistic foci: the oppression and deliverance of the Israelites, and the sufferings and resurrection of Christ. The structure of the novel has been both censured and praised. Shatto Gakwandi, for example, criticizes 'the cumbersome narrative technique' that 'interfere[s] with the sense of continuity'.[9] Nevertheless, it can be argued that the gradual enlarging of the insights of the persistent reader as the same events are depicted from different angles indicates, as David Cook has observed in his study of this novel, that Ngugi has gone beyond the mere flashback technique to a subtle 'interlocking of different phases of time'.[10] Perhaps the most significant result accruing from this sophisticated approach is that the reader is forced to modify his or her judgment of the major characters, who become increasingly difficult to categorize as either villains or heroes.

The thematic kernel of this novel, encapsulated in the title and strategically placed at the outset of the narrative, is a Pauline passage which articulates the profound paradox of life springing out of death:

> Thou fool, that which thou sowest is not quickened, except it die. And that which thou sowest, thou sowest not that body that shall be, but bare grain, it may chance of wheat, or of some other grain (1 Cor. 15.36).

In this novel, there is a proliferation of Moses/Christ figures whose vision and self-sacrifice finally bring Uhuru into being. Ngugi traces

---

8. Ngugi wa Thiong'o, *A Grain of Wheat* (Nairobi: Heinemann, 1967). Page numbers are cited in the text.

9. S. Gakwandi, *The Novel and Contemporary Experience in Africa* (New York: Africana Publishing Company, 1977), p. 188.

10. D. Cook, 'A New Earth: A Study of James Ngugi's *A Grain of Wheat*', *East Africa Journal* 6.12 (December 1969), p. 15.

the 'seed, a grain, which gave birth to a political party whose main strength…sprang from bond with the soil' (p. 13) to the shed blood of a nineteenth-century warrior-leader, Waiyaki (the namesake of the protagonist of *The River Between*), who took up arms against 'the whiteman' (p. 12) who had invaded the land given to the Kikuyus by Murungu. Like the messianic figure whose hands and feet were pierced (Ps. 22.16), Waiyaki had been 'bound hands and feet' (p. 12) and then put to death.

Another defender of the soil of Kenya emerged in Harry Thuku who, like Moses, 'refused to eat the good things of Pharaoh' (p. 13). Kenyans saw in Thuku 'a man with God's message: Go unto Pharaoh and say unto him: let my people go' (p. 13). After Thuku was 'clamped in chains', the common people formed a procession to induce the governor to free him, but were dispersed by a volley of gunfire in which a number of them were killed. Narrowly escaping the fate of Waiyaki, Thuku was exiled for seven years on an island in the Indian Ocean, but came back 'a broken man, who promised eternal cooperation with his oppressors, denouncing the Party he had helped to build' (p. 92). Symbolically, he had abandoned his role as deliverer and joined hands with Pharaoh; a potential saviour figure, he had betrayed his people and become a Judas.

Although Waiyaki and Thuku are peripheral characters in the novel, designed to form part of the historical backdrop of the major events culminating in Uhuru, they nevertheless have a significance that extends far beyond the few lines in which they appear. The Moses-Christ-Judas configuration that emerges is part of a larger pattern that characterizes the pivotal and intertwined actions of the two major figures of the novel: Kihika, the Mau Mau freedom fighter who is eventually betrayed and hanged, and Mugo, a reclusive character whose courageous attempt to save a woman from a beating by a homeguard has so aroused the admiration of his fellow human beings that he has been requested to lead the people of his village in the Uhuru celebrations.

The presence of Kihika dominates *A Grain of Wheat* in spite of, or rather because of, his execution by the British some time before the novel opens. Scriptural passages underlined in red or black in Kihika's Bible, carefully treasured by his surviving fellow revolutionaries, emerge as items for discussion among characters in the novel as well as headings to several chapters in the work. Peter Nazareth sees 'a central irony' in Kihika's receiving his 'inspiration from the Bible'.[11] In a similar vein, Gakwandi views this phenomenon as a 'bizarre interpretation of the Scripture' based on a modification of 'East African evangelism...reinterpreted to suit the people's own aspirations'.[12] Killam also concurs by suggesting that Ngugi uses Christian teaching as an attempt to give 'legitimacy' to the national struggle.[13] From Ngugi's perspective, however, resorting to 'violence in order to change an intolerable, unjust social order is not savagery: it purifies man... Mau Mau violence was anti-injustice.'[14]

The kind of society Kihika envisions is one in which the poor receive justice and the needy receive help, as suggested by a messianic passage from Psalm 72, underlined in red, which includes the clause, 'He...shall break in pieces the oppressor' (p. 72). As a boy, Kihika had been 'moved by the story of Moses and the children of Israel' (p. 75). In one of his final conversations, he appeals to God's judgment on Egypt as the pattern for 'strik[ing] terror' among 'the enemies of black man's freedom' (p. 166). Though Sharma sees no significance in the different colours used by Kihika in underlining key Scriptures,[15] it is apparent that passages relating to the misery of the oppressed are invariably underlined in red, possibly suggesting the need for violent forms of redress.

A measure of Kihika's personal dedication to the liberation of his country from the colonial regime is his willingness to sacrifice his own life for the cause he represents, as indicated by the black ink—presumably symbolizing death—with which he had underlined Jn 12.24, a passage in which Christ prefigures his own death as a pattern for the self-denial demanded of his followers:

> Verily, verily I say unto you, Except a corn of wheat fall into the ground and die, it abideth alone: but if it die, it bringeth forth much fruit (p. 174).

Kihika applies this Johannine paradigm of total sacrificial commitment

11. P. Nazareth, *Literature and Society in Modern Africa* (Nairobi: East African Literature Bureau, 1972), p. 144.

12. Gakwandi, *The Novel*, p. 113.

13. Killam, *An Introduction*, p. 55.

14. Ngugi wa Thiong'o, *Homecoming* (Nairobi: Heinemann, 1972), pp. 28-29.

15. G.N. Sharma, 'Ngugi's Political Vision: Theme and Pattern in *A Grain of Wheat*', in E.D. Jones (ed.), *African Literature Today* (vol. 10; New York: Africana Publishing Company, 1979), p. 174.

to himself or to any other individual who is willing to lay down his or her life for the sake of national freedom:

> ... we want a true sacrifice. But first we have to be ready to carry the cross. I die for you, you die for me... So I can say that you... are Christ. I am Christ. Everybody who takes the Oath of Unity to change things in Kenya is a Christ (p. 83).

Kihika's use of this biblical language can be interpreted as either profoundly reverent or irreverent, if taken out of context. It is certainly not the former, in spite of its echo of the Pauline concept that 'the sufferings of Christ abound in us' (2 Cor. 1.5), since Kihika has just declared that 'Jesus had failed...because his death did not change anything' (pp. 82-83). In terms of its irreverence, Kihika appears to be a voice for Ngugi, who is here depicting Christ's mission in political rather than religious terms:

> All oppressed people have a cross to bear. The Jews refused to carry it and were scattered like dust all over the earth... In Kenya we want a death which will change things... (p. 83).

In any case, Kihika's willingness to carry his 'cross', to be tortured, and to lay down his life for Kenya's freedom inspired his fellow patriots to continue the struggle until the colonial regime collapsed. 'The party...grew...on the wounds of those Kihika left behind' (p. 17).

But how had the almost invincible Kihika been captured? And who had betrayed him? Communal suspicions implicate Karanja, a freedom fighter who eventually surrenders to the British; he narrowly escapes being lynched before the self-effacing Mugo steps forward—not to lead in the Uhuru celebrations but to relieve his tortured soul by publicly confessing that, subsequent to sheltering Kihika one dark night, he had divulged Kihika's whereabouts to the colonial authorities, whereupon Kihika had been tortured and publicly hanged, his body 'dangling on the tree' (p. 17).

Recollections of these events constantly torment him, in spite of his arrest for sheltering Kihika, and they are a weight on his conscience even when he prevents a homeguard from whipping a woman for the fifth time in a trench. This singularly courageous action, with its close parallelism to Moses' defence of the Israelite beaten by the Egyptian taskmaster (Exod. 2.11-12), earns Mugo a reputation as a hero while he, meanwhile, vacillates between his feelings of guilt and his determination to 'lead his people across the desert' to the land of freedom

(p. 118). Kihika's transformation from a Moses figure to a Christ figure has a counterpart in the metamorphosis of Mugo from a Moses to a Judas figure, as Mugo finally acknowledges and confesses:

> You asked for Judas... who led Kihika to this tree, here. That man stands before you, now... He put his life into my hands, and I sold it to the white man. And this thing has eaten into my life all these years (p. 193).

These manifest parallels to the passion accounts in the Gospels can also be linked to the motif of Christ's resurrection, which in Ngugi's novel takes the form of the seeds of political hopes that have finally blossomed into the fruits of Uhuru.

Devil on the Cross

Kenya's transition from its colonial status to independence in 1963 did not result in the kind of society Ngugi had envisioned. His disillusionment with the capitalistic 'imperialism' that had replaced colonialism is expressed in his intensely serious *Petals of Blood*.[16] Though concerned with similar issues, *Devil on the Cross*[17] is a rather bizarre work that addresses Ngugi's concerns by means of satiric inversions and parody. The dominating theme of the novel is the unholy alliance between neo-colonialism and the institutionalized Christianity that has tenaciously survived the political upheavals that led to Uhuru. *Devil on the Cross* is replete with New Testament imagery and motifs, particularly from the Synoptic Gospels and the Book of Revelation, along with clever manipulations of John Bunyan's well-known Christian allegory, *The Pilgrim's Progress*.[18] Apocalyptic elements are incorporated into the setting of the novel, which includes two major cities: Nairobi, the purgatorial setting from which the novel's protagonist, Jacinta Wariinga, escapes, and her destination, Ilmorog, a socially stratified community with an affluent residential area designated as 'Golden Heights' and a dismal slum named Njeruca, popularly referred to as 'the New Jerusalem' (p. 36). The biblical portrait of heaven as a place of perpetual delight and harmony is metamorphosed in Ngugi's

16. Ngugi wa Thiong'o, *Petals of Blood* (Nairobi: Heinemann, 1977), p. 342.

17. Ngugi wa Thiong'o, *Devil on the Cross* (Nairobi: Heinemann, 1982). Page numbers are cited in the text.

18. J. Bunyan, *The Pilgrim's Progress* (1678), in R. Sharrock (ed.), *John Bunyan: Grace Abounding to the Chief of Sinners and The Pilgrim's Progress* (London: Oxford University Press, 1966). Page numbers are cited in the text.

novel, where 'the New Jerusalem' is described as a 'hell...hole full of fleas, lice, bedbugs' (p. 131).

This semi-allegorical political novel incorporates in its title, *Devil on the Cross*, a pivotal event in Bunyan's work. The protagonist in *The Pilgrim's Progress*, Christian, while fleeing from the 'City of Destruction', has a vision of Christ on the cross, whereupon his heavy burden

> ...loosed from off his shoulders, and fell from off his back; and began to tumble; and so continued to do, till it came to the mouth of the Sepulcher, where it fell in, and I saw it no more (p. 169).

Christian then continues his journey to the Celestial City with a 'merry heart' (p. 169). His counterpart in Ngugi's work is the misery-laden Wariinga, who has decided to forsake Nairobi for a new life at her parents' home in 'the New Jerusalem', the slum of Njeruca. Her sense of failure is so extreme that, on her way out of Nairobi, she leaps in front of a bus, but a stranger rescues her by intervening at the crucial moment. In a daze, she rests on the steps of a beauty salon, falls into a reverie, and is revisited by a nightmare she had had while a student attending the Church of the Holy Rosary—a nightmare of 'the Devil on the Cross' (p. 13).

This grotesque transformation of the crucifixion scenes in the Gospels blends with the Beast in the Apocalypse to form Wariinga's glimpse of the Devil with 'seven horns...on his head...with seven trumpets for sounding infernal hymns of praise and glory' (p. 13). The Devil is, however, being propelled 'towards the Cross...by a crowd of people dressed in rags' (p. 13). This parody of Christ's triumphal procession continues after the crucifixion of the Devil, as the people go away, 'singing songs of victory' (p. 13). A counterpart to Jesus' resurrection soon follows. After three days, wealthy men 'dressed in suits and ties', under the cover of darkness, lift 'the Devil down from the Cross' (p. 13) and carry on with their nefarious plundering of the poverty-stricken peoples of the earth.

Emerging from her reverie, Wariinga mounts a matatu (minibus) for Ilmorog and is joined by several characters who, while they do not have overtly symbolic names such as the characters in *The Pilgrim's Progress*, represent various segments of the Kenyan population. Wariinga represents the many young women of her country who are not measured by their talents but by their skirts; she had, in fact, been dismissed from her work in a construction company because of her rejection of her boss's attempts to seduce her. A blacksmith named Muturi enters the bus, and is soon joined by Gatuiria, a researcher into African music at the university; he divulges his revolutionary leanings to Wariinga, and a mutual romantic attraction emerges between them. A destitute woman without shoes introduces herself as Wangari, and she proceeds to boast of her earlier involvement in the Mau Mau struggle. The next entrant is a university graduate, Mwiriri, who is preparing for a career in commerce. Another capitalist turns out to be the driver of the matatu, Mwara, who is described as 'one of those who worshipped at the shrine of the god of money' (p. 32). The license number of the vehicle is MMM333, reminiscent of the mark of the Beast in Rev. 13.18, number 666.

The conversation on the minibus becomes rather animated when the commerce graduate, Mwiriri, offers them all admission cards to 'A Big Feast' and 'Competition in Modern Theft and Robbery' to be held at Ilmorog Golden Heights (p. 76). As if preparing for this great competition, Mwiriri begins to 'talk as if he were at the altar, preaching to a multitude with the Bible before him' (p. 81); this is followed by a reading of the parable of the talents in Matthew 25. Another parody of a church service takes place at the great competition itself, held on a Sunday morning, with the singing of a hymn accompanied by the Hell's Angels band:

> Good news has come
> To our country!
> Good news has come
> About our Saviour! (p. 90).

A sacramental feast soon follows, lubricated by 'whisky, vodka, brandy and gin, or whole cases for each person', with champagne flowing 'like the Ruiru River' (p. 92). Like communion wine, these drinks have symbolic meaning, and they betoken a credal commitment:

> Today we believe in the democracy of theft and robbery, the democracy of drinking the blood and eating the flesh of our workers (p. 89).

The 'Saviour' celebrated is not Christ, however, but the god of finance: 'Money rules the world!' (p. 89).

It is, nevertheless, Jesus' parable of the talents in Matthew 25 that forms the ostensible justification and the rationalization needed for the capitalistic system portrayed in the self-designated 'Christian' society in Ngugi's novel; it thrives on the economic machinations of shrewd investors, whose talents bring colossal profits to their masters. One significant revision of the parable is, however, worth noting. In Matthew 25, the 'unprofitable servant' (v. 30) is castigated for accusing his master of reaping where he has not sown, but in the novel the master of ceremonies boasts that his skill in reaping where he has never sown or 'shed any sweat' is the 'secret' of his success (p. 85).

Ngugi's indictment of institutionalized Christianity as the 'whore of the state' is linked to his description of the badges and the suits of the foreign delegates represented at the International Competition. The suits are designed out of dollars, pounds, Deutschmarks, francs, etc., and the badges each 'bore one or two slogans' such as

> ... World Banks; World Commercial Banks; World's Exploitation Banks; Money-Swallowing Insurance Schemes; Industrial Gobblers of Raw Materials: Cheap Manufactures for Export Abroad; Traders in Human Skins; Loans for a Profit: Aid with Iron Strings; Arms for Murder; Motor-Vehicle Assembly Plants for Vanity Fair at Home and Bigger Profits Abroad; All Products Fair and Lovely to keep Fools in the Dependent Chains of Slavery; Slave for Comfort, Deal with Me; and many others in similar vein (p. 91).

Readers familiar with *The Pilgrim's Progress* will likely detect the parody here of Bunyan's literary technique, as well as theme, in his depiction of the trafficking in Vanity Fair, involving such commodities as

> ... Houses, Lands, Trades, Places, Honours, Preferments, Titles, Countries, Kingdoms, Lusts, Pleasures, and Delights of all sorts, as Whores, Bawds, Wives, Husbands, Children, Masters, Servants, Lives, Blood, Bodies, Souls, Silver, Gold, Pearls, Precious Stones, and what not (p. 211).

While Ngugi's list specifically alludes to Bunyan's inventory, it is highly probable that Ngugi saw the connection between Bunyan's fair and its prototype in Rev. 18.12-13, with its wares of

> ... gold, and silver, and precious stones and of pearls, and fine linen, and purple, and silk, and thyine wood, and all manner vessels of ivory, and all manner vessels of most precious wood, and of brass, and iron, and marble, and cinnamon, and odours, and ointments, and frankincense, and wine, and oil, and fine flour, and wheat, and beasts, and sheep, and horses, and chariots, and slaves, and souls of men (KJV).

These commercial dealings of 'Babylon the Great', who rides 'upon a scarlet coloured beast' (Rev. 17.3-5), have been embraced and perpetuated by nominally Christian nations, as implied by the currencies exchanged in the Great Competition which, in turn, correspond to 'the Britain Row, the French Row, the Italian Row, the Spanish Row, the German Row' in Vanity Fair (p. 211).

A variety of global economic strategies is presented and discussed at Ilmorog's 'Competition in Modern Theft and Robbery' (p. 76), but when Mwiriri challenges 'foreign ideology' by advocating that Kenya should nurture its 'own industrial capitalists' (pp. 161, 171), the conferees 'roared with rage' (p. 172). This perceived threat to international financial connections is deflected by the master of ceremonies, who again appeals to the parable of the talents in Matthew 25, which makes mention of the lord 'travelling unto a far country' (p. 174, cf. v. 14), thereby validating multinational trade. Shortly afterwards, Mwiriri is killed in an 'accident' in Mwara's matatu, Number MMM333.

The other fellow passengers of Wariinga also encounter difficulties. Wangari attempts to persuade some local officials to arrest the conferees as international bandits, but she herself is taken into custody. Muturi, the blacksmith, leads a protest group of fellow workers from the slums to the conference, but is arrested; this leads to a riot in which both he and Wangari mysteriously disappear—presumably executed. Wariinga, on the other hand, rebuilds her life, becomes a skillful mechanic, and proceeds towards marriage to Gatuiria. She is, however, revisited by a variation of her nightmare; this time, tie-wearing men came boldly in 'armoured cars with big guns' and 'lifted the Devil down from the cross' as soon as he had been placed on it (p. 239), indicating Wariinga's subconscious awareness of the ongoing struggle between the wealthy and the poverty-stricken masses. Her personal struggle takes a bizarre turn when Gatuiria introduces her to his father, whom she discovers is the 'Rich Old Man' who, years before, had seduced her onto 'the path that she had thought would lead her to Heaven' but had, in fact, 'led her to a Hell on Earth' (p. 146). When he appeals to her, in private, to cancel her wedding to his son, she pulls out a pistol, shoots him, and stalks out of the house, clearly recognizing that the 'hardest struggle of her life's journey lay ahead' (p. 254). Though melodramatic, this abrupt conclusion to the novel underlines Ngugi's uncompromising stance on the irreconcilable differences that separate the oppressors from the oppressed. For Ngugi, the most blatant form of evil in society is political and economic exploitation—which will continue to manifest itself until this 'Devil' is nailed permanently to the 'Cross'.

Matigari

The shadow of evil imaged in *Devil on the Cross* is matched by the spirit of truth and justice portrayed in Ngugi's *Matigari*.[19] In his note on the English edition of the work, Ngugi tells us that the novel was 'written largely in exile in the quietness of my one-bedroom flat in Noel Road, Islington, London, in 1983' (p. vii); it was published in 'the Gikuyu-language original in Kenya in October 1986', but in 1987 'the police raided all the bookshops and seized every copy of the novel' (p. viii). In spite of this censorship, Wangui wa Goro's translation of the work into English in 1989 made its way into the western world. The author's note to the reader indicates that 'the story has no fixed time' or 'space' (p. ix), as it is intended to be universal in its message of freedom. Although the theme of economic and political oppression in post-colonial Kenya is still a force to be reckoned with, the irrepressible yearnings of the masses—expressed by the workers, the peasants, and the students—will ultimately triumph: 'Victory shall be ours!' (p. 175).

The hero of the novel, Matigari, is depicted as a Christ-figure throughout the work, but in a deliberately less focused manner than with Waiyaki in *The River Between* or Kihika in *A Grain of Wheat*; the centrality of the passion in these novels, as well as in the inverted imagery of *The Devil on the Cross*, is supplemented by numerous and often subtle references to Christ's miracles, message, and both pre- and post-resurrection manifestations. Matigari's sudden appearances, elusive disappearances, and incredible feats create the impression, in the minds of many, that he has divine powers, though a number of these phenomena are later explained in ordinary or naturalistic terms. The full name of this protagonist is 'Matigari ma Njiruungi', a Gikuyu word for 'the patriots who survived the bullets' (p. 20) used in Kenya's struggle for independence.

The story opens with Matigari, a former freedom fighter, coming out of the forests and mountains, after an interval of many years, to find his people and to reclaim the land that Settler Williams

19. Ngugi wa Thiong'o, *Matigari* (trans. Wangui wa Goro; Oxford: Heinemann, 1989). Page numbers are cited in the text.

(representing the colonists) had taken from him long before. He 'hoped that the last of the colonial problems had disappeared with the descent of Settler Williams into hell' (p. 3). On this assumption, he divests himself of his pistol, bullet-belt, and his AK47 rifle and buries them at the foot of a large mugumo (fig) tree, and replaces these vestiges of conflict with a strip of bark: 'I have now girded myself with a belt of peace' (p. 5), he declares.

During the course of his quest, people continually raise queries concerning his identity, reminiscent of the speculations surrounding Christ's ministry:

> Who really was Matigari ma Njiruungi? A patriot? Angel Gabriel? Jesus Christ? Was he a human being or a spirit? A true or false prophet? A saviour or simply a lunatic? Was Matigari a man or was he a woman? A child or an adult? Or was he only an idea, an image, in people's minds? Who was He? (p. 158).

When asked directly, 'Who are you, Mr. Seeker of Truth and Justice?', he replies, 'that is who I am' (p. 75). This response is not as straightforward as it appears to be, however, as the 'I am' ending includes a subtle allusion to Jn 8.58, where Jesus' declaration, 'Before Abraham was, I am', was regarded as blasphemy by the Jews.

Other allusions to the Gospels emerge, apparently randomly, throughout the novel. When Matigari looks for his lost 'children' in a large car-wreckage dump in the slums, some of the boys hurl stones at him, but 'he seemed to be protected by a powerful charm, because not a single stone touched him' (p. 17), recalling Jesus' escape from a similar predicament recorded in Jn 8.59. Matigari's invulnerability finally fails him, however, when stones reach his ear-lobe and the bridge of his nose. This incident was later picked up by popular rumours, which maintained that 'not even one stone touched him', and that he had reportedly said, 'Let the children come to me' (p. 73, cf. Lk. 18.16).

The Johannine account of Jesus' refusal either to condemn or to allow the stoning of the woman 'taken in adultery' (Jn 8.3) has a protracted sequel in Ngugi's novel. When two policemen harass a barmaid who rejects their lustful advances, Matigari publicly intervenes, and authoritatively states, 'Leave her alone!' (p. 31). Guthera's gratitude to her rescuer unravels the sad story of her painful decision to sell her body in order to keep her younger siblings from starvation. She later has an opportunity to repay him when she learns that Matigari and a number of political discontents have been arrested and thrown into gaol. She offers herself to one of the police guards, thereby breaking her 'eleventh commandment' (p. 37) never to have a relationship with a policeman, from whom she procures a key to the cell where Matigari and his companions have been incarcerated. Legends of Matigari's supernatural powers are fueled by this nocturnal escape, which a nameless character compares to 'the case of Paul and the Capernaum prison' (p. 80)—a mutilated rendition of the miraculous release of Paul and Silas in Philippi (Acts 16.25-35), or the angelic deliverance of Peter from prison in Acts 12.

During his short sojourn in the gaol, Matigari, in the light of two candles, took some 'food, broke it and gave it' to his cell-mates; he then 'took the bottle of beer, opened it with his teeth, poured a little of it on the floor in libation and gave them to drink and pass around' (p. 57). This analogy to 'the last supper' in the Gospels does not escape the attention of a drunkard in the cell, who begins to recite the relevant passage from memory before he asks, Pilate-like, 'tell us the truth. Who are you?' (p. 57). When he discovers that he is, indeed, speaking to the elusive patriot, he probes further: 'But how do we know that you are really Matigari ma Njiruungi? How can we identify you? Where is the sign?' (p. 63). Reminiscent of Christ's answer to the Pharisees and Sadducees, whose demand of a sign was peremptorily dismissed by Christ's enigmatic declaration that 'there shall no sign be given...but the sign of the prophet Jonas' (Mt. 16.4), Matigari replies,

> I don't need signs or miracles. My actions will be my trumpet and they shall speak for me. For I will remove this belt of peace and I will wear another, decorated with bullets... I will wear a gun around my waist and carry my AK47 over my shoulder; and I shall stand on top of the highest mountain and tell it to all the people... Let the will of the people be done! Our kingdom come...! (p. 63).

This also somewhat parallels the paradoxical message of 'Christ, the Lord' whose coming was to bring 'Glory to God in the highest, and on earth peace' (Lk. 2.11, 14) but who also stated, 'I came not to send peace, but a sword' (Mt. 10.34).

Like Christ's parables, which encapsulate essential aspects of the nature of the kingdom of heaven, Matigari's parables diagnose some of the most acute social evils on earth:

> The builder builds a house.
> The one who watched while it was being built moves into it.

The builder sleeps in the open air,
No roof over his head.

The worker produces goods.
Foreigners and parasites dispose of them.
The worker is left empty handed.

Where are truth and justice on this earth? (p. 113).

Ngugi's intimate familiarity with the Scriptures, which he handles in ingenious and diverse ways, does not, however, indicate a predilection towards institutionalized Christianity. Presumably a mouthpiece for Ngugi, Matigari states unequivocally, 'I don't belong to your religions or to your churches' (p. 94). When Matigari's quest for truth and justice takes him to a priest, he is advised to seek for 'heavenly truth and justice' from 'the Lord God of heaven, who is the same Jesus Christ who was once crucified on the Cross', but that he should seek 'earthly truth and justice' from 'those who rule on earth' (p. 99). Since, for Ngugi, the current custodians and wielders of power on this earth are the prime perpetuators of social evils, institutionalized religions, including Christianity, are not likely to provide redressive solutions. When asked by some boys if he is 'Jesus Christ…the Lord, who will bring the New Jerusalem here on earth' (p. 156), Matigari shares with them his conviction that there is a 'God' within human beings who, one day, 'will come alive and liberate us who believe in Him' (p. 156). In political and economic terms, this spells the end of the 'imperialism' that 'has tried to kill that God within us' (p. 156). When this 'God' is resurrected, there will be no 'worrying about tribe, race, or colour', for the earth will 'return to those to whom it belongs'—the tillers and the workers who have 'produced all the wealth in this land' (p. 156).

With this vision of an earthly political paradise, Ngugi's eschatology is, of course, radically different from the biblical view. When Matigari escapes from the mental hospital to which he had been escorted by the police subsequent to his eloquent courtroom defence of the rights of the workers, rumours predict 'Matigari's second coming' and 'the Final Judgement' (pp. 164, 158). People of all ranks begin to congregate at Settler Williams's heavily guarded house (now owned by the son of John Boy, Williams's black servant), to which Matigari is expected to return in order to claim what he considers his rightful inheritance, as he had built the house, long ago, with his own hands. The government, though officially Christian, is sufficiently concerned with retaining political control that orders have been given to arrest Matigari or to shoot him 'on sight'—even if he were 'Christ himself' (p. 164).

This satiric touch expands into some hilarious, climactic events. Matigari drives right through the waiting crowds in a Mercedes-Benz he has picked up in the wilderness, as he is assumed to be 'a VIP', and crashes into the main entrance of the house, taking the door with him 'right into the building' (p. 164). The house bursts into flames, which light 'up the whole compound, the fields and the surrounding country' (p. 167). Witnessing this 'judgement' falling on their oppressors, the common people break into song, set further fires, and vow to 'burn the prisons holding all our patriots' (p. 169).

While some soldiers remain at the former settler's house (like the sentinels placed by Jesus' tomb), 'waiting for the fire to die down so that they could look for Matigari's remains' (p. 169), it becomes apparent that Matigari has successfully staged a 'resurrection', as his hat has been spotted in the fields near the gate. While some of the people see this as another miracle, Matigari explains to his reunited companions that he had 'escaped through the window' (p. 170). When the authorities are informed about the lost hat, they launch a major search for Matigari who, along with the redeemed prostitute, Guthera, and Muriuki, a boy from the vehicle dump, is headed for the fig tree where Matigari had hidden his weapons at the beginning of his long search for peace and justice. The pursuers manage to shoot Guthera in the leg, but Matigari carries her to the river, into which they plunge while dogs 'tore at their clothes, their flesh' (p. 173). A deluge falls from the sky, forcing the pursuers to abandon their chase, leaving everyone wondering whether Matigari is dead or alive. The novel ends with Muriuki unearthing Matigari's weapons in order to continue the fight for freedom, while hearing in his mind the voices of the students, peasants, and workers 'singing in harmony: Victory shall be ours!' (p. 175). For Ngugi, the struggle for social, political, and economic equity is not over, but the realization of this ideal can be expedited by Christ-figures whose vision is sustained by total personal commitment, even to the point of death.

IMAGES OF CHRIST IN CANADIAN LITERATURE:
FAITH AND FICTION IN THE NOVELS OF CALLAGHAN,
HOOD AND MACLENNAN

Barbara Pell

There is an inherent tension, even conflict, between faith and fiction.
The modern realistic novel has a professed mimetic relationship to the
post-Christian era we live in that is artistically inimical to acts of
grace and expressions of faith. This conflict is somewhat analogous to
the crisis in modern theology which has attempted to respond to
people's spiritual need in an age bereft of God. Modern Protestantism
seems to have split into its two main constitutive streams of 'revealed'
and 'natural' theology. The neo-orthodox theologians, such as Karl
Barth, advocate a return to the Reformers' emphasis on revelation, the
theology of the Word of God. In contrast, liberal theologians, like Paul
Tillich, deny the relevance of past dogma in a post-Nietzschean world
and repudiate orthodox concepts of God: 'This is the God Nietzsche
said had to be killed...' Tillich redefines God for this century, based
on 'existential experience', as the 'God above the God of theism', 'the
ground of being', the answer to modern doubts and the existential quest
for meaning, and the source of the 'courage to be'.[1] Roman Catholicism
has often seemed much more stable and secure than the Reformers'
fiery faith. However, in the spiritual crisis of contemporary society
and the theological ferments after the Second World War and especially
since Vatican II, Catholics no longer enjoy a complacent spiritual existence. Some Catholic theologians, such as Jacques Maritain, have called
for a more 'incarnational' theology. Both Protestants and Catholics
are today stressing the importance of the existential participation of
Christians in the world—what Karl Jaspers calls 'the limit-situations
of human existence (sin, guilt, strife, suffering, death)'[2]—in order to

1. P. Tillich, *The Courage to Be* (London: Fontana Collins, 1961), pp. 179-83.
2. K.F. Reinhardt, *The Theological Novel of Modern Europe: An Analysis of*

communicate God to a godless world and mediate between theology and culture.

Similarly, the modern religious writer who finds her vision and vocation no longer coincide with the spirit of the age is, like the modern theologian, attempting to portray images of Christ in a post-Christian era. The great Catholic writer, Flannery O'Connor, said,

> The problem of the novelist who wishes to write about man's encounter with this God is how he shall make the experience—which is both natural and supernatural—understandable, and credible, to his reader. In any age this would be a problem, but in our own, it is a well-nigh insurmountable one... I don't believe that we shall have great religious fiction until we have again that happy combination of believing artist and believing society. Until that time, the novelist will have to do the best he can in travail with the world he has. He may find in the end that instead of reflecting the image at the heart of things, he has only reflected our broken condition and, through it, the face of the devil we are possessed by.[3]

O'Connor's final words foreground the connection between religious poetics and the theological debates I have outlined. In simplified terms, the Christian novelist's dilemma resolves itself into two possibilities: does she impose 'the image at the heart of things' onto her characters' struggles for meaning ('revealed theology'), or can she only realize an imaginative solution arising out of the 'broken condition' of her characters ('natural theology')?

Some literary critics, such as Charles Glicksberg and Murray Krieger, have resolved the paradoxical tension inherent within the concept of the 'religious novel' by denying that the genre can even exist. Nevertheless, Glicksberg goes on to say that 'there are novels that are profoundly religious in content without ceasing to be novels', and he cites the universal appeal of Graham Greene and Francois Mauriac: 'In their works, religion is presented as experience, as spiritual conflict, as vision and aspiration, struggle and search and suffering, not as codified theology. What we get is a convincing and comprehensive picture of life in all its irreducible mysteriousness.'[4]

Masterpieces by Eight Authors (New York: Frederick Ungar, 1969), p. 29.

3. F. O'Connor, *Mystery and Manners* (ed. S. Fitzgerald and R. Fitzgerald; New York: Farrar, Straus and Giroux, 1969), pp. 71, 74-75.

4. C.I. Glicksberg, *Modern Literature and the Death of God* (The Hague: Martinus Nijhoff, 1966), p. 72.

We have returned again to the analogy of revealed ('codified theology') versus natural ('experience') theology. The novel has been constructed as a 'realistic' genre, a mimesis of secular life. This theoretical premise has caused some of the most prominent modern Christian writers (for example, C.S. Lewis and J.R.R. Tolkien) to abandon this genre in favour of theological fantasies. Religious novelists, however, who choose to encode the supernatural in the natural cannot deny or distort the latter. Their 'existential participation' in the 'limit-situations' of their readers means admitting the subversions of evil, suffering, and temptation—in other words 'sin'— into their logocentric texts. Above all, they cannot impose a divine metanarrative on the narrative struggles of their characters. Therefore, the struggle for religious meaning cannot be expounded as abstract dogma, but must be integrated into the fabric of the plot, presented as dramatic conflict arising out of the convictions of the characters, and resolved with fidelity to the artistic logic of the fiction and the finite complexities of life.

If critics and writers agree that 'natural theology' is the most promising approach to content in the modern religious novel, is there a theological model to resolve the paradox of sacred form in a secular text? Brian Wicker maintains that metaphor is impossible without a metaphysics of presence, a 'vertical axis' which is the religious worldview.[5] Not surprisingly, the realistic novel is, in contrast, essentially metonymic.

Here, the difference between Protestant and Roman Catholic theologies may be relevant and may provide some explanation for the fact that virtually all of the best religious novelists of this century have been Catholic. As Amos Wilder points out, 'The Roman doctrine of transubstantiation in the Mass is the key to Catholic art. It defines the relation of grace to nature, and the relations of the Catholic artist to the world.'[6] As we shall see in the works of Morley Callaghan and Hugh Hood, Catholic writers realize that, by embodying divine significance in earthly objects, this sacramental theology establishes the basis for symbolism and the metaphoric use of language. In contrast, as the Anglican critic, Malcolm Ross, has complained, 'Protestant theology

---

5. B. Wicker, *The Story-Shaped World: Fiction and Metaphysics: Some Variations on a Theme* (London: Athlone Press, 1975), p. 194.

6. A. Wilder, *Theology and Modern Culture* (Cambridge, MA: Harvard University Press, 1967), pp. 85-86.

rejected the doctrine of transubstantiation, denied the real presence, and allegedly cut off the created world, so that it could no longer be a valid bearer of the divine meaning'.[7] Protestant writers inherit a dualistic theology that privileges the Word but often separates it from the word. The dangers of a Protestant aesthetic, therefore, are twofold: a vaporous spirituality that rejects the natural world as 'fallen' and therefore unworthy of God's grace; and, on the other hand, a subjective, individualistic apprehension of revelation and redemption that is incommunicable to a wider audience. We will find both of these tendencies in the fiction of Hugh MacLennan.

Morley Callaghan

Morley Callaghan was one of the founding fathers of modern Canadian literature. For over sixty years, his novels portrayed the tension between the sacred and the secular in our modern world with fidelity both to the social context and to his personal religious vision. Callaghan's sacramental vision arose naturally out of his Roman Catholic background, but it was more instinctive than intellectual and more empirical than dogmatic. He did not mind being called a 'religious novelist' but insisted that he did not sit down 'to write religious books'. And although he was not as 'hopelessly corrupt theologically' as he said, he was not a consciously orthodox Catholic writer, as Hugh Hood is.

Callaghan began his novels not with a thesis but with a character, and then he wisely allowed the character to determine the action. He always had a customary attitude of deep compassion for and understanding of his characters. But Callaghan was greatly influenced by his friendship with the Catholic philosopher Jacques Maritain in the early 1930s. Subsequently his novels are marked by a strong Christian humanism or personalism, a 'Christ-like identification' with sinful humanity and a respect for human free will and potential—all characteristics of Maritain's philosophy.

These virtues, however, also led Callaghan to his greatest weakness—which seems to be an occupational hazard for religious writers (such as Graham Greene) who demonstrate a theology and technique similar to Callaghan's. His compassionate attitude, his undiscriminating generosity of characterization, his deep involvement in the limit-situations of his characters and the freedom he allows them without the tyranny

---

7.   Wilder, *Theology and Modern Culture*, pp. 86-87.

of plot or theme—all these result in the lack of a definite moral vision. Too often his Christian humanism, with its emphasis on human identi- fication, is not balanced by a clear vision of Christian theology. The Canadian critic Desmond Pacey pointed this out many years ago:

> Callaghan, though himself a Catholic, is a proponent of a liberal and humanitarian Christianity. The defect of that type of Christianity, and of much of Callaghan's work, is that it often loses sight of the reality of evil. One feels the lack, in Callaghan's novels and stories, of any definite stan- dards by which his characters are to be judged. He succeeds admirably in revealing the shoddiness of most of the prevailing standards, but when it is a matter of suggesting alternatives he can offer only vague words like simplicity, tenderness and compassion. The result is that all of Callaghan's work has a certain moral flabbiness... Of the novel, however, we demand a firm philosophy, a clearly articulated sense of values, and instead of that Callaghan invites us merely to a feast of pity.[8]

Unlike Hood, Callaghan was not a scholar or theologian. After dramatizing the existential conflicts of life so faithfully, he either did not know how, or did not wish, to resolve them. In positive terms, he refused to impose arbitrary theological solutions on the mystery of life. In negative terms, he may have finally come to value the ambi- guities of life for their own perverse mystery. Callaghan never ade- quately defined his theological position. In his novels he aroused expectations of a moral and religious context which he never suf- ficiently satisfied. I think the essential pattern in the development of Callaghan's novels was his ongoing search for a solution to the dilemma of dramatizing God's grace in fallen nature, that is of faith in fiction, until he finally in his last novels came to the conclusion that there is no solution.

After early experiments in urban realism and literary naturalism, in 1933 Callaghan published what is still probably his finest novel, *Such Is My Beloved*. Dedicated to Jacques Maritain, it is the first of three novels that portray the incarnational humanist theories of the inevitable conflict between Christian values and the secular life, and the very ambiguous results of any attempt to realize the gospel message in this temporal world. Therefore, these novels are written in the form of biblical parables which operate simultaneously on the levels of realistic fiction and religious belief.

---

8. D. Pacey, *Creative Writing in Canada* (Toronto: McGraw–Hill Ryerson, 2nd edn, 1967), p. 211.

Such Is My Beloved is set in the slums of Toronto during the De-
pression. It is the story of Father Dowling, a young, eager priest who
befriends two prostitutes. They educate him in the socio-economic
realities that oppress his poor parishioners and teach him compassion.
He helps them realize some spiritual self-worth in their degraded
lives. But, in the end, they are all crushed by the combined worldly
wisdom of Church and State. The girls are run out of town, and Father
Dowling, disciplined and heart-broken, is confined to a mental asylum,
writing his commentary on the *Song of Songs* in his brief periods of
lucidity.

The ending of the novel is a source of ambiguity and critical controversy. Callaghan clearly intends us to see Father Dowling's tragedy,
from a religious perspective, as a spiritual triumph, a fictional representation of divine grace in fallen nature. The priest is repeatedly
symbolized as a Christ-figure who achieves 'joy' and 'peace' at Easter in
his self-sacrifice for 'the souls of those two poor girls'.[9] Nevertheless,
this religious interpretation does not solve all the problems with the
ending of the novel. The entire book has emphasized Father Dowling's
struggle to redeem the secular world with the love of Christ. A solution
that is valid only in the spiritual, symbolic realm, and apparently
leaves the secular tragedy unresolved, cannot totally convince the
reader, especially the non-believer, of its existential relevance.

After a silence of ten years, Callaghan published three novels between
1951 and 1961 that resemble his biblical parables in many respects, but
his treatment of the tension between religious vision and the fictional
world was altered. He increasingly concentrated in these novels on the
secular struggle for meaning, refusing to posit theological answers
outside of that situation. It was not, perhaps, a renunciation of Christian
humanism but an emphasis on the 'humanism' at the expense of the
'Christian' because Callaghan found it so impossible to resolve the
tension between them in his art.

After another fourteen year hiatus, Callaghan produced five novels
between 1975 and his death in 1990. In them he reiterated the perennial religious themes of his fiction as they had become defined in an
increasingly secular form. Although his first novel of the 1980s, *A
Time for Judas*, amazed the secular critics with its overtly Christian
subject matter, its clear departure from biblical orthodoxy prompted

9. M. Callaghan, *Such Is My Beloved* (New York: Charles Scribner's Sons,
1934), p. 143.

one Catholic scholar to label it 'a death-dealing absurdity'. Callaghan's last books provide a summary and closure for his fiction by articulating a theological basis for both his humanistic compassion and his aesthetic principles. But it is clearly a theology that finds its ground of being in humanity's divine nature rather than God's transcendent grace.

A Time for Judas was, for Callaghan, a unique departure from fifty-five years of urban realism: an historical-religious romance set primarily in first-century Jerusalem. Using the (rather trite) device of a 'manuscript found in a Greek jar' for verisimilitude, the novel purports to be a 'true' revision of the Gospel story of Christ's crucifixion and resurrection. It supposedly resolves an inconsistency in the original story which depends on Judas Iscariot's betrayal of Jesus. The 'truth' which 'had a wonder and mystery [and]...grandeur of its own' is that Judas only 'betrays' Christ out of love and obedience to him because 'the story requires it'.[10]

Although a shadowy figure in the novel (literally so in the Resurrection scene), Jesus is portrayed as Callaghan's archetypal hero: 'God in man', 'and in everyone alive', the ultimate 'storyteller', isolated, mysterious, magical, full of 'awareness', 'compassion', and imagination, 'bent on overthrowing the real masters of the world', and 'freeing [humanity] from the heavy bondage of the law' so everyone can make their own 'choice' about 'the right action' for 'each situation' (pp. 119-23). Extrapolated from Scripture, Jesus emphasizes humanism, iconoclasm, and situational ethics much more than orthodox theology. Significantly, he is also the lover of Mary Magdalene, who represents Love (p. 230), and the saviour of Mary of Samaria, the 'sacred whore', who represents Beauty (p. 61). According to this biblical revision, the two Marys were censored and conflated by the early Christians into one figure with better public relations value.

In the story of the resurrection Callaghan attempts to integrate religion and realism in an episode unique in his fiction. Unlike Graham Greene, for example, who incorporated supernatural acts (divine intervention and epiphanies) into his religious fiction, Callaghan has always grounded his narratives in the natural world. The appearance of the risen Jesus to the narrator (after he has assisted in the body-snatching from the now-'empty tomb') tries to cover all theological positions without clarifying any: it is neither the physical resurrection

---

10. M. Callaghan, *A Time for Judas* (Toronto: Macmillan, 1975), p. 125. Page numbers are cited in the text.

of orthodoxy nor the spiritual manifestation of liberal theology. Ultimately as theodicy, the ending of this novel is trite and sentimental: 'Where is he? Where there's love' (p. 231).

In Callaghan's works there is a constant, unresolved tension between his religious vision and his fidelity to existential realism. Callaghan always had a profound commitment to portraying the mysterious and sometimes 'rotten' stuff of human existence. And he always attempted, through his iconoclastic but basically religious view of life, to give reality some moral meaning and eternal significance. The ambiguous mixtures of the sacred and the secular in his novels are the result of this tension. The focus of his vision changed over his long career: from a tentative naturalism, to a Christian humanism concentrated at first most strongly in the metaphysical realm and later focused on the secular world, and finally to an emphasis on humanistic struggles almost devoid of theological illumination and form. However, as his religious vision became less theocentric and logocentric in his later works, his images of Christ become less meaningful, both morally and artistically, to a non-Christian world.

Hugh Hood

Hugh Hood was a protégé of Callaghan and in many ways is heir to his spiritual concerns. But he is a much more consciously and intellectually religious writer who has written several essays on the theological basis for his art and calls himself 'a Catholic and through and through a Catholic novelist'. In contrast to Callaghan, who redefines divine grace to fit the dramatic and psychological demands of realistic fiction, Hood redefines fiction to allow him to convey his conservative Catholic vision.

Hood expresses his neo-Thomist theology in an artistic theory called 'super-realism' which exhibits the 'transcendent essences' of things as they are manifest 'in this world'. As he explains in his essays, his philosophy is Aristotelian hylomorphism and his aesthetic is transcendentalism indebted to the Romantics. But his practice is more clearly defined in metaphor: 'If I were a poet, I would write about how things are full of the Holy Spirit, without reference to the Spirit, just to the illuminations in the things. Now I think of it, that's what I try to do in fiction, give the sense of how things are *inflated* like footballs by the indwelling Spirit.'[11] This aesthetic has led Hood increasingly to reject the conventions of realistic fiction and of what he terms the post-Flaubertian 'psychological novel of character and incident'. His alternative is to set his characters within large, metaphoric structures which emphasize the unity and coherence of all time and space in the divine.

Hood's characters, like Callaghan's, search for meaning and grace to illuminate their earthly lives. Unlike Callaghan, Hood seems to have a clear vision of the answer to his characters' quests. But Hood's weakness has always been in the portrayal of the questions. Perhaps because of his own religious optimism, he finds it difficult to depict sin and evil. But, in omitting them, or treating them simplistically within his fiction, he is falsifying life.

Throughout his career, Hood has been seeking—with only some success—a novelistic form to embody his religious vision. *White Figure, White Ground* (1964), Hood's first novel, is still probably his best. He calls it a 'religious allegory' or parable: the existential quest for the hero's father, which is the central action of the book, is paralleled by his spiritual quest for God the Father, and the two levels are synthesized and revealed in the paintings which are the structural metaphors for the novel.

The hero, Alexander MacDonald, travels east from Montreal to his ancestral home in Nova Scotia to search out the mysterious reasons for his father's exile, death, and his own disinheritance. A celebrated Canadian painter on the eve of his New York debut, at thirty-nine Alex also has decided to abandon his gay, popular style and attempt to paint the ultimate in aesthetic illumination in the light of the east coast. In the old gray house where his two maiden aunts and young cousin are prisoners of the past and the memory of his tyrannical grandfather, he finally comes to terms with the family skeletons which have haunted him.

At the same time, Alex also achieves divine illumination in his art. His painting *Light Source #1* is white-on-white, an allegorical celebration of God, what he calls an 'aperture into infinity'. *Light Source #2* represents darkness, night, death, evil, and the absence of God. But it is illuminated by hints of green that represent faith, 'the colour of man in the world God gave him, hoping'. Alex has recognized the *Light Source* paintings to be his best yet, but he will no longer pursue that

11. H. Hood, letter to Dennis Duffy, undated, in D. Duffy, 'Grace: The Novels of Hugh Hood', *Canadian Literature* 47 (1971), p. 10.

potentially dualistic vision. His art will give 'Laus Deo' but be in the 'flesh'.[12]

The primary theme of this novel is the realization of divine grace acting in nature, the spirit in the flesh, 'no ideas but in things' as Hood says. This theme is appropriately embodied in the synthesis of allegorical and realistic elements within this parable. Characterization and action operate quite credibly on the realistic level, and the detailed technical discussions of painting reinforce the authenticity of Alex's craft. On the other hand, the setting, the trinitarian structure, the characters' names, and especially the symbolic use of liturgical colours are all part of a careful design of concrete universals or 'emblems' illustrating a Christian allegory. There are undeniable tensions within this book between the realistic and the allegorical elements, and the result for some readers may be a feeling of unsubstantiality and abstraction beneath the realistic surface. Still, it is an absorbing and persuasive novel, and the most satisfying synthesis of faith and fiction that Hood has yet produced.

In his next three novels Hood deliberately explored other fictional forms in an attempt to find a correlative for his religious vision. *The Camera Always Lies* is a conventional romance, in which a Hollywood heroine is betrayed by villainous movie producers and is saved by a gallant Frenchman who combines romantic heroics with Christian virtues. The villains are punished, and the lovers fly off into the sunrise together. *A Game of Touch* is Hood's only attempt in the mode of the realistic psychological novel. It is a comic slice of Canadian life viewed through the lives of a group of men who play touch football and the woman who sleeps with most of them. During the course of the novel, the two main characters grow up to the realities of the games of life, sex, and politics.

In *A Game of Touch* Hood changed to a secular, not overtly Catholic novel. His next book, *You Can't Get There from Here*, represents the extremity of this development. It is a fantasy satire set in an imaginative hell, Hood's closest approximation to a post-Nietzschean, post-Christian world. In the fictional African country of Leofrica the new president, Anthony Jedeb, is a Christ-figure who, betrayed by his disciples and crucified by his people, descends into hell with no hope of resurrection. This novel indicates the struggle in Hood's work between faith and

12. H. Hood, *White Figure, White Ground* (Toronto: Ryerson, 1964), pp. 217 and 239.

fiction, and it is a transitional phase in his search for a unifying form. Of it he said: 'The problem is that I believe in the heavenly city, the immortal soul and the whole Christian bag of tricks, but I don't know how to make a literary image out of it yet.'[13]

In 1975 Hood embarked on an ambitious vocation to 'endow [Canada] with a great imperishable work of art. If I do, it will be the first one that we have'. Obviously, his immodesty has not endeared him to the critics. He began his twelve-volume series, *The New Age*, twenty years ago with the intention of publishing one novel every two years until the turn of the century: so far he has produced ten volumes.

In *The New Age* Hood definitively turns away from the traditional novel toward the mode of Christian allegory. He says,

> I am trying to assimilate the mode of the novel to the mode of fully-developed Christian allegory, in ways that I don't fully understand. I want to be more 'real' than the realists, yet more transcendent than the most vaporous allegorist... Now let me put it to you that since I am *both* a realist and a *transcendentalist allegorist* I cannot be bound by the forms of ordinary realism.[14]

Now if one accepts Hood's premise that his 'long narratives', particularly *The New Age* novels, should not be judged by the standards of the realistic novel, then the results become simply (as one critic has said) a matter of taste. But Hood has, in fact, also made a commitment to be more 'real' than the realists, and at this point in the series he is failing to satisfy the demands of the realistic novel in terms of character and action. Faith and fiction foregrounds the problem of communication between the religious novelist and the modern non-religious world. It is significant, then, that Hood seems increasingly to appeal to, and perhaps even write for, a coterie audience.

The New Age attempts to create what Hood calls a 'documentary fantasy' or 'social mythology' that will demonstrate within the facts of this real world, and especially within Canada, the transcendental essence that unites all time and space in a divine Eternity. The first volume, *The Swing in the Garden*, tells the story of Matthew Goderich, the central narrator of the cycle, during his first ten years in the thirties. The expanding consciousness of the little boy represents Canadian

---

13. P. Cloutier, 'An Interview with Hugh Hood', *Journal of Canadian Fiction* 2.1 (1973), p. 49.

14. H. Hood and J. Mills, 'Epistolary Conversation', *Fiddlehead* 116 (1978), p. 145.

society in that prelapsarian time before its traumatic maturation in World War II; the theme of the novel is the Fall from Grace to nature and original sin.

The second novel, *A New Athens*, is still probably the best novel in the series to date; it has a better balance of incident and digression and deeper characterization. At thirty-six, the grown-up Matthew narrates the details of his courtship, marriage, and career as an art historian. In his meditations on life in the new Athens, a small town in south-eastern Ontario, and its associations with Loyalist history, he also has a vision of the New Jerusalem through his mother-in-law's visionary art. The theme of the novel is the interpenetration of the earthly and the heavenly cities, the secular and the sacred, the new Athens and the new Jerusalem.

Reservoir Ravine, the third novel, is the story of Matt's pre-history, his parents' courtship and marriage in Toronto during the twenties, that epic time between 'the war' and 'the Crash'. The theme is the unity and continuity of all time and space in the Eternal Will of God. Therefore, as Matt says, there is no break in the continuum of time before and after his birth; it is all accessible to him, part of his personal mythology, and all redeemed as 'being-in-God'.

These first three novels are characteristic of *The New Age* series: it synthesizes time and space within the microcosm of Matt's family and friends, and the macrocosm of Canadian history in order to reveal eternal truth and divine grace. Unfortunately, the critical response to both the fictional form and the religious vision of the modern Christian allegories has changed, over two decades, from respectful attention to derisive dismissal.

The first problem is that Hood rejects the virtues of the realistic novel: there is little action, no dramatic conflict, and no strong narrative line in these books. Characters are evoked through metaphorical incidents and epic motifs rather than psychological depths. The structure consists of a series of short stories or 'spots of time' loosely integrated in a chronological or associative order. These anecdotes are interspersed with digressions on emblems, epic motifs, travelogues, catalogues and full-blown essays in which the author speaks through the narrator. This structure, unenlivened by character development or conflict, can easily become boring. And the narrator, who carries the heavy burden of justifying and organizing these reminiscences, is too often pretentious and tiring—one critic has called him 'a twit'. Hood has committed himself to a representation of real life in these novels, but too often life escapes.

Secondly, there is the problem with Hood's religious vision. His vision is Catholic and Christian, but in his epiphanies of God's grace he does not imaginatively embody humanity's fallen nature. His failure to dramatize that existential struggle against evil and despair that we have seen in the work of Callaghan means that Hood's affirmations of God's grace are too simple and easy, untested and unearned. This conclusion may be the result of his theology: God's grace is unmerited, and evil is the absence of good, therefore theoretically a non-entity and not subject to dramatization. But original sin is also a part of his orthodox Christian thought, realized intellectually but not dramatically.

Hood avoids Callaghan's failing in which sympathetic identification with the sinner tends to preclude discrimination in a 'feast of pity'. But Hood also avoids Callaghan's Christ-like compassion for people in his concentration on things and events, icons and emblems. If he will not plumb the soul of the human being, he perhaps does not imaginatively realize the sin in the human heart. In *Black & White Keys* even the horror of the Holocaust is emotionally disembodied by its integration with wartime domesticity in Toronto. *The New Age* is, ultimately, a cold pastoral. In the conflict between faith and fiction, Hood has explored many options. He has finally chosen to synthesize the novel and the Christian allegory to create a new narrative form. Though theoretically a perfect solution, in practice this hybrid fiction has not been able to communicate his faith to a non-Christian society, perhaps because he ultimately portrays an abstract theology rather than concrete images of Christ.

Hugh MacLennan

Hugh MacLennan, the other founding father of Canadian literature, was also the self-appointed spokesman for Canada in the twentieth century. In four books of essays and seven novels, MacLennan chronicled the historical maturation of Canada from colonial optimism to atomic *angst* and paralleled it with his own personal spiritual journey from Calvinism to Christian Existentialism.

In his book of essays, *Cross-Country*, MacLennan equated Calvinism with a joyless, repressed 'puritan' mentality, a result of his particular upbringing. He believed Canadian society was conditioned from the beginning by Calvinist forces (both Protestant and Roman Catholic Jansenist), and Puritanism as a psychology has prevailed long after the waning of established religion, enormously inhibiting the Canadian character in the process: 'Americans are proud of what they do. The excessive puritanism of Canadians makes them proud of what they don't do.'[15] The Calvinist legacy is a 'futile, haunting, primitive sense of guilt' (p. 139) that has distorted life, degraded sex, devalued aesthetics, and destroyed the creative spirit through the god of materialism. However, MacLennan also warned against the antithesis to traditional religion: 'History reveals clearly that no civilization has long survived after that civilization has lost its religion' (p. 140). And since 'where religion is concerned nature abhors a vacuum', God was replaced by those aberrations of the religious impulse, 'Nationalism, Fascism and Communism' (p. 141). MacLennan said that he, like many of his contemporaries, briefly found an alternative god among these political and social systems of the thirties, and a deceptive peace as a liberal intellectual in the affluent society of the fifties. But he felt his idealistic generation achieved neither personal nor social salvation but only spiritual bankruptcy.

Therefore, since MacLennan did not believe that traditional Christian doctrine contains 'a countervailing idea great enough and sustaining enough to save society from totalitarianism and our own souls from the materialistic desert in which they now wander' (p. 141), he called for a 'reconstruction of Christian theology' to forge 'new symbols' for a 'new vision of God' (pp. 145-48). This vocation led him to search for a 'theology of mediation' in the world of his fiction. His solution to the problem of writing a religious novel in a godless society was a redefinition of God to answer the modern questions about meaning and purpose. His emphasis on natural as opposed to revealed theology indicates an affinity with the branch of modern Protestantism most commonly identified with Paul Tillich and New Theology. The positive result of liberal Protestantism for MacLennan's fiction is that he compassionately identifies with and explores the spiritual struggles of his characters. The negative aspect is that MacLennan's view of God, like that of New Theology, is philosophical, hypothetical, subjective, and therefore difficult to dramatize. This is one of the reasons why, when MacLennan portrays the existential questions

15. H. MacLennan, *Cross-Country* (Edmonton: Hurtig, 1972), pp. 53-54. Page numbers are cited in the text.

with great realism, complexity, and conviction, his theological resolutions often seem arbitrary and unconvincing.

MacLennan's search for a 'new theology' emerges in progressive stages in his first four novels. His heroes repudiate the doctrines of Calvinism but cannot free themselves from its psychological legacy of guilt; they deny the reality of God in the world and then desperately search for alternative 'religions' to console their emptiness and anxiety. But all humanist solutions—social, political, material, even personal relationships—ultimately fail them, and they must eventually find a spiritual Absolute to give their lives meaning and purpose.

MacLennan embodies the whole pattern of his spiritual pilgrimage in his fifth and finest novel, *The Watch that Ends the Night* (1959), and finally arrives at a radical redefinition of God to answer the existential dilemma of modern humanity. The narrator, George Stewart, is the Everyman of 'a generation which yearned to belong, so unsuccessfully to something larger than themselves'.[16] This articulation of the religious theme of the book recalls William James's definition of 'religious experience': 'that we can experience union with *something larger than ourselves* and in that union find our greatest peace'.[17] The search for religious peace—a truce between the human spirit and fate— is the premise and substance of *The Watch that Ends the Night*.

In a pattern repeated throughout the novel, George Stewart prepares us theologically for the events he then dramatizes. He tells us that as a boy he had been religious and believed in a personal, living God. Nevertheless, in the disillusionments of the Thirties, like millions of others, he lost his faith in religion, in himself, and in the integrity of human society (p. 107). And the manifest injustices of the world, symbolized for him in his wife's illness, have increased his rejection of any Divine Power (p. 6). So, in the hubristic, self-centred Fifties he finds his religion, his 'rock' and his 'salvation' in the palpably mortal life and love of his wife, Catherine. She represents a quasi-divine 'spiritual force' in George's life, primarily characterized by the 'Life-Force' which has developed in her in response to her struggle against her 'fate'—her rheumatic heart. And this spirit is the 'sole force which equals the merciless fate which binds a human being to his mortality'

16. H. MacLennan, *The Watch that Ends the Night* (Toronto: Macmillan, 1959), p. 4. Page numbers are cited in the text.

17. W. James, *The Varieties of Religious Experience* (London: Fontana Collins, 1960), p. 499.

(p. 26). It is her strength and her knowledge that 'all loving is a loving of life in the midst of death' (p. 69) that George leans on for years until he is forced to develop his own spiritual resources.

Among George's generation, in which 'so many of the successful ones, after trying desperately to hitch their wagons to some great belief, ended up believing in nothing but their own cleverness' (p. 101), towers the mythological figure of Jerome Martell, Catherine's first husband and George's spiritual father. His life has the symbolic dimension of a modern *Pilgrim's Progress*; during his youth 'he had really thought of himself as a soldier of God. He believed the Gospels literally, and they meant far more to him than they could mean to most people, because he had such a desperate need to belong' (pp. 215-16). But the horror and guilt of World War I destroyed his religion, forcing him to seek absolution in medicine and politics for the senseless killing. Jerome is one of the many who divert the passions that no longer serve a traditional God into a neo-religious faith: 'A man must belong to something larger than himself. He must surrender to it. God was so convenient for that purpose when people could believe in Him. He was so safe and so remote... Now there is nothing but people... The only immortality is mankind' (pp. 270-72).

He abandons his family in order to set up a transfusion unit for the Loyalists in the Spanish Civil War and is reportedly tortured and killed by the Nazis. But he returns from the dead to witness to the second half of the theme: what every man 'requires to know and feel if he is to live with a sense of how utterly tremendous is the mystery our ancestors confidently called God' (p. 324). He has had an unorthodox vision of Jesus in his prison cell: 'He wasn't the Jesus of the churches. He wasn't the Jesus who died for our sins. He was simply a man who had died and risen again. Who had died outwardly as I had died inwardly' (p. 330).

MacLennan resorts to a theological interlude at the end of the novel in which George explains humanity's need for a god and the insufficiency and impermanence of all the various substitutes: reason, success, wife and family, political systems and the state. Faced with mortality, he falls prey to the 'Great Fear', the existential anxiety that God is indifferent and life is meaningless; this *angst* threatens to obliterate his identity. Only a mystical union of the spirit of Everyman with the 'Unknowable which at that instant makes available His power, and for that instant existing, becomes known' (p. 344) defeats the modern death wish, vindicates God to scientific humanity, justifies the human plight and celebrates life: 'it is of no importance that God appears indifferent to justice as men understand it. He gave life. He gave it. Life for a year, a month, a day or an hour is still a gift' (p. 344).

I think this novel can be illuminated by reference to Paul Tillich's ideas. When Jerome Martell's 'courage to be as a part' and George Stewart's 'courage to be as oneself' are ultimately discredited as faiths for the twentieth century, MacLennan turns to 'the courage to be'. The inner harmony and death to self which George finally arrives at are an experience of 'mysticism', defined by Tillich as 'the striving for union with ultimate reality, and the corresponding courage to take the non-being which is implied in finitude upon oneself'.[18] And George's final affirmation of life is what Tillich calls the 'self-affirmation of being-itself: There are no valid arguments for the existence of God, but there are acts of courage in which we affirm the power of being... Courage has revealing power, the courage to be is the key to being-itself.'[19] In this novel MacLennan has attempted to translate this 'natural theology' into dramatic action. Nevertheless, the novel suffers from a non-dramatic ending, a transposition of the existential problem into a metaphysical abstraction. When the world surrounding George becomes 'a shadow' (p. 373), it is no longer the subject of realistic fiction.

The parallels which I have noted with liberal Protestant theology may help to explain some of the problems that critics have had with the ending of *The Watch that Ends the Night* and also with MacLennan's later novels. Tillich, for example, has repudiated 'those elements in the Jewish-Christian tradition which emphasize the person-to-person relationship with God': the personalistic image of God, the personal nature of human faith and divine forgiveness, the idea of divine purpose, and the person-to-person character of prayer and practical devotion.[20] These qualities, traditionally portrayed by religious writers to dramatize God's interaction with this world (for example, in the works of O'Connor and Greene), seem also to be absent from MacLennan's concept of God. His 'new vision of God' is that synthesis of science and mysticism which modern humanity can accept, but God is no longer a Person with an objective reality independent of human

18. Tillich, *The Courage to Be*, p. 156.
19. Tillich, *The Courage to Be*, pp. 175-76.
20. Tillich, *The Courage to Be*, p. 177.

perception of him. A relationship with this transcendent, impersonal Deity is difficult to portray dramatically. As a result, George Stewart's ultimate encounter with the divine is distinguished by didactic sincerity and rhetorical intensity—but metaphysical unreality.

Furthermore, MacLennan has been unable to sustain this optimistic 'new vision of God' in his later novels. *Return of the Sphinx* (1967) is MacLennan's elegy for lost idealism, and there is no attempt at an optimistic fictional resolution. The lesson here is that every generation must repeat the universal religious quest—from the death of God, through false ideologies, to spiritual grace—but now in a world of moral, spiritual and humanistic disintegration. In the Epilogue, therefore, MacLennan is forced to offer his larger vision of the grace operating in nature that he has not honestly been able to dramatize in his plot. The protagonist's vague, pantheistic optimism lacks even the theological content of the resolution of *The Watch that Ends the Night*. Finally, in the ambitious scope of *Voices in Time* (1980) MacLennan portrays a civilization beyond religion, destroyed by humanity's ignorance and evil, offering only a feeble spiritual hope in the mysterious 'God who manifests Himself in evolution'.

Callaghan, Hood and MacLennan have all tried to present logocentric, Christocentric verbal images to a post-Christian era. None has been totally successful in the fusion of faith and fiction. But in an age of unbelief, their unfashionable vocation as Christian writers is all the more to be prized.

'THE SUDDEN LOOK OF SOME DEAD MASTER':
T.S. ELIOT AND DANTE

Kevin McCarron

> We burn with desire to find a firm footing, an ultimate, lasting base on
> which to build a tower rising up to infinity.
>
> Pascal

Kenneth Asher begins his book *T.S. Eliot and Ideology*, published in
1995, with these uncompromising words: 'The past decade has seen
Eliot's reputation recede to its lowest ebb of the century.'[1] Asher, by
no means wholly unsympathetic to Eliot, goes on to note for many
contemporary critics Eliot's claim to establish enduring criteria of
value constitutes 'a futile attempt to legitimate his narrative by reference to a metadiscourse'.[2] In addition to this crime, Eliot has also been
seen as a particularly unabashed advocate of logocentrism and, most
recently, he has been attacked in the name of a multiculturalism that
sees him as the chief modern apologist for a hereditary canon of
western literary classics. All of these criticisms are presented as perceptions on the part of the critic; that is to say, the acumen of the academic critic reveals the deficiencies and unpalatable ideologies, either
overt or covert, enscribed in Eliot's work.

Eliot enjoyed cordial relations with academics throughout his career,
but it perhaps should not be forgotten that he turned down a position
as a lecturer, in philosophy, at Harvard in order to concentrate on
poetry and literary criticism. Moreover, in a letter he wrote to Eleanor
Hinkley in 1914, while studying at Oxford, he wrote,

> I do not want to give the impression that my admiration for Oxford is of a
> grudging sort. I only mean that Oxford is not intellectually stimulating—

---

1. K. Asher, *T.S. Eliot and Ideology* (Cambridge: Cambridge University Press,
1995), p. 1.
2. Asher, *T.S. Eliot and Ideology*, p. 1.

but that would be a good deal to ask of a university atmosphere.[3]

One of the issues I want to raise here is the possibility that academic criticism of Eliot's poetry, in particular, itself forms part of a humanist discourse to which Eliot was implacably opposed. His distaste for humanism is well documented, and perhaps most dramatically expressed in a letter he wrote to Paul Elder More in 1930:

> I am really shocked by your assertion that God did not make Hell. It seems to me that you have lapsed into Humanitarianism... Is your God Santa Claus?... To me religion has brought at least the perception of something above morals, and therefore extremely terrifying; it has brought me not happiness but a sense of something above happiness and therefore more terrifying than ordinary pain and misery; the very dark night and the desert... I had far rather walk, as I do, in daily terror of eternity than feel this was only a children's game in which all the contestants would get equally worthless prizes in the end.[4]

It seems curious, therefore, not to say illogical, to suggest, as Kenneth Asher does, that

> there is a systematic lack of generosity, finally, of humanity, in Eliot's work—both prose and poetry—and, in the last analysis, it is this that will exclude him from the classical company to which he devoted so much of his life.[5]

This does not seem to me to be a literary judgment at all, but rather one tautologously predicated on the humanist notion that only work which celebrates the human can be accepted as having made a valuable contribution. Eliot may well be excluded from the humanist tradition, for which he would be grateful, but to criticize him for his lack of zeal in promoting the humanist cause is surely misguided. Eliot is, certainly in his poetry, among this century's most eloquent advocates of the anti-humanist demand for the annihilation of humanity before God. Humanism is anathema to him, and any literary perspective which itself is predicated on humanist principles (Marxism and Feminism particularly) will necessarily find him wanting. I cannot accept, either, that his position 'excludes him from the classical company to which he

3. *The Letters of T.S. Eliot.* 1. 1898–1922 (ed. V. Eliot; London: Faber and Faber, 1988), p. 61.

4. Cited in M. Jain (ed.), *T.S. Eliot and American Philosophy* (Cambridge: Cambridge University Press, 1992), p. 227.

5. Asher, *T.S. Eliot and Ideology*, p. 165.

devoted so much of his life'. Steve Ellis notes of *Four Quartets* that philosophically 'a Hume-Pascal model of discontinuity between the human/natural and the divine is adopted...'[6] In addition, Eliot's eventual evocation of a Divine Order which penetrates and controls the world's confusions and resolves its contradictions links him with Dante. The central problem here as regards current evaluations of Eliot's work, and one which is inextricably linked itself to humanism, may well be that contemporary literary critics are often ill-equipped, temperamentally and theoretically, to engage with literature that assumes a religious experience is as valid as any other form of experience. What, after all, can the critic who is unsympathetic to religious experience, or even actively hostile to it, make of lines such as these, from 'Little Gidding'?

> We only live, only suspire
> Consumed by either fire or fire.[7]

One strategy, used by a number of critics, is to analyse the poems, particularly the later ones, as though they were cynical, or desperate, attempts on Eliot's part to extricate himself from the implications of the earlier work. Hence Rainer Emig, in *Modernism in Poetry*, notes the striking loss of autonomy experienced by Eliot's early protagonists, and then writes: 'In his later works, Eliot seems to accept this lack of autonomy reluctantly. The deficient subject becomes the basis of a religious framework which pretends to overcome the lack.'[8] We note the word 'pretends'. Similarly, he writes specifically of 'The Hollow Men': 'the recourse to the absolute (whether it is God or death) is necessary to complement the enormous absence of meaning created in the text'.[9] Here, we might note the words 'recourse' and 'necessary'. A more useful way of reading Eliot's poetry, particularly the later work, would be to accept that the reader is being asked to enter imaginatively into states of consciousness which perceive the world, rightly or wrongly, to be animated by a religious power which is not, crucially,

6.   S. Ellis, *The English Eliot: Design, Language and Landscape in Four Quartets* (London: Routledge, 1991), p. 127.

7.   T.S. Eliot, *Collected Poems 1909–1962* (London: Faber and Faber, 1974), p. 221. All subsequent references to Eliot's poetry are to this edition, and are included in the body of the essay.

8.   R. Emig, *Modernism in Poetry: Motivations, Structures and Limits* (London: Longman, 1995), p. 66.

9.   Emig, *Modernism in Poetry*, p. 81.

inside the protagonist, but wholly exterior to him; a force which is totally, and terrifyingly, Other. For Eliot, there is an ontological gulf between God and God's creation—a real difference of being.

A model for a reading of this kind is provided by Eliot himself in his essay on Dante, published in 1929. Here, Eliot writes: 'If you can read poetry as poetry, you will "believe" in Dante's theology exactly as you believe in the physical reality of his journey; that is, you suspend both belief and disbelief'.[10] Eliot first read Dante in 1909, in his second year at Harvard, and the Italian poet remained a powerful influence throughout his life. Eliot admired Dante for his simplicity, lucidity, and economy, and for his ability to employ allegory mediated by clear visual images. In addition, as one of Eliot's biographers has noted 'he found in Dante the highest expression of [the] civilization of Christian Europe… Dante was for him the embodiment of a cultural and social order…'[11]

I want to suggest that Eliot's work, consciously or not, emulates the structure of Dante's *Divine Comedy*. His early poems, which include 'The Love Song of J. Alfred Prufrock', 'Portrait of a Lady', 'Preludes' and, most famously, *The Waste Land* constitute his *Inferno*; 'The Hollow Men', 'Ash Wednesday' and the 'Ariel Poems' are his *Purgatorio*; and *Four Quartets* is Eliot's *Paradiso*. Eliot's protagonists ask questions which are religious throughout all three stages, yet each stage of his work presents a differing image of Christ.

Eliot's early poetry is characterized by disillusion, despair and sensations of disintegration. It is religious poetry by virtue of its doubt. In an essay on Tennyson's *In Memoriam*, Eliot writes,

> *In Memoriam* can, I think, justly be called a religious poem, but for another reason than that which made it seem religious to [Tennyson's] contemporaries. It is not religious because of the quality of its faith, but because of the quality of its doubt. Its faith is a poor thing, but its doubt is a very intense experience. *In Memoriam* is a poem of despair, but of despair of a religious kind.[12]

The famous opening lines of 'The Love Song of J. Alfred Prufrock' set the scene for a powerful examination of loneliness, sickness and estrangement:

10. T.S. Eliot, *Dante* (London: Faber and Faber, 1975), p. 36.
11. P. Ackroyd, *T.S. Eliot* (London: Hamish Hamilton, 1984), p. 179.
12. T.S. Eliot, *Selected Prose* (ed. F. Kermode; London: Faber and Faber, 1975), p. 243.

> Let us go then, you and I,
> When the evening is spread out against the sky
> Like a patient etherised upon a table... (p. 13).

The phrase 'you and I' artfully forces the reader of the poem to collude with the narrator. Throughout the poem the protagonist is aware of the remorseless pressure of time:

> There will be time, there will be time
> To prepare a face to meet the faces that you meet;
> There will be time to murder and create,
> And time for all the works and days of hands
> That lift and drop a question on your plate;
> Time for you and time for me,
> And time yet for a hundred indecisions,
> And for a hundred visions and revisions,
> Before the taking of a toast and tea.
>
> In the room the women come and go
> Talking of Michelangelo (p. 14).

The well-known last couplet has been condemned by several feminist critics for demonstrating a contempt for women, but it is remarkably similar to a comment made in Eliot's later poem 'Portrait of a Lady', in which the male narrator says,

> We have been, let us say, to hear the latest Pole
> Transmit the Preludes, through his hair and finger-tips (p. 18).

The phrase 'let us say' implies that it could have been anybody, playing anything. What is being criticized in both poems, it seems to me, is 'culture' itself. On its own, Eliot suggests, culture is inadequate; it cannot provide the *spiritual* fulfilment which all of Eliot's early characters desire.

> Do I dare
> Disturb the universe? (p. 14)

Prufrock asks. In a sense, all of Eliot's early characters dare to disturb the universe, for the universe they inhabit is a de-sacralized one and, as such, it is insufficient for their needs. In his essay on Dante, Eliot writes of the *Inferno*: 'It reminds us that Hell is not a place but a state...'[13]

---

13. Eliot, *Dante*, p. 25.

A striking feature of Eliot's earlier work is his reliance on metonymy, the use of a part to represent the whole, as occurs, for example, in 'Preludes':

> And short square fingers stuffing pipes,
> And evening newspapers, and eyes
> Assured of certain certainties... (p. 24).

A critic who is irritated by Eliot's intellectual elitism will point to such lines as indicative of the poet's disdain for the masses—metonymy here gives the poet away, it reveals his true feelings. A feminist critic might draw our attention to these lines, from 'Prufrock':

> And I have known the arms already, known them all—
> Arms that are braceleted and white and bare
> (But in the lamplight, downed with light brown hair!) (p. 15).

In this case, it might be argued that by reducing women in this metonymic fashion Eliot betrays confusion, misogyny and even sexual hysteria. Should such a critic have biographical interests, observations and speculations about Eliot's unhappy first marriage might succeed these general criticisms. Similarly, a critic like Terry Eagleton can be used to advance a specifically Marxist argument, and Michael North, for example, writes,

> The general fragmentation of 'The Love Song of J. Alfred Prufrock' is obvious and notorious. The poem seems a perfect example of what Terry Eagleton calls the modern 'transition from metaphor to metonymy: unable any longer to totalize his experience in some heroic figure, the bourgeois is forced to let it trickle away into objects related to him by sheer contiguity'.[14]

However, I would like to suggest that metonymy can be seen in Eliot's work as a figure representing *incompleteness*; it is ubiquitous because, for Eliot, without a spiritual dimension humanity lacks something fundamental to make it whole, something without which it can *only* be depicted metonymically.

A paradox emerges here: metonymy is pervasive because of a lack; that lack, however, is simultaneously, for Eliot, a presence—that of Original Sin. In the *Paradiso*, Beatrice tells the pilgrim that 'the human creature'

> 'never returns to his dignity unless he fills up again the void made by his fault, with just penalties for sinful pleasure. Your nature, when it all

14. M. North, *The Political Aesthetic of Yeats, Eliot, and Pound* (Cambridge: Cambridge University Press, 1991), p. 76.

sinned in its seed, was parted from these dignities, as from Paradise...'[15]

In 1916, defining himself as a classicist, Eliot wrote: 'The classicist point of view has been defined as essentially a belief in Original Sin...'[16] For Eliot, Original Sin is manifested in a sense of estrangement and incompleteness. Culture can, to some degree, fill the gap ('In the room the women come and go / Talking of Michelangelo'), but, not being grounded in the supernatural, is ultimately unsatisfactory. At the end of *The Waste Land*, which is a compendium of literary quotation, annotation, parody and allusion, a voice can say only: '"These fragments I have shored against my ruins..."' (p. 79). Eliot's characters desire, above all else, significance, wholeness, but this can only be found in an image of Christ—at this stage, absent.

While metonymy is the governing rhetorical device of the earlier work (his *Inferno*), the most striking features of the next phase of Eliot's work (his *Purgatorio*) are repetition and anaphora, the doubling of verse beginnings:

> We are the hollow men
> We are the stuffed men... (p. 89).

In his essay on Dante, Eliot writes,

> the *Purgatorio* is, I think, the most difficult of the three parts... Only when we have read straight through to the end of the *Paradiso* and re-read the *Inferno*, does the *Purgatorio* begin to yield its beauty. Damnation and even blessedness are more exciting than purgation.[17]

Eliot's poems from this period are austere, often employing short lines, virtually no punctuation, and frequent enjambement, the running on of line endings, as occurs here in 'The Hollow Men':

> Waking alone
> At the hour when we are
> Trembling with tenderness
> Lips that would kiss
> Form prayers to broken stone (p. 91).

In this poem, Eliot offers a corrective, one he was to develop throughout the rest of his poetic career, to the persistent sense of

15. Dante, *The Divine Comedy: Paradiso* (trans. J.D. Sinclair; Oxford: Oxford University Press, 1979), p. 107.
16. Ellis, *The English Eliot*, p. 3.
17. Eliot, *Dante*, pp. 29-30.

Images of Christ

absence central to his poetry from the beginning. In 'The Hollow Men' he concludes by incorporating specifically Christian phraseology into the work itself: 'For Thine is the Kingdom' (p. 92).

'Ash-Wednesday', as the title suggests, is even more specifically sited within a Christian framework, and concludes with the line: 'And let my cry come unto Thee' (p. 105). What is particularly noticeable about 'Ash-Wednesday' is the sensuousness of the poetry and the vivid sense of loss it evokes, primarily through Eliot's use of repetition:

> And the lost heart stiffens and rejoices
> In the lost lilac and the lost sea voices
> And the weak spirit quickens to rebel
> For the bent golden-rod and the lost sea smell... (p. 104).

What is also stressed is the brevity of human life:

> Wavering between the profit and the loss
> In this brief transit where the dreams cross
> The dreamcrossed twilight between birth and dying... (p. 105).

These lines are strikingly similar to those Pozzo declaims in Samuel Beckett's *Waiting For Godot*, first performed nearly twenty-five years after the publication of 'Ash-Wednesday': '"They give birth astride of a grave, the light gleams an instant, then it's night once more"'.[18] For Beckett's characters, of course, there is no redemption; all that can sustain them is their stoicism in the face of inevitable disintegration and certain annihilation.

Rainer Emig writes of Eliot's later work: 'All modernist endeavours which refuse to accept the irrevocable fragmentation of existence, the loss of firm points of reference, inevitably end up in structures that, although only internally motivated, become universalist and totalitarian'.[19] Such a conception, it seems to me, lies at the centre of contemporary evaluations of Eliot's work. However, Eliot would flatly reject the claim that such structures were 'only internally motivated'. For Eliot, the religious impulse is indeed an internal one, but one which is common to humanity; cultures emerge not to impose religion as a means of social control, as Durkheim suggests, but to facilitate and formalize religious worship.

Beckett's writings do accept 'the irrevocable fragmentation of existence', indeed they comically celebrate it, and for this reason

18. S. Beckett, *Waiting For Godot* (London: Faber and Faber, 1974), p. 89.
19. Emig, *Modernism in Poetry*, pp. 84-85.

Beckett is regarded far more favourably than Eliot by contemporary critics. And yet, is it not part of the artist's task to reject? Eliot rejects the 'irrevocable fragmentation of existence' by consciously aligning himself with the Christian tradition; within this tradition, he suggests, the individual can be redeemed from the tyranny of Time. His sequence of poems collectively entitled *Four Quartets*, 'Burnt Norton', 'East Coker', 'The Dry Salvages', and 'Little Gidding', which effectively concludes his poetic career, is primarily a sustained meditation on time.

In his essay on Dante, Eliot writes of the *Paradiso*: 'We have (whether we know it or not) a prejudice against beatitude as material for poetry'.[20] *Four Quartets*, as I suggested earlier, is Eliot's *Paradiso*—it offers beatitude as subject matter for poetry. In 'Little Gidding', in a passage from which I have taken the title of this paper, the narrator encounters a character commonly accepted as Dante:

> I caught the sudden look of some dead master
> Whom I had known, forgotten, half recalled
> Both one and many... (p. 217).

A similar scene occurs in the *Inferno*, but a contemporary Dante scholar writes of this scene: 'a meeting takes place—not between Dante and Virgil as we tend to think of it, but between two nameless characters whose anonymity confirms the primacy of the meeting itself as a spiritual event'.[21] Similarly, I would suggest the character encountered in 'Little Gidding' is both Dante and other poets; the One and the many. He is a visible embodiment of the historical tradition within which the lives of specific individuals are given meaning and value.

Time permeates *Four Quartets*. Philosophical meditations on the nature of time as it intersects with the four principal elements are intertwined with evocations of subjective time, which, in turn, are placed within the larger framework of sacred time. 'Burnt Norton' begins,

> Time present and time past
> Are both perhaps present in time future
> And time future contained in time past (p. 189).

Yet as the sequence progresses such philosophical appraisals, no less valid for being philosophical Eliot suggests, are succeeded by images

---

20. Eliot, *Dante*, p. 45.

21. D. Heilbronn-Gaines, *'Inferno* 1: Breaking The Silence', in *Dante's Inferno* (ed. and trans. M. Musa; Bloomington: Indiana University Press, 1995), p. 288.

which are presented as more personal; subjective apprehensions which could only be experienced in time:

> But only in time can the moment in the rose-garden,
> The moment in the arbour where the rain beat,
> The moment in the draughty church at smokefall
> Be remembered; involved with past and future.
> Only through time time is conquered (p. 192).

This time, too, is subsumed within another, and in 'The Dry Salvages' Eliot writes,

> The hint half-guessed, the gift half understood, is Incarnation.
> Here the impossible union
> Of spheres of existence is actual,
> Here the past and future
> Are conquered, and reconciled... (p. 213).

In 'East Coker', the Christian mystery is also presented in terms of repetitious violence:

> The dripping blood our only drink,
> The bloody flesh our only food... (p. 202).

Such lines seem to me to exemplify the sense of savagery which Eliot perceived as central to the Christian Mass.

Eliot is clearly closer in thought to, say, Hobbes than he is to Rousseau, whom he blamed for having, virtually single-handedly, initiated Romanticism, a view of life he found even more distasteful than humanism. He writes in an essay called 'Imperfect Critics': 'the only cure for Romanticism is to analyze it'.[22] Dante, *avant la lettre*, and Eliot both reverse the Romantic trajectory which begins in beatitude and ends in disillusionment. In 'East Coker', particularly, Eliot suggests that Nature is not a refuge from time, nor does it provide a convenient opposition to humanity:

> The time of milking and the time of harvest
> The time of the coupling of man and woman
> And that of beasts. Feet rising and falling.
> Eating and drinking. Dung and death (p. 197).

Nature, too, is 'fallen'; it is not possible to find *in* it the creator *of* it. The austerity of Eliot's vision here is unmatched in English poetry. In *Four Quartets* we find none of the benign interaction between humanity

22. T.S. Eliot, *The Sacred Wood* (London: Methuen, 1980), p. 31.

and nature that we find in the Romantics, or even in a writer like Chaucer, who substantially precedes them. (I think it was Dryden who said of *The Canterbury Tales*, 'Here is God's Plenty'. I'm not sure there is 'plenty' in Chaucer, although there is a lot of the same thing, and what there is, is not God's. Apart from those reservations, I suppose I agree with Dryden.)

Dante concludes the *Paradiso* with these lines: 'my desire and will, like a wheel that spins with even motion, were revolved by the Love that moves the sun and the other stars'.[23] John D. Sinclair writes of the *Paradiso*: 'It should be noted, for it is fundamental in Dante, that, while his pilgrimage ends in rapture, it is not mere rapture, but, expressly, a vision which controls his desire and will...'[24] Eliot's last lines are

> When the tongues of flames are in-folded
> Into the crowned knot of fire
> And the fire and the rose are one (p. 223).

Rainer Emig writes of *Four Quartets*: 'A stability and permanence is created which is reassuring, but at the same time isolated and even frigid'.[25] Certainly, Eliot is not emotional. In his Clark Lectures he criticized mystical writers such as St Theresa and St John of the Cross, for, in essence, Romanticism, noting that they were preoccupied with emotion and experiences of ecstatic union. It may well be that the model provided by human sexuality, with its emphasis on consummation, underlies the notion that spiritual union is possible, desirable, and communicable.

Manju Jain notes that Eliot was opposed to such views and preferred 'the mysticism to be found in Aristotle, Thomas Aquinas, Dante, and Richard of St Victor, in which reason and intellect play an essential role and the emphasis is on contemplation...'[26] Eliot's narrator, like Dante's, remains outside his own experience, contemplating it.

Four Quartets is not a poem about time; it is more a contemplation of time. It is not, either, a poem about God; it is a poem about the contemplation of God. Eliot offers three images of Christ throughout his poetry: the absent God, the hidden God, and the transcendent God. In

---

23. Dante, *Paradiso* (trans. Sinclair), p. 484.
24. Dante, *Paradiso* (trans. Sinclair), p. 491.
25. Emig, *Modernism in Poetry*, p. 83.
26. Jain, *T.S. Eliot and American Philosophy*, pp. 190-191.

his essay on Dante he writes 'there is a difference (which here I hardly do more than assert) between philosophical *belief* and poetic *assent*'.[27] To read Eliot with both profit and pleasure, we need not believe, we simply need, for the duration of the text, to assent.

27. Eliot, *Dante*, p. 36.

Part IV

ARTS

JESUS AS MOVING IMAGE: THE QUESTION OF MOVEMENT

John O. Thompson

The story of Jesus has been told directly via the moving image on a number of occasions, and will continue to get told so long as Christianity is with us, but never without generating a sense, especially among 'cultivated' viewers, that this is not the ideal medium for the material. However, Denys Arcand's film *Jesus of Montreal*, which is about a group of people telling the story of Jesus via the medium of theatrical performance, seems to 'get away with it' aesthetically for a large number of satisfied viewers. Why should this be so?

The answer, I will argue, bears on fundamental issues of moving image aesthetics, while having implications as well for the future transmission of the Jesus material within our culture.

Issues of Adaptation

Characters on the screen fall into one of the following categories: (1) real, and really photographed, (2) real, but played by someone else, (3) fictional (so *necessarily* played by 'someone else'). Material on the screen falls into one of the following categories: (1) factual, (2) fictional. It also falls into one of the following categories: (1) original, (2) adapted. It is essential to distinguish between characters and material because of the possibility of real historical characters being made part of fictional constructs, as happens in historical novels.[1]

It might be thought that debate over the historicity of Jesus would raise special problems for narrating the New Testament story, but in

1. On the question of the status of 'real' characters in fiction, and indeed on many other matters relevant to the issues under discussion here, Ruth Ronen's *Possible Worlds in Literary Theory* (Cambridge: Cambridge University Press, 1994) provides an excellent critical discussion of the philosophical and critical literature as well as setting forth her own lucid positive proposals.

fact the problems do not arise there. Real and fictional characters *in adaptations* share more features than separate them, as we will see. To clarify what is involved here I want to use some concepts taken from the great Polish phenomenological aesthetician Roman Ingarden, in his magisterial *The Literary Work of Art*.[2] Ingarden distinguishes between the 'judgmental propositions' that we apply when dealing with the real world, and 'quasi-judgmental propositions' that appear in verbal fiction. Out of the latter are built by the reader, in 'concretizing' a text through reading it, the things and their actions which constitute a fictional world. Real objects, existing in real space-time, are '*unequivocally, universally* (i.e., in *every* respect) *determined*'.[3] The concrete unity of the object, however, means that from a cognitive point of view the totality of those determinations is inexhaustible.[4] But fictional objects, however detailedly described or depicted, are always given only a finite number of determinations in the text. The sentences of fiction, at least of realist fiction, set themselves up as having the same structure as sentences about real objects, but this in fact means that, 'precisely because [each] object is…formally intended as a concrete unit containing an infinite number of fused determinations…"spots of indeterminacy" arise within it, indeed an infinitely great number of them'.[5] Thus, of any real person it can be said that one of his or her determinate features is having or not having children, to a specific number; but Shakespeare's Lady Macbeth, it turns out, has no determinable number of children. Moreover, she has no specified height or weight: if in the theatre on a particular occasion

2. R. Ingarden, *The Literary Work of Art* (Evanston, IL: Northwestern University Press, 3rd edn, 1973). All emphases in quotations from Ingarden are his.

3. Ingarden, *The Literary Work of Art*, p. 246.

4. Ingarden, *The Literary Work of Art*, p. 247: 'The series of cognitive operations in which the individual determinations of one and the same real object are successively apprehended is essentially limitless: however many determinations of a given object are apprehended up to a given moment, there are *always* other determinations still to be apprehended. As a result, in primary cognition, which occurs in a finite manifold of actions, we can never *know* how a given real object is determined in *every* respect; the great majority of its properties is always concealed from us. However, this does not mean that in itself it is not unequivocally, universally determined; it merely means that in this kind of cognition, which proceeds along the path of apprehending the object's individual determinants, it is possible, in accord with the object's essence to apprehend it in a finite series of cognitive operations only *inadequately*.'

5. Ingarden, *The Literary Work of Art*, p. 249.

she 'has', this is in fact because she is being Represented[6] by a real-world person with a particular height and weight and number of children as but three among her (or his, if the part is played by a man) inexhaustible determinations.

It is important to see that 'spots of indeterminacy' are not in any way *blemishes*. Indeed, the structure that Ingarden is describing is not only that which, for Aristotle, allowed poetry to be more highly valued than history,[7] but that which leaves the creator of fiction free to 'get on with it', to give the reader a particular mix of *enough* quasi-judgmental propositions to create the 'reality effect', *not so many* of these as to bog the reader down, and *the right kind* of these as to produce the instruction/entertainment package desired.

The creator of fiction who includes Representatives of real people is involved in a different enterprise from that of the writer of biography, but the difference is a fine one. The biographer can give us only some of the infinite aspects of the person portrayed, because, first, no total grasp of the whole spatio-temporal integrity of a life can be had, in principle; secondly, particular aspects of that life may remain unknown, as a matter of contingency. But the biographer is working from an (inexhaustible) concrete being. Within the pact of fiction, the creator is producing a finite series of quasi-judgmental propositions, albeit concretized in an infinite variety of ways by different readers (your Lady

---

6. In capitalizing 'Represented' here, I am following Ingarden's translator, George G. Grabowicz, who writes, '... Ingarden distinguishes between representation in the sense of "depicting" or "presenting" (*Darstellung*) and representation in the sense of "standing in for" or "imitating" something (*Repräsentation*). Both senses are conveyed by the English term, and, therefore, where necessary, *Repräsentation*, *repräsentieren*, etc., are given as Representation, Representing' (Ingarden, *The Literary Work of Art*, p. 242). The central issue of this paper could be summed up in the question: How is a representation of Jesus to be effected when the Representative of Jesus is a filmed actor?

7. Aristotle, *On the Art of Poetry*, in T.S. Dorsch (trans.), *Classical Literary Criticism* (Harmondsworth: Penguin Books, 1965), p. 43: 'The difference between the historian and the poet... is that the one tells of what has happened, the other of the kinds of things that might happen. For this reason poetry is something more philosophical and more worthy of serious attention than history; for while poetry is concerned with universal truths, history treats of particular facts.' If Lady Macbeth's height and weight had been determinate because she was historically real, this would distract us rather than add to our grasp of the 'universal' aspect of the human possibility that she represents.

Macbeth on the page may be taller and slimmer than mine),[8] and the 'real person' within the fiction remains only partially specified thanks to ontological indeterminacy rather than epistemological limitation. However, because the 'real person' is (a Representative of) a real person, particular debts to and constraints on what *is* made determinate about the character are involved. We know, for instance, how Henry VIII or Napoleon or Lincoln *look*, in a way that we do not, communally, know how Lady Macbeth looks.

The adaptor of a fictional text from one medium to another is indebted to and constrained by the determinacies of the original in much the same way as the historical novelist is indebted to and constrained by the determinacies of the real characters woven into the fictional fabric. If someone *wants* there to be adaptation, movement of material from one telling to another, from one medium to another (and this is certainly what the ongoing importance of adaptation to the moving image arts suggests), part of the demand is for fidelity, for adequate, accurate embodiment. Where fictional originals are involved, the ideally faithful, accurate embodiment of the fiction would be one where *whatever has been made determinate about the characters and settings in the original is carried over into the adaptation.* This can be compared to the ideal historically-accurate fictional rendering of a real-life figure: *nothing that is made determinate about the character in the fiction is inconsistent with what is known of the determinations of the original.*

There are innumerable reasons why both these ideals must and should be deviated from. However, deviation runs a considerable risk of being greeted by disappointment. The counter-move in a quality argument over a fictional adaptation would be that the adaptation is in fact a 'new original': the question is not whether Jonathan Demme's film *The Silence of the Lambs,* and Jodie Foster's and Anthony Hopkins's performances therein, carry across all that could be carried across of the determinations of the characters and the action of Thomas B. Harris's novel *The Silence of the Lambs,* but whether the film's own determinacies and indeterminacies 'work'. But the counter-move to that in turn is to point to how, in being bound by determinacy-

---

8. Or you may be a 'visualizer' who likes to summon up a very concrete Lady Macbeth while reading, complete with near-determinate height and weight (it would be odd to go for *precise* determination), while I am content to read leaving Lady Macbeth's body-shape almost completely 'unfleshed-out', so to speak.

indeterminacy structures of an *autonomous* original, whose creator was in a position to adjust all the quasi-judgments to maximal aesthetic effect and thereby 'get it right', the adaptor is 'creating' with one hand tied behind his or her back. The fictional world was in good shape in the original; what can the most faithful of possible adaptations do but make that shape fuzzier or over-sharp, or knock bits of it out of kilter, via the unavoidable infidelities? Is Demme, committed to a considerable degree of fidelity to the original, in any position to shape his material optimally for the purposes of his 'new original'?

The constraints imposed by the known determinations of a real-life figure similarly run the risk of unduly constraining the shaping power of the creator of the fiction. At the same time, given the plenitude of the real figure, what most risks disappointing the reader or viewer is the incompleteness of the Representative figure. It is always possible to register the move from complete determination to incomplete determination as a loss. We admire the virtuosity of Ben Kingsley's Gandhi, but we may feel this figure in Lord Attenborough's film to be, unavoidably but disappointingly, much *less* than Gandhi. Once this is enunciated, we can see how the case of fictional adaptation is similar: the viewer of Demme's *The Silence of the Lambs* equally risks feeling that the concretization possible through its viewing is much *less*, somehow, than the concretization afforded by a reading of Harris's original novel.

The Jesus Material as Determinate and as Indeterminate

There would seem to be the following possibilities regarding the historical status of Jesus:

1.   There was a historical Jesus, and the New Testament provides us with a reasonable degree of accurate information about him;
2.   There was a historical Jesus, but the New Testament cannot be straightforwardly treated as providing us with the kind of information about him that we would expect from a modern biography;
3.   There may have been a historical Jesus, but the New Testament is so far from providing us with reliable information about him that it might as well be fictional;
4.   There was no historical Jesus, so the New Testament accounts are, simply, fictional.

The curious thing, when one looks at the question of moving-image representation of the Jesus material, is how little difference it would make whether one subscribed to 1 or to 4, in assessing the strengths or weaknesses of any attempt to 'film the New Testament'.

I take it that the Christian doctrine of the incarnation involves claiming (1) that there was a historical Jesus, with a continuous space-time presence from birth to crucifixion on this earth, and (2) that he was God. It is principally the former claim that is pertinent to the considerations we are exploring here, though the latter will turn out to figure in the argument as well.

In what position does the author, or, better, the 'authorial team' in a creative context so collaborative as film or television production is, find themselves when faced with the challenge of 'filming the New Testament'?

As per (1): we know, via the New Testament and any collateral information that is available, *n* number of facts about Jesus and Jesus' acts. A 'Life of Jesus' film will consist of the Representation of all of, or more likely some of, these, as well as other 'quasi-judgmental propositions', verbally and/or visually conveyed, necessary to *fill in the gaps* (the spots of indeterminacy) in the Jesus narrative as we have it, for the purposes of the medium chosen. A photographic narrative medium, for instance, must fill in the details of 'how Jesus looks' in a way that a staged reading of the Gospel narratives does not need to.

However, the criteria for filling in the gaps in visually representing Jesus are neither set by the kind of evidence that constrains the representation of such a figure as Lincoln (photographic) nor by the kind of evidence that constrains the representation of such a figure as Henry VIII (painterly).[9] Unless we were to be convinced that the Shroud of

---

9. I recall being struck by hearing Donald Sinden, speaking on the radio of the experience of playing the King in Shakespeare and Fletcher's *Henry VIII*, stressing how basic a feature of the job it was to *look like* the great Holbein portrait, an image of which somehow 'everyone' brings to the theatre with them in a manner unlike any pre-image they might have of, say, Henry V. No doubt the process is self-confirming, so someone might get a first sense of Henry VIII's 'look' from seeing Sinden or Charles Laughton as the King's Representative. Note, however, how different is the status of the 'known' Holbein image from that of a culturally pervasive image created by an actor without documentary backing. Lawrence Olivier's Henry V, Richard III and Hamlet are apt to be in the minds of a significant number of people in the audience watching Kenneth Branagh or Antony Sher or Mel Gibson represent those characters, but it would be odd indeed for one of the later actors to set himself the task of 'looking

Turin is actually a photograph-like, death-mask-like record of the real features of Jesus, there is no indexical (in C.S. Peirce's sense) evidence of what Jesus looked like. To my knowledge, we do not even have the kind of verbal description of Jesus that exists in the case of, say, Socrates, where we know that 'Plato depicts Socrates as having a snub nose and protruding eyes, typical of a satyr'.[10]

What we have instead, of course, is an extremely powerful *tradition* as to how Jesus looked. That this tradition is not biblically, or otherwise documentarily, grounded seems at first not to make much difference: we can be as sure that Wallace Shawn, the short, balding American stage and film actor perhaps best known for his role in Louis Malle's *My Dinner with André* (itself a rather *Symposium*-like piece), would be excellently cast as Socrates as that he would be grotesquely miscast as Jesus;[11] and, conversely, that Max von Sydow, perfectly reasonably cast as Jesus in George Stevens's *The Greatest Story Ever Told*, would make a very peculiar Socrates.

The arts charged with the duty of developing and maintaining the visual look of Jesus over the centuries were, of course, painting and sculpture, given the 'late' arrival of photography on the scene in terms of the chronology of Christendom. Similarly, the art charged with the duty of developing and maintaining some of the key emotions associated with Jesus and his story has been music, from Gregorian chant through the great tonal tradition to such modernist Christian composers as Messiaen, Penderecki and Tavener. *The Greatest Story Ever Told*, significantly, begins with an imageless opening credits sequence, with music composed with the Christian musical tradition ('late-tonal', Samuel Barber-esque) clearly in mind; when the film moves into the iconic register, it does so via a painted representation of Christ, but painted for the film (with the Byzantine tradition in particular clearly in mind) *and one which is also a painted representation of Max von Sydow*. That is, the image 'signifies' in two directions at once, and in

---

like the Olivier performance'; indeed, this can be felt to be a real danger. On this, see A. Sher, *Year of the King* (London: Methuen, 1985).

10. W.S. Cobb (trans. and ed.), *Plato's Erotic Dialogues* (Albany: State University of New York Press, 1993), p. 185, annotating *Symposium* 215b; Cobb cross-references to *Theatetus* 143e and to Xenophon's *Symposium* 4.19.

11. Note that Shawn would be perfectly 'properly' cast as a *reader*-performer of the Gospel narratives, along the performance line exemplified a few years ago by Alec McCowen, delivering Jesus' words but not *as* Jesus.

this way grounds, or hopes to ground, the performance equation 'Max von Sydow "is" Jesus' through a demonstration that the actor's body-shape and face are consonant with the tradition's ascription to Jesus of a body-shape and a face.[12] The effect is a bit odd, as if a film about Abraham Lincoln starring Henry Fonda as Lincoln had opened with, not a photograph or painting of Lincoln (and why bother with such an opening anyway?), but a photograph or painting of Henry Fonda *as* Lincoln; but in Stevens's defense it could be argued that it is a feature of the tradition of painting Jesus that, while Jesus paintings are united by 'family resemblance', so to speak, each does present a different body and a different face, so there is a perfectly good case for adding to the gallery a Jesus picture which is also a von Sydow picture.

Painting and sculpture, however, are *static arts*, however much, as we have known since Lessing's *Laocoon*, they can imply movement. And it might seem in terms of the nature of the performances which not only von Sydow but the whole cast of *The Greatest Story Ever Told* give, that the static quality of painting in particular has invaded the moving image in the telling of *this* story. My argument is a different one: that the static quality of the acting derives from a problem about the movement from indeterminacy into determinacy required by a *photographic* medium where this particular message is concerned.

Photographing Fiction: The Actor

If there is a particular puzzle about the appropriateness of producing a picture of Jesus which is also a picture of Max von Sydow, this only echoes the endemic 'problem' of photographed fiction, where it is always a question of the production of pictures which are both of the character and of the actor, of Norman Bates and of Anthony Perkins. I put 'problem' in scare-quotes because this is not so much a problem as the founding condition of the fiction film. That there is something problematic here, however, is testified to by the continued grumbling, over the years, about actors who are 'always the same' through their different roles, by the fascination with the use of non-professional

12. A certain crisis in the tradition is felt now to be represented by the 'Victorian' Jesus, the 'gentle Jesus meek and mild' of Victorian high art which feeds the 'everyday devotional art' in kitsch mode. It is no accident that the Jesus painted for *The Greatest Story Ever Told* is *not* the Victorian Jesus, because that image is associated with the (faithful but) tasteless believers.

actors so as to abolish the 'already-seen' problem,[13] and by the numbingly predictable strategy of journalists interviewing actors of trying to establish similarities and dissimilarities between the roles being played and the 'real life' of the actor.[14]

Photography is iconic, presenting us with images *resembling* what they are images of; but equally it is *indexical*, in presenting us with images which are causally linked to what they are images of in a particular way involving a series of mechanical apparatuses operating *in principle* independently of human skill and selection. André Bazin is, within the film theory tradition, the seminal thinker on this subject, with his famous or notorious claims, in 'The Ontology of the Photographic Image':

> The photographic image is the object itself, the object freed from the conditions of time and space that govern it. No matter how fuzzy, distorted, or discoloured [i.e. no matter how iconically inadequate, in Peircean terms]... the image may be, it shares, by virtue of the very process of its becoming [i.e. the mechanical process], the being of the model of which it is the reproduction; it *is* the model...
>
> The photograph as such and the object in itself share a common being, after the fashion of a fingerprint.[15]

On this account, what the camera is 'really' picking up on the set of *Psycho* is, of course, the 'being' of Anthony Perkins (and, now that Anthony Perkins is dead, we are connected to that being/non-being in

13. The great scandal of *The Greatest Story Ever Told*, the thing that gets most remembered and skitted about it, is an element of Representation that falls foul of viewer intuitions on the above two points, namely Stevens's use of John Wayne as the Roman Centurion. In working on the film for this paper I have come to think more and more highly of it, and I believe a strong defense of the Wayne Centurion could be mounted, involving an ascription to Stevens of a sophisticated desire to inscribe 'Hollywood' and 'America' and 'the Western' *explicitly and elegiacally* into his 'late' biblical epic. But there is no space to argue this here, and the outcome suggests that it was a gamble that Stevens lost, so far as the ordinary viewer was concerned.

14. For more on the last of these phenomena, see my 'TV Magazines: Workers' Profiles?', in L. Masterman (ed.), *Television Mythologies* (London: Comedia, 1984), pp. 114-17. It is as well that fictional characters cannot be interviewed, or no doubt they would be constantly called upon to say how they feel their own life differs from the life of the performer playing them.

15. A. Bazin, 'The Ontology of the Photographic Image', in *idem, What Is Cinema?* (trans. H. Gray; Berkeley: University of California Press, 1967), I, pp. 14, 15.

an eerie and poignant way, just as we are through Lincoln photographs to the dead Lincoln). But Perkins is, *within the fictional contract*, Bates, and so we are put in the position of feeling that we are in existential contact with Norman. The destiny of the cinema, Bazin felt, was to find ever-more-perfect ways of rendering *our sense that we are* 'presented with Norman' by the cinematography and editing of the fiction film as close to the *way we really are* 'presented with Anthony' as possible.

How does this relate to Ingarden's doctrine of determinacy (of the real) / indeterminacy (of the fictional)? While the real is fully determined, no representation or rendering of the real can render all those determinations simultaneously, so while there is a certain completeness in the photographic rendering of how Perkins looked at moment *n* during the filming of *Psycho* from the vantage-point of the camera, the completeness does not even run to any specification of *how he looked from another angle* at that moment, much less to such matters as his thoughts and feelings at that moment. Indeed, the whole point of acting is that we should know about the thoughts and feelings of Norman at a given moment, not the thoughts and feelings of Anthony.[16] The gap between completeness of the referent and incompleteness of any conceivable representation of the referent is of course what allows fiction, with its indeterminacy, to feel so much like factual representation, with its partiality. The aim of filmed fiction then becomes the setting-up of a sufficiently 'detailed' set of determinations so that the effect on spectators is as if they were looking at a necessarily partial rendering of a wholly determined set of characters acting in real space and time.

Realistic acting in the cinema (which the 'methods' of Method Acting are directed to achieving, but which is clearly otherwise achievable as well) is acting which gives the viewer the sense of looking at a photographic representation of a real person's body, movement and speech. Where adaptation from a verbal medium is in question, this involves, crucially, *adding* to the account of these things given in the

16. A rather gloomy case in point here is Billy Wilder's deservedly much-loved comedy *Some Like It Hot*, where we are presented with Marilyn Monroe playing a character who, while having her own problems within the fictional world, radiates confidence and fun. We know that the shoot was a very troubled one in terms of the relationships between Monroe and the others involved. Worse, during the filming Monroe suffered a miscarriage. So are we 'really' seeing, via the photographic medium, pictures of a very anxious and unhappy person?

original. This is because no words can fully specify physical presence and action, while the camera cannot but fully catch, from its vantage-point, all of the physical presence and action it 'sees' (is given to 'see'). As real people acting in space and time, we are continuous and complete in action. The task of the realistic actor is to lend the continuity and completeness of his or her physical, existential presence to the fictional 'existence' of someone else.

'Completing' the Original Fictional Character versus 'Completing' the Adaptation Character

In Denys Arcand's *Jesus of Montreal*, the protagonist, Daniel, is a fictional character and as such both radically indeterminate (we know very little about his past, his family, etc.; but also, even respecting the time-period covered by the film, only a small subset of his acts is given to us)[17] and, in audio-visual terms, determinately rendered in the usual cinematic way: we have how he looks and sounds presented to us 'fully', saturatedly, as we would not have if he were a character in a novel. As *Jesus of Montreal* is the only fictional work in which he appears, the totality of the quasi-judgmental propositions true of him is that which is specified in that work, though of course, just as with the real world, counter-'factual' propositions about him can be imaginatively entertained (Daniel as black? Daniel as Bolivian?...). The propositions about Daniel and his circle of friends that are in fact advanced are narratively organized into the story of an actor who finds himself playing Jesus and whose life and death come to parallel those of Jesus.

Daniel is played by Lothair Bluteau. I would want to claim that he is played *strikingly well* by Lothair Bluteau: on what grounds can the argument for such a valuation be mounted?

Fact first, before value: 'Daniel is played by Lothair Bluteau' is a real-world true proposition (while in other possible worlds Daniel is played by other actors). That is, the fully-determinate Lothair Bluteau lends, or, better, donates (for there is no sense of any eventual 'giving

---

17. Especially given that his film has clear generic links to the Hollywood 'putting on a show' musical, with its usual emphasis on the trials and tribulations of the rehearsal process, Arcand effects a striking ellipsis in jumping from the first rehearsal of the passion play directly to the first-night performance. What is elided remains indeterminate. Probably a 'novelization' of the film, had such an unfortunate entity been called into being, would have had to fill in some of the indeterminacy.

back') his determinate body and voice to Daniel. But that donation must be thought of equally as a reverse movement: for a time, Lothair Bluteau's body and voice operate *as determined by* Denys Arcand's scripting of Daniel.

Jesus of Montreal is at the same time a fiction wherein it is the case that 'Jesus is played by Daniel'. Daniel and a group of other actors gathered together by him put on a passion play for the Catholic Church—deviantly, in the commissioning priest's judgment. Daniel is *auteur* of as well as actor in the play, incorporating bits and pieces of recent revisionist scholarship on the historical Jesus as well as, spontaneously it would seem, giving the passion story a strongly 'liberation theology' slant. Within the film, then, a 'Jesus' is created *as the project of a character*. Daniel donates his quasi-determinate body and voice to Jesus, while these reciprocally are determined by the historical/culturally-given 'Jesus material', albeit as inflected by Daniel's theatre-making.

The relationships here are complex when one teases them out, but work straightforwardly for a cinematic audience. The bottom line is that, while Daniel plays Jesus, Bluteau plays not Jesus but Daniel, in an action wherein sometimes we thereby see Bluteau playing Daniel-playing-Jesus.

Daniel plays Jesus in a register which is not method-acting-like but pageant-like. This statement must be modified as soon as it is made. In the fictional world of *Jesus of Montreal*, the Jesus-play being mounted by Daniel and his friends is pageant-like. However, Arcand 'cheats', if you like, by actually getting Bluteau to play a Daniel playing Jesus (and the other actors the other characters) much more *intimately* than could actually work as part of an open-air performance. Thus, when 'Pilate', as incarnated by Robert Lepage, himself of course an enormously talented Canadian director-performer, consults with 'Caiaphas' after the interrogation of Jesus, neither actor delivers the lines in a manner which could in a real-world context actually register on, or even be heard by, a large open-air audience: in this movie they are *actually* acting as if in a movie. This allows the revisionist pageant to feel much more 'naturally' acted than a traditional pageant would or indeed could be. (The film includes video footage of the long-established pageant which Daniel's troop have been commissioned to freshen up, to drive home the contrast: the 'proper' pageant is stagey and corny.) And yet, the film maintains a very clear break between the acting style of the pageant, however intimate and comparatively natural, and the acting style which Bluteau brings to bear upon portraying the *non-performing* Daniel. The latter is what deserves the plaudits, the positive valuation: Bluteau 'is' Daniel, including Daniel-playing-Jesus, in all those hard-to-pin-down ways that constitute great screen acting. (He convinces us thoroughly, and the camera loves him.)

Suppose that a novel called *Jesus of Montreal* had pre-existed the film. Bluteau would then be 'following a blueprint' in a somewhat different way than he actually has to. (Though does not the film-script itself constitute a blueprint?) But because Bluteau can do what has to be done to achieve a credible naturalistic performance, he would in the adaptation case be donating to the character spatio-temporal attributes no less 'full' than he does in the original-script case, although the pre-establishedness of some of these attributes would have a different source and a different status. The *plenitude* of Daniel as a character moving his body and his facial features unbrokenly and fluidly in space-time would need to be rendered by Bluteau no less if the character had a literary origin.

Playing Jesus on Screen: Dare One Move?

The difficulty with playing Jesus on screen, as opposed to playing on screen a man who, *inter alia*, plays Jesus, seems to be this: donating to the Son of God the ordinary plenitude of movement in space-time that naturalistic screen performances donate to characters risks seeming blasphemous or tasteless.

Max von Sydow in *The Greatest Story Ever Told* or Robert Powell in *Jesus of Nazareth* have to move, these being motion pictures, but their movement is quite unlike that of Bluteau. It is itself pageant-like, or hieratical.[18]

The tendency towards the motionless is both general, across the entirety of the films' acting, and relative, as Jesus is put in contrast with others. Everyone within these films gives performances of comparative

---

18. These films can stand as examples of fully 'respectful' treatments of the Jesus story. 'Against' them, so to speak, one could adduce Pasolini's *Gospel According to St Matthew* and Scorsese's *Last Tamptation of Christ*. The essence of the case that could be made about these, in a fuller treatment, is that they so self-consciously de-immobilize the Jesus figure in some respects, while keeping him heiratical in other respects, as to confirm the analysis presented here.

restraint. This is clearest where we are in the presence of actors who, elsewhere, are known for large naturalistic performances with a grotesque or 'tic-ridden' dimension: Donald Pleasance, for instance, in *The Greatest Story Ever Told* (as Satan), or Rod Steiger in *Jesus of Nazareth* (as Pilate). Pleasance and Steiger are, in relation to their other work, strikingly 'toned down'. And yet, at the same time, *in relation to von Sydow or Powell*, they come across as comparatively mobile and 'human'. The Jesus actors keep very still indeed, by contrast. Similarly, when in both films Jesus is in contact with the disciples, everyone on screen is respectfully delineated (where respect, it must be said, can produce an effect of stiffness), but Jesus, as supreme focus of respect, keeps noticeably more still than those around him.

What accounts for this, which, once noticed, begins to feel less like respect and more like inhibition or some sort of block? Perhaps the roots of the immobility of these photographically-rendered Jesuses lie in the paradox of the incarnation itself.

As man, Jesus existed, as fully and continuously as other men and women, in space-time. As divinity, Christ lies outside space and time—outside of the framework of the kind of proposition-advancing that Ingarden discusses, but equally *outside of the realm of the photographable*. An actor playing Jesus exists, of course, in space-time. A fictional character does not actually exist in space and time, because it does not exist; but concretizing that character bestows upon it the quasi-space-time of the fictional world. An actor playing a fictional character donates his or her own spatio-temporal integrity and pleni-tude to the character. (The non-fictionality of a character means that there are in Ingarden's sense judgments rather than just quasi-judgments to be 'equalled' by the actor, but since the real character is being Represented rather than there-before-the-camera in his or her own space-time presence, the process of donation is fundamentally no different.) Insofar as Jesus was a man, von Sydow and Powell donate their bodies to be his Representative. But what can they donate, space-and-time-bound as they actually are, that would correspond to the divine aspect of Jesus?

If continuity and fluidity of movement in space-time constitutes the reality of the human, then might *non-movement itself*, or some sort of 'dis-continuizing' of movement (as in pageant or in ritual), be felt to constitute the divine?

The aesthetic difficulty that arises when this 'solution' is grasped would then have to do with photography's obstinate reluctance, as a spatio-temporal recording medium, to pick up such a performance as embodying an element of the transcendent. Keeping their performances closer to motionlessness than to mobility, the Representatives of Jesus may be aiming to convey the boundless and the eternal; instead, the sceptical viewer may feel that, to put it bluntly, von Sydow and Powell are trapped into being actors photographed acting (*in* space-time) in a certain way—a way for which the word might be 'stiff' or even 'inert'.

The irony is that photography itself can be felt to achieve, non-divinely, a certain emancipation from space and time. Recall Bazin: 'The photographic image is the object itself, the object freed from the conditions of time and space which govern it'. Fiction too achieves, non-divinely, a certain emancipation from (our) space and (our) time. Bazin is often accused in the film theory literature of having so 'documentary' an image of photography as to make his championing of the fiction film incomprehensible. In fact, what Bazin seems to love about the cinema is how it finds ways to wring the most from both forms of 'deathlessness' in mutual imbrocation. And, as Bazin was a Christian, it would seem likely that he saw both photography and fiction as congruent with the redemption both *from* and *of* space and time promised by the Christian message. (Christian anti-stage and anti-cinema traditions may be based on a similar intuition otherwise evaluated: fiction and photography would be felt to be *in competition with* the only true avenue to transcendence.)

The bad news, for anyone who feels that the continued keeping-in-circulation of the Jesus story is of considerable cultural importance, is that (1) moving-photographic narrative in the realist tradition is, by virtue of features of the medium, apt in a strange way to 'freeze' the material, while (2) moving-photographic narrative in the realist tradition is too important in our society to be simply bypassed. The good news is that, once the nature of photography and the nature of narrative fictionality/factuality are taken on board, any number of 'work-arounds' are possible—with *Jesus of Montreal* standing as a highly intelligent, witty, and moving example.

CHRIST IMAGERY IN RECENT FILM:
A SAVIOUR FROM CELLULOID?

David J. Graham

It was several years ago that Marshall McLuhan coined the catch-phrase that 'the medium is the message'. One of the most influential of media is the moving image, as diverse as TV, interactive video and CD-ROM, and now also all that computers and the internet (particularly the World Wide Web) offer.

But despite competition from the new technology, and prognostications of its demise with the rise of TV, the film is still an incredibly popular and powerful medium, not least for the portrayal of religious themes.[1] The centenary of cinema, recalling the pioneering work of the Lumière brothers in Paris in 1895, and London the following year, has reminded us all of the survival—indeed, the ascendancy—of film. The 'mythic power of film' (to use Geoffrey Hill's intriguing phrase) cannot be gainsaid.[2]

Peter Malone has distinguished the 'Jesus' film from the 'Christ' film, which is a useful practical distinction to draw.[3] Theologically, this perhaps finds its antecedent in Martin Kähler's separation, in the post-Straussian era, between the 'historical' (*historische*) Jesus and the 'historic' (*geschichtliche*) Christ.[4] This found expression in later theo-logical discussion in the phrases the 'Jesus of history' and the 'Christ

---

1.   T. Ziolkowski, *Fictional Transfigurations of Jesus* (Princeton, NJ: Princeton University Press, 1972), has previously discussed portrayals of Jesus in fiction.

2.   G. Hill, *Illuminating Shadows: The Mythic Power of Film* (London: Shambala, 1992). Hill gives very creative readings of selected films, using his insights as a Jungian therapist.

3.   P. Malone, *Movie Christs and Antichrists* (New York: Crossroad, 1990), pp. 17-19. He draws on an earlier distinction made by Malachi Martin.

4.   M. Kähler, *The So-Called Historical Jesus and the Historic, Biblical Christ* (ed. C.E. Braaten; Philadelphia: Fortress Press, 1988).

of faith'. Although this is a useful working distinction, the pre- and post-Easter split of the 'earthly Jesus' and the 'risen Lord' is perhaps not so clear-cut. Markus Bockmuehl, for example, has recently questioned this separation and argued for joining together what wo/man has put asunder,[5] and E.P. Sanders, reductionist and procrustean as his methodology may at times be, acknowledges that any coherent understanding of Jesus must also explain the Church, with the implication which that has for the connection between Jesus before and after Easter.[6] So then, the pre-Easter disciples and the post-Easter community cannot be radically divorced from each other. Indeed, much of the pioneering work on the Gospels of form criticism, and then redaction criticism, functioned with the working hypothesis that the information in the Gospels contains at one and the same time material which is informative about the historical Jesus and the concerns of the early Christian communities, that is, they are 'both and' portrayals of the Christ of the Church and historically useful sources for Jesus.

If the Gospels themselves can be regarded as providing at one and the same time complementary descriptions of Jesus (historical), and also portraits or interpretations of his significance as Christ (Kähler's notion of the 'historic'), then perhaps Malone's category of the 'Jesus film' can be functionally regarded in a not dissimilar way. Both are media which provide possibilities for interpretation.

Another reason for considering film, but one which applies more to the 'Christ film' than the 'Jesus film' genre, is that it is a way of exploring the history of influence of biblical ideas. An earlier interest in the 'history of interpretation' in biblical studies is slowly being eclipsed by explorations of the 'history of influence' (or of 'effects'), that is, not just what interpreters thought of texts, but how texts actually affected them as individuals and in community.[7] This enterprise corresponds roughly with Kähler's *geschichtliche* adjective: the 'significant' Christ. Media and cultural artifacts can be used just as usefully as written texts to do this; they record the lasting influence of a text.

In a masterly survey, Jaroslav Pelikan has chronicled the significance

5. M. Bockmuehl, *This Jesus: Martyr, Lord, Messiah* (Ediburgh: T. & T. Clark, 1994), esp. pp. 21-23.

6. E.P. Sanders, *Jesus and Judaism* (London: SCM Press, 1985), pp. 18-22.

7. E.g. U. Luz, *Matthew 1–7: A Commentary* (Minneapolis: Augsburg, 1989).

of Christ in Christiaculture and history.[8] But this significance immediately raises the question or problem of diversity: when we speak of
Christ images, exactly which ones do we mean? As Pelikan shows,
many interpretations of Jesus as Christ are possible, and not all of
them are immediately obvious on reading the Gospels. But before we
discuss the more explicit Christ typologies such as those in Pelikan's
categories, we must first mention what we will term implicit Christian
imagery, that is, film as a medium for conveying the numinous.

Schrader refers to this as the 'transcendental'.[9] Apart from the three
directors who are the focus of Schrader's study, his own celebrated
partnership with Martin Scorsese exemplifies his phrase (which originated as the title of his university thesis) 'transcendental style'. While
stating that there is little agreement on what constitutes transcendence,
he defines it as 'beyond normal sense experience, and...by definition,
the immanent'.[10] Schrader tries to see the 'spiritual universality' of a
film: something, he believes, which can only be demonstrated by
critics, even though it may be interpreted variously by theologians,
aestheticians, and psychologists.[11] This is not the same, he contends, as
a 'religious' film. He explores the (rather limited) concept of transcendentalism, stating that 'The proper function of transcendental art
is, therefore, to express the Holy itself (the Transcendent), and not to
express or illustrate holy feelings'.[12] This is a limited remit for the
function of art in the expression of the religious, and may indeed
conflict with the view of John May, that the emotional precedes the
cognitive. Schrader's work consists mainly of a detailed study of three
directors, with reference to others. For that reason, it is a useful and
pioneering study, but of necessity limited in scope. It is also a study of
style, and therefore restricted to 'general representative form'.[13] The
work of others, especially Mircea Eliade and René Girard, may be

8.   J. Pelikan, *Jesus through the Centuries* (New Haven and London: Yale
University Press, 1985).
9.   P. Schrader, *Transcendental Style in Film: Ozu, Bresson, Dreyer* (Berkeley:
University of California Press, 1972). See also the discussion of this in K. Jackson
(ed.), *Schrader on Schrader* (London: Faber and Faber, 1990), pp. 27-28.
10. Schrader, *Transcendental Style*, p. 5.
11. Schrader, *Transcendental Style*, p. 3.
12. Schrader, *Transcendental Style*, p. 7.
13. Schrader, *Transcendental Style*, p. 8. See Jackson (ed.), *Schrader on Schrader*, p. xv.

used to complement Schrader's study. But before we proceed, allow him to conclude in his own words: 'Transcendental style can take a viewer through the trials of experience to the expression of the Transcendent; it can return him [*sic*] to experience from a calm region untouched by the vagaries of emotion or personality. Transcendental style can bring us nearer to that silence, that invisible image, in which the parallel lines of religion and art meet and interpenetrate.'[14]

If we are exploring its effective history, we must also recognize that film is a powerful affective medium.[15] Film of course shares this with other sensory media, which then raises a more general question: what role can art (in general, of which film is a part) play in any exploration of religion? Mircea Eliade, in ways reminiscent of the ideas of Rudolf Otto, has made us aware of the function of 'hierophanies', where the sacred is manifested through some other thing or person.[16] Paul Tillich comments that 'everything that expresses ultimate reality expresses God whether it intends to do so or not'.[17] Langdon Gilkey describes this as a prophetic role, when art becomes a critic of culture.[18] Art can thus enhance our experience, and when it does so, 'Art opens up the truth hidden behind and within the ordinary', 'the transcendent appears through art, and art and religion approach one another'.[19]

Some writers would claim that the traditional language and symbols of religion are passé, and that new media are needed to express religious phenomena. Eliade is one such thinker. After discussing the 'death' of God in Nietzsche, and the 'eclipse' of God in Buber, he says that the 'death' of God 'signifies above all the impossibility of

---

14. Schrader, *Transcendental Style*, p. 169.

15. See J.R. May (ed.), *Image and Likeness: Religious Visions in American Film Classics* (New York: Paulist Press, 1992).

16. Eliade, classically, in his *The Sacred and the Profane* (New York: Harper & Row, 1961). See also his 'The Sacred and the Modern Artist', in D. Apostolos-Cappadona (ed.), *Art, Creativity, and the Sacred* (New York: Crossroad, 1984), pp. 179-83.

17. P. Tillich, 'Art and Ultimate Reality', in Apostolos-Cappadona (ed.), *Art, Creativity, and the Sacred*, p. 220. He also gives a useful five-fold categorization of religious experience and the art forms associated with each.

18. In Apostolos-Cappadona (ed.), *Art, Creativity, and the Sacred*, p. 190.

19. In Apostolos-Cappadona (ed.), *Art, Creativity, and the Sacred*, p. 189.

expressing a religious experience in traditional religious language'.[20] The sacred is buried by the profane in art, he says, but the religious survives in the human unconscious, despite all protestations to be areligious.

How do we identify, categorize, and analyse these, whichever description we actually prefer? The work of other scholars is useful in this regard. Apostolos-Cappadona and others have, as we have already seen, used insights from Eliade to explore the interconnectivity of art and religion.[21] Apart from the 'numinous', we must mention briefly the use of christological typology in morality tales, which may include redeemers or saviour figures, rites of passage, holy men and the like. How they function is by taking ethical themes, either from within a specific religious tradition or independently. The work of Kieslowski, for example his 'Three Colours' trilogy, would be a notable example.[22]

Some directors see their work as directly and specifically religious. Bergman, Scorsese, Schrader, Buñuel and Verhoeven are all examples of self-consciously religious practitioners, some of whom are even self-confessedly Christian. The whole area of 'religion in film' is therefore a rich subject to explore as an implicit subtext. But let us turn now to more explicit motifs. I will give some examples, focusing mainly on principles, problems, and methodology. A number of books give useful descriptive surveys and readings of selected films.[23] I will concentrate

20. 'The Sacred and the Modern Artist', in Apostolos-Cappadona (ed.), *Art, Creativity, and the Sacred*, p. 179.

21. Apostolos-Cappadona (ed.), *Art, Creativity, and the Sacred*; D. Adams and D. Apostolos-Cappadona, *Art as Religious Studies* (New York: Crossroad, 1987).

22. E.g. his 'Decalogue'. The film 'Seven' may be another more recent example, based as it is on the moral concept of the seven deadly sins.

23. E.g. B. Babington and P.W. Evans, *Biblical Epics: Sacred Narrative in the Hollywood Cinema* (Manchester: Manchester University and St Martin's Press, 1993); W. Brueggemann, *Texts Under Negotiation: The Bible and Postmodern Imagination* (Minneapolis: Augsburg–Fortress, 1993); G.E. Forshey, *American Religious and Biblical Spectaculars* (New York: Praeger, 1992); W. Hamilton, *A Quest for the Post-Historical Jesus* (London: SCM Press, 1993); Hill, *Illuminating Shadows*; R. Holloway, *Beyond the Image: Approaches to the Religious Dimension in the Cinema* (New York: World Council of Churches, 1977); R. Jewett, *Saint Paul at the Movies: The Apostle's Dialogue with American Culture* (Louisville, KT: Westminster/John Knox, 1993); L.J. Kreitzer, *The New Testament in Fiction and Film: On Reversing the Hermeneutical Flow* (Sheffield: JSOT Press, 1993); idem, *The Old Testament in Fiction and Film: On Reversing the Hermeneutical Flow* (Sheffield: Sheffield Academic Press, 1994); Malone, *Movie Christs and Antichrists*;

more on method and theological issues than some of these do.

What I have described earlier as the effective cultural history of Christ has given us a legacy of two millenia of motifs, symbols and images. To produce a reading of a film, the Christ(ian) symbolism must be recognizable, able to be interpreted that way. Most films— perhaps all of them in fact—are open to a religious reading. But that does not necessarily mean a specifically Christian one. O'Grady presents us with six 'models' of Christ.[24] Some can obviously be represented on screen. But can others? The crucifixion imagery in 'Boxcar Bertha' is hard to miss; so is the martyrdom theme in 'On the Waterfront'. But Disney's 'Lion King' was hailed in the popular press as an authentically 'Christian' film, with its resurrection motifs and the victory of good over evil. But it backfired. Soon it was claimed as more authentically 'eastern', perhaps Hindu or Buddhist, the 'circle of life' theme resonating of karma or shiva the lord of the dance, or reincarnation, or the universal religious experience.[25] The film was then 'demonized' by some of the Christian right, as dangerously 'new age' and syncretistic.

A not dissimilar thing happened with George Lucas's 'Star Wars' trilogy. Alec Guinness, the spiritual demon and inspiring genius of 'Luke Skywalker' (who popularized the phrase 'may the force be with you'), can be and was read pneumatologically or christologically.[26] But then elements of dualism were thought to be unworthy of trinitarian orthodoxy, and more akin to Gnosticism. Similar points might be made of Richard Bach's 1973 'Jonathan Livingston Seagull', with its celebrated and popular music by Neil Diamond.[27]

J. Martin and C.E. Ostwalt, *Screening the Sacred: Myth, Ritual, and Religion in Popular American Film* (Boulder, CO: Westview, 1994); May, *Image and Likeness*; B.B. Scott, *Hollywood Dreams and Biblical Stories* (Philadelphia: Fortress Press, 1994). I will not go over this ground, nor anticipate the contents of the forthcoming book *Movies and Meaning: Explorations in Theology and Film* (ed. C. Marsh; Oxford: Basil Blackwell, 1997), to which I am a contributor.

24. J.F. O'Grady, *Models of Jesus Revisited* (New York: Paulist Press, 1994). He lists (1) the incarnate second person, (2) the mythical Christ, (3) the liberator, (4) the man for others, (5) the lord and saviour, (6) the human face of God. Each, he says, is useful in different contexts (p. 208).

25. Interesting to compare with this is Sydney Carter's use of the Hindu idea of 'The Lord of the Dance' for a modern *Christian* hymn.

26. Moreso in the Johannine sense, with the paraclete as Jesus' alter ego.

27. Halliwell's film guide comments that 'the bird photography is much more

When is a motif 'Christian'? O'Grady has eight criteria for his Jesus models (which are actually, as he notes, models of Christ):[28] they must have a firm basis in Scripture, show compatability with Christian tradition, help Christians to believe in Jesus, help believers fulfil the Church's mission, relate to Christian experience, show theological fruitfulness, foster a good sense of Christian anthropology and support good preaching and religious education.[29] But he recognizes the difference between individual personal understandings of Jesus, and theological models of Christ.[30] Also, each 'model' does not offer identical potential. His own view is that the 'human face of God' has the most potential, while the 'second person of the blessed trinity' is the least interesting.[31] Other 'models' might equally well be used. Pelikan's survey of the history of Christology gives no less than eighteen ways in which Jesus has been understood, each one corresponding approximately to each of the centuries.[32] This may seem somewhat contrived (for example we might note that there is no mention of Christ as intercessor). But for our purposes, it is apparent that not all would be either easily visually portrayed, or if they were, necessarily recognized as Christian images. And therein lies one of the problems of a religious reading of film. For instance, 'Superman' may in one sense be a saviour figure, but he is hardly 'one of us': he also has his weaknesses (at least, when confronted with kryptonite!). Could he be read as a Christian saviour figure in any incarnational sense? Perhaps only if we adopt a semi-arian Christology. Likewise with E.T., the lovable extra-terrestrial, who Malone sees as a Christ figure.[33] If superman is semi-arian, then E.T. most nearly resembles the Johannine

successful than the mysticism'; J. Walker (ed.), *Halliwell's Film Guide: 11th Edition* (New York: HarperCollins, 1995), p. 609.

28. O'Grady, *Models*, p. 3.

29. O'Grady, *Models*, pp. 198-200.

30. O'Grady, *Models*, p. 3.

31. O'Grady, *Models*, p. 205.

32. Pelikan lists 'the rabbi', 'the turning point of history', 'the light of the gentiles', 'the king of kings', 'the cosmic Christ', 'the son of man', 'the Image', 'Christ crucified', 'the monk who rules the world', 'the bridegroom of the soul', 'the divine and human model', 'the universal man', 'the mirror of the eternal', 'the prince of peace', 'the teacher of common sense', 'the poet of the spirit', 'the liberator', 'the man who belongs to the world'.

33. Malone, *Movie Christs and Antichrists*, p. 59, suggests that Christian abbreviations should include OT, NT, and E.T.!

Christ, who (like the player in jail on the Monopoly board) is 'just visiting'! But the comparisons soon break down. E.T. is not really in any sense human, even if he does show love, inspire others, 'die' and is resurrected.

But we have judged these on the basis of Nicean or Chalcedonian orthodoxy. Should it set the agenda? Trinitarian orthodoxy was the end of a protracted process (which, it may be argued, is not yet completed in theological discussion).[34] Just as the Christian Scriptures and traditions were read in different ways, so also film is open to many readings; many trajectories are possible. The sinless one of the *Gospel of the Nazarenes*, or the 'Wunderkind' of the *Infancy Gospel of Thomas*, may be more like Superman or E.T. than the Christ of credal orthodoxy. And they may give us closer parallels to Christ figures, albeit heterodox ones incorporating mixed images.

Martin Scorsese's remarkable 1991 remake of 'Cape Fear' is a case in point. The anti-hero Max Cady (Robert de Niro) is all of an avenging angel, a destroyer, a bringer of justice, the Bible itself (with his quotations of Scripture), even a Christ figure (unjustly punished, later vindicated). Towards the end, he is even 'resurrected'. Several readings are possible. Cady is a Christ and an antichrist figure, with the intricate suspense of justice and retribution.[35] In one and the same film, then, characters or motifs can function in almost contradictory ways, reinforcing and undermining the reader's pre-existing typology.

The distinction between myth and parable may prove to be useful here. A myth is world-establishing, while a parable undermines or challenges it. I would contend that Jesus rightly belongs in the category of parable, but Christ—that is, the christological constructs of the Church through the ages—has made him myth. It is no surprise that in Pelikan's list the images of Christ throughout the centuries have reflected the politics of the age. This is not an author's convenience for the sake of contents page, but reflects the reality that

34. See H. Koester, *Ancient Christian Gospels: Their History and Development* (London: SCM Press, 1990), who follows the approach of W. Bauer. G.W.P. McFarlane, *Christ and the Spirit: The Doctrine of the Incarnation according to Edward Irving* (Exeter: Paternoster Press, 1996), part I, discusses the ongoing work of Christology, with particular reference to one Scottish theologian.

35. I differ here somewhat from Kreitzer's attempts to 'reverse the hermeneutical flow'. See his *The New Testament in Fiction and Film* and *The Old Testament in Fiction and Film*.

images of Christ have been used as powerful political tools to establish a particular political order. Some 'Jesus' films (using Malone's categories again) are similar. They domesticate Jesus and reinforce stereotypical attitudes. Zeffirelli's 'Jesus of Nazareth' manages to tame the radically subversive sermon on the mount with one flash of Robert Powell's watery eyes and pale skin.[36] Of course, there are exceptions, even in 'Jesus' films: 'Jesus of Montreal' is one, 'The Last Temptation' is another, and 'The Life of Brian' another (admittedly, offbeat!) example. Surely the most effective attempts to use Christ imagery are those which challenge the image of the comfortable Christ by presenting one who is precisely the opposite.[37] They are creative, rather than boringly stereotypical. I say that also because readers today are less accepting of traditional Christ figures; they find them incredible. The inner struggle between sin and redemption, like the rabbinic doctrine of the 'two inclinations', is perhaps closer to the experience of many than a sinless saviour or perpetually virgin mother. Society both reflects and responds to its own struggles and developments, and the recognition that it is fundamentally flawed looms high in a culture where the hope that science and evolution and development would themselves be saviours has faded.[38]

Marie Connelly shows how John Ford and Frank Capra chronicled the simpler life of 1930s and 1940s America, when issues were much more clear-cut than today.[39] However, with social upheaval, the second World War and the holocaust, more recent film has shown a much greater complexity in understanding and portraying salvation. The search for salvation is not always beyond us, in the triumph of good, but often and also within ourselves. Some of the characters played by Clint Eastwood are both saviours and demons (e.g. in 'Unforgiven'); Spielberg's Oskar Schindler is also such an ambivalent figure; Forrest Gump an equivocal gauche 'everyman' who yet changes history and is

36. The question of whether such portrayals are also antisemitic must be asked.

37. Compare, for example, Anton Wessels's work on non-European Jesus images: A. Wessels, *Images of Jesus: How Jesus is Perceived and Portrayed in Non-European Cultures* (London: SCM Press, 1990).

38. Tomlinson, interestingly, thinks that much (evangelical) Christianity is still addressing the questions of the modernist agenda, which no-one is now asking, while largely ignoring the postmodern: D. Tomlinson, *The Post-Evangelical* (London: Triangle, 1995), esp. pp. 139-45.

39. M.K. Connelly, *Martin Scorsese: An Analysis of his Feature Films* (London: McFarland, 1993).

a saviour. Quentin Tarantino's films are an example of the human potential both to create and to destroy.

It may be that theological reflection to some extent always reflects culture: Cecil B. de Mille, Nicholas Ray, George Stevens and Franco Zeffirelli spoke to, and from, their own day. Interpreting and communicating images of Christ in generations after them requires different approaches.[40] The more complex use of Christian imagery, which we have briefly surveyed through film, is as much a comment on a changing culture as it is on a changing Christology. But we will give the last word to that doyen of film directors, Martin Scorsese. He has done much to explore religious—even explicitly Christian—motifs in film. And he has done so self-consciously. Commenting on Elia Kazan's film about immigrants, 'America, America', Scorsese says:

> Actually I later saw myself making the same journey, but not from Anatolia, rather from my own neighbourhood in New York—which was in a sense, a very foreign land, I made that journey from that land to movie making—which was something unimaginable. Actually, when I was a little younger there was another journey I wanted to make—a religious one. I wanted to be a priest. However, I soon realised that my real vocation, my real calling was the movies.
>
> I don't really see a conflict between the church and the movies, the sacred and the profane. Obviously, there are major differences, but I could see great similarities between a church and a movie house. Both are places for people to come together and share a common experience, and I believe there's a spirituality in films, even if it's not one which can supplant faith.
>
> I find that over the years many films address themselves to the spiritual side of man's nature: from Griffiths' 'Intolerance' to John Ford's 'The Grapes of Wrath', to Hitchcock's 'Vertigo', to Kubrick's '2001'... and so many more. It's as if movies answer an ancient quest for the common unconscious. They fulfil a spiritual need that people have, to share a common memory.[41]

In a society which is increasingly driven by images, and held together by communication (ironically, often at the cost of isolating individuals by using less personal communication media), perhaps the cinema for many people is the focus of their religious experience, and the film directors their priests.

40. The reaction of a class of students to whom I recently showed a clip of Zeffirelli's 'Jesus of Nazareth' was a spontaneous outburst of laughter!

41. *A Personal Journey through American Movies* (Channel Four Television, 4 June 1995).

THE ICONOGRAPHY OF CORPUS CHRISTI

Pamela Tudor-Craig

The Doctrine of Transubstantiation was defined at the fourth Lateran
Council in 1215, and at the same time regulations were laid down
concerning the reservation of the consecrated host. The formulations
of that year, leading to the new summer feast of Corpus Christi, to the
vision of the Blessed Juliana in about 1230, to the Papal Bull of 1264,
and to two glorious hymns associated with St Thomas Aquinas, had
widespread implications for the visual arts. But, as is the way
with formulations, they codified a trend which had already begun.
St Aelred's 'Life of Edward the Confessor',[1] written in the mid-
twelfth century, vouches to him two visions, both closely associated
with his attendance at the mass. In one of them the king sees the infant
Christ sitting upon the altar. By the time, a hundred years later, this
story came to be illustrated the Christ Child is in the hands of the
priest at the elevation.[2] Lay communion was already rare. The laity
were encouraged to regard that moment of elevation of the host as the
climax of the service.

However, devotion to the consecrated host itself, displayed in a
monstrance on the altar, was a comparatively late development. There
was one at Innsbruck by c. 1400. In 1415 the administration of the
chalice to the laity was banned at the Council of Constance, and from
that time the emphasis on the wafer became more pronounced,
especially in Germany, where, from 1451, the host could only be
exposed during the octave of the Feast of Corpus Christi.[3] Spectacular

1. F. Barlow (ed. and trans.), *The Life of King Edward who Rests at
Westminster* (Oxford: Clarendon Press, 2nd edn, 1992), pp. 72-75.
2. M.R. James, '*La Estoire de Seint Aedward le Rei*' (Oxford: Roxburghe Club,
1920), from the Manuscript, Cambridge University Library Ee 3.59, f. 21 (or 37),
and introduction p. 52.
3. M. Rubin, *Corpus Christi: The Eucharist in Late Medieval Culture*

monstrances were described at Lubeck and at Basel. At Ulm, in 1498, a Dominican account praises the splendid monstrance and describes the fifteen thousand Easter communicants. So, if the consecrated host upon the altar had to remain hidden for the rest of the year, in northern Europe a spectacular *Sakramenthaus* was made to enshrine it. Apparently the Ghent altarpiece by the van Eyck brothers is such a sacrament house, containing a hidden tabernacle. Hence the iconography of the lower register is not just the adoration of the lamb, but of the perpetual Eucharist.

Raphael's famous *Disputa* in the Stanza della Segnatura in the Vatican is indeed a dispute about the nature of the host in its monstrance on the altar. On the earthly plane theologians are discussing and defining. In the heavenly sphere the Corpus Christi is displayed at the heart of the Trinity, flanked closely by Our Lady and St John the Baptist, with the Apostles in attendance. This calm and balanced description of the Catholic position on the theology of Corpus Christi was painted precisely five years before Luther pinned his thesis to the doors at Wittenburg, plunging the western world into battle over the nature of the Eucharist and of the authority of those presiding at it, a battle which rages yet.

Nor is it only the Protestant north and Catholic south which have engaged in this subject. The great Emile Male[4] claimed that the iconography of a half-length upright figure of the dead Christ (plate 1A), the form in which the fourteenth and fifteenth centuries discovered the Corpus Christi, was of Byzantine origin. He knew an early sixteenth-century engraving of it by Israel van Mecheln on which the inscription IC XC takes the Greek form, and the label across the top of the cross behind the figure, the INRI label, is in misunderstood Greek. His deduction has been vindicated by the publication by H.W. van Os[5] of a number of Byzantine images of this format. His examples go back to two images in the Katahissar Gospels in St Petersburg Public Library, and a stone icon in the Moscow National Museum, all of the twelfth century. He has an icon of about 1200 with a Dominican painted c. 1300

(Cambridge: Cambridge University Press, 1991), pp. 291-92. This book is an indispensable tool for the study of the subject.

4. E. Male, *L'Art Religieux de la Fin du Moyen Age en France* (Paris: n.p., 1908), pp. 93-96.

5. H. van Os, 'The Discovery of an Early Man of Sorrows on a Dominican Triptych', *Warburg and Courtauld Journal* 41 (1978), pp. 65-75, illus.

on the back, and a Franciscan MS in the Bibliotheca Laurenziana in Florence of 1293. The Franciscan miniature is associated with a picture of St Bernard, and the text from St Bernard's writings, so popular with the Franciscans, is an example of the affective mysticism which is the mainspring of devotion to the Corpus Christi:

> O how intensely thou embraced me, Good Jesu,
> when the blood went forth from thy heart, water from thy side
> and the soul from thy body. Most sweet youth, what hast thou done that
> thou shouldst suffer so? Surely I too am the cause of thy sorrow.[6]

From 1300 onwards Italy, especially Venice, and then France are flooded with this half-length figure.

The source, however, at least for the West, may be in the ghost of such a figure, with again a Greek inscription, in a later frame of the early fourteenth century in the Treasury of the Holy Sepulchre at Jerusalem, in Rome. This picture purports to represent the form of the vision which St Gregory had while celebrating mass at the high altar there. The version of the miracle of St Gregory in the thirteenth-century Golden Legend,[7] however, knows nothing of the appearance of the figure of the dead Christ, but only reports that the host became a piece of flesh in order to convince the doubting lady who had baked the Eucharist bread that morning. St Gregory and his vision, however, was universally popular throughout the rest of the Middle Ages. Its popularity was no doubt due to the number of days off purgatory that were associated with meditation on the image. That image was without question regarded as a manifestation of the Corpus Christi. It is carved on the Desiderio da Settignano's Sacrament altar of 1461 at San Lorenzo in Florence. In Andrea Ferrucci's engraved brass door of a tabernacle of c. 1490 now in the Victoria and Albert Museum, London, the out-stretched pierced hand,[8] and its relationship with the loin cloth, prove that the single hand surviving from a wall painting in the chapel of

---

6.   Van Os, 'The Discovery of an Early Man of Sorrows', p. 74 n. 36, 'O quam vehementi amplexu amplexasti me bone jesu quando sanguis exivit de corde aqua de latere anima de corpore. O amantissime, iuvenis, quid fecisti ut talia patereris Certe et ego sum causa doloris tui' (Florence Bibl. Laurenziana MS. Plut XXV, f. 183v).

7.   J. de Voraigne, *The Golden Legend*, I (trans. Caxton, 1483; London: William Morris, Kelmscott Press, 1892), pp. 409-16, esp. p. 415.

8.   J. Dunkerton *et al.*, *Giotto to Durer: Early Renaissance Painting in the National Gallery* (New Haven and London: Yale University Press, 1991), p. 23 fig. 5.

St John's College in Cambridge belonged to a Corpus Christi (plate 2A).[9] From the fourteenth century, the figure could be alone, or supported, as we have seen, by Mary and John, or supported by angels. The Giovanni Bellini example in the Vatican Collection (plate 2C) formed the apex of an altarpiece. Something like a third of the output of Giovanni Bellini and a substantial amount of Andrea Mantegna's (plate 2B) workshop was devoted to this theme.

The most explicit of all examples is the lunette in the Doges's Palace, where the dead Christ is held upright by Mary and St John (plate 2C). The object before them is certainly an altar, for it has a candlestick either end.[10] The picture, dated 1472, was largely repainted and enlarged after the fire, and the alterations are dated 1571. The accuracy of the iconography, however, is confirmed by a copper gilt and bronze morse in the Victoria and Albert Museum of c. 1500, where the identical disposition is found.

It would seem that the very slight incident recorded in earlier medieval legends of St Gregory had grown, by association with a Byzantine icon of the half-length Christ above the altar where that Father of the Church was reported to have had his vision as he consecrated the host, into an identification of the sacrament with a figure of the dead Christ in half-length representation. In an exquisite drawing in a monastic missal of the fourteenth century at Subiaco (plate 1B), the figure is placed just above the words of consecration. This image is usually called the 'Christ of Pity', a relatively modern name for it. I am claiming that it would be more appropriate to call it the 'Corpus Christi'.

In the later fifteenth century a more graphic representation of the Mass of St Gregory was popular all over western Europe. The rendering by the Maestro de Santa Maria del Campo in the Monastery of Santa Clara at Palencia gives the fully developed form. A miniature

9.   See the E.W. Tristram Archive in the Conservation of Wall Paintings Department of the Courtauld Institute. I am grateful to David Park for giving me access to this valuable material. The circulation of this half-length figure of the dead Christ in England in the later Middle Ages is further illustrated by a woodcut tipped into the only known complete copy of Clement Maydestone's 'Directorium Sacerdotum', printed by Caxton in 1486 (pl. 1C). See *William Caxton: An Exhibition to Commemorate the Quincentenary of the Introduction of Printing into England* (London: British Library, 1976), p. 75 no. 78 and pl. opp. p. 76.

10.   A. Tempestini, *Giovanni Bellini: Catalogo Completo* (Florence: n.p., 1992), p. 56 no. 13.

full-length Christ appears on the altar, surrounded by the instruments of the passion, the 'Arma Christi', and blesses Gregory. The version by the Master of the Aachen Altarpiece, in the work of that name in the Walker Art Gallery in Liverpool,[11] goes further (plate 3A). As the miniature Christ leans forward, the blood from his side sprays into Gregory's chalice. The Mass of St Gregory was carved in relief on the Kirkham Chantry at Paignton (plate 3B).[12] In the hand of Giovanni Bellini (plate 3C),[13] the more macabre elements of this theme are subsumed by the power of the artist. This panel was again the door of a tabernacle, declaring that it must represent the Corpus Christi.

Divorced from the context of St Gregory, the standing Christ offers his blood to a kneeling donor in the carved group by Pedro Millan of c. 1490 at El Garroba in Spain.[14] The standing figure of the dead Christ, for this is in no sense a resurrected figure, occurs in an alabaster of the Trinity of the late Middle Ages,[15] supported either side by a twin pair of the Father and Holy Spirit (plate 4A). The appeal of this attenuated and tragic figure in the late Middle Ages is attested, I believe, by the altar piece in Prince Arthur's Chantry, where the central figure alone has been defaced (plate 4B). The narrowness of the niche, contrasting with the swelling proportions of the saints on either side, declares that nothing less significant could have been placed here. There remain the attendant angels. At Winchester the fragments of such a Corpus Christi survive.

Durer's print of the Trinity of 1505 showed the Father with his dead Son hanging from his arms. This poignant image was widely circulated in Italy, influencing Michelangelo in all his depositions and entombments, culminating in the Rondanini Pieta, where it is Mary alone who offers her dead son. She had done the same in all late fifteenth-century Pieta's—the last work of Donatello in San Lorenzo, Florence of 1460, the piercingly tragic Pieta by Ercole Roberti of the

11. Dunkerton *et al.*, *Giotto to Durer*, p. 42 fig. 35.

12. G.McN. Rushforth, 'The Kirkham Monument in Paignton Church', *Transactions of Exeter and Diocesan Architectural Society*, 3rd Series 4 (1929–37), pp. 1-37, esp. pp. 21-24.

13. Dunkerton, *et al.*, *Giotto to Durer*, pp. 22 and 24 fig. 6.

14. The group by Pedro Mellan is illustrated by T. Muler, *Sculpture in the Netherlands* (Pelican History of Art; Harmondsworth: Penguin Books, 1966), pl. 153b.

15. F. Cheetham, *English Medieval Alabasters* (Oxford: Phaidon, 1984), p. 310 no. 236.

1480s or the elegaic early Michelangelo of 1498–99. It was Catholic belief in the Middle Ages that the Virgin was a priest in her act of making incarnate the Word of God. It was also believed that she foresaw her son's death. This sense of doom was inherent in every solemn virgin and child group, as when the baby was represented asleep, and when the group was surrounded with prophetic children or angels, or in a hundred little touches, like giving the child a goldfinch to play with. A lullaby of c. 1370 makes this explicit:[16]

> Lullay, lullay, litel child, child rest thee a throwe,
> From heighe hider art thou sent wyth us to wonen lowe;
> Poure and litel art thou made, uncouth and unknowe,
> Pyne and wo to suffren heer for thyng that nas thyn owe.
> Lullay, lullay, litel child, sorwe myghte thou make;
> Thou art sent into this world, as thou were forsake.

The most constant subjects for an altarpiece are the crucifixion, Christ in majesty or the virgin and child. Altarpieces themselves were created in response to the formal enhancement of eucharistic worship in the thirteenth century.[17] The priest now officiated with his back to the congregation, and both he and his audience needed a new focus beyond him. Most of these early altarpieces were long and low, and at this stage the frontals, which had been till that time placed along the altars themselves, were sometimes repositioned behind the altar. Suger's frontal for St Denis was reused in this way. It was generally found by the mid-fourteenth century that a taller focal point rising above the priest was needed. In addition to a main theme concentrating on Christ and his Mother, an element specifically concerned with the Corpus Christi was often incorporated, sometimes in the Predella. Would Uccello's Predella of 1475–78 painted for the Confraternity of the Holy Sacrament in Urbino make such a popular postcard if more people knew that it described the story of the wicked Jewish family who bought over the counter a consecrated host? When they attempted to cook it, blood poured from it. They were discovered, and the family were all burnt alive.[18] This is but one of several stories

---

16. J. Martineau (ed.), *Andrea Mantegna* (London: Royal Academy of Arts, 1992), p. 205 no. 41. Poem quoted from R.D. Stevick (ed.), *One Hundred Middle English Lyrics* (New York: Norton, 1964), p. 67 no. 42, from the unique text: Edinburgh Advocates Library 18.7.21.

17. Dunkerton *et al.*, *Gilotto to Durer*, pp. 25-37.

18. Rubin, *Corpus Christi*, p. 287. The 'Jeu de la Sainte Hostie'.

of a bleeding host current in the fifteenth century. The Urbino example ran beneath Justus of Ghent's picture of Christ administering the host at the last supper.

We have by no means exhausted the imagery whereby devotion to the sacrament of the altar was encouraged. From the early fourteenth century the liturgy of Maundy Thursday involved the placing of the consecrated host in a specially arranged Easter sepulchre to the north of the high altar, whence it was retrieved for the Mass of the Pre-Sanctified on Holy Saturday. Some Easter sepulchres survive, in this country notably in Lincolnshire.[19] In the fifteenth century, however, it was regarded as highly desirable to have an altar tomb with a flat top which could be used as the sepulchre. Many of these survive, sometimes with indented brasses, which might be covered for the annual ceremony with rich cloths. People bequeathed actual bed linen for the purpose. The tomb of Sir John Hopton, died 1489, at Blythborough, for example, has the linen carved along the front. Moreover, the ceremony of lying in state was a familiar event of the later Middle Ages, so the juxtaposition of bed and tomb was familiar.

Yet even this was not enough. In northern Europe in the fifteenth century there was a fashion for life-size carved and painted groups of the entombment. They survive in several Burgundian churches: Solesmes, Joigny, Tonnerre, Dijon (plate 5) have good examples. At Joigny the dead Christ is laid on a bier which is in the form of an altar. At Gisors, unfortunately, the central group is missing. There is such a Christ figure from an entombment group at Regensburg. Dr Joan Evans identified one from Mercer's Hall in London.[20] The carved groups were neglected after the Reformation even in Catholic countries, and destroyed in Protestant ones. The impetus would have been, of course, to celebrate the Eucharist exactly here, but the potential altar top is occupied by the life-size figure of the dead Christ. The logical

19. V. Sekules, 'The Sculpture and Liturgical Furnishings of Heckington Church and Related Monuments: Masons and Benefactors in Early Fourteenth Century Lincolnshire' (PhD thesis, University of London, 1991): and 'The Tomb of Christ at Lincoln and the Development of the Sacrament Shrine', *British Archaeological Association Conference Transactions* 8 (1986), pp. 118-31.

20. J. Evans and N. Cook, 'A Statue of Christ from the Ruins of Mercers' Hall', *Archaeological Journal* 111 (1954), pp. 168-80, with many illustrations of French examples, some in wood, and a wooden Christus from Rostagsbro, Uppland. I believe the small figure of the dead Christ now in the St Albans Cathedral Watching Chamber came from a miniature entombment group.

step was taken. In the famous Isenheim altarpiece by Grünewald the predella is occupied by a painting of the dead Christ laid just here, on the altar. A predella by Holbein of the same subject is at Basel. It is possible this iconographic theme of the entombment, made familiar by endless paintings, gives a clue to the inner meaning of that most beautiful and mysterious lament, beginning with a lullaby, and therefore sung by the Virgin Mother in her prophetic role:

> Lully, lulley; lully, lulley;
> The falcon hath borne my make away.
> He bare him up, he bare him down;
> He bare him into an orchard brown.
> In that orchard there was an hall,
> That was hanged with purple and pall.
> And in that hall there was a bed;
> It was hanged with gold so red.
> And in that bed there lyeth a knight,
> His wounds bleeding day and night.
> By that beddes side there kneeleth a may,
> And she wepeth both night and day.
> And by that beddes side there standeth a stone,
> CORPUS CHRISTI written thereon.[21]

I have already pointed out the links between the Christ Child and the goldfinch, seen, f instance, in the Royal Academy's Michelangelo roundel. A goldfinch would be vulnerable to a falcon. The 'bearing up' is the crucifixion; the 'bearing down' the deposition; the bearing into the hall the carrying to the tomb. The orchard brown is an orchard of dead trees or Calvary. We have seen the knight whose wounds bleed day and night. The may or maiden has to be the Virgin again.

The whole dark pageant of the passion is the setting of the Corpus Christi. Nor have we exhausted it yet. In the Michelangelo roundel in the Royal Academy in London the Christ Child flees to the protection of his Mother's arms from the ominous bird, which is presented to him by the infant Baptist. The Baptist, who declared the Christ in the words used in the canon of the mass and set to much imperishable music—'Behold, the Lamb of God, behold him who taketh away the sins of the world'—was an ever more popular saint in both eastern and western church up to the Reformation. His constant emblem is the

21. Published in many anthologies of English Medieval Pottery. For this version, see H. Gardner, *Religion and Literature* (London: Faber and Faber, 1971), pp. 154-55.

Lamb of God, carried on a dish, as it were the paten which held the Host.[22] With the urge towards literalism of the later Middle Ages, the association of the Baptist with the Eucharist was pressed. One inventory of 1379 describes a figure of the Baptist with an aperture for relics behind the Agnus Dei.[23] On the feast of Corpus Christi the relics were taken out and replaced by the consecrated wafer in a transparent rock crystal. The plot thickens. There are two feasts of the Baptist, his birth on January 6, the same day as Epiphany, and the other on August 29, his Decollation: not just his martyrdom, but his beheading and the presentation of his head on a dish or paten to Herod. It is most unfair that the Knights Templar were condemned for venerating a bearded head on a plate, since in the fifteenth century that veneration would become uncannily common.

In October 1491 an image maker, Nicholas Hill, brought an action against William Bott for the value of 58 heads of the Baptist. In 1495 Robert Tull charged an alabaster man, the same Nicholas Hill, for failing to pay costs for taking drivers from Nottingham to London with heads of St John the Baptist.[24] Most of the surviving English renderings of the head of the Baptist on a charger are of alabaster, and carved en suite with the dish. Such an image, tip tilted upon an altar and flanked by candles, appears in a Bavarian picture of 1511, with a crowd of people praying before it. Nor was it only the custom in Bavaria. Elizabeth de la Pole, Duchess of Suffolk, who died in 1470, had a St John's head upon the altar of her private chapel at Ewelme, and Archbishop Warham had another on the altar of his private chapel at Lambeth. In the Welsh version of the grail legend, *Peredur*, the grail appears as a bleeding head in a dish. According to Cretien de Troyes's version of the Holy Grail, written not long before 1174, the grail was lit from within. It is a delightful property of alabaster that it is translucent. In the Victoria and Albert there is one North German

22. A.A. Barb, 'The Round Table and the Holy Grail', *Warburg and Courtauld Journal* 19 (1956), pp. 40-67, esp. pp. 46 and 60 and pl. 17.

23. Barb, 'The Round Table', p. 60 n. 51, quoting *Analecta Bollandiana* 68 (1950), pp. 408-409.

24. For the whole subject of St John's heads and their mass production in Nottinghamshire in the later Middle Ages, see Cheetham, *English Medieval Alabasters*, p. 317. Cheetham illustrates (pls. 244-56), a whole range of alabasters showing the St John's head on a dish with beneath it either a diminutive Lamb of God or a half length Christ. He has ten examples of this second formula, all drawn from the one collection in the Victoria and Albert Museum.

example (plate 6A and 6B) which is actually hollowed at the back, and at the top of the hollow there is evidence that a candle has been burnt in it.[25] A Bavarian head in their National Museum is of wood, with glass eyes backed with parchment. It is hollowed, and the open mouth opens into the hollow. How much intensity of light would have to be placed behind such a work, especially if it was of alabaster, for it to appear to be illuminated from within? What are these ghostly luminous carvings of the decapitated head doing on late medieval altars? It is appropriate that the answer should be found in York, home of the Corpus Christi plays. The York breviary reads: 'Caput Johannis in disco signat Corpus Christi que pascimur in sancto altari...' This is a summary of the post communion prayer for the Feast of the Decollation of the Baptist given in the Sarum Missal: 'Conferat nobis domine quesumus sancti iohannis baptiste utrumque sollempnitas. Ut et magnifica sacramenta que sumpsimus patribus nostris significatur ueneremur, et in nobis pocius edita gaudeamus...'[26] This conflation of the sacrament of the altar with the decollation of the Baptist is not confined to the west. A late fifteenth-century icon of the beheading of the Baptist from Novgorod[27] shows the Baptist standing beside a chalice-like vessel containing his head. There is a direct reference to the Byzantine convention of showing the 'Agnus Dei' in the form of the Holy Child lying in a chalice.

We have come so far without reference to the obvious illustration of Corpus Christi, the representation of the last supper. While many medieval examples concentrate on the moment of betrayal there are last suppers where the eucharistic content is emphasized. The greatest rendering of that subject, Leonardo's of the 1490s, was not placed over an altar but in the Refectory of Sta Maria della Gracie in Milan. The reference is to the consecration of all meals after the prism of the Cena. The picture is answered by the gigantic crucifixion on the opposite wall, so the weight of the sacrifice is not underplayed. Leonardo, being Leonardo, has contrived to incorporate both the

25. W.L. Hildburgh, 'A Curious Type of St John's Head', *Antiquaries Journal* 17 (1937), pp. 419-23, esp. pp. 421-23; and P. Williamson, *Northern Gothic Sculpture 1200–1450* (London: Victoria and Albert Museum, 1988), pp. 192-95.

26. For the text of the post-communion prayer of the Sarum rite, see J. Wickham Legg (ed.), *The Sarum Missal* (Oxford: Clarendon Press, 1916), p. 315.

27. See R. Grierson (ed.), *Gates of Mystery: The Art of Holy Russia* (Cambridge: Lutterworth Press, 1994), catalogue no. 10, pp. 86-90, entry by I. Soleveva.

climaxes of the last supper in his composition. With his right hand the Christ stretches out to dip his sop in the dish with Judas. The apostles behind them register their dismay and horror. With his left hand he indicates the bread, 'This is my body', and the apostles on his left side are caught up in awe. One finger points upwards, in the gesture Leonardo always used to suggest the spiritual dimension.

So what happened at the Reformation? We may prefer to draw a veil over the several German paintings in which Luther and Melancthon themselves are portrayed as apostles at the last supper. On the whole the Protestant north recoiled from the gory detail of much of the imagery we have been examining. Some of the paintings and carvings discussed here are perhaps proof enough that devotion to the Eucharist was in need of a less creaturely interpretation. Even in the Catholic countries subject matter of this kind appears to have dwindled.[28] Tintoretto developed a more dramatic last supper, Rubens painted an electrifying deposition from which Rembrandt extracted the tragic essence. Rembrandt also found the most satisfying representation of the supper at Emmaus, 'They knew him in the breaking of the Bread'. The Roman Church appears to have adopted a more allusive approach to the sacrament of the altar, setting the actual mass or the monstrance in Baroque clouds and artificial sunshine. Where, as in the Wies in Bavaria, a church was built around a figure of the suffering Christ, the statue and its veneration predated the church. The unquenchable thirst for violence was usually diverted to endless and sickening representations of cruel martyrdoms.

The northern Protestant countries, deprived of a liturgical framework, diverted that dubious taste for the sensational back to what might be regarded as its ancient classical home, the stage. What about *Titus Andronicus*? What about Marlowe's *Tamburlaine* of 1590, Webster's *Duchess of Malfi* or the *White Devil*? What about John Ford's *Tis Pity she's a Whore*? All popular in revival now. It is about time we faced this thirst in human nature, and tried, as the Middle Ages tried, to harness it to the love of God. As the passion of Christ is the crux of our destructive nature, so the Corpus Christi is, at its best, the most heart-rending appeal to our better nature:

---

28. However, seventeenth- and eighteenth-century St John's heads in Granada and Seville, in Karlsruche and Breitnau, are noted by Barb, 'The Round Table', pp. 60-61 n. 59. It may be they had acquired the status of folk religion.

Upon this mount I found a tree;
Under this tree a man sittyng.
From hed to foot wounded was he,
His herte blood I saw bledyng;
A seemly man to ben a kyng,
A gracious face to loke unto.
I axed him how he hadde peynyng:
He seyed, '*Quia amore langueo.*

'I am trewe-love that fals was nevere;
My suster, mannes soule I lovede hire thus;
Bicause I wolde on no wyse dissevere
I lefte my kyngdom glorious;
I purveide hire a place ful precious.
She flitte, I folwed, I lovede hire so
That I suffred thise peynes piteous,
Quia amore langueo. . . [29]

It is all in Col. 1.19-22: 'For it pleased the Father that in him all full-ness should dwell. And having made peace through the blood of his Cross, by him to reconcile all things to himself... In the body of his flesh through death, to present you, holy and unblameable...'

(Please note that all of the following plates are used by permission.)

29. Stevick, *One Hundred Middle English Lyrics*, pp. 88-91 no. 50, quoting Cambridge University Library, Hh.4.12. and the text in Lambeth Manuscript 853, both of c. 1430.

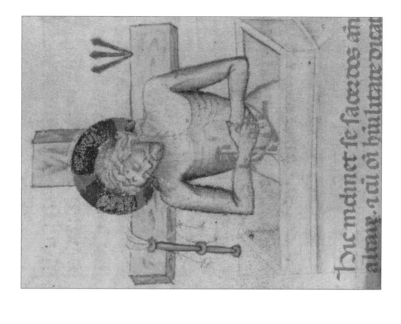

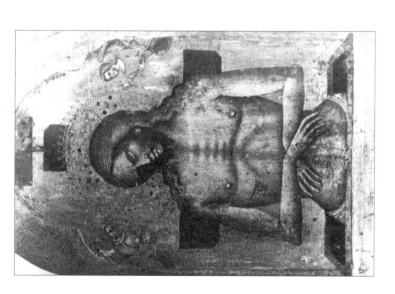

Plate 1a. Corpus Christi. Venetian, second half of the fourteenth century. Panel painting, London, National Gallery 3893.

Plate 1b. Missal of the mid-fourteenth century. Subiaco, S. Scolastica. Preamble to words of consecration.

Plate 1c. Corpus Christi surrounded by emblems of Passion. Woodcut
presumably available in England in late-fifteenth century as single sheet.
Here tipped into only known copy of Clement Naydestone's Directorium
Sacerdotum as printed by William Caxton at Westminster in 1486.
By permission of the British Library.

Plate 2a. Fragment of Wounded outstretched hand of Christ from wall painting of Corpus Christi.
Late fifteenth century. St John's College Chapel Cambridge. (Photograph courtesy of Courtauld Institute.)

Plate 2b. Andrea Mantegna, Corpus Christi with attendant angels c. 1500.
Tempera on wood. Statens Museum fur Kunst, Copenhagen.

Plate 2c. Giovanni Bellini, Adoration of the Corpus Christi upon the altar, 1472. Enlarged, repaired and transferred to canvas, 1571. Venice, Palazzo Ducale.

Plate 5. Entombment group late fifteenth century. Chapel of the Holy Cross in Dijon. (Photograph copyright Courtauld Institute.)

For Plate 3b see p. 333.

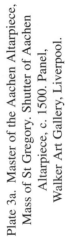

Plate 3a. Master of the Aachen Altarpiece, Mass of St Gregory. Shutter of Aachen Altarpiece, c. 1500. Panel, Walker Art Gallery, Liverpool.

Plate 3b. Mass of St Gregory, c. 1490–1500. Kirkham Chantry at Paignton.
(Photograph courtesy of Courtauld Institute.)

Plate 3c. Giovanni Bellini, Tabernacle door with panel painting of Corpus
Christi, c. 1460–65. London, National Gallery 1233.

Plate 4a. The Trinity compromising the Corpus Christi, with the globe of the universe between his feet, upheld by the Father and Holy Spirit, represented identically The hole may have taken an attachment for the Dove. The Annunciation is shown above. Alabaster, late fifteenth century. (Photograph courtesy of Victoria and Albert Museum.)

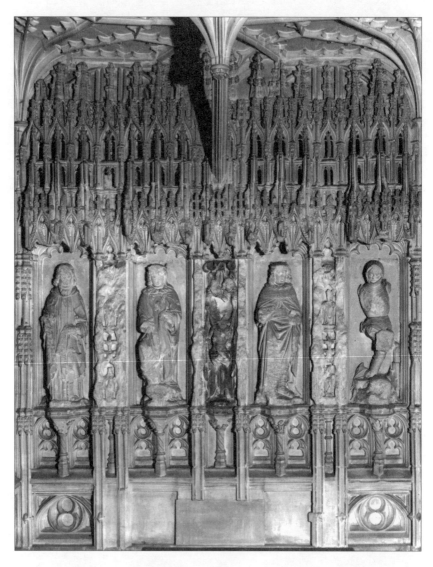

Plate 4b. Reredos of Prince Arthur's Chantry Chapel, Worcester Cathedral, 1502–1505. The central figure, deliberately mutilated at the Reformation, showed the full-length Corpus Christi attended by angels. (Photograph courtesy of Courtauld Institute.)

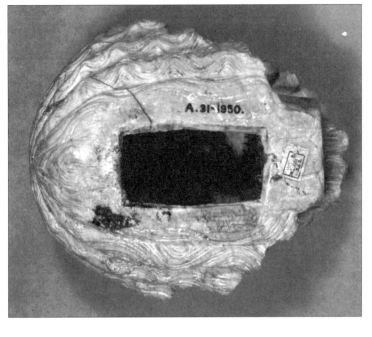

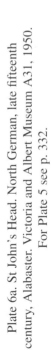

Plate 6a. St John's Head. North German, late fifteenth century, Alabaster. Victoria and Albert Museum A31, 1950. For Plate 5 see p. 332.

Plate 6b. Back of the same St John's Head, showing recess (which has been used) for candle. (Photographs courtesy of Victoria and Albert Museum.)

IMAGES OF CHRIST IN THE WORKS OF REMBRANDT

John Barber

It has always seemed to me that a proper understanding of drawing as a primary human language is vital to the appreciation of all traditional art, but that drawing is so sadly undervalued in our educational system that many find that art is inaccessible and peripheral to their lives. The word language itself, springing as it does from Lingua–Tongue, is inappropriate to a universal means of communication which owes nothing to speech. I believe that mime and music were followed by drawing, speech may have come later and writing evolved from drawing.

The first drawing caught a thought within a line; it was our first evidence of human intellect. Before drawing, all the aeons of time since the creation had left no trace of an object that expressed a thought. Within the outline was thought, outside was the chaos of nature and the tyranny of time. From the drawing point, whether pencil, pen, or crayon, the line snakes out, catching the seen object in a permanent unbreakable snare. This element of the hunting and trapping of an image is particularly relevant to the study of Rembrandt. If a good drawing is one that expresses the greatest number of thoughts by the least number of lines, then the consummate draughtsmanship of Rembrandt brings him more frequently close to this ideal than any other artist, with the possible exception of Hokusai.

Rembrandt was, from early boyhood, a catcher of images, compulsively snatching scenes from life with a few rapid lines, developing and refining his thoughts, making many variants of his compositions so that when he stood in front of his canvas the picture already existed in his visual imagination. The overall design could be orchestrated and enriched by details of character and pose from his rich store of drawings of unsurpassed accuracy and economy of line. For him the large scale preparatory drawing, or cartoon scaled up to the size of the canvas, was simply not needed. A few strokes of the reed pen dipped in bistre were enough, they held all the information he needed.

In his finest paintings Rembrandt achieved a highly individualistic realism in which we will seek in vain for stylised beauty of colour or elegance of line; he offers us instead a truly compassionate revelation of the dignity of human nature. This is his unique legacy to anyone who will stand in front of his pictures with an humble mind and a calm spirit. In his portraits and his biblical subjects it is his intense identification with his subjects which is the key to his ability to engage and move us despite the three centuries between. Rembrandt's devotion to meditation on the life of Christ and his life-long personal exploration of the Gospels and the expression of his profound philosophy in graphic art were utterly different from the many superb and impressive works of his Flemish contemporaries.

Even an artist as original as Rembrandt is better understood in context with his influences and contemporaries, and a much deeper understanding can come from some attempt to trace the more obvious precedents in his work. I say the more obvious since there is this strange anomaly that the more original and revolutionary an artist appears to be, the more eager they seem to be to plunder the past.

For instance, Manet frequently took his compositions from the engravings of Mantegna and the etchings of Goya. Degas based many of his figures on Italian or Classical models, particularly sculpture. Van Gogh copied the dramatic book illustrations of Gustave Doré; developed his famous brush style from Monticelli; and admired Luke Fildes R.A.! In music, Igor Stravinsky, a great original, was also a great borrower and admitted the fact, calling himself a kleptomaniac. His contemporary Picasso who trawled through the history of art for his images was never so honest. In this context the dictum that 'All art is theft' does have a certain ring of truth. Rembrandt himself bought paintings by living artists which he copied as models for his own compositions.

Of all the influences that Rembrandt absorbed, that of Caravaggio was the strongest. This is hardly surprising since so many otherwise independent-minded artists fell under the spell of Caravaggio's powerful realism. His dynamic use of light is as controlled as a theatre spotlight and gives equally theatrical effects. Light, often from a single source shining from the top left of the picture, and which John Ruskin compared to the lighting in a coal cellar (meaning that the only light was coming through the open coal hole), rakes across the forms of the figures set against a dark background. This lighting which is so essential in the imitation of the texture of materials and the articulation of forms in a painting was adopted by Rembrandt and evolved in his work as a pictorial language capable, through the alchemy of his genius, of hinting at the universal and the spiritual by the detailed delineation of the particular forms of his often unprepossessing subjects.

Neither did Rembrandt escape the all-pervading influence of Rubens who, while arguments will always exist as to his absolute quality as an artist, created a style by which the sheer illusionistic power of paint could be adapted for almost any artistic purpose. Muscular vigour and healthy, glowing carnality were his constant delight. But nowhere in the art of Rubens do we sense the spiritual hinterland that makes itself felt in everything that Rembrandt touches. Contrast the opulent forms and writhing bodies in the 'Coup de Lance' of Rubens (1620 Antwerp) with Rembrandt's 'Raising of the Cross' (1633 Munich). Here the body of Christ is as straight as a shaft of light, almost as ethereal in its colouring, and totally devoid of the anguished contortions of other painters. On horseback in the background the still figure of his favourite model for old men once again wears the turban that is often Rembrandt's only concession to historical costume. At centre stage stands Rembrandt himself, not in vainglory as in his early work, but to stress his involvement and publicly proclaimed guilt.

What a poor mutilated piece of flesh he shows us in his 'Descent from the Cross' of the same year. Here is no gracious, serene Saviour: no elegant limbs arranged into a perfect composition; but a pathetic wounded corpse, tenderly lowered by grieving friends. The sense of weight tearing at the one hand still nailed to the Cross is for me unbearable, as it was surely meant to be. Most painters of the period used familiar models for their Christ, copying the portrait of an individual who happened to be available—a full beard and long hair seem to have been qualification enough. Rembrandt's archetype for the Christ, sought for so long through countless drawings and etchings, is strangely generalized, as if he looked not for an historical individual, but for a human visage able to accommodate our own imaginative contribution. As his vision became more profound he abandoned the violent drama and theatrical gestures and in their place the slightest nuance of movement became significant. His 'Supper at Emmaus' (1648 Louvre) takes this trend in his work toward the ultimate economy of pictorial means. How calm is the quiet scene. Three people sit at table; the Christ, isolated against the great visual silence of the blank wall, gently raises his hands. The servant carries the dish to the table, oblivious of his part in this moment of mind-bending revelation. Here Rembrandt has perfected his type of the Christ which seems to me to question the need to seek the face in an historic human form.

Let us finally, since they are so accessible, compare two pictures in the National Gallery. Caravaggio's 'Supper at Emmaus' is a theatrical tableau indeed. Dramatic gestures force us to admire the skill of the artist, but these are gestures without movement, the famous fore-shortened hand is as much a still-life as the fruit one can almost lift from the table. His Jesus is the round-faced, beardless friend we know from other performances of this static artistic repertory company of the artist's cronies. Rembrandt's Jesus in 'Woman taken in Adultery' is almost featureless. The picture relies on the perfect grouping of the figures for its expressive power and layered meaning. The technique is perfect and, therefore, invisible. 'The art that conceals art' is here truly an apt phrase.

Go, if you will, to Trafalgar Square again, look afresh at these two paintings and spare time to see the 'Christ before Pilate'. Here is Rembrandt at his most descriptive, drawing on all his knowledge of pose and gesture in a well-wrought monochrome that was probably the pattern for an etching. Observe the High Priest. Can you not hear his shout of 'Give us Barabbas' as Pilate recoils in horror showing how unwilling is his involvement? How appalling it all is! Rembrandt uses ugly forms for ugly subjects. Potiphar's naked wife in the etching is repulsive in a way which brings home the distasteful sexual harass-ment, but by our own revulsion we are convinced of the innocence of Joseph. In these ways Rembrandt, the greatest illustrator of the great-est book, reveals the depth of his identification with his subjects and demonstrates his own deep faith. What I feel in all his works is com-passion. Compassion for the monk copulating in the cornfield; com-passion for the pig in the wheelbarrow, waiting for the butcher's knife; compassion for the baby girl in her padded helmet taking her first steps.

In looking at Rembrandt's work we can still share in his humanity and life-long pilgrimage towards a personal image of Christ, achieved by his daily contemplation of the Gospels and his tireless devotion to his art.

IMAGES OF CHRIST IN THE PAINTINGS OF JAMINI ROY*

Suman Gupta

1. *Addressing the Audience*

I want my audience to look at Jamini Roy's paintings of Christ. You are my audience: scholars of theology, literature, culture and sociology who are, for the larger part, resident in Britain. Christ is in this environment: in the manifold twists of its history, amongst the folds of its cultural expressions, between the semes of its languages, wrapped up within the layers of its politics and ideological state apparatuses. Jamini Roy was not of this environment. But you cannot really look at the paintings of one of the most admired artists of modern India without pausing a bit. In this pause you would probably negotiate the strange mixture of nostalgia for the Raj, condescension towards the 'third world', pride or (perhaps) guilt of the ex-colonizer, remoteness from the 'orient', ignorance or knowledge of an immensely complex and heterogeneous culture, and the proximity (in several senses) of the impression that Britain has necessarily made on India and vice versa.

I want you then to look at Jamini Roy's paintings of Christ. In this moment of contact all the complicated factors enumerated above are jostled against each other. The gaze which you extend to Jamini Roy's paintings of Christ cannot be a simple one. Most of all, it shouldn't be an indifferent one. It is this indifference which this paper wishes to resist. If I wanted you to glance at Jamini Roy's paintings of Christ I might have organized an exhibition and sent you special invitations—with a glass of sherry thrown in. But the complex gaze which Jamini Roy's paintings of Christ demand needs something more. It needs preparation, some reflection, a few preliminary observations. That is what this paper tries to provide. I will leave it to you to look at Jamini

* Thanks are due to Shrimati Anjali Sen, Director of the National Gallery of Modern Art, New Delhi, for permission to publish the plates appearing at the end of this essay.

Roy's paintings of Christ after that, to interpret the lines and delve into the forms.

2. Biographical Sketch

To begin with then, a brief biographical sketch of Jamini Roy. Jamini Roy was born into a land-owning Hindu family of Beliatore, a village in the Bankura District of West Bengal, in April 1887. In 1903 he joined the Government School of Art, Calcutta. After completing studies there Jamini Roy established himself as a painter in the familiar European styles and media. Sometime around 1921 he decided to adopt a more indigenous form of artistic expression. Consequently, he studied and adapted from the tradition of folk painting in rural Bengal, and gradually evolved the strength of line and the palette which give his paintings their peculiar flavour. Paintings were usually devoted to a limited number of recurring themes, one of which dealt with various episodes of the Christ-myth. The first significant exhibition of this new style of paintings was held in 1938 in Calcutta. Between 1940 and 1970 he executed as many as twenty-six works devoted to the Christ-myth. A series of exhibitions of these and other paintings at home and abroad (London in 1946, for example, and New York in 1953) marked the growth of an international reputation. He died in April 1972.

This skeletal biographical outline is merely a gesture towards the historical, social, cultural context from which Jamini Roy's paintings of Christ emerge to meet your gaze.

3. Influences

Implicit in that brief biographical sketch are hints of a specific kind of artistic education, an exposure of the sensitive artist to a certain set of influences. Three levels of influence are to be kept in mind.

First, the influence of the formal education in western techniques, western art media, and the history of western art (which has to be necessarily understood if its practice is to be mastered). Jamini Roy's earlier paintings clearly demonstrate a certain mastery of the western practice of art. Discerning art critics have shown that his engagement with western art and its techniques affected even his later paintings, which are more obviously indebted to Bengali folk art. Sovon Som,

for instance, has observed that the significance of Jamini Roy's technique is not that he uses features of traditional Bengali folk art (the
patua painters, for instance), but that he transforms these features to
accommodate a formalistic intention which derived from an urbane
and primarily western perspective:

> The abbreviated nature of form, the gesture of line, the use of colour for
> the sake of colour, the total compositional clarity and the frontal placement
> of the form without illusionist depth, were the qualities he made use of for
> evolving his style. With this formalistic notion he copied the Kalighat Pats.
> During the first decade of this century Henri Matisse in Le Luxe and La
> Danse paintings had modified forms in the interest of a total harmony. He
> sought to eliminate the traces of illusionism of depth and volume empha-
> sizing the flatness of forms, the abstract quality of line, the decorative
> patterns and the flat colour. Jamini Roy showed the same hedonistic
> response to the configurative elements of paintings as Matisse showed.[1]

Of more immediate interest to us is the fact that Jamini Roy's education
in the techniques and history of western art has a direct bearing on his
conception of the Christ-myth. Evidence of this is found in comments
such as the following:

> The sophisticated art of Europe could and did for a long time thrive on the
> Christ-myth. And so long as this was possible there was no unrest. After
> Rembrandt, however, belief in such a myth was shattered by changed
> social circumstances. Art abandoned faith but courted unrest. Gauguin and
> Van Gogh made their last desperate effort to revive the Christ-myth. But
> this was just impossible. The contemporary art of Europe shows a desperate
> effort to cling to some belief-system or other, but the modern mind would
> not allow any. So there is no end to unrest.[2]

This comment is interestingly placed amongst observations regarding
the *patua*-paintings of Bengal—which leads to the second level of
influence on Jamini Roy's work.

Secondly, the influence of folk art. He had clearly studied the technical nuances and the philosophical and sociological import of Bengali
folk in some detail. This consisted in an assimilation of then recent
developments in the study of the folklore and folk art in Bengal: studies

---

1. S. Som, 'The Art of Jamini Roy and the Bengal Folk Paradigm', in
A. Mukhopadhyay (ed.), *Jamini Roy* (Delhi: Lalit Kala Akademy, 1992), p. 29.

2. J. Roy, 'The Patua-Art of Bengal' (translation from article based on interviews
by Debiprasad Chattopadhyaya), *Jamini Roy (1887–1972): Centenary Exhibition*
(Delhi: National Gallery of Modern Art, 1987), p. 72.

initiated and conducted by Revd James Long, Revd Lalbehari Dey, Taraknath Mukherji, Abanindranath Tagore, Dineshchandra Sen, and Gurusaday Dutta, amongst others. More importantly, this entailed a detailed study of art forms with which he was familiar in his childhood: the art of the tribal *santhals*, the village *patua*-painters (wall or scroll painting), the *kantha*-makers (quilt embroidery), those who modelled in clay, and those who built the terracotta temples in the Bankura District. He made copies of (and refined) Kalighat *pat* paintings—an urbanized form of *pat* painting to be found at the Kali Temple of Kalighat in Calcutta. He began using indigenously produced materials and colours which have been described by Dey and Irwin in the following fashion:

> Expensive oils were given up in favour of tempera and the cheap materials of the village craftsmen. His palate was usually limited to only seven colours: Indian red, yellow-ochre, cadmium, green, vermillion, grey, blue and white. The first four were made from local rock-dust, mixed with the glue of tamarind seeds, or occasionally white-of-egg, to give adhesion. Vermillion was made from the mercury powder used by Hindu women in their ritual-worship. Grey was a composition of alluvial mud; blue was made from indigo, and white was common chalk. The linear brush-drawings were done in lampblack. Using for canvas the cheap home-spun cloth of his village, he prepared it as a basis for paint by coating it with a mixture of alluvial soil and cow-dung, followed by whitewash. At other times he painted directly on cheap three-ply wood (having first prepared the surface in a similar manner) or else on cheap handmade cardboard, or the rough side of poster-paper.[3]

This evidence of Jamini Roy's striving after purity in the folk technique and form he chose to adopt can perhaps be understood by taking cognizance of his general conception of folk art. Evidently, Jamini Roy was not attempting merely to create the *effect* of folk painting, he actually wanted to reproduce the primary experience of that form of painting. He hoped to rekindle the conditions of its reception and transmission by recreating the conditions of its production. In other words, Jamini Roy hoped to recreate an entire milieu of engagement with art by refashioning the artistic conditions which gave birth to that milieu. Oddly enough this was not incompatible with his urbanity, with his exposure to western art and its practice, because

---

3. B. Dey and J. Irwin, *Jamini Roy* (Calcutta: Indian Society of Oriental Art, 1944), pp. 22-23.

Jamini Roy was able to discern something universal and primal and beyond all crudity or sophistication in the *patua* painting of Bengal:

> What is it that the *patua*-art wants to express? It is certainly not a meticulous copy of nature; it is as certainly a conveying the essence thereof. For it had for its aim a direct expresion of the emotion aroused by the universal nature of the essence of the nature around. A tree painted by the *patua* is unmistakably a tree: but you can hardly call any actual tree of your concrete experience. In other words, it has everything that is essential for a tree, though nothing that belongs to the limitation of any individual tree. In this, the *patua*-art of Bengal resembles the primitive art of any other country.[4]

He goes on to clarify that the *patua* art of Bengal differs from that of other countries in adopting the coherent belief-system of Hindu mythology, distinct from but in effect the equivalent of say the belief-system of the Christ-myth. At any rate, by locating his search for formal purity within the milieu of Bengali folk art Jamini Roy deliberately distanced himself from the mainstream nationalist movement in Indian painting. This leads to the third level of influence (more appropriately, negative effect) to be discerned in his work.

Thirdly, Jamini Roy's growth as a painter was largely impelled by his reaction against the Nationalist School which had spearheaded a revival in Indian painting. Jamini Roy's strong lines, his slabs of unadulterated colour, his sturdy forms, present an exact contrast of technique to the blurred washes, the gentler shades, the delicately curvaceous, almost wispy, forms of say Abaninadranath Tagore's or Nandalal Bose's paintings. Where Jamini Roy traces the universal behind the particular of *patua* folk painters, these pioneers of Indian art were attempting to construct a specific national consciousness from the high art of the past: mainly the Ajanta cave frescos, for example. Jamini Roy's understanding of painting clearly defined itself against those of most of his contemporaries, as is apparent when he puts his seal of approval on the work of another of his contemporaries. In Rabindranath Tagore's comparatively untaught abstract drawings Jamini Roy saw something of his own quest for the universal behind the particular: hardly surprising in a writer of Rabindranath Tagore's philosophical, albeit mystical, nature. In his writings Rabindranath Tagore had contemplated and expressed the 'Universal Mind' more explicitly than Jamini Roy expressed the 'universal' aspect of folk art in his paintings. It is interesting that in giving his seal of approval to

4.   J. Roy, 'The Patua-art of Bengal', p. 71.

Rabindranath Tagore, Jamini Roy could not but ironize the wispy forms of paintings of the Nationalist School:

> Rabindranath doesn't have an exact understanding of anatomy but there is a sense of anatomy in his paintings. His human figures do not seem to collapse supinely or waver weakly in the wind, one feels that his figures possess backbones. What is powerful about Rabindranath's paintings is the strength of the backbone in the figure, not the balance and rhythms of the composition. It seems Rabindranath wants to protest against the loss of that which has affected Indian painting over the last two hundred years, from the times of the Rajputs to the present—a strong and sturdy backbone.[5]

Clearly, Jamini Roy's resistance to the techniques of the Nationalist School was not for lack of nationalist sentiment. I do not, however, intend to dwell on Jamini Roy's brand of nationalism here.

4. *Images of Christ*

The complex of skills and techniques, ideas and aspirations, accomplishments and disagreements acquired in the course of Jamini Roy's growth as an artist was undoubtedly expended on, amongst other themes, the image of Christ. Why Christ? one feels compelled to ask. And not for the first time. Here are Bishnu Dey and John Irwin posing and trying to answer the same question (possibly with the aid of Jamini Roy himself):

> It is sometimes asked why an orthodox Hindu who has never even read the New Testament should be interested in the subject of Christ. Jamini Roy gives several reasons. In the first place, he wanted to find out if his new technique could be applied with equal effect to a subject remote from his personal life. And for this purpose the christian myth seemed a suitable choice. He was further encouraged by the fact that he had seen photo-reproductions of the Renaissance masterpieces which had left him dissatisfied. It was wrong, he thought, that these painters should attempt to convey the essentially human character of Christ by naturalistic or representational means, and he wanted to show that the human and the divine could be made one only by abstract, symbolic means.[6]

That Jamini Roy wanted to portray the meeting of the divine and the human by taking recourse to 'abstract, symbolic means' seems to be

---

5.   J. Roy with D. Chattopadhyaya, '*Rabindranather Chhabi*' (1940), in M. Dutta (ed.), *Selections from* Kavita *edited by Buddhadeb Bose*, I (Calcutta: Gyaniram, 1987), p. 136. My translation.

6.   Dey and Irwin, *Jamini Roy*, pp. 25-26.

consistent with his search for the universal behind the specific, for the primal oneness behind human diversity; with, in other words, his quest for essential form through folk-art. That he should choose the remote theme to demonstrate this is also consistent with what we have seen of his ideas of art and life: what better way is there to grasp universality than by showing a comprehension of the most remote? Perhaps this is a sufficient explanation—a search through his art, and through his self-consciousness regarding art, for a holistic vision and expression of life. It is mystical rather than religious. More importantly it is mystical in the same sense that all modernist quests in Europe, as in Bengal by repercussion and assimmilation, were mystical. Jamini Roy tried to reinstate a grand narrative (he would call it a 'belief system') when grand narratives were crumbling. The realization of a universal vision and expression, a realization of universal forms symbolized through past myths (like the Christ-myth), is not a religious statement but a modernist and mystical quest.

To demonstrate at any rate that this was a symptom of Roy's Hindu upbringing is certainly tenuous. All who are aware of the politics of religion would recognize the vested interests which inspire such a claim. All who are aware of the social and communal ramifications of religion in an Indian context (and arguably in most contexts where religion captivates the communal imagination) would recognize the untenability of the claim. But the claim exists. Bishnu Dey and John Irving, despite the above explanations, are also the first to make the claim:

> The genuine religious feeling in Jamini Roy's Christ studies is striking; and here again we trace the assimmilating mind of Hinduism at work, for perhaps it would be true to say that only the Hindu (who 1900 years ago gave asylum to St. Thomas) can experience genuine feeling for a religious myth that is essentially foreign to his own belief.[7]

It is seconded by scholars who have a religious presumption worked into their scholarly perceptions. In attempting to understand the phenomenon of non-Christian painters painting on Christian themes in India (for there are others[8]) John F. Butler, for instance, generalizes the claim. His manner of doing so is worthy of note: his argument

7.   Dey and Irwin, *Jamini Roy*, pp. 26-27.
8.   For example, G. Tagore, P. Karmakar and N. Biswas in Calcutta; A. Das in Delhi; K.C.S. Paniker in Madras; S.D. Chandra in Murabai; S.Y. Malak in Nagpur.

begins with an analysis of the phenomenon as a 'triumph of Christ'[9] and then subtly balances this with:

> ...this plethora of Christian paintings by non-Christians in India is mostly a triumph not of Christ, but of Hinduism, that is, of the 'Higher Hinduism' which holds, roughly, that 'All religions are the same' (though, to be fair to it, that summary requires more careful wording).[10]

Here is evidence of the caution, the careful diplomacy which the politics of religion (precariously poised on divisiveness and distrust in its social effects) demands.

It seems to me that to read a religious feeling into Jamini Roy's paintings of Christ is to detract from the far more sophisticated modernist, albeit mystical, quest which underlies them; it is to disregard the considerable intellectual effort and self-awareness of Jamini Roy's art. However, finally it is up to the observer to decide whether there is any religious feeling. Certainly those educated in religious doctrine— Hindu and Christian alike—would have much to ponder here. They may compare Jamini Roy's paintings of Christ with Jamini Roy's paintings of Indian gods and godesses and their mythology. They may wonder how faithful his paintings are to biblical descriptions. Why does Jamini Roy's Christ carry a transparent cross (plates 2 and 3)? Is it a prefiguration of the symbolism of crucifixion? Does it bear some relation to the rock crystal cross of John the Baptist in Raphael's 'Ansidei Madonna',[11] for instance? Why is Christ on the cross (plate 1) and elsewhere painted yellow? Does this have something to do with Gauguin's portrayal of Christ or is there some deeper significance? But that is not my topic here.

5. *Modernism Transformed*

Finally I am interested in the social implications of Jamini Roy's paintings of Christ. This brings us back to the gaze that you, the British connoisseur, may bestow on these paintings.

You should recognize much that underlies these paintings. These are

---

9. J.F. Butler, *Christian Art in India* (Madras: Christian Literature Society, 1986), p. 128.

10. Butler, *Christian Art in India*, p. 129.

11. Raphael's *Virgin and Child Enthroned with Sts John the Baptist and Nicholas of Bari* (the Ansidei alterpiece), oil on panel, 1505(?), 209 × 148 cm. (London, National Gallery).

modernist paintings, drawn from a modernism rooted in the west, in
Europe, and inevitably translated to a colony which cultivated a western
education. After a hundred years of debating the relative advantages
of providing the native with a Sanskritic or English education[12] the
latter had firmly established itself in the metropolitan university in
India. English was a doorway to Europe. Almost all the important
poets and painters of the forties and fifties (when Jamini Roy painted
most of his Christ paintings) were engaged, in a slightly belated
fashion, with the poetry and art of European modernists. Most of the
Calcutta Group of Painters derived inspiration from the impressionists,
fauvists, cubists, vorticists, dadas, surrealists, expressionists; most of
the important Bengali poets and writers read and adopted from the
work of the modernists. Rabindranath Tagore, Jibanananda Das,
Bishnu Dey, Sudhindranath Datta, Premendranath Mitra, Buddhadev
Bose, amongst others, interacted with the modernist writers in
Europe, adopted some of their attitudes, and translated their work
fairly extensively. Jamini Roy lived in this milieu, was provided with
an education in western art, discussed his work with and was discussed
by his contemporaries—his preoccupation with the familiar strains of
European modernism was inevitable. And, I think, you would
probably recognize some of this: would perceive in the unremittingly
flat forms, stretched evenly across the board, centred to perfection,
balanced carefully, confident in its awareness of its own medium,
something of the search for a holistic vision and expression of life
which inspired them. The flat and deliberately ethereal forms might
recall for you the paintings of Matisse, of Madigliani, the later paintings
of Picasso—the desire for a visual grandnarrative which could conquer
or compress all perspectives. And because of the theme, the familiar
invocation of the Christ figure, you would undoubtedly recognize the
modernist nostalgia of the European artist-thinker: the nostalgia which
made Eliot and Pound and Aldington neoclassicists; which encouraged
Eliot to find his place in tradition, and Pound turn to Chinese and
Japanese classics and medieval romance language poetry, and Joyce

12. Accounts of this are to be found in G. Vishwanathan, *Masks of Conquest:
Literary Study and British Rule in India* (London: Faber and Faber, 1989); and K.
Sanghari, 'Relating Histories: Definitions of Literacy, Literature, Gender in Nineteenth
Century Calcutta and England', pp. 32-123, and B. Raina, 'A Note on Language,
and the Politics of English in India', pp. 264-97, in S. Joshi (ed.), *Rethinking
English: Essays in Literature, Language, History* (New Delhi: Trianka, 1991).

draw on the *Odyssey* for inspiration; which made Yeats dream up an idealized Byzantium; and led Roger Fry to reflect on the so-called 'primitive' art of Africa. Jamini Roy's Christ paintings reflect the nostalgia of the western modernists, almost deliberately gestures towards it. There is an air of calculated nostalgia, almost a pastiche (not a parody) of modernist nostalgia in the west, when he recreates the effect of the Byzantine mosaic (plate 2). His Christ paintings are most often compared to Russian icons, a personalized and homely conception of Christ.

But the modernism which is translated from the west is also inevitably transformed. Behind the modernist nostalgia and holistic desire which is encapsulated in the paintings of Christ is the sense of awkwardness, the rigidity, the remoteness of the Christ-myth in the context of the paintings. Compared to the sinuous curves in his paintings and drawings of Hindu deities, *Santal* men and women, Bengali women, and cats, the Christ figure is usually presented in a few rigid lines, standing erect, inflexible, unyielding. Figures move and hang like puppets in his paintings of Christ—whether in his depiction of the *Crucifixion* (plate 1) or in his presentation of the *Flight to Egypt*.[13] Indeed the Christ figure seems to almost disappear into the environment created in the painting. The lines which delineate the Christ figure do not differentiate him from the lines which delineate his companions. The three crucified figures in the *Crucifixion* (plate 1), or the thirteen figures of the *Last Supper* (plate 5) are indistinguishable in that respect. Christ may almost merge in the bland remoteness of his environment, the motionless ogling crowd which surrounds him: there is no halo to mark him out, no evident sign of divinity. And yet he does stand out, just barely—he seems just a jot narrower, sharper, more angular than the other apostles in the *Last Supper* (plate 5); and he glows with the difference of his colour in the *Crucifixion* (plate 1), in stark contrast to the other crucified.

It is a modernism which is wrung dry of its agony and its passion. It is a vision of a belief-system so static, so paralyzed, that it seems a remote frozen thing. If it is evoked in the style of the *pat* painters of Bengal it is only to emphasize the distance of this theme, to underline the awkwardness of its evocation.

Perhaps this was natural. For Jamini Roy Christianity is an inevitably

13. J. Roy's *Flight to Egypt*, tempera on cloth, 119 × 52.7 cm., Acc. No. 3149 (New Delhi, National Gallery of Modern Art).

remote belief-system which impinges upon his consciousness and enters his environment in an uneasy fashion. It might fit in well with his urbane quest for universal forms through folk art, but the immediate reality was that Christianity sat in his part of India awkwardly at the time. It rested in the proselytizing and doctrinaire charity of the missionary institutions of Bankura; in the distant western paintings he studied but had never actually seen; in a text which converts around him tried to assimilate and accommodate and which he never read. It was all around him, unavoidably, and yet uncomfortably. Is that why Jamini Roy painted Christ as he did?

Or is it actually your gaze which places Jamini Roy's paintings of Christ at a distance, as hidden behind a veil of inscrutability, the remoteness of a context which you had approached but failed to meet or understand?

Plate 1. *Crucifixion*, tempera on canvas, 88.5 × 68.5 cm., Acc. No. 157.

Plate 2. *Christ with Cross*, 39 × 64 cm., Acc. No. 3159.

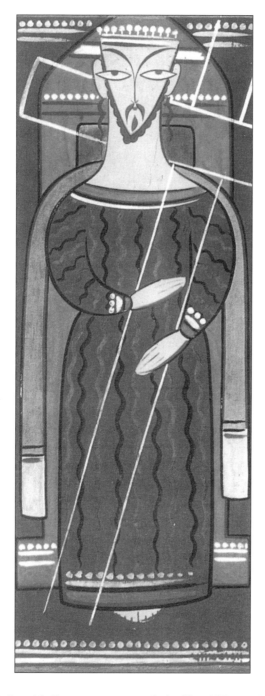

Plate 3. *Christ with Cross*, tempera on cloth, 42 × 107 cm., Acc. No. 65.

Plate 4. *Christ*, tempera on paper, 16.2 × 26.2 cm., Acc. No. 3112.

Plate 5. *Last Supper*, tempera on cloth, 42 × 189.5 cm., Acc. No. 3152.

CHRIST ON THE ROAD TO BELLEVILLE:
CHRISTOLOGY THROUGH CONVERSATION
WITH GEORGES ROUAULT (1871–1958)

Clive Marsh

1. *Introduction*

The extent to which art with a Christian theme contributes substantively to Christian theology remains insufficiently explored.[1] Books on religious art abound. Books and articles on the possible links between art and theology have been produced in fits and starts over the years, yet are still few in number.[2] A full theological assessment of the contribution of the visual arts to Christian theology from either a historical or a methodological perspective has, however, yet to be written. A constructive Christian systematics which takes the visual arts seriously seems even more distant.[3] A step in the right direction can, however, be taken piecemeal by theologians undertaking small (ad)ventures in branches of Christian systematic theology, using artistic works as legitimate *theological* resources. To be successful, such ventures need to be theologically constructive in the present and informed by Christian tradition, while at the same time upholding artistic integrity. They need, in other words, not merely to quarry (plunder?) the world of the

---

1.   I avoid use of the term 'Christian art' in order to allow a possible contribution of art with a Christian theme by those who may not call themselves 'Christian' to Christian theology.

2.   Especially useful are Begbie 1991; Jane Dillenberger 1986; John Dillenberger 1987; Dixon 1978; Tillich 1989; and the work of Diane Apostolos-Cappadona.

3.   John Dillenberger (1987: 219-24) notes theologians who appear to find a place for the visual arts in their theological methodologies, yet do not seem to carry through their espoused methodology in practice. In his treatment, he mentions Farley, Gilkey (more promising than most), Lindbeck, Tillich, Cobb and M.C. Taylor. Even von Balthasar and Rahner—who appear to find a key place for the visual arts— do not realize their vision (John Dillenberger 1987: 225-26).

visual arts in search of good illustrative material. The very content of the resulting theological proposal must in some way be shown to derive from the form and content of the art considered.[4] It is to this constructive end that I offer this present chapter. I shall offer a contemporary contribution to Christian Christology in dialogue mainly with Georges Rouault's 1920s painting *Le Christ dans la banlieue (Christ in the Suburbs/Christ in a Depressed Suburb[5])*. The conversation will, however, bear in mind Rouault's *oeuvre* as a whole.

2. *Rouault as Painter*

Georges Rouault was a pious French Roman Catholic, born into the sounds of civil unrest in Paris in 1871.[6] Much of his artistic work, particularly in later life, was devoted to Christian subjects, and to portrayals of Jesus the Christ in particular. He is perhaps best known for his print series *Miserere* (1916–1927; published 1948) for some striking images of sad clowns, and for his tragic *Head of Christ* (1905). We shall consider *Christ in a Depressed Suburb* (1920–1929) for a number of reasons. First, it encapsulates many of Rouault's theological convictions in a way which enables us to examine them further. Secondly, it is relatively unusual to find Rouault placing the figure of Jesus the Christ in sympathetic company and in a contemporary setting. Thirdly, it is striking that in this painting, the figure of Jesus has no halo. The painting thus enables us to examine the relationship between portrayals of Jesus and so-called 'Christ figures' in visual art, bearing in mind our contemporary western context, when literacy in such artistic and theological traditions can no longer readily be assumed.

4. I should add here that I include in my own definition of 'visual arts' film and TV, even though I am here using an example from painting in the tradition of fine art.

5. The different English translations of the French title illustrate well an important feature of the painting's contribution to Christology: 'in the suburbs', though adequate as a translation, implies a level of material well-being in English translation not reflected either in the painting itself or in Rouault's primary concerns. The translation offered in Dorival 1984—*Christ in a Depressed Suburb*—is thus to be preferred.

6. The most readily available studies in English are those by Courthion 1978 and Dorival 1984. See also Venturi 1948 (French text); Hergott and Whitfield 1993; and Hergott 1993 (German text). Dyrness (1971) offers the fullest extended treatment of Rouault's work from the perspective of Christian theology, though Jane Dillenberger (1986: 206-13), John Dillenberger (1987) and Tillich (1989) also make reference to him.

In the painting we see an adult figure accompanying two children on a street in a smoky, run-down city quarter. The street is dirty and in the background there is a factory chimney. The adult figure is either speaking in a caring, concerned fashion or listening attentively to the children, his head humbly bowed towards them. Leaving the title of the painting aside, we are expected to see this figure as Jesus the Christ. The resemblance to the iconic, stain-glass influenced portrayals of Jesus the Christ, which can be said to have become Rouault's artistic trademark, is clear.[7] Two figures are walking on the road and Christ is their companion: there is thus an allusion to the Emmaus Road story.[8] Even if this is not Belleville, where Rouault grew up, Rouault is certainly locating Jesus the Christ as companion in a contemporary French context amongst people with whom Rouault believed Christ would most clearly identify.[9]

How does this painting contribute to the task of formulating a contemporary Christology? In order to do justice to the artistic integrity of the work, it is important that we begin with the interpretation of an art critic rather than launch into a theological discussion immediately. We shall therefore engage critically with the words of Pierre Courthion. Of this picture, Courthion writes,

> Rouault's Christ has no need of a halo to identify Him. The painter has crowned Him with something very different from the false brilliance of gold: He has stamped Him with his own faith, with his own gratitude, and has shown Him as the greatest hope of suffering humanity. All this is communicated to us through the artist's hand, through the emotion that it has instilled in this paint, this pigment, that has been touched and worked, until its essence has been transfigured in this unforgettable creation.[10]

7.   See, for example, *Christ Mocked* (1932), *Ecce Homo (The Passion)* (1936), *Head of Christ (The Passion)* (1938), and *Christ and Children* (1931–39).

8.   Lk. 24.13-35. Dyrness (1971: 30) quotes Rouault's own comment that Rembrandt's *Christ at Emmaus* had influenced him generally, even if not in direct relation to this picture.

9.   Dyrness (1971: 21) notes that Belleville was not part of Paris at the time of Rouault's birth, but a 'village' outside. When working in the centre of Paris, however, Rouault became well acquainted with the difficult conditions endured by the working class in Paris. His own roots as an artisan (he began work as a stained-glass apprentice) remained important for him and he concurred with the view of his artistic mentor, Gustave Moreau, that an artist needed an experience of poverty to have any chance of understanding the world in which most people lived (Dyrness 1971: 24, 61).

10.   Courthion 1978: 98.

A number of key discussion points should be drawn from this quotation. First, something is said about the content of Rouault's own Christology. Christ is, as expressed in Rouault's art, the 'greatest hope of suffering humanity'. Rouault was preoccupied with the passion of Christ in equal measure with the suffering of humanity he witnessed during the first half of the twentieth century. He recognized that suffering could not be evaded, yet knew from his faith that it could not be allowed to have the last word. Much of his art takes human suffering, and the confrontation of that suffering in relation to the figure of Jesus the Christ, as its subject-matter. This painting is no exception.

Secondly, Courthion indicates to us Rouault's method in Christology. In offering interpretations of Jesus as the Christ, Rouault is not working as an official church spokesperson.[11] Yet in putting something of himself into his paintings, as he believes, on artistic grounds, he must, Rouault is not striving to be idiosyncratic or unorthodox in his reading of Jesus the Christ. He wishes simply to continue the Christian tradition about Christ within which he finds himself in a way that will be comprehensible and persuasive to those who view his paintings.[12] Rouault is thus speaking through his visual creations not simply of how Christ has had an impact upon him. But in speaking of the Christ whom he believes he has encountered, and in whom he believes, he can do no other than also speak personally. His Christology is thus both *popular* and *subjective*, and for those very reasons all the more powerful.[13] If we term Rouault's Christology an 'Expressionist

11. Rouault received no church commission until 1945—when asked to design windows for a church in Assy; see Dyrness 1971: 14-15.

12. Whether this was in any way a 'missionary' motive for Rouault, in the way it is possible to contend for Rembrandt, is open to question. Arguably, Rembrandt may have preferred etchings to oil paintings for some of his studies of Jesus in order to 'get his message across' more widely. He did, after all, have some links with Christians influenced by the Radical Reformation. Rembrandt was certainly an artistic influence on Rouault, as noted by Bloy (Dyrness 1971: 42; see also Courthion 1978: 17), who considered Rouault 'perhaps the only [painter] who can still remind us somewhat of Rembrandt' (cited in Dorival 1984: 18). But Rembrandt's capacity 'to incarnate' a particular quality of faith into his paintings also seems to have left its mark on Rouault (Dyrness 1971: 30).

13. I am here applying in a theological sphere words used by Dorival (1984: 45) of Rouault's art: '...Rouault...spent the rest of his life expressing Jesus' universal and perpetual agony in an art that was doubly direct because it was an art that was at

Images of Christ

Christology' then we would not be far wrong. We must, however, be cautious on at least two fronts. Artistically, though Rouault has close affinities with Expressionism, he cannot simply be labelled such.[14] Evidence of Munch's influence on Rouault or of a clear link to German Expressionism is lacking. But Rouault does paint in vivid colour from inner necessity with a prophetic strength and sense of urgency, even if 'the Expressionist painters shout, vomit, and ejaculate their paintings' while 'Rouault...builds them with love'.[15] Nevertheless, to call Rouault's an 'Expressionist Christology' does not mean that he is simply a theologian of the Expressionist movement in painting. The second note of caution is theological. 'Expressionism' in theology need not receive the critique levelled by George Lindbeck at the 'experiential-expressivist' approach to Christian doctrine.[16] Rouault cannot, as we have said, simply be accused of speaking of his *own* experience of Christ. He knows, as an artist, he will not paint authentically if he fails to infuse his work with his own experience. But his choice of subject-matter indicates that he is attempting to do more. Our conversation with Rouault, in other words, opens up for us an avenue along which Lindbeck's rather sweeping rejection of 'experiential expressivism' must be challenged.[17]

A third point to be drawn from Courthion's observation takes us into his somewhat overpowering rhetoric. The painting does indeed

once popular and subjective'. Note should also be taken of Rouault's own words, spoken in relation to his treatment of nature, but of clear relevance here too: 'They think that I am a "subjectivist". But actually I am both an "objectivist" and a "subjectivist"' (cited in Dyrness 1971: 174).

14. See the discussions in, for example, Dyrness 1971: 47-48, 168-69 and 213; Dorival 1984: 17, 84 and 89; and Hergott 1993: 18.

15. Dorival 1984: 89.

16. Lindbeck 1984: 16-17 and 31-32 for his understanding of 'experiential-expressivism'; 34-41 for a critique from the perspective of his own 'cultural-linguistic' model in which, he argues, 'experience and expression are no less important' (36). They are simply viewed 'in a different way' (35).

17. McGrath (1990: 26) echoes such a challenge. In a helpful discussion of Schleiermacher, McGrath becomes an unexpected ally of that nineteenth-century Liberal Protestant: 'The delicate interplay between language and experience suggested by Schleiermacher does not appear to be vulnerable to Lindbeck's critique, and does not even appear to fall within its scope. The example of Schleiermacher serves to remind us that not all experiential approaches to doctrine can be dismissed with quite the ease Lindbeck appears to suggest.' Rouault's delicate interplay of pigment and experience could be said to offer a similar challenge to Lindbeck.

carry a sombre beauty. Its subject-matter combines the lofty (Christ) with the lowly (a depressed suburb), the sublime with the seemingly trivial. As with all great art, however, the ugliness is made beautiful through the painter's skill and it is this achievement to which Courthion's words bear witness. But how is this achievement to be understood *theologically*? Are we to read theology's work as an essentially *aesthetic* act, according to which theological resources are used to accompany a sufferer in the reinterpretation of their suffering in order to make it bearable? Are we to live with ugliness, and merely understand it differently, *creating* something beautiful out of that which is not? Is theology then, when all is said and done, really merely a human work? Rouault clearly thought not. His was faith in a God who is real. His persuasive art, however, is now viewed in a generation less sure of referentiality beyond the text (viz. canvas). What Rouault may have felt firmly to be the case may not actually be so. His art may stand as a memorial to past attempts to undertake realist theology and serve as a stimulus to the inevitably non-realist theologies which must be ventured in the present.[18] Christology may thus prove to be an exercise in aesthetics.[19]

A fourth and final point to be drawn from Courthion's observation takes consideration of the contemporary context within which Rouault's work is now viewed a stage further. Courthion's comment that 'Rouault's Christ has no need of a halo to identify Him' is worth critical scrutiny. Rouault's Christ may well not need a halo to identify him in a setting where it is assumed that Rouault is wanting to portray *Christ*, that is, in the still largely Christian West and bearing in mind Rouault's general interests and *oeuvre*. In such a context, it is even possible that the allusion to the Emmaus Road may be recognized. At the end of an increasingly secularized century, however, such inter-

18. In the contemporary British scene, Don Cupitt stands as the clearest and most popular exponent of Christian 'non-realist theology', i.e. Christian theology which deems that theology remains necessary, that the Church still has an important role to play in society and in helping people to shape their spiritualities, but which accepts that there is no objective reality 'God'; see, for example, Cupitt 1980, 1982, 1987 and 1991.

19. This point directly relates to those interpretations of Rouault (as cited, for example, in Dyrness 1971: 206) that see his art as having only aesthetic significance: a form of symbolism which was so keen to express its meaning in painted presentation that it survives when the reference-point/s beyond the symbols are held to have gone, but negates any (realist) theological intent which the painter may have had.

textual links may be less easy to make. Western secularity may not be wholly what was once thought (religious interests persist in western culture even if not in mainstream religions), but a working cultural background is needed for such allusions to carry their full weight. Be that as it may, Rouault's resulting secular, incognito Christ may have more to teach us than even he himself expected.

3. *Rouault and Christology*

These four points drawn from interaction with Courthion's obser-vations about the painting—Christ as suffering figure, Rouault's Christology as 'Expressionist', Christology as an aesthetic task, and the unhaloed Christ in a secular context—must now be put to theo-logical use. We must now address more explicitly the theological task of constructing a Christian Christology today and determine how Rouault may be of assistance. In this process, we shall also bear in mind the factors which led to our being drawn to the painting in the first place: Rouault is direct about his theological interests (inside and outside his paintings); this painting is striking in placing Jesus the Christ in a contemporary setting; and Rouault invites us through his unhaloed Christ to consider the relationship between Jesus and Christ figures. The constructive part to follow comes under six headings: Christology as Experiential, Christ among the Poor, Christ as Companion, Christ as Co-Sufferer, the Hidden Christ, and Revisioning the Body of Christ.

Christology as Experiential
In the same way as art which fails to embody the life experience of the artist is inauthentic so also Christology which fails to incorporate the life experience of the theologian will prove second-hand and unreal. This is the main methodological lesson to be drawn from dialogue with Rouault's *Christ in a Depressed Suburb*. Rouault is able to portray Christ as companion with conviction and in persuasive fashion because Christ accompanies him. Rouault is driven to portray Christ as companion in a rough and dirty part of the city because that is where he believes Christ is most likely to be found. That is, after all, where most people live (in the sense that most struggle to make a living and cannot choose where they live). Rouault's was not a condescending and false identification with materially poor working people precisely

because of the beginnings of his own working experience and his own observations throughout his time in Paris. Furthermore, though it cannot be said that he remained poor, it is also true that he resisted being sucked into the world of artistic convention throughout his life.[20] Of Rouault it is undoubtedly true that fame was of little interest to him.

However, though Rouault himself is identifying fully with the context of his creation and with the figures in the picture who themselves are encountering Christ the companion, this does not exhaust the painting's experiential dimension. For it instructs the viewer who *cannot* identify with the figures portrayed on where to look for the Christ. 'If you do not know who Christ is', Rouault is saying, 'then you must look among the people where he is most likely to be found'. Rouault thus relates his own experience to a firmly orthodox message about the location of Christ in the present in creating a picture which functions kerygmatically for searching enquirers or disinterested observers.

Christ among the Poor
'Christ will be found', the painting proclaims, 'among the poor'. The painting will even challenge the context within which it will later be exhibited. Christ is not readily to be found in art galleries of West or East. Those who view the painting are encouraged to look elsewhere: Christ will be found as the companion of children, of travellers on the road, of those on the streets, of those inhaling the pollution caused to line the pockets of those who live elsewhere. The conviction that Christ will be found among the poor raises an important theological challenge. If Christology is to be experiential, and Christ is found among the poor, then does this mean encountering Christ entails becoming poor? In the light of Rouault's experience as an artist, the answer must be 'yes': as we saw, one cannot communicate as an artist unless one knows how most people actually live. How must Rouault's artistic response be understood in terms of practical Christology? How can Jesus' response, as portrayed by Mark in his Gospel, to the rich man who felt unable to sell all he had in order to give that money to the poor, be understood satisfactorily in the light of Rouault's painting?

20. From 1913, when he began to purchase Rouault's works, to his death in 1939, Ambroise Vollard effectively functioned as a patron to Rouault and set him up financially as a result. Rouault was sceptical of the words of art critics (Dyrness 1971: 77) and refused to paint pictures simply because they would be likely to sell (Dyrness 1971: 85).

The conviction that Christ is to be found among the poor suggests at the very least that the experience of the poor is a powerful, and perhaps essential, starting-point for Christian theological reflection. Christians who attempt to undertake theology Christianly (which inevitably entails putting Christology at the heart of a theology[21]) will thus have to go by the way of the poor. They will undoubtedly in some sense have to become poor, or else they will not have rendered into the terms of their own experience their encounter with the Christ who is to be found among the poor. What that 'in some sense' must mean probably cannot be neatly defined. But it needs to be seen as a feature of *theology* (viz. Christology) and not just be related to ethical consequences.[22] And it probably must be seen, partially at least, in material terms, so long as the 'becoming poor' is not merely abandonment of riches without a change of heart. Giving away one's wealth might indeed be an indication of a change in the orientation of one's life. Yet it might not be. Or it might be an indication that God's grace could somehow be earned. Neither could be seen as an encounter with Christ on the road to Belleville as understood by Rouault, or on the road to Emmaus as seen by Luke.

Finding Christ among the poor is, of course, a contemporary emphasis in much Christian theology. Latin American Liberation Theologians have drawn such an approach to the attention of theologians of the affluent North West to considerable effect.[23] In modern discussion prior to the emergence of Liberation Theology, and sadly to some extent since, exploration of the topic of Christ and the poor has often been quickly stifled by reference to the supposedly failed

21. This means that despite the many current voices which suggest the contrary, Christocentrism in Christian theology has a future. As John Cobb Jr has noted, the issue is not whether Christian theology is Christocentric or not, but whether a theology is working with a good or bad Christocentrism. Christocentrism is not the opposite of Theocentrism, but the Christian form of Theocentrism. See Cobb in Davis (ed.) 1988: 28. I am (still!) working on a book on this theme, *A Particular Faith: The Future of Christocentrism in Christian Theology*.

22. Ethics is often seen to be derivative of theology proper, though why ethical considerations should be any less important than theology is a mystery to me.

23. See, for example, the work of Berryman 1987; the Boffs 1987; Gutierrez 1978 and 1983; Pixley and Boff 1989; and Sobrino 1978 and 1987. Berryman (1987) and the Boffs (1987) are useful introductions to readers exploring Liberation Theology for the first time.

project of the 'Social Gospel'.[24] One wishes that many of Walter Rauschenbusch's critics had been as courageous as he in his New York ministry. Striking, however, is that the theme of Christ's presence among the poor persists despite all failures to reflect it adequately in Christian activity, and all ecclesiastical tendencies to suppress its full significance. What is more, the popular (populist?) Christ of the poor has a lively role to play in art and literature, fields in which Christian theology itself should feel free to roam, yet does all too little.[25]

Christ as Companion

Christ is among the poor as their companion. The Christ figure in Rouault's *Christ in a Depressed Suburb* accompanies the walking children. They may well be heading somewhere, but there is no indication that they will escape the smoke, grime and grim darkness of their surroundings. Nor is there any indication that Christ will, or can, lift them out of it. But Christ is with them: listening and perhaps speaking. He may also be incognito, just as on the road to Emmaus. Perhaps Rouault was more acute in his portrayal of Christ at this point

24. Seen to emerge out of nineteenth-century Liberal Protestantism, reaching, and being developed in, the United States via Walter Rauschenbusch (who studied under Albrecht Ritschl). See Rauschenbusch 1984 for a general selection of his work and Dorrien 1990 for a recent reassessment. The relationship between the Social Gospel and Liberalism is intriguing. Both movements have their flaws. But some of their critics are inconsistent. The Social Gospel is usually viewed as coming from Liberalism, even though Liberalism is seen simply as an individualistic product of the Enlightenment. Thus, if the derivation is accurate, the Social Gospel is not 'social' at all. However, if it is 'social' (no matter how inadequate its analysis of structural life may be), and has a link with Liberalism, then Liberalism may not simply be the individualist monster it is often portrayed as being. More work needs undertaking in this important area of historical theology.

25. To cite just a few examples at random: Rembrandt's etchings of Christ portray him among the ordinary people of Amsterdam (see e.g. *Christ Preaching* c. 1650). James Ensor's *The Entry of Christ into Brussels* (1889) notoriously nearly loses Christ in the crowd (see John Dillenberger 1987: 114-16). In 1940, Michael Rothenstein painted a 'matter of fact' Deposition in watercolour and ink (in Jones [ed.] 1993: 54). In the 1960s, Adrian Henri undertook in both poetry and paint for Liverpool what Ensor had done for Brussels (in Lucie-Smith 1970: 349-52), and Denis Potter portrayed Jesus as a working Son of Man. These examples, with the exception of Rembrandt, can hardly be called straightforward orthodox interpretations. But they by no means constitute a mocking form of ordinariness. Rather, they represent a respectful exploration of what Christ is to mean in contemporary life.

Images of Christ

than Courthion allows. But what is he doing here? Is Christ's role to be the artist who will help his companions spin something beautiful out of the grime? Is he to try and convince them that their lot really is a happy one after all, and that perhaps their poverty is blessed? Rouault would be uncomfortable with such a thought precisely because his own faith (and art) enables him to transcend the material particularity of life as he experienced it, even if he knew also that the materiality of his existence could not be evaded. But we confront again the question whether we can share so easily in Rouault's optimistic referentiality.

Let us be clear: non-realism in Christian theology is a persuasive option for contemporary Christian theology in a postmodern world. The reality of God has been under siege for some time in western culture and post-Feuerbach and post-Holocaust Christianity understandably finds reassertion of God's reality rather difficult. But truth seems to require the reassertion of God's reality if for no other reason than to prevent the atomistic fragmentation of western culture. Rouault's visual Christology relates well here to contemporary explorations of the transcendence of interpersonal relations.[26] Christ may not be constituted by friendship but is certainly disclosed in friendship. Christ does not lie behind friendship, but may be said to be discovered between people who are friends. Christ is thus identified in contemporary terms with no individual, nor with any disembodied spirit. Christ is truly 'other' yet is radically particular in the relationships which forge the deepest friendships between people.

Such a reading of Christ is even possible through attention to Rouault's own life experience.

> Rouault...defined his life in a few friendships. They were attachments of the spirit that far surpassed mere comradery, unions on which the spirit of the painter could feed and nourish itself.[27]

It can thus be said of Rouault, then, that he reflected at a subconscious level a direct and deep corollary between his understanding of deep friendship and the intensity of his encounter with Christ through the development of his art in the company of close friends. Neither Bloy

26. Farley has been exploring the importance of intersubjectivity in Christian thought and practice for two decades (1975, 1982, 1991).

27. Dyrness 1971: 26. Dyrness refers here directly to Rouault's friendships with the writer Léon Bloy (1846–1917; see Dyrness 1971: 32-45), Joris-Karl Huysmans (1848–1907; see Dyrness 1971: 64-67), Jacques and Raïssa Maritain and André Suarès.

nor Huysmans was Christ for him. But Christ was present in the inter-relationship between Rouault and Bloy, and Rouault and Huysmans. It is through this insight that it is possible to claim that *Christ in a Depressed Suburb*, despite the gloom which pervades the work, is more optimistic than many of Rouault's portrayals of Christ where Christ is alone, or presented in the context of the passion story. Transcendence is achieved less through art than through companion-ship:

> Like the son of the Miller of Leyden, this cabinetmaker's son had a sense
> of community and possessed the gift of expressing it in his art.[28]

The lonely Christ, though it has become very much a hallmark of Rouault's work, thus represents only a part of Rouault's exploration in Christology. Dyrness's linking of Rouault to Bloy's contention that 'God is the great Lonely One who speaks only to the lonely' is thus only partly true.[29] Rouault was indeed reflecting upon loneliness, and the loneliness of Christ, very often in his work. But his insight into Christ the companion also enabled him to address the world of the lonely with his conviction, born of faith, that God in Christ is along-side the lonely, even if hidden (unhaloed).[30]

Christ as Co-Sufferer

Such a message was deemed by Rouault to have especial significance for the lonely who suffered, either due to or in their loneliness. It was Rouault's concern to address the needs of the suffering and the outcast, born of his own experience, which drew him to Bloy and his work.[31] His early exploration of lonely figures—sad clowns and prostitutes, paintings especially undertaken as he moved through his own crisis of spiritual exploration following the death of his artistic mentor Moreau in the first decade of this century—provides the background for his later exploration of the sad figure of the suffering Christ. The two phases of Rouault's work relate to each other in that they both explore loneliness and suffering, and the means of dealing with them.

28. Courthion 1978: 20. The allusion is to Rembrandt.

29. Dyrness 1971: 38.

30. Dyrness's observation of the tendency in Rouault's work 'to de-emphasize the individual' (1971: 198), which runs counter to the evident theme of loneliness, is relevant here.

31. Dyrness 1971: 41.

Rouault's is no easy view of resurrection.[32] Though transcendence through relationship maintains belief in a real God who co-suffers with people in Christ, Rouault's vision is not one with an obviously happy ending. Friendship in Christ *is* resurrection. There is no speculation in the paintings as to what that may mean beyond this life. But to have one's suffering shared, and to have one's loneliness relieved, by the presence of Christ the companion is more than a mere resurrection hope. It is a presence of communal life in Christ.

Rouault's work resists speculation, too, as to whether the Church should understand itself as the redemptive community: the body which should so shape its own life under God as to enable those who suffer to find Christ the companion within it, and to go out and seek the lost and the lonely so that isolation may be overcome in the friendship of Christ. In that sense Rouault's corporate vision is underdeveloped. There may, however, be a challenge from Rouault even here. Rouault resisted having his art categorized as Christian art. He sat loose to church structures in his working life, even while espousing an orthodox faith. The reason for this is simple: 'Rouault did not treat sacred art as something separate...'[33] So great, in other words, was Rouault's sense of the grace of God operating sacramentally in the world at large, that it appeared not to have occurred to him to see the corporate aspect of his vision in primarily ecclesiastical terms. People are, after all, not saved by the Church. They may be saved within it. But definitions of what the Church is may best come from the communities of the redeemed, among whom Christ the companion of the poor and the suffering may be found, rather than being presupposed on other grounds. Perhaps this apparent lacuna in Rouault's Expressionist Christology is not so significant after all.

The Hidden Christ
Christ is without a halo in *Christ in a Depressed Suburb*. Either we must say, with Courthion, that this is because Christ has no need of a halo: his identity is obvious. Or we can say that it is important he is

---

32. On Rouault's understanding of resurrection, see Dyrness 1971: 193-95. Some of Rouault's interpreters clearly think Rouault spent too long in hell (Dyrness 1971: 86 and 89-90).

33. Courthion 1978: 34. As Rouault himself remarked, 'All my work is religious for those who know how to look at it' (cited in Dyrness 1971: 79).

unknown to the children. Were he haloed he would be all too recognizable and detached from his surroundings. His incarnation would be devalued, and our redemption less possible. The latter message may be Rouault's own. Be that as it may, it is the one most necessary at the end of the century. From a Christian theological perspective, we would do well to make Christ more visible in the West. But Christ's hidden presence makes more sense to us, not because it is a last ditch effort by Christianity to try and convince a sceptical world that the language of 'presence'really does mean something, but simply because hiddenness relates to ordinariness, concreteness, particularity, the everyday, the mundane, the cut and thrust of life. If incarnation cannot be maintained in the midst of such life, then it cannot be maintained at all.

Rouault's unhaloed Christ is thus useful as a contemporary symbol for Christian Christology. Only an unhaloed Christ will do. Christ does not thereby cease to be God for us or God with us. The hidden, unhaloed Christ simply reminds us of the kind of God that Christians have, from the first, been trying to tell the world that God actually is: God is as God is in Jesus. We can gloss this statement with insights from Rouault: God is as God is in Jesus, and that means being the companion of those who are willing to let Jesus the Christ walk with them. God is as God is in Jesus as the one who enables relationships to happen. God is as God is in Jesus is therefore best told about in stories and in paintings which best highlight Jesus as himself in a set of relationships: with fishermen, perhaps, or with travellers on the road to Emmaus, or to Belleville.

Revisioning the Body of Christ
Our dialogue with Rouault's art thus leaves us at the crossroads of a corporate Christology. As many forms of contemporary Christology (feminist, above all[34]) are reminding us, there have been too many drawbacks to overemphasizing the individual male figure, Jesus of Nazareth, in Christology. Christology may be rooted in Jesus, but it is never exhausted by Jesus.[35] Rouault's own Expressionist Christology provides an exemplary reminder of what Christianity has always done: spoken about contemporary experience of Christ, of human experience,

34. See, for example, Brock 1991; Herrara 1993.
35. Thus, for example, Brock 1991: 52: '... I will be developing a christology not centered in Jesus but in relationship and community as the whole-making, healing center of Christianity. In that sense, Christ is what I am calling Christa/Community.'

of traditions about Christ, and of God, even while saying, or painting, something about Jesus. Christologies which are Jesusologies are simply not Christian. More than ever now in the present we are seeing the need to question the individualism of so much western Christology. Locating Christology firmly in a trinitarian framework may well be one way of addressing this need. It is not the only way. There are biblical resources which invite further development in this regard. Perhaps the time has come to revision Paul's understanding of 'the body of Christ'. Using our dialogue with Rouault as a basis we can maintain afresh a sense in which the body of Christ is a term for the Christian Church in all its many and diverse forms. But we can also be stimulated not to begin with the Church as it is. Following Rouault's lead, we can look for Christ among the poor, as their companion. We can find Christ also among the suffering. Christ is likely to be a hidden presence, waiting to be revealed, a community-creator forging relationship in the face of lonely suffering. From such liberating communities understandings of the body of Christ would thus arise. From experience of such liberating communities, it may then, at last, be possible to speak of an encounter with Christ, and of 'church'.

4. Conclusion

Our dialogue with Rouault has enabled us to highlight some key concerns of contemporary Christology. In wrestling with his wordless Christology, we have had our own insights sharpened. He has offered challenging content—a contribution to, not merely an illustration of, contemporary needs. He by no means addresses, let alone answers, all our questions. But he does seem to be speaking a similar language in the sense that he addressed issues which remain ours. In this way he is no less a useful discussion partner than a more traditional wordsmith in theology. If our engagement with Rouault has been illustrative, then, it can only be in the sense that it illustrates the value of contemporary Christian systematic theologians taking the arts much more seriously.

BIBLIOGRAPHY

Begbie, J.
    1991   *Voicing Creation's Praise* (Edinburgh: T. & T. Clark).
Berryman, P.
    1987   *Liberation Theology* (London: Tauris).

Boff, C., and L. Boff
1987   *Introducing Liberation Theology* (Tunbridge Wells: Burns & Oates).
Brock, R.N.
1991   *Journeys by Heart: A Christology of Erotic Power* (New York: Crossroad).
Courthion, P.
1978   *Georges Rouault* (London: Thames and Hudson).
Cupitt, D.
1980   *Taking Leave of God* (London: SCM Press).
1982   *The World to Come* (London: SCM Press).
1987   *The Long-Legged Fly* (London: SCM Press).
1991   *What is a Story?* (London: SCM Press).
Davis, S.T. (ed.)
1988   *Encountering Jesus: A Debate on Christology* (Atlanta: John Knox).
Dillenberger, Jane
1986   *Style and Content in Christian Art* (London: SCM Press).
Dillenberger, John
1987   *A Theology of Artistic Sensibilities* (London: SCM Press).
Dixon, J.W., Jr
1978   *Art and the Theological Imagination* (New York: Seabury).
Dorrien, G.
1990   *Reconstructing the Common Good* (Maryknoll, NY: Orbis Books).
Dorival, B.
1984   *Rouault* (trans. G. Apgar; Naefels: Bonfini).
Dyrness, W.A.
1971   *Rouault: A Vision of Suffering and Salvation* (Grand Rapids: Eerdmans).
Farley, E.
1975   *Ecclesial Man* (Philadelphia: Fortress Press).
1982   *Ecclesial Reflection* (Philadelphia: Fortress Press).
1991   *Good and Evil: Interpreting the Human Condition* (Philadelphia: Fortress Press).
Gutierrez, G.
1978   *A Theology of Liberation* (London: SCM Press, 2nd edn).
1983   *The Power of the Poor in History* (London: SCM Press).
Herrera, M.
1993   'Who Do You Say Jesus Is? Christological Reflections from a Hispanic Woman's Perspective', in M. Stevens (ed.), *Reconstructing the Christ Symbol* (New York: Paulist Press).
Hergott, F.
1993   *Rouault* (Recklinghausen: Bongers).
Hergott, F., and S. Whitfield
1993   *Georges Rouault: The Early Years 1903–1920* (London: Royal Academy/Lund Humphries).
Jones, T.D. (ed.)
1993   *Images of Christ: Religious Iconography in Twentieth Century British Art* (Northampton: St Matthew's Centenary Arts Committee).

Lindbeck, G.
1984   *The Nature of Doctrine* (London: SPCK).
Lucie-Smith, E. (ed.)
1970   *British Poetry since 1945* (Harmondsworth: Penguin Books).
McGrath, A.E.
1990   *The Genesis of Doctrine* (Oxford: Basil Blackwell).
Pixley, G., and C. Boff
1989   *The Bible, the Church and the Poor* (Tunbridge Wells: Burns & Oates).
Rauschenbusch, W.
1984   *Walter Rauschenbusch: Selected Writings* (New York: Paulist Press).
Sobrino, J.
1978   *Christology at the Crossroads* (London: SCM Press).
1987   *Jesus in Latin America* (Maryknoll, NY: Orbis Books).
Tillich, P.
1989   *On Art and Architecture* (New York: Crossroad).
Venturi, L.
1948   *Georges Rouault* (Paris: Albert Skira).

BACH, BEETHOVEN AND STRAVINSKY MASSES:
IMAGES OF CHRIST IN THE CREDO

Wendy J. Porter

1. *Introduction*

Three composers who deviated from their normal patterns to use the Latin text of the mass are Bach, Beethoven and Stravinsky. Bach normally wrote in German, Beethoven did not write religious music as a rule, and Stravinsky might reasonably have been expected to use Russian. Each set the mass in a way that depicts a unique image of Christ. This image becomes apparent in a comparison of the Credo sections of Bach's *Mass in B Minor*, Beethoven's *Missa Solemnis*, and Stravinsky's *Mass*. By focusing briefly on the overall structure of each mass, and then specifically on the central Credo sections as they relate to the Christ figure, some instructive observations can be made. Without using the works to speculate on each composer's religious faith, certain personal details of the composer and his known intentions for the mass do shed light on the particular image of Christ that is created, as do the musical and textual details of each composition.

In an attempt to draw theological characteristics out of sacred musical compositions there is a tendency to read into the music and text insights that may well not be there. As a case in point, M. Cooper uses the opening bars of Beethoven's Credo to caricature theological speculation:

> Is the orchestra's initial leap...a leap of faith? and are the rugged entries of the first theme, with its suspensions and ascents into the void symbolical of Beethoven's battle against doubt? are the suspensions, as it were, suspensions of disbelief? and when the bass line in bar 8 climbs towards an E flat that is in fact sung by the sopranos while the basses break off prematurely, are we to believe that Beethoven dispatched the basses to the heights in search for a God that they never found, and that the sopranos take up the search instead—to discover a God whose omnipotence keeps

them, twelve bars later, on a top B flat for the best part of five bars? It is difficult to believe in detailed symbolism of this kind.[1]

I agree—this is difficult to believe. As fascinating as such speculation might be, there is little in the music or in Beethoven's life that allows us to make such correlations of music and biography.

However, apart from this kind of biographical interpretative reading, how the composer emphasizes certain words or phrases of the text or selects keys or musical motifs to indicate related sections all combine to form a certain picture or image of the subject. As Marshall says, 'the text of the Mass Ordinary—at least in the two lengthy sections, the *Gloria* and the *Credo*—does not unambiguously suggest any particular subdivision or formal ordering. The design is therefore up to the composer.'[2] Rather than use the works to try to view the *composer*, I will show how certain choices the composer has made in setting the Credo section of each of the following masses allows for a certain way of viewing the *subject*, in this case the image of Christ.

2. *Bach's Mass in B Minor*

a. *Background to the Mass in B Minor*
J.S. Bach (1685–1750) wrote—or compiled and re-wrote—the *Mass in B Minor* (1749) near the end of his life. There are two issues that continually emerge in establishing the proper background for understanding this mass. The first is its composite nature. The issue of parody is continually raised regarding the *Mass in B Minor*. The practice of using past material or borrowing music and reworking it into new compositions was a common one in Bach's day.[3] Today this borrowing might be viewed unfavourably, but it is in large part what makes the *Mass in B Minor* enduring.[4] The majority of these earlier sources are Bach's own religious works. When Bach used movements from his earlier church cantatas, he did not take them over as they were, but rewrote them to a higher degree of perfection than the

1. M. Cooper, *Beethoven: The Last Decade 1817–1827* (London: Oxford University Press, 1970), pp. 241-42.

2. R.L. Marshall, *The Music of Johann Sebastian Bach: The Sources, the Style, the Significance* (New York: Schirmer, 1989), p. 182.

3. Marshall, *Music of Johann Sebastian Bach*, p. 32.

4. J. Butt, *Bach: Mass in B Minor* (Cambridge: Cambridge University Press, 1991), p. 42.

model.[5] Bach often took sections of his own secular work, for example music written for a one-time occasion such as a coronation, and rewrote them into his sacred music—but never the reverse. Whether secular or sacred in its original form—perhaps an instrumental line rewritten for voices or a chorus rewritten to fit a slightly different text—the setting of the *Mass in B Minor* became the final form. Wolff comments that 'as the result of further compositional refinements, the Mass movements whose parody models are known invariably surpass the pieces on which they are based'.[6]

The second issue is the theological implications of Bach's *Mass in B Minor*. The work has caused much speculation and debate, partly because, although Bach had set the mass several times, for this, his greatest and final sacred work, he again chose the Latin text rather than the customary German of his cantatas. Therefore musicians and theologians question why he chose to compose the work and why he did so in a language that appears to be in some conflict with both the theology and practices of the German Lutheran Church. Some suggest that Bach was leaning towards Catholicism, although even in post-Reformation Germany there were certain Protestant cities and churches, including Leipzig where Bach lived for the last 25 years or so of his life, where the mass was celebrated in ways identical to the Catholic mass,[7] and the use of the Latin texts in Leipzig were 'in keeping with its liturgy, which had continuously employed the language of medieval Christendom for these parts of public worship'.[8] In any case, there are numerous hypotheses regarding how this work fits with the rest of Bach's sacred compositions. Wolff calls it a 'political move...with the aim of obtaining the title of court composer',[9] but Schweitzer states about the mass: 'It is as if Bach had here tried to

5. K. Geiringer, *Johann Sebastian Bach: The Culmination of an Era* (London: George Allen and Unwin, 1967), p. 207.

6. C. Wolff, *Bach: Essays on his Life and Music* (Cambridge, MA: Harvard University Press, 1991), p. 333.

7. P. Spitta, *Johann Sebastian Bach: His Work and Influence on the Music of Germany, 1685–1750* (trans. C. Bell and J.A. Fuller-Maitland; 3 vols.; London: Novello, 1889; repr. New York: Dover, 1951), II, p. 263.

8. C.S. Terry, *The Music of Bach: An Introduction* (London: Oxford University Press, 1933), p. 88.

9. See Wolff, *Bach*, p. 35, where he further comments that the 'choice of this "interdenominational" subject was precisely because of the conversion of the reigning electoral house to Catholicism...'

write a really *Catholic* Mass; he endeavours to present faith under its larger and more objective aspects'.[10]

Despite all of this speculation regarding his motives, we can reasonably conclude that Bach probably did not expect the work as a whole to be performed in church, particularly as the music alone can take over two hours to perform. J. Butt writes: 'The conclusion which many writers...are reluctant to reach is that Bach may have compiled the work with no specific practical end in mind, an act which would clearly be more appropriate for a composer of a later age, when music had become an "autonomous" art'. However, Butt goes on to say, '...perhaps the most useful means of summing up its meaning and content is to consider its "universality", with regard both to its place in Bach's oeuvre and [to] its apparent ecumenicism...he seems to have had one aim in mind: the summation and perfection of his entire lifework.'[11] Although it is difficult to prove what Bach may have thought, an argument can be made that the mass is in fact a summative and emblematic work of Bach's musical career, certainly of his sacred vocal music.

Although there is still doubt regarding Bach's intentions for the complete mass, the five main sections of the mass—Kyrie, Gloria, Credo, Sanctus and Agnus Dei—are well-suited to Bach's sense of proportion and balance. Within these five sections, the Credo is situated in the middle of the text as the theological centre and the 'intellectual formulation', as Cooper calls it.[12] It is probable that he wrote at least the Credo, or what he himself titles as the *Symbolum Nicenum* (Nicene Creed), to be used in its entirety for the liturgy. The manuscript of the *Symbolum Nicenum* has its own title page, which suggests that it was designed to exist on its own and marks its potential use as a separate work.[13] Bach's musical treatment of the words of the Credo shows the significance of this central movement and how he focuses it on the image of the crucified Christ.

b. *An Image of the Crucified Christ*
Bach divides the Credo text into nine sections with the *crucifixus* at the centre. He uses this division along with the relationships of time

10. A. Schweitzer, *J.S. Bach* (trans. E. Newman; 2 vols.; London: Breitkopf, 1911), II, p. 314.

11. Butt, *Bach*, p. 24.

12. M. Cooper, *Beethoven*, p. 240.

13. Butt, *Bach*, p. 15.

signatures and keys, the musical forms of the sections and the choice of choir versus soloists to frame the middle movement, the *crucifixus*. Ultimately, the image of the crucified Christ emerges as the most significant image of Bach's Credo. His use of archaic elements gives a sense of continuity with a past tradition that also focuses on the *crucifixus*. The various elements that Bach uses leave little ambiguity as to the centrality of the crucified Christ.

The nine sections into which Bach divides the Credo are as follows:

1. *credo in unum deum*
(I believe in one God)

2. *credo in unum deum, patrem omnipotentem, factorem coeli et terrae, visibilium omnium et invisibilium*
(I believe in one God, the Father Almighty, maker of heaven and earth and of all things visible and invisible)[14]

3. *et in unum dominum Jesum Christum, filium dei unigenitum, et ex patre natum ante omnia saecula, deum de deo, lumen de lumine, deum verum de deo vero: genitum, non factum, consubstantialem patri per quem omnia facta sunt qui propter nos homines et propter nostram salutem descendit de coelis*
(and in one Lord Jesus Christ, the only begotten son of God, begotten of his Father before all worlds, God of God, light of light, very God of very God, begotten, not made, being of one substance with the Father by whom all things were made who for us men and for our salvation came down from heaven)

4. *et incarnatus est de spiritu sancto ex Maria virgine et homo factus est*
(and was incarnate by the Holy Spirit of the virgin Mary and was made man)

5. *crucifixus etiam pro nobis sub Pontio Pilato passus et sepultus est*
(was crucified also for us under Pontius Pilate, he suffered and was buried)

6. *et resurrexit tertia die secundum scripturas et ascendit in coelum sedet ad dexteram dei patris et iterum venturus est cum gloria judicare vivos et mortuos cujus regni non erit finis*
(and rose again the third day according to the Scriptures and ascended into heaven and sitteth on the right hand of God the Father, and he shall come again with glory to judge both the quick and the dead, whose kingdom shall have no end)

14. Bach repeats the phrase from the first chorus in this section.

7. *et in spiritum sanctum dominum et vivificantem qui ex patre filioque procedit qui cum patre et filio simul adoratur et conglorificatur qui locutus est per prophetas et unam sanctam catholicam et apostolicam ecclesiam*
(and in the Holy Spirit, the Lord and giver of life, who from the Father and the Son proceedeth, who with the Father and the Son together is worshipped and glorified, who spake by the Prophets; and in one holy catholic and apostolic Church)

8. *confiteor unum baptisma in remissionem peccatorum et expecto resurrectionem mortuorum*
(I acknowledge one baptism for the remission of sins and I look for the resurrection of the dead)

9. *et expecto resurrectionem mortuorum et vitam venturi saeculi. amen.*
(and I look for the resurrection of the dead and the life of the world to come. Amen.)

Nos. 1 and 2 are linked ideologically in expressing belief in God the Father and nos. 8 and 9 are linked in dealing with the Christian Church. Nos. 3 and 7 are linked by each being about one other member of the Trinity. The middle three—nos. 4, 5 and 6—relate to the details of Christ's life and are the central focus of the text on which Bach builds the symmetry of his work. Of these three—incarnation, crucifixion and resurrection—he places the crucifixion at the heart of the Credo.

Bach uses the time signatures of these nine sections to reinforce the central placement of the *crucifixus* :

```
Section 1: ¢
(credo)
Section 2: ¢
(credo/patrem)
                Section 3: 4/4
                (et in unum)
                                Section 4: 3/4
                                (et incarnatus)
                                                Section 5: 3/2
                                                (crucifixus)
                                Section 6: 3/4
                                (et resurrexit)
                Section 7: 6/8
                (et in spiritum)
Section 8: ¢
(confiteor)
Section 9: ¢
(et expecto)
```

Figure 1.

The two outer movements at the beginning and at the end of the Credo are all marked ¢ (= cut-time); the three central movements are all set in three beats to the bar. Of the three middle movements, the two outer ones are in 3/4, giving three quarter notes to the measure. Only the *crucifixus* in the centre is set in 3/2 (figure 1). The 3/2 setting of the *crucifixus*, which gives three half-notes to each measure, allows the central section to move at a slower pace to accommodate the slowly repeated descending bass line. The third section, *et in unum dominum*, is the only section in 4/4 and deals with the subject of Jesus as the second person of the Trinity, while the seventh section, *et in spiritum*, is the only setting written in 6/8 and is about the Spirit. Perhaps the 4/4 as a multiple of two can be seen to represent the second person of the Trinity and the 6/8 as a more complex multiple of three than 3/4, for instance, can be seen to represent the third person of the Trinity. Obviously too much can be—and has at times been—made of this symbolism, but the structural and theological correlates do seem to exist.

The relationship of the keys focuses on the *crucifixus* as central as well. Although the work is referred to as the B minor mass, the predominant key in the Credo (and in fact the entire mass) is that of D major. The first two sections of the Credo are in D major, although to be more accurate the first movement is in the archaic Mixolydian mode. This is in keeping with Bach's use of an archaic Gregorian chant melody in this first section. The last two sections also have this kind of integral relationship, making use of an archaic mode and a Gregorian melody in the first of the two sections. The duet that deals with the second person of the Trinity, section 3, is in the key of G major, which is closely related to D major by being built on the subdominant of the D scale. The key of A major is the other major key most closely related to D major, built on the dominant, and it is no surprise to discover that Bach set the solo in section 7, which deals with the third person of the Trinity, in A major. These two movements, the duet and the solo, surround the three middle choruses that focus on Christ's birth, death and resurrection. The setting of the *crucifixus* is in E minor. Figure 2 (following page) shows the arrangement of the keys. The key of E minor is somewhat unusual for the Credo, or at least a less predictable key for D major than the rest of the Credo. As the relative minor of G major, it relates most closely to the duet, *et in unum dominum*, which expresses belief in the Lord Jesus Christ.

Section 1: D mode
(*credo*)
Section 2: D major
(*patrem*)
        Section 3: G major
        (*et in unum*)
                Section 4: B minor
                (*et incarnatus*)
                        Section 5: E minor
                        (*crucifixus*)
                Section 6: D major
                (*et resurrexit*)
        Section 7: A major
        (*et in spiritum*)
Section 8: F# mode
(*confiteor*)
Section 9: D major
(*et expecto*)

Figure 2.

This is not an unexpected relationship, as Bach has placed great emphasis on the complexity of the second person of the Trinity in the *et in unum dominum* (mentioned below), and shows the connection of the person of the *et in unum dominum* with the person of the *crucifixus* as fundamental to the significance of the crucifixion.

Bach uses soloists in the Credo only to depict the second and third persons of the Trinity.[15] For instance, Bach chooses a duet for *et in unum dominum* as a way of describing the internal relationship of Father and Son. Here Bach writes for two independent voices, soprano and alto soloists, to portray the difficult concept of the oneness of Jesus and God, yet the separateness of Jesus as Son and second person of the Trinity. The *et in unum dominum* was originally music from a love song by Bach, which quite naturally was set as a duet. The 'two-in-oneness' of this setting is appropriate for a text depicting the second person of the Trinity, Jesus Christ. Written as a strict canon, with one part closely imitating the other, the notes are separated by a fourth and each musical statement is echoed by the other as if to emphasize how one follows the other.[16] It is not always the same voice that leads,

15. Spitta (*Bach*, III, p. 46) notes that the solos 'assume a less personal character than is usual even with Bach', which is perhaps in keeping with depicting persons of the Trinity.

16. See Spitta, *Bach*, III, p. 31, where he says that the 'intention is unmistakable,

suggesting the intertwining of the two-in-one. Evidence for this symbolism comes from Bach's own words on the manuscript, where he wrote 'Two voices express 2'.[17] The only other section to be written as a solo is *et in spiritum*, which is about the Holy Spirit. Otherwise all the main sections of the creed are sung by the choir, perhaps to keep extraneous personalities out of the picture and to more closely align it with the actual corporate confession of the creed by a church congregation.

While Bach emphasizes this two-in-one image, it is not his main focus; nor is the *et incarnatus*, as lovely as it is. The *et incarnatus* and the *et resurrexit* on either side contrast with the *crucifixus*. There is a strong sense of progression through the three events—from the incarnation through the crucifixion to the resurrection. But the focus that Bach presents as central to interpretation of the Credo text is that of the crucifixion. By the very manner in which Bach lays out the entire *Mass in B Minor*, there is a sense of orderliness and symmetry. This holds true not only for the musical ideas, but also for the textual ideas. Everything is presented within the boundaries of this symmetry and especially the words of the creed are laid out with great attention to detail and overall form. As a result of this orderliness and logic, the image of the crucifixion of the living Christ that Bach depicts forms the apex of the work, but is also portrayed as part of a greater plan and *not* simply as an extremely emotional image.[18] Grief is represented through recognized musical symbolism without being trivialized. The passacaglia, a slowly descending bass line that moves chromatically, is a well-recognized Baroque musical symbol used to depict grief.[19] Daw's comment is that 'the bass-line of the great "Crucifixus" has the universally understood poignancy of the lament'.[20]

Although Bach had implemented this particular musical idiom in various ways periodically throughout his life, it is noteworthy that,

since the musical scheme allows of the canonic imitation on the fourth below from the very beginning'.

17. Butt, *Bach*, p. 52.

18. Contrast Bach's and Beethoven's approaches in D. McCaldin, 'The Choral Music', in D. Arnold and N. Fortune (eds.), *The Beethoven Companion* (London: Faber and Faber, 1971), pp. 387-410 (405).

19. Geiringer, *Bach*, pp. 261-62.

20. S. Daw, *The Music of Johann Sebastian Bach: The Choral Works* (East Brunswick, NJ: Fairleigh Dickinson University Press/Associated University Presses, 1981), p. 161.

for one of his most significant and enduring musical images, he chose
what for him was already thirty-five years old: the opening chorus of
the cantata no. 12, *Weinen, Klagen, Sorgen, Zagen*. To this he adds an
introduction, changes some of the instrumentation, intensifies the pulse
of the passacaglia bass line, and adds 'a textually motivated a cappella
concluding phrase ("...passus et sepultus est") that modulates from E
minor to G major',[21] but it is familiar nonetheless.[22]

However, drawing from much further back than even his own early
writing, Bach based his Credo on archaic traditions in several ways.
First, Bach used the archaic language of the creed, as mentioned above.
Mann remarks that 'Bach's remarkable use of the entire Catholic Mass
text linked his work to that of the great composers of the past; the B
Minor Mass may be considered a conscious contribution that Bach
made to that genre of composition which had been the noblest musical
form since the days of Dufay, Josquin, and Palestrina'.[23] Secondly, he
used ancient modes and Gregorian melodies or chants to form the
basis of several sections (i.e. sections 1 and 8). Wolff comments on
Bach's use of two pairs of opening and ending choruses that incorporate
'a *stile antico* movement, with liturgical *cantus firmus*...' followed by
a full chorus movement. Wolff further identifies how inside these
framing choruses, the arias further frame the central three choruses
'whose texts, in turn, mark the Christological center of the Nicene
dogma. In this chiastic-symmetrical form...the stile antico emerges as
a palpable architectonic unit.'[24] Mann also comments that chant 'had
served through the ages as thematic material upon which composers
based their compositions in more and more complex structures. Bach
had used chant melodies on various occasions, but they became of
primary importance to him when he turned his full attention to the
composition of the Mass text.'[25] Thirdly, Bach also refers to earlier
practices by his use of five parts in the choir, rather than the customary

21. Wolff, *Bach*, p. 333.
22. It would be useful here to listen to a recording of the *crucifixus* of Bach's
Mass in B Minor, noting especially his use of the underlying passacaglia, the repeated
bass line.
23. A. Mann, 'Bach Studies: Approaches to the B Minor Mass', *American Choral
Review* 27.1 (1985), p. 8.
24. Wolff, *Bach*, p. 102. See also p. 87: '...traditional vocal polyphony was
almost entirely bound to liturgical practice, predominantly in works with Latin texts;
it became the *stile antico*'.
25. Mann, 'Bach Studies', pp. 29-30.

four parts.[26] For instance, where there would normally be soprano, alto, tenor and bass, he has written two soprano parts as well as alto, tenor and bass. 'This may seem to be a small difference, but in reality it signifies a different orientation of style; the five-part texture was prevalent in the century before Bach, not in his own...'[27] In Bach's later years he devoted serious study to the compositional techniques and styles of Italian composers, such as Palestrina (c. 1525–1594), who wrote for these same five parts for choir, and here we see Bach drawing on that earlier tradition.

Bach's integration of archaic elements both stylistically and structurally into the *Mass in B Minor* connects it with much earlier Church practice and results in a sacred work that establishes continuity with a long history of Church music. His division of the text, his use of various elements to identify chiastic, symmetrical structure and focal point such as the pattern of time signatures and key signatures and the use of soloists to frame central choruses, all unerringly point to the Christ figure in the *crucifixus* as central to Bach's setting of the Credo, and ultimately of his setting of the mass. All of these factors contribute to Bach's setting of the Credo image of Christ having an archaic and timeless sense, and, perhaps, a universal and ecumenical one.

3. Beethoven's Missa Solemnis

a. *Background to the Missa Solemnis*
Ludwig van Beethoven (1770–1827) intended his *Missa Solemnis* or Mass in D Major for the occasion of the enthronement of Archduke Rudolph as Archbishop in 1820. Beethoven started on the work in 1819, but continued working on it until 1823 and, needless to say, missed the intended occasion. The work was first performed on 7 April 1824, in St Petersburg, and was published in 1827, soon after the composer's death.

There have been numerous theories regarding the origins of Beethoven's *Missa Solemnis*. A common theory is that it depicts Beethoven's personal religious experience and beliefs.[28] For example, Bekker relates the entire composition of the mass as growing out of a

---

26. Geiringer, *Bach*, p. 208.
27. Mann, 'Bach Studies', p. 21.
28. M. Solomon, 'Beethoven: The Quest for Faith', in *Beethoven Essays* (Cambridge, MA: Harvard University Press, 1988), pp. 227-28.

spiritual crisis Beethoven had in 1819.[29] Kirkendale proposes that the *Missa Solemnis* directly conforms to the rules and accepted forms of religious music of the day.[30] According to B. Cooper, who takes a slightly jaundiced view of Beethoven and his reasons for composition, the three motivating forces for Beethoven's creativity were performance, publication and payment, as some of his shrewd business dealings even for the *Missa Solemnis* suggest.[31] However, as pragmatic as Beethoven may have been, there is no doubting the depth of emotion he explores nor the level of creativity he displays in this work. In a letter of 1824, Beethoven writes about the *Missa Solemnis*: 'it was my chief aim to awaken, and to render lasting, religious feeling as well in the singers as in the hearers'.[32] B. Cooper comments that Beethoven '...used in his setting every means of musical imagery to enhance the meaning of the text and make it more intelligible to the listener'.[33] Without attempting or presuming to understand Beethoven's intentions or his theological preferences, there is one aspect of the Christ figure that he makes very visible—the humanity of Christ.

b. *An Image of the Humanity of Christ*
An image that Beethoven focuses on and develops throughout his Credo in the *Missa Solemnis* is the human aspect of Christ. Although it is common to associate the *Missa Solemnis* with Beethoven's own experience and to presume that the work is an expression of his own emotions,[34] what is more pertinent to my particular study is that he depicts an image of Christ with a pronounced emphasis on Christ's human characteristics. This human side is developed by attention first of all to the statement that he is human, and secondly to the exploration of human emotion that Christ experiences, especially the suffering of his death by crucifixion. While settings of the Credo text naturally include *et homo factus est* —'and was made man'—Beethoven

29. P. Bekker, *Beethoven* (trans. M.M. Bozman; London: Dent, 1925 [originally published in Berlin, 1912]), pp. 269-70.
30. W. Kirkendale, 'New Roads to Old Ideas in Beethoven's *Missa Solemnis*', *Musical Quarterly* 56 (1970), pp. 676-77, 699-700.
31. B. Cooper, *Beethoven and the Creative Process* (Oxford: Clarendon Press, 1990), p. 30.
32. *Beethoven's Letters*, with notes by A.C. Kalischer (trans. J.S. Shedlock; selected and edited by A. Eaglefield-Hull; New York: Dover, 1972 [1926]), p. 331.
33. B. Cooper, *Beethoven*, p. 57.
34. Bekker, *Beethoven*, p. 273.

sets this statement in a new way. He uses various elements to identify *et homo factus est* as central to the Christ-figure as seen in the Credo, such as his division of the text, his use of tempos and keys and their interrelationships to identify the structural layout of the work, his attention to certain words and ideas in the various sections, and his integration and contrast of soloists and chorus.

Beethoven's division of the text is a significant factor in determining his image of Christ. He creates fifteen independent sections of the words of the Credo, dividing the text as follows:

1. *credo in unum deum, patrem omnipotentem, factorem coeli et terrae, visibilium omnium et invisibilium*
(I believe in one God, the Father Almighty, maker of heaven and earth and of all things visible and invisible)

2. *[credo] in unum dominum Jesum Christum, filium dei unigenitum, et ex patre natum ante omnia saecula*
([I believe] in one Lord Jesus Christ, the only begotten son of God, begotten of his Father before all worlds)[35]

3. *deum de deo, lumen de lumine, deum verum de deo vero: genitum, non factum, consubstantialem patri per quem omnia facta sunt*
(God of God, light of light, very God of very God, begotten not made, being of one substance with the Father by whom all things were made)

4. *qui propter nos homines et propter nostram salutem descendit de coelis*
(who for us men and for our salvation came down from heaven)

5. *et incarnatus est de spiritu sancto ex Maria virgine*
(and was incarnate by the Holy Spirit of the virgin Mary)

6. *et homo factus est*
(and was made man)

7. *crucifixus etiam pro nobis sub Pontio Pilato passus et sepultus est*
(was crucified also for us under Pontius Pilate, he suffered and was buried)

8. *et resurrexit tertia die secundum scripturas*
(and rose again the third day according to the Scriptures)

9. *et ascendit in coelum sedet ad dexteram dei patris et iterum venturus est cum gloria*
(and ascended into heaven and sitteth on the right hand of God the Father and he shall come again with glory)

35. Here, as well as in nos. 11 and 12, Beethoven substitutes the word *credo*, 'I believe' (noted in square brackets), for the original word *et*, 'and'.

10. *judicare vivos et mortuos cujus regni non erit finis*
(to judge both the quick and the dead whose kingdom shall have no end)

11. *[credo] in spiritum sanctum dominum et vivificantem qui ex patre filioque procedit qui cum patre et filio simul adoratur et conglorificatur qui locutus est per prophetas*
([I believe] in the Holy Spirit, the Lord and Giver of life, who from the Father and the Son proceedeth, who with the Father and the Son together is worshipped and glorified, who spake by the Prophets)

12. *[credo] in unam sanctam catholicam et apostolicam ecclesiam confiteor unum baptisma in remissionem peccatorum et expecto resurrectionem mortuorum et vitam venturi saeculi. amen.*
([I believe] in one holy catholic and apostolic Church; I acknowledge one baptism for the remission of sins and I look for the resurrection of the dead and the life of the world to come. Amen.)

13. *et vitam venturi saeculi. amen.*
(and the life of the world to come. Amen.)

14. *et vitam venturi saeculi. amen.*
(and the life of the world to come. Amen.)

15. *et vitam venturi saeculi. amen.*
(and the life of the world to come. Amen.)[36]

In dividing the sections as he does, Beethoven identifies several phrases as distinctive that Bach, for instance, does not. For example, Beethoven sets *et homo factus est* separately, rather than including it with *et incarnatus est*. The separation of the phrase 'and was made man' from the previous words that began 'and was incarnate' gives a new emphasis to Jesus becoming human. Where typically the statement is: 'and was incarnate by the Holy Spirit of the virgin Mary and was made man', here 'and was made man' becomes an entirely separate statement.

There is ambiguity on several levels as to whether the central focus of Beethoven's Credo consists of three or four sections. If there are three, *et homo factus est* is placed in the middle of the three sections. If there are four, then even if the more complex and weighty movement of the *crucifixus* is central by intention, the symmetrical balance does not fully support this arrangement. The question relates partly to the

36. The entire Credo text is completely stated in the first twelve divisions that Beethoven has made, with the last line repeated in each of the final three sections. For the purpose of identifying the main focus of the body of the text and musical work, these last three sections will be left on their own as an appended musical unit, functioning separately as the closing fugue of the work.

passage that follows immediately after the *crucifixus*—the *et resurrexit*. In some ways *et resurrexit* seems to belong to the previous group and in some ways to the following group. Undoubtedly, this ambivalence is not entirely unintentional nor is it particularly inappropriate. In either instance, Beethoven uniquely emphasizes the humanity of Christ by giving special attention to the announcement: *et homo factus est*.

The tempos of the first twelve sections give an indication of inner groupings within the work, as well. Fiske says,

> the Viennese Credo was almost always in three sections:
> Fast: Credo in unum Deum, etc.
> Slow: Et incarnatus est, etc.; in a contrasting key
> Fast: Et resurrexit tertia die, etc.
> Often the Credo ended with a fugue to the words 'et vitam venturi saeculi.
> Amen'... Beethoven was content to write in the usual three main sections
> and to end conventionally with a fugue...[37]

Indeed, sections 1–4 are at a fairly fast tempo, sections 5–7 are at slow tempos, and the following five sections, 8–12, are again at fast tempos, followed by the massive closing fugue. If these tempos indicate divisions, as they seem to, they first of all identify the traditional middle section of the Credo text but then secondarily identify the middle section of nos. 5–7 as the pivotal point of those three, which places *et homo factus est* at the centre. Although the *crucifixus* is the more traditional place of focus, Beethoven draws our attention instead first to the phrase 'and was made man'.

The keys and their relationships throughout the Credo and particularly in the central section also bring a pronounced emphasis to the phrase *et homo factus est*, rather than focusing entirely on the *crucifixus*. While the *Missa Solemnis* is also known as the Mass in D, the Credo itself is structured around the key not of D major but of B flat major, as the two beginning and two ending sections of the Credo are all in B flat major. The central section of the Credo is set in various keys around the tonality of D. The *et incarnatus* is in an archaic mode, centred on D and sounding somewhat like D minor, and the *crucifixus* is in D minor, although frequently sounding like it is trying to move away from the key. The only section in the Credo that is set in the home key of the mass, D major, is *et homo factus est*. In Drabkin's commentary on the key for this section he puts it in the

37. R. Fiske, *Beethoven's Missa Solemnis* (London: Paul Elek, 1979), p. 11.

context of the entire mass: 'It is sometimes remarked that this passage helps unify the mass by recapitulating its home key, thus linking the one movement not in D major—the Credo—to the rest of the work'.[38] But he suggests that D major is a sidetrack from the 'quasi-minor' Dorian mode of the *et incarnatus* as a way of setting up the D minor of the *crucifixus*, which implies the centrality of the *crucifixus*.[39] However, perhaps this one instance of D major in the Credo is better understood as a clue to Beethoven's own perspective on the significance of *et homo factus est*. This section does not involve the complexity of writing that is found in the *crucifixus*, but it does accentuate and dramatize a high point of tension and release in the work. This isolated return to the home key of the entire work perhaps indicates that Beethoven has shifted the balance slightly from the traditional focus of the *crucifixus* to give tremendous import to the words preceding it, *et homo factus est*.

Beethoven places the following section, *et resurrexit,* in the archaic Mixolydian mode. It is difficult to determine whether by this he intended it to be linked to the earlier section, *et incarnatus,* which is also set in an archaic mode, as this would frame the inner sections of *et homo factus est* and *crucifixus,* or merely as an archaic way of making a pronouncement before entering into the following section, *et ascendit.* The ambiguity and lack of schematized symmetry in Beethoven's setting of the Credo mark a shift in focus from the icon-like predictability of the Christ figure to one that has more evolving human dimensions.

Even the words that Beethoven chooses to emphasize contribute to a certain image of Christ in this work. In the second movement, he uses *fortissimos* on the word *dominum,* 'Lord', and then later on the word *natum,* 'born' or 'begotten'. In the fourth movement, the hymn-like *qui propter,* he vividly highlights the words *descendit de coelis,* using familiar word-painting that makes use of descending scales to depict descending from heaven. By commanding attention to the words *dominum, natum* and then *descendit de coelis,* he sets up an image that is later revealed, that of the humanity of Christ in *et homo factus est.* Here the word that is dwelt upon and developed is *homo,* 'man'. The concept of humanity is further developed in the *crucifixus,* where the

38. W. Drabkin, *Beethoven: Missa Solemnis* (Cambridge: Cambridge University Press, 1991), p. 107.
39. Drabkin, *Beethoven,* p. 107.

word explored to the greatest degree is *passus*, 'suffered'. Here Beethoven gives each soloist a specific role to play in bringing out the individual and human quality of Christ's suffering.[40] The interaction and contrast of the soloists and the chorus directs yet more attention to the human image that Beethoven dwells on in *et incarnatus*, *et homo*, and *crucifixus*. All four soloists are used in *et incarnatus*, singing in a *mezza-voce* or semi-spoken style. The chorus enters about half-way through this section, *pianissimo*, in a semi-spoken style of chant. Fiske describes the combination of 'the unusual simplicity of two-part counterpoint with modalism' as 'mysterious and awesome'.[41] The combination does create a sense of mystery that underlines the text at this point: the inexplicable concept of how God could in some way become human. Fiske gives a further impression of this section: 'When these same words are intoned on one note, *pianissimo*, by the whole chorus, the effect is for a brief moment like the murmured undertones of the congregation at a normal church service'.[42] From this quiet and intense chanting section the tenor emerges singing the word *et* on the high note E, the same note all the upper voices of the choir have been chanting. As the music abruptly changes from the archaic mode into D major the tenor note moves up a tone to F# to begin the full phrase, *et homo factus est*.[43] In this shift to D major and to the higher tone, Beethoven has used the *tierce de picardie*, the sudden and rather unexpected change from ending on a minor chord to a major chord, to make a dramatic transition from high suppressed tension to bold release, as vivid as the first breaking through of sunlight in a sunrise. The tenor at this point depicts *et homo factus est* as though he himself were surprised and utterly delighted to discover that he is human and truly alive.[44] Beethoven

---

40. Two words that are *not* given prolonged emphasis in the *et resurrexit* are the very words, *et resurrexit*. Compared with Bach's use of all the voices of the choir in a fairly lengthy section of the *et resurrexit* in his mass, Beethoven's use of one voice to make the solitary statement of *et resurrexit* in less than two measures is short indeed. Whether this is for dramatic effect—a bold quick pronouncement—or because the concept of resurrection is difficult to believe and Beethoven chose to move as quickly through it as possible, is difficult to say.

41. Fiske, *Beethoven's Missa Solemnis*, p. 58.

42. Fiske, *Beethoven's Missa Solemnis*, p. 59.

43. McCaldin, 'Choral Music', p. 404 n. 1.

44. See D. Matthews, *Beethoven* (London: Dent, 1985), p. 204, where he comments on the tenor as he 'breaks into the warm D major harmony of "et homo

sets the next repetitions of *homo* and *et homo factus est* as an exchange back and forth between tenor and chorus, both of whom treat the words with tenderness, even awe, yet in a manner of conversation. Here Beethoven develops the central image of his mass—the humanity of the Christ figure—with tremendous emotion and sensitivity. The single voice of the tenor conversing with the chorus allows one to imagine the Christ figure represented as one who has a natural and earthly relationship with humanity because of his own humanity.[45] In the *crucifixus* that follows the human-ness of this figure is treated in greater detail. Here Beethoven returns to using all four soloists. Each one separately emphasizes *passus*, drawing out the sense of human emotion and human suffering. This contributes to Beethoven's Christ image by filling in the depth of his humanity.

Beethoven's approach to the text, sometimes giving more than one perspective, emphasizes an unwillingness to force every detail into a pre-set mould, giving a human dimension to his image that perfect symmetry would not. He uses archaic features in a way that seems to underline that he is *not* conforming to ancient patterns but creating new ones, and, in this case, giving a new perspective on the humanness of Christ. The way one section musically grows out of the previous one, as in *et homo factus est* moving right out of *et incarnatus*, gives Beethoven's image of Christ a depth and warmth that may not be found in a truly liturgical setting of the text. Perhaps as a result there is a sense of three dimensions in his image of Christ that is not typical of earlier settings of the mass. The image of Christ that Beethoven depicts seems to live and breathe, and even seems quite modern.

4. *Stravinsky's Mass*

a. *Background to the Mass*

Igor Stravinsky (1882–1971), who is probably still most well-known to the general public for his unprecedented use of rhythm and percussion in his ballet of 1911, *The Rite of Spring*, had moved an incredible distance from that work by the time he composed the *Mass*

---

factus est". This is surely one of the Mass's most inspired moments, coming as it does before the agonised D minor of the "Crucifixus"...'

45. At this point, it would be helpful to listen to an excerpt of a recording of Beethoven's *Missa Solemnis*, beginning in the *et incarnatus* to hear the contrast of the tenor line in *et homo factus est*.

in the mid-1940s. Stravinsky wrote his *Mass* (1944–48) for mixed chorus and double wind quintet in the latter part of what some term his neo-classical period (Stravinsky himself would not necessarily have agreed with this designation). The first public performance of the *Mass* was at La Scala, Milan, on 27 October 1948, although this was not his choice of venues. Stravinsky wrote the mass with the intention that it be used liturgically, not as a concert performance piece.[46] Stravinsky's often-quoted comment is that his *Mass* 'was partly provoked by some Masses of Mozart that I found in a second-hand music store in Los Angeles in 1942 or 1943. As I played through these rococo-operatic sweets-of-sin, I knew I had to write a Mass of my own, but a real one.'[47] This is one of his few uncommissioned works, which suggests that he wrote out of genuine piety, as opposed to simply writing for a business contract.

The *Mass* is not long, especially when compared with Bach's *Mass in B Minor* and Beethoven's *Missa Solemnis*. The score indicates 17 minutes, although Stravinsky actually intended it to take longer—but only by six minutes. Within these small parameters, Stravinsky uses the classical element of symmetry, shaping the *Mass* as a formal arch, with the longest movement being the Credo.

He chose the Latin text of the mass, having gained experience with the language in *Oedipus Rex* (1927),[48] although the natural choice would seem to have been his native Russian, particularly as he had rejoined the Russian Orthodox Church in the late 1920s. Stravinsky's own practical reason for writing for the Catholic mass as opposed to the Russian Church was that, as Stravinsky himself says, '…Orthodox tradition proscribes musical instruments in its services…' And he was not prepared to write a mass for unaccompanied voices.[49]

The *Mass* is written for trebles and altos (both upper parts designated for children's voices), tenors and basses. Although since the earliest performances of the *Mass* women's voices have frequently been used, Stravinsky's explicit direction was that the upper parts be

46. I. Stravinsky and R. Craft, *Igor Stravinsky: Expositions and Developments* (London: Faber and Faber, 1959), p. 76.

47. Stravinsky and Craft, *Expositions and Developments*, p. 77.

48. G. Amy, 'Aspects of the Religious Music of Igor Stravinsky', in J. Pasler (ed.), *Confronting Stravinsky: Man, Musician, and Modernist* (Berkeley, CA: University of California Press, 1986), pp. 195-206 (196).

49. Stravinsky and Craft, *Expositions and Developments*, p. 77.

sung by children. In one of his letters he writes that for a New York recording of the *Mass* he used children who were 'not at all first-rate', but he chose them, nevertheless, 'because the presence of women in the music of the mass, no matter how perfect they might be, would be a more serious mistake for the sense and spirit of this music than the imperfection of a chorus of children'. A woman's voice, he claimed, 'is always too passionate for liturgical chant'.[50] Along with one of his numerous strong and now politically unacceptable opinions we also see his intended use for the *Mass*—the liturgy.

b. *A Symbolic Image of the Crucified Christ*
The image Stravinsky creates is a somewhat flat symbolic figure of the crucified Christ. As G. Amy points out, one would have difficulty in finding sentimentalism in any of Stravinsky's portrayal of the sacred,[51] and this is particularly true of his *Mass*. Stravinsky identifies significant elements, but does not particularly develop or interpret them. This is evident by the length of the entire *Mass,* as well as the length of the Credo within the mass. Since the Credo lasts only about four minutes in performance, there is little time with a text of this length and complexity to develop any one phrase either musically or textually. This is obviously Stravinsky's intention. The Credo is written in one movement and is scored for voices to sing in a semi-chanted style. The first phrase is sung by the priest, reinforcing that the proper setting be the liturgy.

Apart from the priests's intonation, the setting is one long, practically unbroken chant. The instrumentation is an unusual combination of 2 oboes, cor anglais, 2 bassoons, 2 trumpets and 3 trombones, which creates a sound not unlike that of an organ. This also marks the Credo's suitability for the traditional liturgy. The dynamics of the Credo rarely vary from the *piano* marking. The dynamic range is fairly narrow and the vocal range also is quite limited. There are few, if any, dramatic effects or ornamentation. In fact, there is little that draws attention to itself. Further evidence of this is that Stravinsky uses no soloists in the Credo—no one individual emerges in this section at all. Stravinsky focuses attention on the function of the text. He draws attention to several textual details that are essential to the Christ

50. R. Craft (ed. and with commentaries), *Stravinsky: Selected Correspondence* (London: Faber and Faber, 1982), I, pp. 246-47.
51. Amy, 'Aspects', p. 195.

of the creed, but does not elaborate them or interpret them. As a result, Stravinsky creates in this section of his mass an image of Christ that is almost featureless and flat. The Credo has few elements of dramatic contrast and practically no emotion that would suggest the warmth of a living Christ. The image is a symbolic one that does not seem intended to display a natural life-likeness, or an ethereal other-worldliness, but a functional image. Walsh notes that Stravinsky avoids 'elaborately evolved musical structures...that do not have to do with a straightforward declamation of the words'.[52] Stravinsky himself gives us the key to his Credo: 'In making a musical setting of the Credo I wished only to preserve the text in a special way. One composes a march to facilitate marching men, so with my Credo I hope to provide an aid to the text. The Credo is the longest movement. There is much to believe.'[53] Since a march is not written for contemplation and interpretation but rather as a functional tool to allow the marchers to move systematically and rhythmically forward, so Stravinsky has created a setting of the Credo—and ultimately an image of Christ— that is to be used functionally to move one along in liturgical worship.

Stravinsky makes use of forms that are classical or baroque in nature, emphasizing for instance the symmetrical features of some of these early works. He also uses a more severe or unornamented style. Druskin calls it 'an anticipation of the strictness and austerity of the composer's "late" manner'.[54] Siohan emphasizes that the 'austere polyphony of this score harks back to the past, and in some of its passages to an almost medieval hieraticism'.[55] The *Mass* uses Gregorian chant as well as polyphony and counterpoint with more emphasis than previous works of Stravinsky, contributing to its archaic nature.[56] The use of features such as plainsong and syllabic word-setting, among others, points to the *Mass* being based on traditional Church idioms.[57]

52. S. Walsh, *The Music of Stravinsky* (Oxford: Clarendon Press, 1993), p. 193.

53. 'Stravinsky's Mass: A Notebook', in M. Armitage (ed.), *Symposium on Stravinsky* (New York: G. Schirmer, 1949), cited in E.W. White, *Stravinsky: The Composer and his Works* (London: Faber and Faber, 1979), p. 447.

54. M. Druskin, *Igor Stravinsky: His Life, Works and Views* (trans. M. Cooper; Cambridge: Cambridge University Press, 1983 [Original Title: *Igor Stravinsky— lichnost', tvorchestvo, vzhlyady*; Gosizdat, 1979]), p. 26.

55. R. Siohan, *Stravinsky* (trans. E.W. White; Paris: Editions du Seuil, 1959; London: Calder and Boyars, 1965), p. 129.

56. White, *Stravinsky: The Composer and his Works*, p. 100.

57. Walsh, *Music of Stravinsky*, p. 193.

Contributing to the symbolic image of Christ is Stravinsky's use of symmetry in dividing the text into sections. After the priest's intonation, the work can be divided into three nearly equal-length sections of 52 measures, 49 measures and 52 measures. The first section begins at *patrem* (compare Bach nos. 2–3; Beethoven nos. 1–4), the second section at *et incarnatus est* (Bach nos. 4–6; Beethoven nos. 5–10), and the third section at *et in spiritum sanctum* (Bach nos. 7–9; Beethoven nos. 11–12). These are fairly consistent with traditional divisions of the text. The text that is given the most unusual rhythmic treatment is *et homo factus est*—'and was made man'. The rhythm of the voices and text at this point and the pulling of the instruments—notably the two trumpets—against the voices, distinguish it from the rest of the work. But there is little here to suggest that Stravinsky is trying to interpret this phrase in any particular way or to give any indication of his own personal view of the meaning of the text. The only place where there is more than one measure of rest in the voices—in this case there are five measures in a row—is just following *et homo factus est* and just prior to *crucifixus*. Again, without giving much elaboration to the phrases, Stravinsky presents them in such a way that the traditional heart of the Credo text, the *crucifixus*, is definitely identified. Stravinsky has thus drawn attention to the phrase 'and was made man' but has not amplified it. He then sets up the phrase dealing with the crucifixion by using the five measures of rest. The *crucifixus*—written for five voices, with the tenor in two parts—is distinct from the four voice parts of the rest of the Credo. The only instruments at this point are the cor anglais and bassoons until the words *passus et sepultus est,* where the oboes dispassionately enter. Stravinsky has highlighted the recognizable and significant details of the image of Christ, especially his being made human and then his resurrection, but the composer has not tried to fill in any kind of meaning around them. The words of the crucifixion are prepared and presented, but not given emotional expression of any kind. The *crucifixus, et resurrexit* and *et ascendit* are all delivered in the semi-chant of the earlier sections of the Credo with little variation.[58]

---

58. At this point, it would be helpful to listen to a recording of the Credo of Stravinsky's *Mass*, particularly noting the rhythmic interest in *et homo factus est*, the several measures of instruments only that follow it and then the chant-like nature of the *crucifixus*.

The first and only crescendo in the Credo begins at *cujus regni* 'whose reign', increasing in pitch and volume on the *non erit finis* 'will never end', with a *fermata* or pause on the second syllable of *finis*. The tenor line moves upward where one might expect a unison octave, but results in a major ninth instead. The unison is reached at the next sentence of the text, when the voices move back to semi-chant on an E major chord at *et in spiritum sanctum*. The next words that are emphasized are done so in several ways. Stravinsky marks these words *poco più f*, 'a little louder', and changes from using eighth notes and combinations of eighth notes and quarter notes to using four straight quarter notes on the words *ecclesiam, peccatorum*, and *mortuorum*. The corresponding marking in the score for the instruments is *marcato*. Although these words may have been marked simply to make them more interesting or to aid the memory or the ear, their emphasis contributes to the functional image of Christ that is depicted in relationship to the words highlighted—'church', 'sin' and 'death'. The whole movement ends with an unexpectedly lovely *amen* written for voices without accompaniment, marking the end of Stravinsky's aid to the text of the Credo.

In this setting of the mass there is an element of timelessness. Boucourechliev comments that the *Mass*'s 'ascetic character, the attempt to achieve a timeless language and the instrumentation...places it outside chronological considerations'.[59] I think that Stravinsky was attempting to do just that—to write a setting of the Credo in particular that would transcend normal time boundaries. These elements also contribute to the *Mass*'s symbolic function, a function that links what Souris calls 'consecrated musical forms' and the traditions and nature of the Church.[60] By setting the Credo in this manner, Stravinsky showed himself to belong, at least in this instance, to the long historical line of Church composers. He captured the essence of the Church dogma and presented it in a form that could be equated with the tradition of the great icon painters of the Orthodox Church, always basing this work on a traditional form and preserving the sense of the archaic, but not without giving it somewhat of a personal stamp.

59. A. Boucourechliev, *Stravinsky* (Librairie Arthème Fayard, 1982; trans. M. Cooper; London: Victor Gollancz, 1987), p. 228.

60. A. Souris, 'Le sens du sacré dans la musique de Stravinsky', *Conditions de la musique, et autres écrits* (Brussells: Editions de l'Université; Paris: Editions du Centre National de la Recherche Scientifique, 1976), p. 49.

5. *Conclusion*

Both Bach and Stravinsky allow the traditions of the Church and the creed to determine how they portray their images of Christ. All three composers use archaic elements in their works, but Bach and Stravinsky use them to draw lines of connection to the Church and Church composers of the past, while Beethoven uses them to emphasize that he is trying to develop a completely new view of the subject. Where Bach and Stravinsky use symmetry, for instance, as an integral means of shaping their work and ultimately their forms of the image of Christ, Beethoven uses elements of symmetry only to move away from them. Beethoven's image seems to be set very much in the present, requiring little effort on the part of the listener to gain its moving emotional impact. Bach's and Stravinsky's images seem to be set in antiquity, requiring a certain amount of effort to understand the larger significance of them, and perhaps resulting in a more cerebral perception of the image of Christ. Where Bach tries to elucidate elements that are inexplicable, like the concept of the second person of the Trinity, Beethoven elaborates on the elements that are humanly understandable and passes rather superficially over things that are difficult to understand. Beethoven does not concentrate on *how* Christ could be human, but brings out the human emotions that simply emphasize his humanity. Stravinsky does not stop to evaluate any one area but creates a measured rhythmic setting by which one can move efficiently through the words of the Credo. Obviously the composers have used the techniques of their individual periods to create these compositions, but they have also drawn from a wide range of compositional elements from earlier and contemporary periods in providing new ways of interpreting—or not interpreting—the text. Each has demonstrated that the image of Christ that is created is altered by the weight, development and placement of a phrase or section of the text, especially dealing specifically with Christ. Each has given us a perspective on the intrinsic meaning of the creed and, more specifically, a particular view of the image of Christ.

INDEX OF AUTHORS AND PROPER NAMES